ANNUAL EDITIONS

Marketing 13/14

Thirty-Sixth Edition

EDITOR

Nisreen N. Bahnan

Dr. Nisreen Bahnan is Associate Professor of Marketing at Salem State University's Bertolon School of Business. She has earned her PhD in Business Studies from Temple University in Philadelphia. She teaches several marketing courses at the undergraduate and graduate levels, including Principles of Marketing, Consumer Behavior and Nonprofit Marketing. She has presented at conferences and published articles in the fields of services marketing and consumer behavior.

ANNUAL EDITIONS: MARKETING, THIRTY-SIXTH EDITION

Published by McGraw-Hill, a business unit of The McGraw-Hill Companies, Inc., 1221 Avenue of the Americas, New York, NY 10020. Copyright © 2014 by The McGraw-Hill Companies, Inc. All rights reserved. Printed in the United States of America. Previous edition(s) 2013, 2012, 2011, 2009, and 2008. No part of this publication may be reproduced or distributed in any form or by any means, or stored in a database or retrieval system, without the prior written consent of The McGraw-Hill Companies, Inc., including, but not limited to, in any network or other electronic storage or transmission, or broadcast for distance learning.

Some ancillaries, including electronic and print components, may not be available to customers outside the United States.

This book is printed on acid-free paper.

Annual Editions® is a registered trademark of the McGraw-Hill Companies, Inc.
Annual Editions is published by the **Contemporary Learning Series** group within the McGraw-Hill Higher Education division.

1 2 3 4 5 6 7 8 9 0 QDB/QDB 1 0 9 8 7 6 5 4 3

ISBN: 978-0-07-352876-2
MHID: 0-07-352876-5
ISSN: 0730-2606 (print)
ISSN: 2159-0621 (online)

Acquisitions Editor: *Joan L. McNamara*
Marketing Director: *Adam Kloza*
Marketing Manager: *Nathan Edwards*
Developmental Editor: *Dave Welsh*
Senior Project Manager: *Joyce Watters*
Buyer: *Nichole Birkenholz*
Cover Designer: *Studio Monatage, St. Louis, MO*
Content Licensing Specialist: *Beth Thole*
Media Project Manager: *Sridevi Palani*

Compositor: Laserwords Private Limited
Cover Image Credits: © Fancy Collection/SuperStock (inset), © The McGraw-Hill Companies, Inc./Jill Braaten, photographer (background)

Editors/Academic Advisory Board

Members of the Academic Advisory Board are instrumental in the final selection of articles for each edition of ANNUAL EDITIONS. Their review of articles for content, level, and appropriateness provides critical direction to the editors and staff. We think that you will find their careful consideration well reflected in this volume.

ANNUAL EDITIONS: Marketing 13/14
36th Edition

EDITOR

Nisreen N. Bahnan
Salem State University

ACADEMIC ADVISORY BOARD MEMBERS

Preface

In publishing ANNUAL EDITIONS we recognize the enormous role played by the magazines, newspapers, and journals of the public press in providing current, first-rate educational information in a broad spectrum of interest areas. Many of these articles are appropriate for students, researchers, and professionals seeking accurate, current material to help bridge the gap between principles and theories and the real world. These articles, however, become more useful for study when those of lasting value are carefully collected, organized, indexed, and reproduced in a low-cost format, which provides easy and permanent access when the material is needed. That is the role played by ANNUAL EDITIONS.

The new millennium should prove to be an exciting and challenging time for the American business community. Recent dramatic social, economic, and technological changes have become an important part of the present marketplace. These changes—accompanied by increasing domestic and foreign competition—are leading a wide array of companies and industries toward the realization that better marketing must become a top priority now to assure their future success.

How does the marketing manager respond to this growing challenge? How does the marketing student apply marketing theory to the real-world practice? Many reach for the *Wall Street Journal, BusinessWeek, Fortune,* and other well-known sources of business information. There, specific industry and company strategies are discussed and analyzed, marketing principles are often reaffirmed by real occurrences, and textbook theories are supported or challenged by current events.

The articles reprinted in this edition of *Annual Editions: Marketing 13/14* have been carefully chosen from numerous public press sources to provide current information on marketing in the world today. Within these pages you will find articles that address marketing theory and application in a wide range of industries. In addition, the selections reveal how several firms interpret and utilize marketing principles in their daily operations and corporate planning.

The volume contains a number of features designed to make it useful for marketing students, researchers, and professionals. These include the *Topic Guide* to locate articles on specific marketing subjects; *Internet References* pages; the *Table of Contents* abstracts, which summarize each article and highlight key concepts; and a *Glossary* of key marketing terms. Also included are Learning Outcomes at the beginning of each Unit, as well Critical Thinking study questions after each article to help students better understand what they have read.

The articles are organized into four units. Selections that focus on similar issues are concentrated into subsections within the broader units. Each unit is preceded by a list of unit selections, as well as a list of key points to consider that focus on major themes running throughout the selections, web links that provide extra support for the unit's data, and an overview that provides background for informed reading of the articles and emphasizes critical issues.

This is the thirty-sixth edition of *Annual Editions: Marketing.* Since its first edition in the mid-1970s, the efforts of many individuals have contributed toward its success. We think this is by far the most useful collection of material available for the marketing student. We are anxious to know what you think. What are your opinions? What are your recommendations? Any book can be improved and this one will continue to be, annually.

Nisreen N. Bahnan
Editor

The Annual Editions Series

VOLUMES AVAILABLE

Adolescent Psychology

Aging

American Foreign Policy

American Government

Anthropology

Archaeology

Assessment and Evaluation

Business Ethics

Child Growth and Development

Comparative Politics

Criminal Justice

Developing World

Drugs, Society, and Behavior

Dying, Death, and Bereavement

Early Childhood Education

Economics

Educating Children with Exceptionalities

Education

Educational Psychology

Entrepreneurship

Environment

The Family

Gender

Geography

Global Issues

Health

Homeland Security

Human Development

Human Resources

Human Sexualities

International Business

Management

Marketing

Mass Media

Microbiology

Multicultural Education

Nursing

Nutrition

Physical Anthropology

Psychology

Race and Ethnic Relations

Social Problems

Sociology

State and Local Government

Sustainability

Technologies, Social Media, and Society

United States History, Volume 1

United States History, Volume 2

Urban Society

Violence and Terrorism

Western Civilization, Volume 1

World History, Volume 1

World History, Volume 2

World Politics

Contents

Preface   iv

Series   v

Correlation Guide   xi

Topic Guide   xii

Internet References   xiv

UNIT 1
Marketing in the 2000s and Beyond

Unit Overview   xvi

Part A. Changing Perspectives

1. **Marketing in 2012: The End of the Middle?,** Christine Birkner, *Marketing News,* January 31, 2012

   Marketplace watchers proclaim that the recession in the American economy may call for a new definition of the middle class, prompting many marketers to shift everything within their marketing mixes.   **2**

2. **Hot Stuff: Make These Top Trends Part of Your Marketing Mix,** Gwen Moran, *Entrepreneur,* August 2006

   Gwen Moran uncovers some hot trends in marketing and suggests ways that these trends should be part of one's *marketing mix.*   **5**

3. **Evolve,** Chris Penttila, *Entrepreneur,* May 2009

   Chris Penttila provides seven ways game changers can pull levers that affect a *market* or create an entirely new one.   **8**

4. **The Unmarketables,** Piet Levy, John N. Frank, and Allison Enright, *Marketing News,* July 30, 2009

   For *brands* and businesses that have fallen out of favor with *customers,* marketers have to craft messages and *promotions* that can revitalize lackluster images.   **10**

5. **Six Strategies for Successful Niche Marketing,** Eric K. Clemons, Paul F. Nunes, and Matt Reilly, *The Wall Street Journal,* May 23, 2010

   The article supplies thoughtful ideas of how to become successful in *niche marketing.*   **15**

6. **The Branding Sweet Spot,** Kevin Lane Keller and Frederick E. Webster, Jr., *Marketing Management,* July/August 2009

   One of the realities of modern *brand* marketing is that many of the decisions that marketers make with respect to their brands are seemingly characterized by conflicting needs.   **19**

Part B. The Marketing Concept

7. **Marketing Myopia (with Retrospective Commentary),** Theodore Levitt, *Harvard Business Review,* September/October 1975

   According to Theodore Levitt, shortsighted managers are unable to recognize that there is no such thing as a growth industry—as the histories of the railroad, movie, and oil industries show. To survive, he says, a company must learn to apply the *marketing concept:* to think of itself not as producing goods or services, but as buying customers.   **25**

8. **Putting Customers First: Nine Surefire Ways to Increase Brand Loyalty,** Kyle LaMalfa, *Sales & Marketing Management,* January/February 2008

   Kyle LaMalfa explores nine surefire ways to increase *customers' brand loyalty.*   **36**

The concepts in bold italics are developed in the article. For further expansion, please refer to the Topic Guide.

9. **Making the Most of Customer Complaints,** Stefan Michel, David Bowen, and Robert Johnston, *The Wall Street Journal,* September 22, 2008
    Customers are constantly judging companies for **service** failures large and small, from a glitch-ridden business-software company to a hamburger served cold. **39**

10. **When Service Means Survival,** Jena McGregor, *Bloomberg BusinessWeek,* March 2, 2009
    Keeping **customers** happy is more critical than ever. **Service** champs economize on everything but TLC. **43**

11. **Become the Main Attraction,** Piet Levy, *Marketing News,* July 30, 2010
    Piet Levy gives some good suggestions for successful **event marketing.** **47**

Part C.   *Services and Social Marketing*

12. **How to Make Marketing Brilliance,** Jason Daley, *Entrepreneur,* February 2011
    This article provides a look at the best marketing moves of 2010. **50**

13. **Imaginative Service,** Chip R. Bell and John R. Patterson, *Leadership Excellence,* May 2009
    The authors discuss ways to deliver unique value and faster **service** to meet and exceed **customer** expectations. **55**

14. **Walking the Talk,** Katherine Ling, *Marketing News,* March 15, 2012
    Eco-minded retailer, Patagonia, caused a stir with its recent "conscious-consumption" holiday campaign that told consumers **not** to buy the featured product. **57**

Part D.   *Marketing Ethics and Social Responsibility*

15. **Honest Innovation,** Calvin L. Hodock, *Marketing Management,* March/April 2009
    Ethics issues in **new product development** could be stalling **innovation** growth. **61**

16. **It's Hard to Be Good,** Alison Beard and Richard Hornik, *Harvard Business Review,* November 2011
    The article chronicles five companies whose success is built on responsible business practices. **65**

UNIT 2
Research, Markets, and Consumer Behavior

Unit Overview **70**

Part A.   *Market Research*

17. **A Step-by-Step Guide to Smart Business Experiments,** Eric T. Anderson and Duncan Simester, *Harvard Business Review,* March 2011
    Every company can profit from testing customers' reactions to change. The authors provide companies guidance on how to start. **72**

18. **Know What Your Customers Want before They Do,** Thomas H. Davenport, Leandro Dalle Mule, and John Lucker, *Harvard Business Review,* December 2011
    Retailers need to target customers with the right deal at the right time. Here's how to nail the "next best offer." **78**

The concepts in bold italics are developed in the article. For further expansion, please refer to the Topic Guide.

Part B. Markets and Demographics

19. **Respect Your Elders,** Tom Stein and Tim Devaney, *Marketing News,*
April 30, 2012
Digital marketing techniques may be young and flashy, but conventional marketing strategies have not lost their impact. The ideal modern marketing mix makes room for both.   **83**

20. **Marketing to Kids Gets More Savvy with New Technologies,**
Bruce Horovitz, *USA Today,* August 2011
This article tackles the sensitive issue of the increased practice of targeted advertising to tech-savvy children.   **85**

21. **It's Cooler than Ever to Be a Tween,** Sharon Jayson, *USA Today,*
February 4, 2009
The **tweens** are a hot market—they're complicated, and there are two in the White House.   **87**

22. **Segmenting the Base of the Pyramid,** V. Kasturi Rangan, Michael Chu,
and Djordjija Petkoski, *Harvard Business Review,* June 2011
Decent profits can be made at the base of the pyramid if companies link their own financial success with that of their constituencies, whereby these constituencies acquire basic services and grow more affluent.   **90**

Part C. Consumer Behavior

23. **Can More Information Be a Bad Thing?,** Robert S. Duboff,
Marketing Management, Summer 2012
Despite researchers' best efforts, consumer decision-making will always have subjective components.   **95**

24. **The Tyranny of Choice: You Choose,** *The Economist,* December 18, 2010
If you can have everything in 57 varieties, making decisions becomes hard work.   **99**

25. **Tapping the Untapped,** Diana Derval, *Marketing Management,* Spring 2012
Marketers can learn from product preferences that are simply linked to consumers' physiology.   **103**

UNIT 3
Developing and Implementing Marketing Strategies

Unit Overview   **106**

26. **The CMO and the Future of Marketing,** George S. Day and Robert
Malcolm, *Marketing Management,* Spring 2012
This article examines how the roles, responsibilities and influence of the chief marketing officer will evolve in the future.   **109**

Part A. Product

27. **Innovate or Die,** Stephen C. Harper and Thomas W. Porter, *Industrial
Engineer,* September 2011
Many companies are not as innovative as they could be because their search for market opportunities is too narrow and they fail to funnel innovation into their product and process development.   **114**

28. **Brand Integrity,** Tom Peters and Valarie Willis, *Leadership Excellence,*
May 2009
The authors advocate that excellence is achieved when the brand, the talent, and the **customer experience** are all in alignment.   **119**

The concepts in bold italics are developed in the article. For further expansion, please refer to the Topic Guide.

29. **Brand Apathy Calls for New Methods: Turn Customer Preference from "No Brand" to "Some Brand,"** Don E. Schultz, *Marketing Management,* Winter 2010

Building market share requires a new set of tools and brand strategies designed to shift ongoing consumer preference and purchase from competitive brands to yours. **121**

30. **Branding's Big Guns,** Paula Andruss, *Entrepreneur,* April 2012

This article chronicles the success of the10 most trusted U.S. brands that have become household names. **123**

31. **Playing Well Together,** Jason Daley, *Entrepreneur,* April 2012

Emerging co-branding concepts prove that strategic business combinations can cut costs and broaden the customer base. **128**

Part B.   Pricing

32. **Competing against Free,** David J. Bryce, Jeffrey H. Dyer, and Nile W. Hatch, *Harvard Business Review,* June 2011

Free offerings are rapidly spreading beyond online markets to the physical, brick and mortar world. The authors give pointers on how incumbents can fight back. **130**

33. **Ditch the Discounts,** Rafi Mohammed, *Harvard Business Review,* January/February 2011

The author discusses pricing strategies and tactics that are more appropriate for economic recovery than the adaptive pricing companies adopted during the recession. **136**

Part C.   Distribution

34. **The Devolution of Marketing: Is America's Marketing Model Fighting Hard Enough to Keep Up?,** Andrew R. Thomas and Timothy J. Wilkinson, *Marketing Management,* Spring 2011

This article argues that the current American marketing model is dysfunctional, and small and medium-sized businesses operate under a misconceived ideology of producing and selling. **139**

35. **In Lean Times, Retailers Shop for Survival Strategies,** Jayne O'Donnell, *USA Today,* February 28, 2008

During the difficult *economic* times, according to the author, *retailers* are in search of tenable survival *strategies.* **142**

36. **The Rebirth of Retail,** Jason Ankeny, *Entrepreneur,* March 2011

This article discusses the inspiration and vision behind Shopkick, a new shopping application. **146**

Part D.   Promotion

37. **Marketing Communication in a Digital Era: Marketers Should Focus Efforts on Emerging Social, Mobile and Local Trends,** Donna L. Hoffman and Thomas P. Novak, *Marketing Management,* Fall 2011

Marketers should focus efforts on emerging social, mobile and local trends. **149**

38. **Selling Green,** Matt Villano, Entrepreneur, November 2011

A five-step guide to correctly market a business as green is presented here. **154**

39. **What's Your Social Media Strategy?,** H. James Wilson et al., *Harvard Business Review,* July/August 2011

This study describes four ways companies are using technology to form connections. **158**

40. **Advertising's New Campaign,** Jennifer Wang, *Entrepreneur,* April 2012

The author discusses BlogFrog's new advertising campaign which capitalizes on the massive influence of mom bloggers with its brand-sponsored communities. **161**

The concepts in bold italics are developed in the article. For further expansion, please refer to the Topic Guide.

UNIT 4
Global Marketing

Unit Overview   **164**

41. **Emerging Lessons,** Madhubalan Viswanathan, José Antonio Rosa, and Julie A. Ruth, *The Wall Street Journal,* October 20, 2008

    For *multinational* companies, understanding the needs of poorer *consumers* can be both profitable and *socially responsible.*   **166**

42. **KFC's Radical Approach to China: To Succeed, the Fast-Food Giant Had to Throw Out Its United States Business Model,** David E. Bell and Mary L. Shelman, *Harvard Business Review,* November 2011

    To succeed, the fast-food giant had to go beyond adapting and localizing their offerings to throw out its United States business model.   **169**

43. **Retail Doesn't Cross Borders,** Marcel Corstjens and Rajiv Lal, *Harvard Business Review,* April 2012

    In contrast to other industries, grocery retail is still dominated by local players in most countries. International players are almost entirely absent from even the largest retail markets, and every grocery retailer that has ventured overseas has failed as often as it has succeeded.   **174**

Glossary   **180**

Test-Your-Knowledge Form   **185**

The concepts in bold italics are developed in the article. For further expansion, please refer to the Topic Guide.

Correlation Guide

The *Annual Editions* series provides students with convenient, inexpensive access to current, carefully selected articles from the public press. **Annual Editions: Marketing 13/14** is an easy-to-use reader that presents articles on important topics such as *the future of marketing, developing marketing strategies,* and many more. For more information on *Annual Editions* and other *McGraw-Hill Contemporary Learning Series* titles, visit www.mhhe.com/cls.

This convenient guide matches the units in **Annual Editions: Marketing 13/14** with the corresponding chapters in three of our best-selling McGraw-Hill Marketing textbooks by Perreault et al., Kerin et al. and Grewal/Levy.

Annual Editions: Marketing 13/14	*Essentials of Marketing,* 13/e by Perreault et al.	*Marketing,* 11/e by Kerin et al.	*Marketing,* 3/e by Grewal/Levy
Unit 1: Marketing in the 2000s and Beyond	**Chapter 2:** Marketing Strategy Planning	**Chapter 3:** Scanning the Marketing Environment **Chapter 4:** Ethical and Social Responsibility in Marketing	**Chapter 3:** Marketing Ethics **Chapter 12:** Services: The Intangible Product
Unit 2: Research, Markets, and Consumer Behavior	**Chapter 2:** Marketing Strategy Planning **Chapter 5:** Final Consumers and Their Buying Behavior **Chapter 6:** Business and Organizational Customers and Their Buying Behavior	**Chapter 1:** Creating Customer Relationships and Value through Marketing **Chapter 5:** Understanding Consumer Behavior **Chapter 8:** Marketing Research: From Customer Insights to Actions	**Chapter 4:** Analyzing the Marketing Environment **Chapter 5:** Consumer Behavior **Chapter 9:** Marketing Research and Information Systems
Unit 3: Developing and Implementing Marketing Strategies	**Chapter 2:** Marketing Strategy Planning **Chapter 3:** Evaluating Opportunities in the Changing Marketing Environment **Chapter 4:** Focusing Marketing Strategy with Segmentation and Positioning **Chapter 13:** Promotion—Introduction to Integrated Marketing Communications **Chapter 15:** Advertising, Publicity, and Sales Promotion **Chapter 16:** Pricing Objectives and Policies **Chapter 17:** Price Setting in the Business World	**Chapter 2:** Developing Successful Marketing and Organizational Strategies **Chapter 3:** Scanning the Marketing Environment **Chapter 6:** Understanding Organizations as Customers **Chapter 13:** Building the Price Foundation **Chapter 14:** Arriving at the Final Price **Chapter 15:** Managing Marketing Channels and Wholesaling **Chapter 16:** Customer-Driven Supply Chain and Logistics Management **Chapter 17:** Retailing **Chapter 18:** Integrated Marketing Communications and Direct Marketing **Chapter 19:** Advertising, Sales Promotion, and Public Relations **Chapter 21:** Implementing Interactive and Multichannel Marketing **Chapter 22:** Pulling It All Together: The Strategic Marketing Process	**Chapter 2:** Developing Marketing Strategies and a Marketing Plan **Chapter 6:** Business-to-Business Marketing **Chapter 8:** Segmentation, Targeting, and Positioning **Chapter 10:** Product, Branding, and Package Decisions **Chapter 11:** Developing New Products **Chapter 13:** Pricing Concepts for Establishing Value **Chapter 14:** Supply Chain Management **Chapter 15:** Retailing and Multichannel Marketing **Chapter 16:** Integrated Marketing Communications **Chapter 17:** Advertising, Public Relations, and Sales Promotions
Unit 4: Global Marketing		**Chapter 7:** Understanding and Reaching Global Consumers and Markets	**Chapter 7:** Global Marketing

Topic Guide

This topic guide suggests how the selections in this book relate to the subjects covered in your course. You may want to use the topics listed on these pages to search the Web more easily.

On the following pages a number of websites have been gathered specifically for this book. They are arranged to reflect the units of this *Annual Editions* reader. You can link to these sites by going to www.mhhe.com/cls.

All the articles that relate to each topic are listed below the bold-faced term.

Advertising
2. Hot Stuff: Make These Top Trends Part of Your Marketing Mix
12. How to Make Marketing Brilliance
14. Walking the Talk
19. Respect Your Elders
20. Marketing to Kids Gets More Savvy with New Technologies
30. Branding's Big Guns
37. Marketing Communication in a Digital Era: Marketers Should Focus Efforts on Emerging Social, Mobile and Local Trends
38. Selling Green
40. Advertising's New Campaign

Branding
2. Hot Stuff: Make These Top Trends Part of Your Marketing Mix
4. The Unmarketables
6. The Branding Sweet Spot
28. Brand Integrity
29. Brand Apathy Calls for New Methods: Turn Customer Preference from "No Brand" to "Some Brand"
30. Branding's Big Guns
31. Playing Well Together

Competition
18. Know What Your Customers Want before They Do
32. Competing against Free

Consumer behavior
2. Hot Stuff: Make These Top Trends Part of Your Marketing Mix
8. Putting Customers First: Nine Surefire Ways to Increase Brand Loyalty
23. Can More Information Be a Bad Thing?
24. The Tyranny of Choice: You Choose
25. Tapping the Untapped

Consumer demographics
2. Hot Stuff: Make These Top Trends Part of Your Marketing Mix
19. Respect Your Elders
20. Marketing to Kids Gets More Savvy with New Technologies
21. It's Cooler than Ever to Be a Tween
22. Segmenting the Base of the Pyramid

Distribution planning
34. The Devolution of Marketing: Is America's Marketing Model Fighting Hard Enough to Keep Up?
35. In Lean Times, Retailers Shop for Survival Strategies
36. The Rebirth of Retail
43. Retail Doesn't Cross Borders

Economic environment
1. Marketing in 2012: The End of the Middle?
22. Segmenting the Base of the Pyramid
33. Ditch the Discounts

Event marketing
11. Become the Main Attraction

Franchising
31. Playing Well Together

Global marketing
3. Evolve
34. The Devolution of Marketing: Is America's Marketing Model Fighting Hard Enough to Keep Up?
41. Emerging Lessons
42. KFC's Radical Approach to China: To Succeed, the Fast-Food Giant Had to Throw Out Its United States Business Model
43. Retail Doesn't Cross Borders

Innovation
3. Evolve
7. Marketing Myopia (with Retrospective Commentary)
15. Honest Innovation
27. Innovate or Die

Internet marketing
2. Hot Stuff: Make These Top Trends Part of Your Marketing Mix
20. Marketing to Kids Gets More Savvy with New Technologies
37. Marketing Communication in a Digital Era: Marketers Should Focus Efforts on Emerging Social, Mobile and Local Trends
39. What's Your Social Media Strategy?
40. Advertising's New Campaign

Lifestyle marketing
21. It's Cooler than Ever to Be a Tween
22. Segmenting the Base of the Pyramid

Marketing and technology
3. Evolve
17. A Step-by-Step Guide to Smart Business Experiments
39. What's Your Social Media Strategy?

Marketing concept
7. Marketing Myopia (with Retrospective Commentary)
24. The Tyranny of Choice: You Choose

Marketing ethics
15. Honest Innovation
16. It's Hard to Be Good
20. Marketing to Kids Gets More Savvy with New Technologies

Marketing mix
1. Marketing in 2012: The End of the Middle?
2. Hot Stuff: Make These Top Trends Part of Your Marketing Mix

Marketing research
17. A Step-by-Step Guide to Smart Business Experiments
18. Know What Your Customers Want before They Do
23. Can More Information Be a Bad Thing?
25. Tapping the Untapped

Marketing strategies
1. Marketing in 2012: The End of the Middle?
2. Hot Stuff: Make These Top Trends Part of Your Marketing Mix
34. The Devolution of Marketing: Is America's Marketing Model Fighting Hard Enough to Keep Up?

Market share

32. Competing against Free

New product development

3. Evolve
15. Honest Innovation
27. Innovate or Die

Niche marketing

5. Six Strategies for Successful Niche Marketing

Price competition

32. Competing against Free

Pricing strategy

33. Ditch the Discounts

Product development

3. Evolve
15. Honest Innovation
27. Innovate or Die

Product differentiation

3. Evolve
32. Competing against Free

Product positioning

3. Evolve

Promotion development

4. The Unmarketables

Retailing

35. In Lean Times, Retailers Shop for Survival Strategies
43. Retail Doesn't Cross Borders

Services marketing

2. Hot Stuff: Make These Top Trends Part of Your Marketing Mix
3. Evolve
10. When Service Means Survival
13. Imaginative Service

Social responsibility

14. Walking the Talk
15. Honest Innovation
16. It's Hard to Be Good
38. Selling Green

Target marketing

19. Respect Your Elders
20. Marketing to Kids Gets More Savvy with New Technologies
21. It's Cooler than Ever to be a Tween
22. Segmenting the Base of the Pyramid

Technology

3. Evolve
20. Marketing to Kids Gets More Savvy with New Technologies
37. Marketing Communication in a Digital Era: Marketers Should Focus Efforts on Emerging Social, Mobile and Local Trends
39. What's Your Social Media Strategy?
40. Advertising's New Campaign

Internet References

The following Internet sites have been selected to support the articles found in this reader. These sites were available at the time of publication. However, because websites often change their structure and content, the information listed may no longer be available. We invite you to visit www.mhhe.com/cls for easy access to these sites.

Annual Editions: Marketing 13/14

General Sources

Baruch College BusinessWeek—Harris Poll Demographics
www.businessweek.com/1997/18/b352511.htm

The Baruch College–Harris poll commissioned by *BusinessWeek* is used at this site to show interested businesses that are on the Net in the United States.

General Social Survey
www.webapp.icpsr.umich.edu/cocoon/ICPSR-SERIES/00028.xml

The GSS (see DPLS Archive: http://DPLS.DACC.WISC.EDU/SAF/) is an almost annual personal interview survey of U.S. households that began in 1972. More than 35,000 respondents have answered 2,500 questions. It covers a broad range of variables, many of which relate to microeconomic issues.

BestOfAdvertising.net
www.bestofadvertising.net

This is a complete list of sites that include information on marketing research, marketing on the Internet, demographic sources, and organizations and associations. The site also features current books on the subject of marketing.

STAT-USA/Internet Site Economic, Trade, Business Information
www.stat-usa.gov

This site, from the U.S. Department of Commerce, contains Daily Economic News, Frequently Requested Statistical Releases, Information on Export and International Trade, Domestic Economic News and Statistical Series, and Databases.

U.S. Census Bureau Home Page
www.census.gov

This is a major source of social, demographic, and economic information, such as income/employment data and the latest indicators, income distribution, and poverty data.

UNIT 1: Marketing in the 2000s and Beyond

American Marketing Association Code of Ethics
www.marketingpower.com

At this American Marketing Association site, use the search mechanism to access the organization's Code of Ethics for marketers.

Futures Research Quarterly
www.wfs.org/frq.htm

Published by the World Future Society, this publication describes future research that encompasses both an evolving philosophy and a range of techniques, with the aim of assisting decision makers in all fields to understand better the potential consequences of decisions by developing images of alternative futures. From this page explore the current and back issues and What's Coming Up!

Center for Innovation in Product Development (CIPD)
web.mit.edu/cipd/research/prdctdevelop.htm

CIPD is one of the National Science Foundation's engineering research centers. It shares the goal of future product development with academia, industry, and government.

UNIT 2: Research, Markets, and Consumer Behavior

Canadian Innovation Centre
www.innovationcentre.ca

The Canadian Innovation Centre has developed a unique mix of innovation services that can help a company from idea to market launch. Their services are based on the review of 12,000 new product ideas through their technology and market assessment programs over the past 20 years.

BizMiner—Industry Analysis and Trends
www.bizminer.com/market_research.asp

The importance of using market research databases and pinpointing local and national trends, including details of industry and small business startups, is emphasized by this site of the Brandow Company that offers samples of market research profiles.

Small Business Center—Articles & Insights
www.bcentral.com/articles/krotz/123.asp

This article discusses five market intelligence blunders made by the giant retailer K-Mart. "There were warning signs that K-Mart management mishandled, downplayed or just plain ignored," Joanna L. Krotz says.

Maritz Marketing Research
www.maritzresearch.com

Maritz Marketing Research Inc. (MMRI) specializes in custom-designed research studies that link the consumer to the marketer through information. Go to Maritz Loyalty Marketing in the Maritz Companies menu to find resources to identify, retain, and grow your most valuable customers. Also visit Maritz Research for polls, stats, and archived research reports.

USADATA
www.usadata.com

This leading provider of marketing, company, advertising, and consumer behavior data offers national and local data covering the top 60 U.S. markets.

WWW Virtual Library: Demography & Population Studies
http://demography.anu.edu.au/VirtualLibrary

More than 150 links can be found at this major resource to keep track of information of value to researchers in the fields of demography and population studies.

UNIT 3: Developing and Implementing Marketing Strategies

American Marketing Association Homepage
www.marketingpower.com

This site of the American Marketing Association is geared to managers, educators, researchers, students, and global electronic members. It contains a search mechanism, definitions of marketing and market research, and links.

Internet References

Consumer Buying Behavior
www.courses.psu.edu/mktg/mktg220_rso3/sls_cons.htm

The Center for Academic Computing at Penn State posts this course data that includes a review of consumer buying behaviors; group, environment, and internal influences; problem-solving; and post-purchasing behavior.

UNIT 4: Global Marketing

International Trade Administration
www.ita.doc.gov

The U.S. Department of Commerce is dedicated to helping U.S. businesses compete in the global marketplace, and at this site it offers assistance through many web links under such headings as Trade Statistics, Cross-Cutting Programs, Regions and Countries, and Import Administration.

World Chambers Network
www.worldchambers.net

International trade at work is viewable at this site. For example, click on Global Business eXchange (GBX) for a list of active business opportunities worldwide or to submit your new business opportunity for validation.

World Trade Center Association OnLine
http://iserve.wtca.org

Data on world trade is available at this site that features information, services, a virtual trade fair, an exporter's encyclopedia, trade opportunities, and a resource center.

UNIT 1

Marketing in the 2000s and Beyond

Unit Selections

1. **Marketing in 2012: The End of the Middle?** Christine Birkner
2. **Hot Stuff: Make These Top Trends Part of Your Marketing Mix,** Gwen Moran
3. **Evolve,** Chris Penttila
4. **The Unmarketables,** Piet Levy, John N. Frank, and Allison Enright
5. **Six Strategies for Successful Niche Marketing,** Eric K. Clemons, Paul F. Nunes, and Matt Reilly
6. **The Branding Sweet Spot,** Kevin Lane Keller and Frederick E. Webster, Jr.
7. **Marketing Myopia (with Retrospective Commentary),** Theodore Levitt
8. **Putting Customers First: Nine Surefire Ways to Increase Brand Loyalty,** Kyle LaMalfa
9. **Making the Most of Customer Complaints,** Stefan Michel, David Bowen, and Robert Johnston
10. **When Service Means Survival,** Jena McGregor
11. **Become the Main Attraction,** Piet Levy
12. **How to Make Marketing Brilliance,** Jason Daley
13. **Imaginative Service,** Chip R. Bell and John R. Patterson
14. **Walking the Talk,** Katherine Ling
15. **Honest Innovation,** Calvin L. Hodock
16. **It's Hard to Be Good,** Alison Beard and Richard Hornik

Learning Outcomes

After reading this Unit, you will be able to:

- Dramatic changes are occurring in the marketing of products and services. What social and economic trends do you believe are most significant today, and how do you think these will affect marketing in the future?

- Theodore Levitt suggests that as times change, the marketing concept must be reinterpreted. Given the varied perspectives of the other articles in this unit, what do you think this reinterpretation will entail?

- In the present competitive business arena, is it possible for marketers to behave ethically in the environment and both survive and prosper? What suggestions can you give that could be incorporated into the marketing strategy for firms that want to be both ethical and successful?

Student Website

www.mhhe.com/cls

Internet References

American Marketing Association Code of Ethics
    www.marketingpower.com

Futures Research Quarterly
    www.wfs.org/frq.htm

Center for Innovation in Product Development (CIPD)
    www.web.mit.edu/cipd/research/prdctdevelop.htm

"If we want to know what a business is we must start with its purpose. . . . There is only one valid definition of business purpose: to create a customer. What business thinks it produces is not of first importance—especially not to the future of the business or to its success. What the customer thinks he is buying, what he considers 'value' is decisive—it determines what a business is, what it produces, and whether it will prosper."

— Peter Drucker, *The Practice of Management*

When Peter Drucker penned these words in 1954, American industry was just awakening to the realization that marketing would play an important role in the future success of businesses. The ensuing years have seen an increasing number of firms in highly competitive areas—particularly in the consumer goods industry—adopt a more sophisticated customer orientation and an integrated marketing focus.

The dramatic economic and social changes of the last decade have stirred companies in an even broader range of industries—from banking and air travel to communications—to the realization that marketing will provide them with their cutting edge. Demographic and lifestyle changes have splintered mass, homogeneous markets into many markets, each with different needs and interests. Deregulation has made once-protected industries vulnerable to the vagaries of competition. Vast and rapid technological changes are making an increasing number of products and services obsolete. Intense international competition, rapid expansion of the Internet-based economy, and the growth of truly global markets have many firms looking well beyond their national boundaries.

Indeed, it appears that during the new millennium marketing will take on a unique significance—and not just within the industrial sector. Social institutions of all kinds, which had thought themselves exempt from the pressures of the marketplace, are also beginning to recognize the need for marketing in the management of their affairs. Colleges and universities, charities, museums, symphony orchestras, and even hospitals are beginning to give attention to the marketing concept—to secure funds and donations and to provide what the consumer wants to buy. The selections in this unit are grouped into four areas. Their purposes are to provide current perspectives on marketing, discuss differing views of the marketing concept, analyze the use of marketing by social institutions and nonprofit organizations, and examine the ethical and social responsibilities of marketing.

The articles in the first subsection provide significant clues about salient approaches and issues that marketers need to address in the future in order to create, promote, and sell their products and services in ways that meet the expectations of

McGraw-Hill Companies, Inc./Gary He, photographer

consumers. Berkner's "Marketing in 2012" raises the intriguing concept that the recession in the American economy may call for a new definition of the middle class, prompting many marketers to shift everything within their marketing mixes.

The selections that address the marketing concept include Levitt's now classic "Marketing Myopia," which first appeared in the *Harvard Business Review* in 1960. This version includes the author's retrospective commentary, written in 1975, in which he discusses how shortsightedness can make management unable to recognize that there is no such thing as a growth industry. Also in this area is "Putting Customers First," which suggests nine ways to increase customers' brand loyalty. The next two articles in this subsection reflect the importance of companies focusing on customer satisfaction and customer service. The last article, "Become the Main Attraction", gives some practical suggestions for successful event marketing.

In the *Services and Social Marketing* subsection, the first article, "How to Make Marketing Brilliance" presents some of the best marketing moves of 2010. The second article discloses the importance of delivering unique value and faster service to meet and exceed customer expectations. The final article in this subsection discusses how eco-minded retailer, Patagonia, caused a stir with its recent "conscious-consumption" holiday campaign that told consumers not to buy the featured product.

In the final subsection, *Marketing Ethics and Social Responsibility,* a careful look is taken at the strategic process and practice of incorporating ethics and social responsibility into the marketplace. "Honest Innovation" reveals that ethical issues in new product development could be hampering innovation growth, and "It's Hard to be Good" chronicles five companies whose success is built on responsible business practices.

Marketing in 2012: The End of the Middle?

A new and more segmented American marketplace has risen from the ashes of the recession, prompting some marketplace watchers to proclaim the demise of the middle class—or, at the very least, to call for a new definition of that expansive consumer group. Once marketers' bread and butter, middle-class consumers are being pushed to the periphery of many marketers' targeting strategies as they focus, instead, on a more cut-and-dry division of the socioeconomic spectrum: into the "haves" and "have-nots." Experts predict that this polarized view of the marketplace could prompt many marketers to shift everything from their product portfolios and pricing to their messaging strategies and marketing mixes this year.

CHRISTINE BIRKNER

The Economic Outlook

More sophisticated segmentation practices have been parceling out the once-generic middle-class consumer group for years, but now, from a socioeconomic standpoint, the definition of a middle-class consumer—and particularly his wallet size—is anything but generic, and many successful marketers are taking a high-low approach to their targeting and segmentation practices. "There's been a notion in retailing for a long time that you could do better targeting the top end or the bottom end, and you could get lost if you're in the middle. We're seeing more companies focusing on that notion now than ever before," says Jonathan Asher, senior vice president at Perception Research Services International Inc., a consumer research firm based in Fort Lee, N.J.

Given the years of financial unease that many consumers have experienced since the United States economy faltered, it comes as no surprise that "trading down" has become a central consumer behavior. Although not quite as bleak as they were at the beginning of the recession in late 2007, economic statistics and consumer attitudes remain grim. The United States unemployment rate stood at 8.6 percent in November 2011, according to the United States Bureau of Labor Statistics, and while consumer confidence rose in November entering into the holiday shopping season, the United States Consumer Confidence Index, an economic indicator that measures the degree of optimism that consumers feel about the state of the economy, had declined to 39.8 the month before, a level last seen during the 2007–2009 recession. Consumers' overall optimism about the economy slumped to 23 percent in October 2011, down from 35 percent in March 2011 and 41 percent in September 2009, according to a survey on shopper and consumer insights by global management consulting firm McKinsey & Co. Those results don't bode well for marketers targeting beleaguered consumers in 2012, experts say.

"Consumers are still spending money, but they're not feeling good about it. Prices have been increasing and wages are not increasing. The median family income has also fallen three years in a row and a lot of households have lost their net worth. When people don't have any assets, they pursue less. It's very evident that the middle market is being squeezed," says Chris Christopher, senior principal economist at IHS Inc., an Englewood, Colo.-based global research and consulting company. IHS projects that income inequality will increase in the United States in 2012.

Economic conditions in 2012 will foster a recovery for the upper class in terms of consumer spending, but there will be continued malaise in the middle and lower classes, according to Michael Englund, principal director and chief economist at Boulder, Colo.-based Action Economics, a market analysis firm. "At the low end of income distribution, people dependent on wage income are going to find that labor markets are going to get increasingly dysfunctional. We're not entirely sure the middle class is getting smaller, but what we are finding is people who are depending on wage income can't simply assume ongoing climbs in wage income going forward . . . and they just don't have the income to finance the kind of spending that we've seen in [times of economic] expansion."

Adds Christopher, "We know from economic data that income inequality has increased since the recession hit and that's being reflected in how retailers are approaching things."

Retail and CPG as a Microcosm of the Marketplace

For a barometer of the changing consumer marketplace, look no further than recent moves by Cincinnati-based Procter & Gamble Co. According to *The Wall Street Journal*, P&G expanded its research on low-income households over the past two years and this fall, in response to consumers' needs for lower-cost options, P&G launched bargain-priced Gain dish soap, its first dish soap launch in 38 years. In an attempt to secure the other end of the economic spectrum, P&G introduced higher-priced versions of its Olay and Gillette product lines in 2009 and 2010, respectively. P&G declined to comment for this story.

Shrinking package sizes are another consequence of Americans' shrinking incomes. P&G reduced the size of some Tide laundry detergent packages from 100 oz. to 75 oz., allowing it to sell the smaller package size at under $10 at Wal-Mart compared with $12 for the 100-oz. version, according to *Ad Age*. In October, H.J. Heinz announced plans to produce smaller-sized versions across its product portfolio to target low-income consumers and Coca-Cola introduced 12.5 oz. bottles that sell for less in convenience stores than its 16-and 20-oz. versions.

Consumers still want name-brand products, but they want them for less, says Marshal Cohen, chief industry analyst at Port Washington, N.Y.-based research firm The NPD Group Inc. who specializes in consumer behavior, retail and fashion. "Today, when you ask the consumer, 'What is value?' the No. 1 answer they give is 'brand names for less.' That justifies why companies like Coca-Cola and Procter & Gamble [are cutting package sizes]. All of those things are a direct reflection of customers saying, 'I want the quality of the trusted brand, the reputation of the product, but I want it at a better value price and I'm willing to pay less to get the experience.' "

The success of discount retailers such as Family Dollar and Dollar General—both of which posted earnings increases in 2011—is evidence of a more permanent shift in purchase behavior than just a reactionary response to the recession's pressures, experts say. "The dollar stores have done a very good job of retaining a customer that gravitated towards them during the recession out of necessity to save money and make their paycheck go further," Cohen says. "The lower-middle and lower-income consumer have engaged with dollar stores and stayed there, and that's why dollar stores continue to grow, because they've offered a more diversified product range, because they've offered new sizes of product at advantageous prices."

On the higher-income end of the spectrum, luxury retailers now are faring well. Tiffany's sales increased 21 percent over the prior year in the third quarter of 2011 and Neiman Marcus Inc. reported total revenues of $1 billion in the first quarter of the 2012 fiscal year compared with $927.2 million in the prior year. "We've been doing a lot of work over the past couple of years on the polarized consumer. Those with incomes of over $100,000 are back in the game. The recession has ended for them. All other income groups are cutting back in terms of spending," says Todd Hale, senior vice president of consumer and shopper insights at the New York-based Nielsen Co.

Granted, experts say that the luxury consumer of 2012 is more cautious than the pre-recession luxury consumer. "The luxury consumer's mindset is one of eagerness and anticipation, but there's also a heavy dose of caution. [Luxury brands] are performing well but not necessarily at pre-recession rates,"

says Justin Wartell, executive director of brand strategy at Interbrand Design Forum, the shopper sciences and retail arm of Interbrand, a New York-based global branding consultancy.

Pamela Danziger, founder of Unity Marketing, a Stevens, Pa.-based marketing firm that specializes in luxury goods, says that luxury stores have held their own because they've adapted to the changing economy. "Shopping in those stores today is very different than shopping in those stores in 2007. They've opened their doors to lower-priced product lines. Saks is doing more with their own private label, which is more value-oriented, more dollar-friendly. Neiman just started taking MasterCard and Visa, whereas before it was only their own credit cards and American Express. The stores are being rewarded for [their] effective response to the economic climate. They're very smart marketers and as a result, they're showing positive results," Danziger says.

While low-end and high-end retailers have hit their stride in targeting more discerning consumers who've been trained to mind their credit lines by a painful recession, many middle-range retailers haven't been as successful. As *Marketing News* has reported, middle-market retailer Gap Inc. has faltered throughout 2011, with both marketing and earnings troubles. Gap's third quarter 2011 earnings dropped 36 percent and it announced the closure of 21 percent of its United States-based Gap stores in October. Other mid-market retailers struggled in late 2011 as well: J.C. Penney's total company sales in November 2011 decreased 5.9 percent and Sears' domestic comparable sales declined 0.7 percent in the third quarter of 2011.

"We're watching the consumer try to figure out where they belong. Not all of the mass merchants have done as good of a job as the others at reclaiming that lower-end consumer and not all the luxury retailers have recovered from the loss of that aspirational middle-class customer," Cohen says.

"As we see the middle class get stretched further and further into having to buy more diversified product with less income power, luxury is going to get back to pure luxury," he adds. "You're also seeing the low end being able to raise the bar again to at least engage the consumer in figuring out how to put a little bit of luxury there. We're seeing the polarization of luxury very strongly exemplified: the luxury market doing better and the low-end market dipping their toe into affordable luxury, which is eroding the middle even more."

The world of retail is trying to figure out how to reach the two ends of the economic spectrum, Cohen says. And with the disappearance of the aspirational middle-class consumer—or at least with middle-class consumers who are willing and able to spend on aspirational products—some luxury brands are developing products for the middle- or lower-class market, such as fashion retailer Missoni's line of products for Target. "It sold out within two and a half hours in 89 percent of stores they put the product in. That's a phenomenal success story, so successful it crashed Target's website," Cohen says.

And as the marketplace bifurcates based on wallet size, price is, of course, paramount. "If you're going to make price some sort of driver of your message, it has to stand for something, and the middle means nothing. It's either price because it's value, or luxury because it's pricey," says Scott Lucas, executive director of Interbrand Cincinnati. "We're seeing our clients make a clear distinction that if it's going to be a price-based conversation with consumers, it has to be meaningful and that middle tier isn't as rich of a story because price is tied to just being in the middle. . . . It has to be value or premium."

The Broader Implications

Retailers' responses to consumers' new spending behaviors are, of course, emblematic of what's going on throughout the global marketplace, as restaurants, airlines and tourist destinations, service providers, B-to-B organizations, you name it, rethink their targeting and pricing strategies, unbundle or resize their offerings and adjust their thinking to focus on customers who sit right or left of middle on the financial spectrum. In 2012 and beyond, offering a middle-range, average-priced product or service is no longer an enticing marketing proposition for many customers, experts say. Either you beat your competition by offering the most attractive price, or you beat them by convincing customers that the quality and value of your offering is worth the extra cost.

Asher of Perception Research says that for customers across the marketplace, their purchase behavior has become a cost-conscious, either-or proposition: "It's either, 'I'm looking totally for price,' or 'I'm going to spend more for quality because it's going to be worth it in the long run.'"

Critical Thinking

1. What is the United States Consumer Confidence Index?

2. In your opinion, what is the direct and indirect impact of the United States Consumer Confidence Index on consumer consumption patterns and habits?

3. With a small group of peers from your class, brainstorm some alternative strategies that companies could pursue to better target the contracting United States middle class.

Hot Stuff

Make These Top Trends Part of Your Marketing Mix

Gwen Moran

Still using the same marketing tactics you were using five years ago? Those won't work with today's shifting demographics and preferences. The U.S. population is older, more multicultural, more time-pressed and more jaded toward overt sales pitches than ever before. And your marketing strategy should be built accordingly.

So what's working? After consulting over a dozen experts in the field, we've uncovered the following hot trends in marketing.

Market on the Move

According to the Mobile Marketing Association, by 2008, 89 percent of brands will use text and multimedia messaging to reach their audiences, with nearly one-third planning to spend more than 10 percent of their marketing budgets on advertising in the medium. As phones with video capability become more prevalent, expect more rich media marketing options. Plus, now that mobile phone service providers are dipping their toes into the credit card pool—soon your phone or PDA may make plastic obsolete—customers will be relying on these devices more than ever.

"There are some low-cost mobile marketing onramps for small businesses," says Kim Bayne, author of *Marketing Without Wires*. "Businesses can implement opt-in text messaging services and coupons with their loyal customers. We've already seen local restaurants send the day's specials to nearby lunch patrons. The cost is fairly low, and it can be done from a PC, without involving a pricey service provider."

Go Online

"Think globally, act locally" is now the mantra for entrepreneurs advertising online. Online ad spending is up as much as 33 percent over last year, says David J. Moore, chairman and CEO of digital marketing firm 24/7 Real Media Inc. in New York City. Earlier this year, Google announced a new local advertising program linked to its map service and AdWords program, allowing businesses to drive some of Google's traffic to their brick-and-mortar locations.

"[Entrepreneurs] should pay attention to any targeting that allows them to increase advertising efficiency by reaching users in their particular geographic area," says Moore. Online ads are also migrating to podcasts and blogs, where advertisers can reach very specific niche audiences. And with increased access to broadband and the falling cost of video production, Moore foresees a rise in online video ads for businesses as well.

Court the Boom

A baby boomer turns 50 every 7 seconds—joining a population segment that will grow by 25 percent in the next decade while other segments remain flat.

Matt Thornhill, founder of consulting firm The Boomer Project, which helps businesses reach adults born between 1946 and 1964, says it's time for marketers to recalibrate their thinking about marketing to older adults. Boomers are a dynamic group that's much more open to new experiences and brands than previous generations of older adults have been.

Stephanie Lakhani found that to be true at her upscale Breathe Wellness Spas (www.breathetoheal.com) in Boise, Idaho. Catering primarily to boomers, the two spas bring in about $1.2 million per year. She says boomers are an excellent target, with disposable income and a tendency to refer business. "They expect perfect service," says Lakhani, 35, who adds, "They tend to travel and buy in groups, so giving them an incentive to refer a friend in the form of an upgrade or a thank you [gesture] works very well. They are also very responsive to direct mail."

Thornhill adds that marketers should target boomers by what they're doing instead of how old they are. "Boomers are living such cyclical lives. In their 40s or 50s, they could be going back to college, be empty nesters or be married a second time and raising a young family," he explains. "You wouldn't sell the same vacation package to all these people. So pick the lifestyle segment you're targeting, and focus on that."

Sindicate Simply

For something that's named Really Simple Syndication, few tools are more misunderstood or misused than RSS. Provided by such companies as Bloglines (www.bloglines.com) and News-Gator (www.newsgator.com), RSS lets you send and receive information without using e-mail. Instead, the information is sent directly to a subscriber, who receives it through an RSS reader. With browsers like Internet Explorer integrating such readers, we'll be seeing more information feeds. That could be a good thing—or not—depending on whether businesses use them properly.

"You don't need to blog to offer an RSS feed," says online marketing consultant Debbie Weil, author of *The Corporate Blogging Book*. "But you should have a blogging mind-set. Show the reader what's in it for them. Write clear and interesting headlines. There's a bit of an art to writing RSS [content]." She adds that you should break up your feeds by audience—customers, investors, media and the like—just as you would any other message distribution.

Jim Edwards, 38, uses a blog and RSS to promote his business, Guaranteed Response Marketing. "Whenever I publish an article, either through my blog [www.igottatellyou.com/blog] or through another site's RSS feeder, I expect to get 100 to 300 references back to me in a week," says Edwards, whose $2 million Lightfoot, Virginia, business provides electronic tutorials and publications. "It's a quick way to get links back to you, as well as to get on sites that people are actively looking at."

Use Social Networks

Customers are making friends online through social networking sites like MySpace.com. The massive site—boasting millions of users, all segmented by age, geography and interests—offers an unbridled opportunity for marketers, according to Libby Pigg, senior account manager at Edelman Interactive in New York City.

"You [can] launch a profile for your business and give it a personality," says Pigg, who has launched MySpace marketing campaigns for major consumer products companies. "It's simi-

lar to a dating site, where you tell people a bit about yourself. Then, you use the search function to find the group you want to target—maybe single people in New York [City] between 24 and 30—and contact them to become your 'friends.'"

A MySpace profile helped Taylor Bond generate interest in Egismoz.com, the electronics division of his $20 million retail company, Children's Orchard, in Ann Arbor, Michigan. Earlier this year, Bond sent invitations to some of the site's young, tech-savvy users. The key to maintaining their interest, he says, is to provide fresh content and special offers.

"We're seeing more people come into the store saying that they saw us on MySpace," says Bond, 44. "We're definitely seeing more traffic and feedback on the profile, and we're getting some incredible feedback about what's hot and what people want, so it's good for market research, too." Opportunities also exist on other networking sites like Friendster.com, LinkedIn.com, and even niche sites like Adholes.com, which focuses on the advertising community.

Advertise in Unusual Places

From valet tickets and hubcaps to T-shirts emblazoned with video displays, advertising is popping up in new places. A March survey of marketing executives by Blackfriars Communications entitled "Marketing 2006: 2006's Timid Start" found that business spending on traditional advertising continued its decline, and spending on nontraditional marketing methods—from online promotions to buzz marketing—rose 12 percent since late 2005.

Scott Montgomery, principal and creative director of Bradley and Montgomery, an advertising and branding firm in Indianapolis, says the shift in ad spending will continue as advertisers look to make their ad dollars more effective.

Make It Stick

Tap these marketing trends to get into customers' hearts and minds.

- **Multicultural Market:** By 2010, the buying power of American blacks and Hispanics is expected to exceed the gross domestic product of Canada, according to the Selig Center for Economic Growth at the University of Georgia in Athens. Make sure you're not overlooking this market. Rochelle Newman-Carrasco, CEO of Enlace Communications, a Los Angeles multicultural marketing firm, advises companies not only to translate materials when appropriate, but also to be conscious of cultural images: "In lifestyle shots, go beyond multicultural casting. Show scenes where the clothing, food and other backgrounds reflect different cultures."
- **Experiential Marketing:** Kathy Sherbrooke, president of Circles, an experiential marketing firm in Boston, says businesses must figure out the key messages of their brand and find ways for their staffs and locations to reflect that image—young and trendy, sophisticated and elegant, and so on. "Create an environment that's consistent with your brand," she says. She points to Apple Computer's retail stores, where clerks use handheld

checkout machines and pull product bags out of their back pockets to reinforce the ease-of-use and streamlined processes for which Apple is known.
- **Customer Evangelism:** From hiring word-of-mouth marketing companies to creating incentives for customer referrals, businesses are placing more importance on customer evangelism, says Andrew Pierce, senior partner at New York City branding firm Prophet. "Companies need to be customer-centric for this to happen," he explains. "If you're not finding ways to increase value and inspire loyalty, it won't work."

At the simplest level, Pierce advises using customer testimonials to add credibility to marketing efforts, including webinars where customers talk about your company. More extreme examples include buzz marketing campaigns where happy customers talk up the product, or inviting customers to trade shows or other events where they can show their enthusiasm in person.

Montgomery and his team were the first to develop advertising programs on electrical outlets in airports. Reasoning that business travelers—one of the holy grail audiences marketers love—power up portable technology while waiting for their planes, it seemed a natural place to reach them.

"Smart marketers are looking [for] places where people are engaged," says Montgomery. "You have to target your message in a way that makes sense for [how] people behave."

Premiumize Your Brand

Brands like Coach and Grey Goose vodka have mastered the art of taking everyday items and introducing luxe versions at much higher price points. Now, growing businesses are also going upscale with their products or services.

Andrew Rohm, professor of marketing at Northeastern University's College of Business Administration in Boston, says smaller businesses can often "trickle up" more easily than large brands, which may find that customers are resistant to accepting their more expensive offerings. "A small brand can reinvent itself without having to swim upstream against its image," says Rohm.

To posh up your product, he advises the same best practices as with any new offering: Do your research, and make sure there's a market for the product or service before you make your brand go bling.

Blog On

With the blogosphere more than 43.1 million blogs strong, according to blog search engine Technorati, it appears everyone and his grandmother are blogging. Robert Scoble, technical evangelist at Microsoft and author of *Naked Conversations: How Blogs Are Changing the Way That Businesses Talk With Customers,* believes blogs are important for businesses that want direct customer feedback. And development blogs, where businesses get direct input about products and services from readers, will soon become even more important, he says.

Scoble predicts a rise in regional blogs linked to Google's new local advertising program and Mapquest.com for quick access to directions, giving people more insight into the local businesses they want to frequent. He also says we'll see more video blogs, which won't replace text blogs but will more effectively communicate with some audiences. "If I'm trying to explain to you what [video game] Halo 2 is, I can write 10,000 words and I'm not going to get it right, but you can see a 2-minute video and you'll understand," he says.

Take these trends into consideration as you plan for the coming year. Not every idea may apply to your company, but most are market forces you can't afford to ignore.

Critical Thinking

1. Discuss some recent shifts in the demographic and sociocultural environments in the United States.
2. Explain how technology impacts marketing strategies and decisions, namely promotional tactics.

GWEN MORAN is *Entrepreneur's* "Retail Register" and "Quick Pick" columnist.

Evolve

The old business methods won't work anymore. It's time to evolve.

CHRIS PENTTILA

For companies feeling their way through the worst recession since the 1930s, it's easiest to stay focused on next quarter's numbers, improving operations and lowering costs where possible. Just stick with the playbook and keep your head down, and things will be fine, right?

Wrong. This recession is different from other recessions in its scope and depth, and the worst thing you can do is more of the same. Staying the course with your current business model "might let you survive a little bit longer, but you're not going to create that competitive advantage necessary for the long term," says Scott Anthony, president of Innosight, an innovation consulting firm, and author of next month's new book *The Silver Lining: An Innovation Playbook for Uncertain Times.*

You've got to change your game. But how can you do it? Here are seven ways to be a game changer right now:

Get comfortable with chaos. Globalization and technology are leading to constant economic turbulence. Being a game changer begins with a recognition of this new normality, says John A. Caslione, founder of GCS Business Capital, an M&A advisory company with offices worldwide, and co-author of *Chaotics: The Business of Managing and Marketing in the Age of Turbulence.* "[There's] going to be continuous turbulence punctuated by spurts of prosperity and downturns," he explains. "Understand that you're not going to be able to count on uninterrupted periods of prosperity."

Reassess your customers' values. This recession is changing people's mind-sets, not just their spending habits. It's still too early to tell what long-term impact this recession will have on customer behavior, but a more cautious, anxiety-ridden consumer has arisen in the short term. People are reevaluating their values and their purchases. How have your customers' values changed in the past six months, and how have their needs changed? The answers could spark new product and service ideas aimed at value-conscious consumers. Your company's closeness to customers is a huge advantage, so talk to them or work up a simple survey. Says Caslione, "You've got to be talking to your customers more than ever before to be able to understand how their needs are changing."

The Dos and Don'ts of Game Changing

Do

- Look at your business through the lens of another industry to find new ways to operate. If you're in manufacturing, how would you operate as a retailer, or vice versa?
- Talk to your customers about what they need today. This will help you find new competitive advantages.
- Get employees on the front lines talking about how customer mind-sets have changed and how the company can better reach consumers.
- Reexamine your business model for products, processes, promotions and so on that are no longer effective.
- Constantly look for ways to add value to your company, product or service. This doesn't have to be expensive. A retailer, for example, might set up a small play area with secondhand toys to keep kids busy while parents shop. It's the small things that can boost a revenue line.

Don't

- Stay the course. Realize the economy has changed and your company must change with it.
- Stop marketing your product or service. You need to actually communicate with customers now more than ever.
- Assume your suppliers, vendors and distributors are doing fine. Go see them in person. Check in with their suppliers, too.
- Get complacent if margins are still good because rapid industry transformations rise to the surface in tough times. The newspaper industry, for example, saw trouble coming for years, but healthy sales kept it from making necessary changes.
- Stop being creative. Aim for discipline in your core business balanced with a willingness to try new things and create new markets.

Understand that a good product always sells. A startling number of companies and game-changing products were actually launched in very tough times. Campbell's Soup was introduced in the 1890s. IBM launched its personal computer in 1981. The first iPod came out in late 2001. These periods were economic low points and seemingly not the time to launch new products. Marketing research company Nielsen found customers' willingness to purchase innovative products in good times and bad times has stayed remarkably constant over the past 30 years. "Just because times get tough," says Anthony, "doesn't mean people aren't willing to pay for things that help them solve problems."

Think new markets, not just cost cutting. Trimming costs where you can (renegotiating prices with suppliers and distributors and lowering your overhead) is very important, but don't stop there. Game changers see levers they can pull (e.g., affordability, convenience, accessibility, location and cost) that change a market or create an entirely new one. When MinuteClinic, a timesaving one-stop shop for simple ailments, launched in 2000 inside select CVS pharmacies, its model changed the game-and consumers responded.

View scarcity as a good thing. When sales are good, there's no urgency or any real need to be innovative. Feeling like your back is against the wall actually forces you to try new things. Now's the time to ramp up a few low-cost experiments and reexamine your entire business model for weaknesses in light of the economy. What have you got to lose? Welcome the challenge.

Stop defending the status quo. An idea sounds great—until you realize the operating margin or some other metric will be lower than expected. Microsoft had all the tools to create Google's search advertising business but abandoned the idea when search produced a paltry (by Microsoft standards) $1 million in sales during its first few months. By the time Microsoft finally recognized the importance of search, Google had a commanding lead in the market. Bending a little bit could pay off big time.

Serve the customers you hate. Every company has customers it sees as undesirable from a cost or profit perspective. Consider Netflix, which started out with a traditional pay-per-rental model in which customers paid late fees. In early 2000, 45-employee Netflix switched to a subscription model without late fees, a move that appealed particularly to customers who have trouble returning movies on time. Today, Netflix has around 250 employees and its business model is thriving in the recession. "It's not just the customers you've learned to love but, in fact, customers you've learned to hate and figuring out ways to innovate to make them great customers," Anthony says.

Every game has winners and losers. Which side will you be on? "Continue to dream, continue to experiment, continue to think differently," Anthony says. "But you've got to prove your dream more quickly than you ever did before." Now hurry—your customers are waiting.

Critical Thinking

1. In your perspective, what recent economic forces require companies to transform their business approach?

2. List and summarize the seven changes that the author of the article recommends businesses make.

CHRIS PENTTILA is a freelance journalist in the Chapel Hill, North Carolina, area.

The Unmarketables

Tough times call for new marketing strategies and tactics. Here are five approaches that these practitioners hope will revitalize their images and put them on the road to business recovery.

PIET LEVY, JOHN N. FRANK, AND ALLISON ENRIGHT

Brands, products and business segments have their ups and downs. The downs challenge marketers to find new approaches to revitalize and rejuvenate images to reconnect with key audiences.

This feature looks at a cross-section of businesses and products that are down for a variety of reasons. Some, like restaurants, financial services companies, and business travel and meeting resources, have been pushed out of favor because of the recession. Others, like U.S. automakers GM and Chrysler, need to battle the negatives that come with filing for bankruptcy protection. And another, high fructose corn syrup, faces image and health issues.

The first lesson for any brand, company or business segment facing similar challenges is that adversity means it's time to find new approaches for marketing, says brand guru David Aaker, vice chairman of Prophet, a San Francisco-based branding and marketing consultancy.

"I just don't think you can do business as usual and continue to spend money the way you've been spending money; you just need to be really creative," he counsels. Look to connect with your key audiences in new ways, with approaches that help you stand out dramatically from competitors, he says. You'll find more advice from Aaker, who also is *Marketing News*' newest columnist, throughout this piece. Look for his first *Marketing News* column in our Aug. 30 issue.

Restaurants: Value Tops the Menu

When your stomach's growling but your wallet's whimpering, a restaurant meal isn't as appetizing as it may have been in better times.

As a result, restaurant chains are hurting. Fine dining and casual dining sales likely will drop 10 to 15% and 5 to 8% respectively this year, says Darren Tristano, executive vice president of Chicago-based food industry consulting firm Technomic Inc.

Trying to do better than those predictions, many restaurant groups are stressing value and unique experiences in their marketing efforts.

Denny's Corp., for example, grabbed attention with its Grand Slam giveaway advertised during the Super Bowl. It gave away nearly 2 million free meals on Feb. 3, introducing consumers to its recently revamped menu in the process. It also provided incentives for return trips, says Mark Chmiel, executive vice president and chief marketing and innovation officer for the Spartanburg, S.C.-based company. Sales dropped in the first quarter but beat analyst expectations. In a statement, Denny's CEO Nelson Marchioli said the promotion was an "overwhelming success" and that the company "made significant progress on our primary goal of improving sales and guest traffic trends." Denny's continues to offer free meals through Twitter.

Besides value, Denny's is targeting niche audiences with new items and campaigns. Health nuts finally have some Denny's options, including chicken sausage and granola, which debuted in June. The company also has been stepping up early morning, young adult business with a funky social media campaign involving emerging rock bands and a talking unicorn.

Like Denny's, The Cheesecake Factory Inc., based in Calabasas Hills, Calif., had better than expected sales in the first quarter. Mark Mears, the company's senior vice president and CMO, says one reason for that is the chain's "Small Plates & Snacks" menu, nationally released in March. Meanwhile, the 200-item main menu trumpets variety and sharable meals as value options, Mears says.

Cheesecake Factory's "Share the Love" and "Share the Celebration" campaigns offered dine-again incentives during select weeks; the former touted a design-a-cheesecake feature online, and the latter encouraged fans to post descriptions of events they celebrated at Cheesecake Factory for entry into a sweepstakes.

At the higher end of the dining price chain, Morton's Restaurant Group Inc. in Chicago experienced a 24.1% decrease in comparable restaurant revenues in the first quarter of its fiscal 2009 because of cutbacks in business-related dining.

Aaker Advice
Restaurants

Find True Points of Difference

"You really need to help generate really different ideas that will break out of the clutter. You always need to find new things, but these days [it's] the only way."

Aaker Advice
Financial Services

Target Consumer Education

"If they really want to educate, the problem becomes how do you do it effectively? You need to segment the population. You need to target people."

It's trying to turn things around with value messaging driven by social media. Morton's blog recently featured recipes for meals and details on a new Morton's cookbook being promoted on a national tour at Morton outlets. Roger J. Drake, the company's chief communications officer, says the book pushes brand awareness and the book events drive restaurant traffic.

The company's biggest social media success has been through Twitter, with 1,424 followers as of late June. Twitter was exclusively used to promote a networking event at the new Bar 1221 inside a Chicago Morton's restaurant; Drake says sales were so successful that the strategy will be used at other locations.

Morton's Facebook page showcases other events like an absinthe tasting experience and price promotions such as a $99.99 deal for a pair of three-course steak and seafood dinners.

Value messaging, to many consumers, equals lower prices. So offering value through too many price promotions carries its own problems for when the economy improves. "It's not something you want consumers to get used to," Technomic's Tristano says. "It's hard to go back to the regular price points."

The Problem	Consumers are less likely to eat out in a bad economy.
The Fix	Create value messaging via price promotions, lower-cost menus and new food offerings.
Potential Pitfall	Consumers will continue to demand lower prices even in a healthier economy.

Financial Services:
Listen to Customers

Financial services firms have seen better days.

"Banking as a business and bankers in a generic sense have been getting bashed pretty badly," acknowledges long-time banking consultant Bert Ely, founder of Ely & Co. in Alexandria, Va.

Indeed, the credit card corner of the banking world became one of the first hit with new legislation this year when Congress passed a bill restricting a wide range of card issuer practices.

In the face of such negative perceptions, credit card companies are stressing their core brand values in marketing. They're also talking about responsible borrowing and financial education. Banks are trying a variety of approaches, including changing their names and their product offerings in response to consumer input.

Credit card companies such as Discover Financial Services "face a major challenge to their business models because now they have to invest an enormous amount of money changing all their systems to conform with new rules," Ely says. They need to do that while cutting overall spending in response to shareholder concerns. This recession is the first in which the major credit card companies—Discover, MasterCard and Visa—all are publicly traded companies. "The fact that they're public could change marketing spending. . . . You have to meet investor expectations," says Michael Kon, a senior analyst who follows credit cards at Morning-star Inc. in Chicago. Visa cut spending on marketing, advertising, sales and promotions by 8.8% in the first quarter of 2009 compared with the same period in 2008; MasterCard cut such spending 35%, Discover 21% and American Express Co. 42%, Kon notes.

Harit Talwar, CMO at Riverwoods, Ill.-based Discover, says he's using more online tools in his marketing mix and working to better integrate all his marketing efforts. Messaging stresses what he calls Discover's core brand mission, which is "helping consumers spend smarter, manage debt better, save more," he says. Discover in February introduced its Paydown Planner, Purchase Planner and Spend Analyzer on its website, three financial management tools that speak to its core mission, he says.

At rival MasterCard Worldwide, "we focus on what the Priceless campaign [MasterCard's ongoing advertising effort] has always been about; [it's] not about conspicuous consumption, it's about things that matter most," says Chris Jogis, vice president of U.S. consumer marketing for the Purchase, N.Y. company.

MasterCard's digital efforts center on financial education and the utility of using MasterCard. An iPhone application, for example, helps people find the nearest MasterCard-accepting ATM.

In an effort to get a more up-to-the-minute read on consumer sentiment, MasterCard has stepped up the frequency of economic focus groups to ask consumers how they're feeling financially.

Asking consumers what they want led to new products and a new name at what was known as GMAC Bank, an online banking operation owned by General Motors' financing arm, GMAC.

The newly named Ally kicked off its marketing campaign May 15, offering consumer-requested products like no withdrawal penalty CDs and less legalese in describing its offerings, notes Vinoo Vijay, product, brand and marketing executive at Ally. "Consumers are going to demand that banks do better by them, recession or not," Vijay says.

11

The Problem	Counter negative consumer and legislator perceptions.
The Fix	Stress responsible borrowing and spending, and offer financial education.
Potential Pitfall	Consumers will see new financial education efforts as disingenuous.

Business Travel: Go to Washington

As they boarded their luxury corporate jets last fall to testify before Congress about their incredibly, painfully red financial statements, the heads of GM, Ford and Chrysler probably couldn't fathom the storm they were flying into. Nor, perhaps, could the meeting planners for AIG, who hosted a $440,000 corporate retreat at a California luxury resort in September, less than a week after accepting $85 billion in bailout funds from taxpayers. Certainly, a large part of their collective actions were rooted in habit and pre-planning—albeit executed in a state of economic tone-deafness.

The resulting press coverage and 'can-you-believe-it' water cooler conversations produced a devastating effect on the related industries—private jet travel and the meeting planning and hotel industries—by default.

Faced with the enormous challenge of changing consumer sentiment and revving up business, the two industries quickly created separate integrated marketing efforts that shared similar messaging and intent. The National Business Aviation Association (NBAA) and the General Aviation Manufacturers Association jointly created "No Plane No Gain," while the U.S. Travel Association (USTA) tried to shore up its interests via a "Meetings Mean Business" campaign, coordinated with eight other travel-oriented association groups. The messages for both stressed the impact the negativity and related business losses had on front-line employment among employees serving these industries and the businesspeople that benefit from using those services. Both made a strong effort to change the tenor of statements coming from influential voices on Capitol Hill.

"We watched [the Meetings Mean Business] campaign with great interest because there is so much commonality there. . . . For us, it's 'how did you get there?' In [USTA's] case, it's 'where did you go?'" says Dan Hubbard, vice president of communications for NBAA and the in-house manager of the No Plane No Gain campaign in Washington, D.C.

"The tenor of the conversation had neglected a lot of facts. . . . [The campaign] helped frame it in the right terms, to help politicians understand that when you make off-the-cuff comments, you are putting people out of a job," says Chris Gaia, vice president of marketing for meetings, events and travel incentive planner Maritz Travel in St. Louis.

Maritz Travel's leadership worked with USTA to develop the Meetings Mean Business effort. Gaia estimates that Maritz Travel saw a 30% decline in the November time frame from 2007 to 2008. "A large portion of that was driven by [clients] not wanting to be targets of the media. They didn't want to get

---

called out for excesses. There were genuine economic problems [and adding the] political thing was icing on the cake," he says.

Both marketing efforts included intense communication efforts in the Washington area—No Plane No Gain included ad buys on local cable and in *Roll Call, Politico, USA Today* and *The Wall Street Journal*—and culminated in separate meetings at the White House with President Obama.

Business is trickling back at Maritz Travel, Gaia says. "In the last 60 days, we've had clients who cancelled stuff scheduled two years out come back and say: 'We need to add a short-term incentive sprint. We need to do a CEO roadshow to increase communication,'" he says.

At NBAA, Hubbard is optimistic that the efforts are taking hold. "A lot of that has come together in recent weeks and we're hopeful. It seems to have had a helpful impact."

The Problem	Condemned by the excesses of a few, the private aviation and corporate travel and meetings industries are hit hard by the economy.
The Fix	Industry groups installed intensive marketing initiatives to challenge and correct the public comments made by influencers.

See more, www.NoPlaneNoGain.com and www.MeetingsMeanBusiness.com

Bankrupt Automakers: Come Back, Shoppers

To say that U.S. automakers are facing marketing challenges this year is a bit akin to saying the crew of the Titanic had some problems with ice—the scale involved dwarfs anything Detroit has faced before.

"This is not an auto recession, it's an auto depression. The challenge everyone is facing is just staying alive," says David Cole, chairman of the nonprofit Center for Automotive Research, an Ann Arbor, Mich.-based auto think tank. U.S. car and light truck sales had been between 16.5 million and 17 million units annually two years ago. They fell to 13.5 million in 2008 and this year have been hovering around the 9 to 10 million annual rate.

The market dive drove Chrysler and General Motors into bankruptcy court by the start of June.

The marketing battle for each company has become a two-front war. Each needs to convince consumers it will still be in business once the recession ends. They also need to get reluctant buyers back into showrooms.

Regain Consumer Trust

"You need a branded program that packages the logic of why [consumers] should trust you and why it's going to be OK. Just to run ads that say 'we're trustworthy' [is] a complete waste of time. There needs to be substance."

Combat Rumors with Facts

"Find out what the facts are [about HFCS] and find a way to communicate them."

Chrysler addressed the first challenge with an advertising campaign starting May 3 that included print ads in 50 large U.S. newspapers, including the *New York Times, Wall Street Journal* and *USA Today.* "The tagline is, 'We're building a new car company, come see what we're building for you,'" says Jodi Tinson, Chrysler's manager of marketing communications.

"The whole purpose of the campaign is to let people know, yes, we're still out there for you."

The "We Build" campaign also includes five TV ads, two discussing restructuring and three featuring Chrysler, Dodge and Jeep products. The product ads focus on various Chrysler products in efforts to distinguish them from the competition. The Auburn Hills, Mich.-based automaker continues to work with its ad agency of record, BBDO, on the campaign, which also will have some online elements, Tinson says.

General Motors has joined industry efforts to assure people they won't get stuck with a new car and no regular paycheck. It's offering a payment protection plan to pay up to $500 a month for nine months to any buyer who loses a job, explains John M. McDonald, GM's manager for pricing incentives and market trends. It's also touting a vehicle protection plan that addresses trade-in values by offering buyers up to $5,000 if they trade in a GM car in the next two-and-a-half years and find the trade-in value has fallen below the amount of their auto loan.

For its Cadillac and Hummer lines, marketing has focused on letting people know financing is available, McDonald says. GM partnered with credit unions earlier this year to get discounted financing for credit union members buying GM products.

Cole thinks automakers should be touting the fact that the deals being offered now won't last once the economy revives. "One of the things that gets Americans to move is a deal or the potential loss of a deal," he says.

McDonald agrees that deal messaging will help with anyone already thinking about buying, but adds that "the issue right now is getting people into the marketplace."

The Problem	Convince consumers the companies won't go out of business; get consumers into a buying mood again.
The Fix	Stress corporate staying power, product attributes and financial concerns.
Potential Pitfall	Only those already thinking about a purchase will care; the rest will stay on the sidelines.

Corn Syrup: Sticky Sweet Truths

Give me your gut reaction: Is high fructose corn syrup (HFCS) good or bad?

It is generally agreed that most consumers' first reactions fall somewhere on the scale from negative to neutral. And that's meant marketing troubles for the HFCS business. Indeed, 67% of consumers indicated they were trying to consume less HFCS last year, up from 60% in 2007 and 54% in 2006, found the Washington-based International Food Information Council's 2008 Food & Health Survey.

Turning negative perceptions around has become a major industry challenge. The marketing response from the Washington-based Corn Refiners Association (CRA), which represents the largest corn refiners in the United States including Archer Daniels Midland and Corn Products International, has been a consumer education campaign begun in June 2008. The Sweet Surprise integrated campaign produced with agency DDB Chicago presents the scientific data about HFCS via TV ads, print and online elements, and includes a PR media outreach effort coordinated by Weber Shandwick. The CRA won't disclose spending, but industry estimates put the campaign in the $20-$30 million range.

"The reason [for the campaign] is to correct the significant misinformation being given to consumers about our corn sweetener," says Audrae Erickson, the president of the CRA. "Most of that information was misleading and completely inaccurate. Our goal is to ensure that consumers have the facts [and] that they understand that these two sweeteners [sugar and HFCS] are essentially the same."

HFCS is a corn-derived sweetener that is nearly identical in chemical composition to sugar. It has the same calorie count per gram and numerous scientific studies have indicated that the human body processes the product the same way. And government subsidies made to U.S. corn farmers also makes it a cheaper ingredient for food and beverage makers to use than sugar, which is why it appears in food and beverage products that formerly contained natural sugar.

Since the ingredient is found in few products produced outside the United States—it is cheaper to use sugar elsewhere—and frequent news headlines at home alert us that we are turning into a nation of chunks, some health and dietary groups assert that a connection can be made between our obesity problem and the growth of HFCS consumption during the past 30 years. Those headlines appear to be having an impact on consumer consumption patterns.

The per capita delivery of HFCS for food and beverage use declined 16.4% from 1999 (HFCS's peak year) to 2008, according to U.S. Department of Agriculture statistics. Worried about a consumer backlash, food and beverage marketers have begun to try to distinguish their products as containing no HFCS; 146 products carried the claim in 2007, up from just six products in 2003, according to London-based Datamonitor.

The Sweet Surprise campaign's target market is mothers, says Don Hoffman, executive vice president and managing director of accounts with DDB Chicago. "The tone of the communications is simple and straightforward. It is targeted to women as decision makers and good communicators. . . . [Women] find the right facts and disseminate the right facts," he says.

Early returns are limited, but Erickson says the campaign is helping. "We have been very successful in making a difference in correcting the record. But based on the stories that continue, there is more work to be done to ensure that consumers get the truth."

The Problem	High fructose corn syrup is getting a bad rep in the media and among consumers.
The Fix	The Corn Refiners Association launched an integrated media blitz to disseminate scientifically backed facts about the ingredient. For more, see www.SweetSurprise.com.
Trivia	The average U.S. consumer consumed 40.1 pounds of HFCS and 44.2 pounds of refined sugar in 2007, according to the U.S.D.A. Economic Research Service.

Critical Thinking

1. Describe the effects of the current economic recession on various industries and sectors.

2. Explain how technology impacts marketing strategies and decisions, namely promotional tactics.

From *Marketing News*, July 30, 2009, pp. 10–14. Copyright © 2009 by American Marketing Association. Reprinted by permission.

Six Strategies for Successful Niche Marketing

How to win big by thinking small.

Eric K. Clemons, Paul F. Nunes, and Matt Reilly

There's been a lot of buzz about the long-tail phenomenon—the strategy of selling smaller quantities of a wider range of goods that are designed to resonate with consumers' preferences and earn higher margins. And a quick scan of everyday products seems to confirm the long tail's merit: Where once we wore jeans from Levi, Wrangler or Lee, we now have scores of options from design houses. If you're looking for a nutrition bar, there's one exactly right for you, whether you're a triathlete, a dieter or a weight lifter. Hundreds of brewers offer thousands of craft beers suited to every conceivable taste.

It's not surprising that so many companies have embraced this strategy. It allows them to avoid the intense competition found in mass markets. Look at the sales growth that has taken place in low-volume, high-margin products such as super-premium ice cream, noncarbonated beverages, heritage meats and heirloom vegetables.

But the case for the long tail has frequently been overstated. This strategy can be expensive to implement, and it doesn't work for all products or all categories. It's surely better to produce a blockbuster film, for instance, than a smattering of low-volume art films.

In other words, simply avoiding the clutter of mass markets isn't enough. Companies need to stake out unique market *sweet spots*, those areas that resonate so strongly with target consumers that they are willing to pay a premium price, which offsets the higher production and distribution costs associated with niche offerings. We call this approach resonance marketing.

The vast amount of information available on the Internet has made this kind of niche marketing more important than ever and easier to do. More important because all that information encourages comparison shopping, putting tremendous downward pressure on prices and profits in highly competitive mass markets. And easier because it eliminates much of consumers' uncertainty about new

Questions to Ask Yourself

1. As part of a strategy of selling a wider range of high-margin goods, are you being careful to distinguish potential future market sweet spots from valueless niches that produce needless complexity?
2. Are you listening carefully to what consumers are saying online about your products, not just to you but also to each other, and are you reacting quickly to make improvements that address any negative comments?
3. Are you standardizing design components as much as possible to limit the costs of producing an extensive product line?
4. Are you aggressively keeping inventory and distribution costs down with strategies that allow you to configure finished products quickly when orders arrive, swap inventory among outlets or share distribution with other producers?
5. Are you continually reviewing your product portfolio to weed out those products that aren't contributing to profits, while being careful not to dump products that aren't big sellers but still contribute to the portfolio's overall profitability?

If you answered no to any of these questions, you're not getting the most out of what we call resonance marketing—selling a variety of precisely targeted goods designed to resonate with consumers. Following the steps in this article will help you manage the complexity of this strategy and reap superior profitability.

For Further Reading

These related articles from MIT Sloan Management Review can be accessed online

From Niches to Riches: Anatomy of the Long Tail

Erik Brynjolfsson, Yu "Jeffrey" Hu and Michael D. Smith (Summer 2006)

The Internet marketplace allows companies to produce and sell a far wider range of products than ever before. This profoundly changes both consumer behavior and business strategy.

Harnessing the Power of the Oh-So-Social Web

Josh Bernoff and Charlene Li (Spring 2008)

People are connecting with one another in increasing numbers, thanks to blogs, social networking sites and countless communities across the Web. Some companies are learning to turn this growing groundswell to their advantage.

Cracking the Code of Mass Customization

Fabrizio Salvador, Pablo Martin de Holan and Frank Piller (Spring 2009)

Most companies can benefit from mass customization, yet few do. The key is to think of it as a process for aligning a business with its customers' needs.

But that's not as easy as it might sound. Finding profitable new niches requires a set of skills different from those needed to build market share or to create variations of an existing product—you're looking for places where no offerings exist, not one where consumers are complaining about existing choices.

Consider the success of Toyota Motor Corp.'s Lexus line of luxury cars. Toyota's research indicated there was an untapped market in the U.S. for Mercedes-quality luxury cars at a lower price, rather than superior quality at a comparable price. The Lexus line was designed to offer quality at a price that indicated the owners could afford whatever they wanted but also were smart enough to get it at a great price. The brand fulfilled an unmet need in the market and enjoyed immediate success.

Simply identifying gaps in the market isn't enough, though. Plenty of unique consumer products have failed to capture the imagination of shoppers. There's no guaranteed way to avoid such failures, but extensive research is essential. Often an ethnologist can help. Many companies use these analysts to explore why consumers buy what they do and what they would buy if it were available.

Listen to Your Customers. Really Listen.

Traditional advertising campaigns don't make sense for most niche markets; they're too expensive and too difficult to target precisely enough. Indeed, there are entire product categories, including nutrition bars and craft beers, where most products are never advertised. Their producers have learned how to work with consumer-generated content online—reviews, ratings or just chatter about a product. They don't just listen when customers talk to them; they listen just as carefully when customers talk about them.

The beauty of consumer-generated content is that companies get immediate and continuous feedback about their products. The key here is to listen closely and react quickly. Marketing executives should watch for the first online comments about their wares with the same excitement and apprehension as Broadway producers waiting for opening-night reviews. Consumers will make it clear right away what they like about the product and what they don't.

Harsh reviews can have devastating consequences. We analyzed two years of data on hotel bookings and found that the length, specificity and detail of negative online reviews are the best predictors of a hotel's inability to sell itself online.

niche products, since they can easily find reviews, ratings and comments on everything that hits the market. For decades consumer uncertainty blocked the launch of new offerings that were too focused to be supported by national ad campaigns; today's empowered consumer is truly listening to word-of-mouth.

Finding sweet spots in the market is especially important in these tough economic times, when so many consumers are strapped for cash. Many shoppers will compromise whenever possible by looking for cheaper alternatives to the things they usually buy—but keep buying products that don't have any direct substitutes.

With the right approach, resonance marketing can fulfill its promise. We have found that six marketing principles, taken together, will allow a company to manage the complexity of this strategy and reap superior profitability.

Target Carefully

Sweet-spot offerings aren't better than other products in any absolute sense; they simply have to be different from existing options and better for their target consumers. They have to resonate powerfully with them.

So what do you do if the product you so carefully crafted to appeal to a particular market segment is trashed by those very consumers? Fix it immediately.

If defects pointed out by consumers are fixed quickly, more-favorable comments will emerge just as quickly. But companies should never assume that they've gotten it right and can stop listening. Continuous monitoring of online comments will alert executives to any new issues that arise, any improvements consumers might like to see as they become more familiar with the product, and even the emergence of any competitors or alternatives that might siphon off buyers.

Some traditional marketing still has its place, and indeed has become more powerful thanks to the way word-of-mouth spreads so quickly over the Internet. Companies can generate positive buzz for niche products with events like the Great American Beer Festival that small, specialty brewers attend every year. The brewers make sure to attract both professional critics and passionate amateur bloggers alike.

Moreover, craft brewers have learned to work together to make these events successful; they understand that at this point in their industry's development, their greatest danger comes not from each other but from consumer acceptance of mass-produced, generic beers.

Control Production Costs

Selling a large number of narrowly targeted products may sound like a production nightmare, but it doesn't have to be. There are several ways to maintain economies of scale over a broad range of product offerings.

Variety and standardization can coexist. For instance, Callaway Golf Co. offers buyers of its drivers multiple options for a club's head, loft angle and shaft—several hundred different combinations in all. But the company doesn't manufacture every variety separately. Any configuration of the various components can be readily assembled, since the interconnections are standardized.

Manufacturing processes can also be standardized to a large extent. While pumpkin spice ice cream appeals to a very different group of consumers than vanilla does, the manufacturing process is nearly identical for both flavors and any others. Brewing involves cold-fermenting lagers in one set of tanks and warm-fermenting ales in another, but the two varieties share many other processes: mashing grains, adding hops, bottling.

It also pays for a company to have a high-volume product in its portfolio that will keep its manufacturing equipment and employees from sitting idle for stretches of time. The relatively low volume of sales in narrowly targeted markets means production plants might not need to work to their full capacity to meet demand. A high-volume, if less profitable, product can take up the slack.

Control Distribution Costs

It's not just production costs that will determine the profitability and ultimate success of resonance offerings. Distribution costs are also important. There are ways here, too, to keep costs under control.

It can be difficult to forecast demand for products with limited sales, but that doesn't necessarily mean a company needs to stockpile high levels of inventory to keep from getting caught short. Companies that offer many varieties of a product based on different combinations of components, as Callaway does with its golf clubs, can keep inventory low by postponing final assembly until a particular product is ordered—there's no need to keep a given number of every combination in stock.

Flexible inventory allocation is another way to keep from having to stockpile goods. Auto makers, for instance, often swap needed items. If a customer in New Jersey wants a copper-colored Infiniti FX35 and his dealer has the car in silver, while a customer in Pennsylvania wants the same car in silver and his dealer has the copper, the dealers can arrange an exchange.

Shared distribution is another option worth considering. Small brewers, for instance, cut costs this way.

Selling to customers directly from a company website can reduce costs by eliminating intermediaries. But companies should be aware that shoppers can be less forgiving online than they are offline. A consumer who visits a store to buy a product or orders it from a catalog may be miffed if it is temporarily out of stock. But frustration may rise to the level of anger if the same consumer orders the product online and isn't notified until three days later that the item is out of stock, because of a glitch in the site's inventory software.

Some Apparent Losers Are Worth Keeping

Even with the best research and the most careful marketing, production and distribution, some products will be unprofitable or only marginally profitable. But before discontinuing a product, a company should consider the product's value in broader terms.

Some products that don't generate significant profit directly still help make a company's other products more profitable. Feeder routes on airlines transport customers to more-profitable routes, such as trans-Atlantic flights. Likewise, niche books that don't account for a significant portion of Amazon.com Inc.'s sales are valuable to the company because they contribute to its reputation as a one-stop source for any book.

Prune Your Portfolio Ruthlessly

Companies must relentlessly drop niche offerings that don't contribute to profitability directly or indirectly. The scores of flavors discontinued over the years by Ben & Jerry's Homemade Inc., remembered fondly in the "flavor graveyard" on the company's website, serve as a reminder to all companies that the flip side of creative expansion of a product line is eliminating those that no longer resonate with consumers. And the success of Ben & Jerry's is a reminder of the power of resonance marketing done right.

Critical Thinking

1. List a possible seventh strategy and explain why you came up with it.
2. What questions would you ask in the pursuit of an additional niche market(s)?

DR. CLEMONS is a professor of operations and information management at the Wharton School of the University of Pennsylvania. MR. NUNES is executive director of research at the Accenture Institute for High Performance and is based in Boston. MR. REILLY is a senior executive in Accenture's management-consulting business, global managing director of the firm's Process and Innovation Performance practice and global co-leader of its Operational Excellence service. They can be reached at reports@wsj.com.

The Branding Sweet Spot

KEVIN LANE KELLER AND FREDERICK E. WEBSTER, JR.

One of the realities of modern brand marketing is that many of the decisions that marketers make with respect to their brands are seemingly characterized by conflicting goals, objectives and possible outcomes. Unfortunately, in our experience, too many marketers define their problems in "either/or" terms, creating situations where one idea, one individual or one option wins out. Opportunities are missed for finding an even better solution, a new idea that could have been discovered and developed by combining and refining conflicting points of view. As a result, resources may be squandered, consumers may be left unsatisfied or confused and the organization may find itself struggling with lingering internal conflict.

We submit that this is dangerously wrong, and there is a better way to approach such problems, one which we call "marketing balance." Achieving marketing balance requires understanding and addressing conflicting objectives and points of view, taking into account and resolving multiple interests. It is synonymous with moderation, and the opposite of self-indulgence or turbulence. It involves finding "win-wins"—the branding sweet spot—so that vulnerable extreme solutions and suboptimal compromises are avoided.

Marketing Trade-offs

Conflict and trade-offs are inherent in marketing decision making, and are the most fundamental challenge of marketing and brand management. Table 1 organizes these trade-offs or conflicts into four broad categories—strategic, tactical, financial or organizational decisions—which we briefly highlight here.

Strategy trade-offs. Marketing strategy trade-offs involve decisions related to targeting and positioning brands. Some involve trade-offs in growth strategies, such as concentrating marketing resources on expanding the brand into new product categories vs. fortifying the brand and further penetrating existing product categories. Another growth trade-off is emphasizing market retention and targeting existing customers vs. emphasizing market expansion and targeting new customers.

Whether to use funds to build and retain existing customer relationships or spend resources to develop new customers is certainly a dilemma that many firms face.

Other marketing strategy trade-offs revolve around how brands are competitively positioned in the minds of customers—such as an emphasis on brand tangibles (product performance) vs. brand intangibles (user imagery); a classic vs. contemporary image; an independent vs. universal image; and so on. Some of the product-related performance trade-offs in brand positioning are between attributes and benefits—such as price and quality, convenience and quality, variety and simplicity, strength and sophistication, performance and luxury and efficacy and mildness.

One common trade-off is whether the marketing program should stress points of difference (i.e., how the brand is unique) or points of parity (i.e., how the brand is similar), with respect to competitors' offerings. Product development decisions are often defined in terms of whether to bring the next generation of products in line with a major competitor's level of performance, or to commit more research and development funds and time to achieving a technological breakthrough.

Tactics trade-offs. Marketing tactic trade-offs involve decisions related to the design and implementation of marketing program activities. Some of the more common trade-offs evident with marketing programs are push (intermediary-directed) vs. pull (end-consumer-related) strategies or how the program is updated over time (emphasizing continuity vs. change).

A real dilemma for many companies is whether to support existing channels or to develop new ones, which usually means creating competition for the companies' traditional outlets. The problem often comes down to a stark choice: Given evolution in customer buying patterns and preferences, and significant declines in the market position of our traditional dealers, do we create a whole new system for going to market or do we re-segment the market,

Table 1 Representative Marketing Trade-offs

Strategic (Targeting and Positioning)
- Retaining vs. acquiring customers
- Brand fortification vs. brand expansion
- Brand awareness vs. brand image
- Product performance vs. user imagery
- Points of parity vs. points of difference

Tactical (Design and Implementation)
- Push vs. pull
- Continuity vs. change
- Existing vs. new channels
- Direct market coverage vs. use of middlemen
- Selling systems vs. selling components
- Creative, attention-getting ads vs. informative, product-focused ads

Financial (Allocation and Accountability)
- Short-run vs. long-run objectives
- Revenue-generating vs. brand-building activities
- Easily measurable marketing activities vs. difficult to quantify marketing activities
- Quality maximization vs. cost minimization
- Social responsibility vs. profit maximizing

Organizational (Structure, Processes, and Responsibilities)
- Central vs. local control
- Top-down vs. bottom-up brand management
- Customized vs. standardized marketing plans and programs
- Internal vs. external focus

refine our strategy and strengthen our position with our traditional distribution partners?

Financial trade-offs. Marketing financial trade-offs involve decisions related to the allocation and accountability of investments in marketing program activities. In arriving at marketing investment decisions, these are some common trade-offs:

- Invest in generating revenue vs. building brand equity.
- Go for clearly measurable effects vs. "softer" effects that are more difficult to measure.
- Maximize product or service quality vs. minimizing costs.

Perhaps the most common trade-off is the tension on long-term brand-building strategies created by pressure for short-term earnings results and "making the numbers." Marketing expenditures, especially for advertising and brand development, are among the most vulnerable when management is looking for ways to improve the bottom

Executive Briefing

One of the challenges in modern brand marketing is the many strategic, tactical, financial and organizational trade-offs that seem to exist. Successfully developing and implementing marketing programs and activities, to build and maintain strong brands over time, often requires that marketers overcome conflicting objectives and realities in the marketplace. Guidelines and suggestions are offered on achieving marketing balance, to hit the branding sweet spot by arriving at "win-win" decisions that successfully reconcile marketing trade-offs.

line, because the long-term effects of most marketing expenditures are so hard to determine due to the problem of multiple causation.

Unfortunately, the paths of commerce are strewn with the debris of once-powerful brands that were milked for profit and cash, based on the mistaken belief that they were strong enough to sustain major spending cuts for improving the bottom line. As one example, Coors Brewing cut advertising spending in the 1990s for its flagship Coors beer brand—from $43 million annually to a meager $4 million. Not surprisingly, the brand's market share subsequently dropped in half.

Organization trade-offs. Finally, marketing organization trade-offs involve decisions in the structure, processes and responsibilities involved in marketing decision making. For large global organizations especially, trade-offs found in this area include centrally mandated vs. locally controlled authority and standardized vs. customized marketing approaches. As effective a marketer as Nike has been, the company has often lamented that it has not historically balanced global objectives with local realities as well as it would have liked. Walt Disney Co. has been even more blunt in its belief that it has needed to achieve more cultural relevance in its global pursuits.

In terms of brand management, trade-offs often emerge between top-down (corporate-level) vs. bottom-up (product/market level) and internal vs. external focus. Strong business-to-business brands, such as GE, often find themselves challenged with managing their corporate brand in the face of diverse business units with different competitive challenges and potentially different stages of brand development in the marketplace and in different countries.

Marketing Balance Levels

Although we discussed marketing trade-offs within our four main categories, trade-offs certainly exist across the categories too. Pressure to achieve certain earnings targets may lead to an emphasis on short-term tactical moves, for example. One response to these trade-offs is to adopt an "extreme" solution and maximize one of the two dimensions involved with the trade-off. Many management gurus advocate positions that, in effect, lead to such a singular, but clearly limited, focus. These approaches, however, obviously leave the brand vulnerable to the negative consequences of ignoring the other dimension.

The reality is that for marketing success, both dimensions in each of these different types of decision trade-offs must typically be adequately addressed. To do so involves achieving a more balanced marketing solution. Marketing balance occurs when marketers attempt to address the strategic, tactical, financial and organizational trade-offs as clearly as possible in organizing, planning and implementing their marketing programs.

There are three means or levels of achieving marketing balance—in increasing order of potential effectiveness as well as difficulty.

Alternate. The first means would be to identify and recognize the various trade-offs, but to emphasize one dimension at a time, alternating so that neither dimension is completely ignored. Although potentially effective, the downside with this approach is that the firm often experiences a "pendulum effect," as there can be a tendency to overreact to a perceived imbalance on one dimension leading to a subsequent imbalance on the other dimension. Too often, there is too much of the wrong thing at the wrong time.

Divide. The second means of achieving marketing balance would be to "split the difference" and do a little of both to "cover all the bases." The idea here is to mix and match marketing efforts, so that both dimensions are covered. For example, at one point, Dewar's Scotch ran two print ad campaigns simultaneously. "Portraits" offered descriptive "personals" type of information of young scotch drinkers in an attempt to make the brand more relevant to a younger audience. And "Authentics" focused on the heritage and quality of the scotch, appealing to an older audience that was already part of the brand franchise and presumably valued more intrinsic product qualities.

Clearly, such solutions can be expensive and difficult, as two distinct marketing programs have to be successfully designed, financed and implemented. They can also result in conflicting messages and customer confusion. Although potentially effective if properly executed, this approach may suffer if insufficient or inadequate resources are put against the two objectives, with critical mass not being achieved. Attempting to do "a little of this and a little of that" may be too wishy-washy and lack sufficient impact.

Reconcile. Finally, perhaps the best way to achieve marketing balance is by reconciling the differences and achieving a positive synergy between the two dimensions. Marketing balance in this way occurs by shrewdly addressing the decision trade-offs head-on (i.e., by resolving the conflicting dimensions in some uniquely creative manner). Hitting the branding sweet spot in this way may involve some well thought out moderation and balance throughout the marketing organization and its activities. Top marketing organizations such as Procter & Gamble (P&G), Nike, LVMH, Virgin and Toyota differ in many ways, but they share one characteristic: They have been remarkably adept at balancing trade-offs in building and managing their brands.

Achieving Marketing Balance

A two-step approach can help in achieving marketing balance: First, the extent and nature of the marketing trade-offs faced by the organization must be defined. Then, appropriate solutions must be developed to address the trade-offs as carefully and completely as possible.

To understand the nature and extent of the marketing trade-offs, some key questions must be answered: How severe are they? Are they unavoidable, inherent in the nature of the decision problem and situation? How have they been dealt with before? Of particular importance is to recognize whether the trade-offs result from internal, organizational considerations or external, structural issues inherent in the marketing environment where management has less control.

Next, marketers must develop effective means for achieving marketing balance. Given the wide range of marketing trade-offs that exists, it is perhaps no surprise that a correspondingly wide range of solutions is also typically available. We briefly outline six different options that are available to marketers to achieve marketing balance in Table 2.

Breakthrough Product or Service

One compelling way to resolve potential marketing strategy trade-offs is through product or service innovations. For example, Miller Lite became the first successful nationally marketed light beer through an innovative brewing formulation that was able to retain more of the taste profile of a full-strength regular beer, while still having a lower calorie count. Breakthrough product or service innovations

Table 2   Achieving Marketing Balance

- Breakthrough product or service innovation
- Improved business models
- Expanded or leveraged resources
- Embellished marketing
- Perceptual framing
- Creativity and inspiration

may not necessarily always require such significant initial investments. Decades later, Miller Lite was able to re-assert its straddle "Tastes Great, Less Filling" brand promise through an intensive ad campaign that focused on its low carbohydrate levels. Miller Lite had always had a performance advantage on the basis of "low carbs," but it only became a positioning advantage when the company could tap into a growing consumer health trend.

As another example, when BMW first made a strong competitive push into the U.S. market in the early 1980s, it positioned the brand as being the only automobile that offered both luxury and performance. At that time, American luxury cars were seen by many as lacking performance, and American performance cars were seen as lacking luxury. By relying on the incomparable design of their car—and to some extent their German heritage too—BMW was able to simultaneously achieve (1) a point of difference on performance and a point of parity on luxury with respect to luxury cars and (2) a point of difference on luxury and a point of parity on performance with respect to performance cars. The clever slogan, "The Ultimate Driving Machine," effectively captured the newly created umbrella category: luxury performance cars. Product differentiation can occur through technological innovation or creative repositioning.

Improved Business Models

Sometimes the solution is broader than just the product itself, and encompasses other aspects of the business. For example, P&G's switch to every-day low prices (EDLP) necessitated that the company overcome the potential trade-offs between high-quality products vs. the high costs and prices that are typically involved in delivering high levels of quality. P&G knew it could not deliver everyday low prices without having low everyday costs.

To reduce costs, P&G implemented a number of changes, simplifying the distribution chain to make restocking more efficient through continuous product replenishment. The company also scaled back its product portfolio by eliminating 25 percent of its stock-keeping units. Importantly, all of these cost-reduction changes were done without sacrificing product quality, allowing P&G to maintain much of its market leadership.

Expanded or Leveraged Resources

Another means of achieving balance and overcoming the inherent trade-offs in marketing decision making is to find ways to expand or leverage existing resources to make them more productive. For example, one approach often employed in addressing positioning trade-offs—albeit not without some investment implications—is to use ingredient brands (e.g., "Intel Inside") or a celebrity spokesperson/endorser. Ingredient brands or celebrities can reinforce a potentially weak area of a brand image. For example, General Motors used the popular appeal of golfer Tiger Woods for a number of years, to give its aging Buick brand a potentially more youthful and contemporary image.

Skillfully expanding resources is another means to adequately address more dimensions in a trade-off. For example, taking the cue from Harley-Davidson, Apple and others, many firms are attempting to build online and/or off-line brand communities. Building brand communities allows firms to tap into the passions and dedication of existing customers, reinforcing their loyalty and motivating and empowering them to serve as brand ambassadors or even brand missionaries with other consumers. In this way, existing customers help to bring new customers into the fold. Brand communities can thus be an effective means to help a firm both acquire and retain customers for its brands.

Embellished Marketing

Another potentially productive strategy is to find ways to embellish existing marketing programs to encompass a neglected or even missing dimension. In what ways can a marketing decision or action that typically emphasizes one dimension be modified or augmented to also encompass another dimension at the same time?

For example, many sales promotions emphasize price or discounts at the expense of product or service advantages, and thus the equity of the brand. Bucking that trend, however, P&G ran a clever promotion for Ivory soap that reinforced its key attribute of "floating" and its key benefit of "purity" while also providing an incentive for purchase: A select number of bars of soap were weighted such that they sank in the bathtub, giving the purchaser the right to enter a contest to win $250,000. Equity-building promotions that introduce key selling points into traditionally price-focused sales promotions are thus one way to incorporate an important but underemphasized dimension into marketing decisions.

Perceptual Framing

Trade-offs vary in terms of whether they are based in reality, reflecting inherent "laws" of the marketplace or, instead, are based on perceptions—thus reflecting the potentially biased or maybe just idiosyncratic views of the parties involved. The more the latter is the case, the more opportunities there are for marketing efforts to overcome potentially inaccurate or incorrect perceptions.

Perceptual framing can be an especially powerful way to achieve robust brand positions and, thus, marketing balance. For example, when Apple Computer Inc. launched the Macintosh, its key point of difference was "user friendly." Many consumers valued ease of use—especially those who bought personal computers for the home, but customers who bought personal computers for business applications inferred that ease of use meant that the computer must not be very powerful—a key choice consideration in that market.

Recognizing this potential problem, Apple ran a clever ad campaign with the tag line "The power to be your best," to redefine what a powerful computer meant. The message behind the ads was that because Apple was easy to use, people in fact did just that—they used them! It was a simple, but important, indication of "power." From that point of view, there was a positive, not negative, correlation between the two choice criteria.

Creativity and Inspiration

One powerful solution to reconcile conflicts in marketing decision making is to find potentially overlooked synergies. Perhaps the common denominator to all the different advocated solutions reviewed in this article is marketing creativity and the ability to address seemingly insurmountable problems through imaginative marketing solutions. Achieving marketing balance requires penetrating insights, shrewd judgments and a knack for arriving at solutions that go beyond the obvious. Creativity, the combination of previously unrelated ideas into new forms, is often the inspiration to achieve marketing balance.

For example, in the early 1990s, the California Milk Processor Board (CMPB) uncovered an insight that had been overlooked by marketers of milk all over the world. Unlike traditional and increasingly ineffective marketing campaigns that emphasized the healthful benefits of milk (e.g., how it made people look and feel good), the CMPB recognized that one powerful advantage of milk was as an indispensable companion or even "ingredient" with certain foods (e.g., cookies, cakes, etc.). With their ad agency Goodby Silverstein, the CMPB took that insight and developed the highly

creative Got Milk? ad campaign that entertained and engaged consumers and sold milk in the process. The amusing and beloved ads ensured that its humor did not detract from its fundamental message: Running out of milk is a pain!

The Implications of Marketing Balance

One of the challenges in modern brand marketing is the many strategic, tactical, financial and organizational trade-offs that seem to exist. Successfully developing and implementing marketing programs and activities to build and maintain strong brands over time often requires that marketers overcome conflicting objectives and realities in the marketplace. After reviewing the nature of these trade-offs, a set of guidelines and suggestions was offered toward achieving marketing balance and hitting the branding sweet spot—by arriving at "win-win" decisions that successfully reconcile marketing trade-offs.

Marketing balance can actually be more difficult to achieve than more extreme solutions that only emphasize one option, involving greater discipline, care and thought. To use a golf analogy, the golfer with the smoothest swing is often the one who hits the ball farther and straighter. Marketing balance may not be as exciting as more radical proposed solutions, but it can actually turn out to be much more challenging and productive.

It is all about making marketing work harder, be more versatile and achieve more objectives. To realize marketing balance, it is necessary to create multiple meanings, multiple responses and multiple effects with marketing activities. Marketing balance does not imply that marketers not take chances, not do different things or not do things differently. It just emphasizes the importance of recognizing the potential downside of failing to reconcile marketing trade-offs.

That said, there certainly may be times that given extreme circumstances, dire straits or an overwhelming need to achieve one objective at all costs, radical solutions are warranted. But even in these cases, marketers would be well-served to recognize exactly the extent and nature of the decision trade-offs they face, and the consequences of ignoring other options. Radical solutions should be thoroughly vetted and contrasted to more balanced solutions that offer more robust and complete solutions.

Marketing balance implies an acceptance of the fact that marketing is multi-faceted and involves multiple objectives, markets and activities. Marketing balance recognizes the importance of avoiding over-simplification: Marketers must do many things, and do them right. Fundamentally, to achieve marketing balance and truly hit the branding sweet spot, marketers must understand and fully address important marketing trade-offs.

Critical Thinking

1. Define marketing balance.
2. According to the article, why is maintaining marketing balance superior to the existence of strategic, tactical, financial, and organizational trade-offs?

KEVIN LANE KELLER has served as brand confidant for some of the world's successful brands, including Accenture, American Express, Disney, Intel, Levi-Strauss, Procter & Gamble, Samsung and Starbucks. His textbook, *Strategic Brand Management,* is in its 3rd edition and has been adopted at top business schools and firms around the world. He may be reached at kevin.keller@dartmouth.edu **FREDERICK E. WEBSTER,** Jr. is widely recognized for his extensive research, writing, teaching and consulting in the field of marketing strategy and organization. Author of 15 books and more than 75 academic and management journal articles, his executive program teaching and consulting clients have included Ford, Mobil, IBM, DuPont, Monsanto, Praxair, General Electric, ABB, Chase Manhattan, Volvo and Phillips. He may be reached at fred.webster@dartmouth.edu.

Reprinted with permission from *Marketing Management*, July/August 2009, pp. 13–17, published by the American Marketing Association. Copyright © 2009 by American Marketing Association.

Marketing Myopia
(with Retrospective Commentary)

Shortsighted managements often fail to recognize that in fact there is no such thing as a growth industry.

Theodore Levitt

[handwritten margin notes: HBR - Harvard Business Review; myopia: nearsightedness]

How can a company ensure its continued growth? In 1960 "Marketing Myopia" answered that question in a new and challenging way by urging organizations to define their industries broadly to take advantage of growth opportunities. Using the archetype of the railroads, Mr. Levitt showed how they declined inevitably as technology advanced because they defined themselves too narrowly. To continue growing, companies must ascertain and act on their customers' needs and desires, not bank on the presumptive longevity of their products. The success of the article testifies to the validity of its message. It has been widely quoted and anthologized, and HBR has sold more than 265,000 reprints of it. The author of 14 subsequent articles in HBR, Mr. Levitt is one of the magazine's most prolific contributors. In a retrospective commentary, he considers the use and misuse that have been made of "Marketing Myopia," describing its many interpretations and hypothesizing about its success.

Every major industry was once a growth industry. But some that are now riding a wave of growth enthusiasm are very much in the shadow of decline. Others which are thought of as seasoned growth industries have actually stopped growing. In every case the reason growth is threatened, slowed, or stopped is *not* because the market is saturated. It is because there has been a failure of management.

Fateful purposes: The failure is at the top. The executives responsible for it, in the last analysis, are those who deal with broad aims and policies. Thus:

- The railroads did not stop growing because the need for passenger and freight transportation declined. That grew. The railroads are in trouble today not because the need was filled by others (cars, trucks, airplanes, even telephones), but because it was *not* filled by the railroads themselves. They let others take customers away from them because they assumed themselves to be in the railroad business rather than in the transportation business. The reason they defined their industry wrong was because they were railroad-oriented instead of transportation-oriented; they were product-oriented instead of customer-oriented.

- Hollywood barely escaped being totally ravished by television. Actually, all the established film companies went through drastic reorganizations. Some simply disappeared. All of them got into trouble not because of TV's inroads but because of their own myopia. As with the railroads, Hollywood defined its business incorrectly. It thought it was in the movie business when it was actually in the entertainment business. "Movies" implied a specific, limited product. This produced a fatuous contentment which from the beginning led producers to view TV as a threat. Hollywood scorned and rejected TV when it should have welcomed it as an opportunity—an opportunity to expand the entertainment business.

Today TV is a bigger business than the old narrowly defined movie business ever was. Had Hollywood been customer-oriented (providing entertainment), rather then product-oriented (making movies), would it have gone through the fiscal purgatory that it did? I doubt it. What ultimately saved Hollywood and accounted for its recent resurgence was the wave of new young writers, producers, and directors whose previous successes in television had decimated the old movie companies and toppled the big movie moguls.

There are other less obvious examples of industries that have been and are now endangering their futures by improperly defining their purposes. I shall discuss some in detail later and analyze the kind of policies that lead to trouble. Right now it may help to show what a thoroughly customer-oriented management can do to keep a growth industry growing, even after the obvious opportunities have been exhausted; and here there are two examples that have been around for a long time. They are nylon and glass—specifically, E. I. duPont de Nemours & Company and Corning Glass Works.

Both companies have great technical competence. Their product orientation is unquestioned. But this alone does not explain their success. After all, who was more pridefully product-oriented and product-conscious than the erstwhile New England textile companies that have been so thoroughly massacred? The DuPonts and the Cornings have succeeded not primarily because of their product or research orientation but because they have been thoroughly customer-oriented also. It is constant watchfulness for opportunities to apply their technical know-how to the creation of customer-satisfying uses which accounts for their prodigious output of successful new products. Without a very sophisticated eye on the customer, most of their new products might have been wrong, their sales methods useless.

Aluminum has also continued to be a growth industry, thanks to the efforts of two wartime-created companies which deliberately set about creating new customer-satisfying uses. Without Kaiser Aluminum & Chemical Corporation and Reynolds Metals Company, the total demand for aluminum today would be vastly less.

Error of analysis: Some may argue that it is foolish to set the railroads off against aluminum or the movies off against glass. Are not aluminum and glass naturally so versatile that the industries are bound to have more growth opportunities than the railroads and movies? This view commits precisely the error I have been talking about. It defines an industry, or a product, or a cluster of know-how so narrowly as to guarantee its premature senescence. When we mention "railroads," we should make sure we mean "transportation." As transporters, the railroads still have a good chance for very considerable growth. They are not limited to the railroad business as such (though in my opinion rail transportation is potentially a much stronger transportation medium than is generally believed).

What the railroads lack is not opportunity, but some of the same managerial imaginativeness and audacity that made them great. Even an amateur like Jacques Barzun can see what is lacking when he says:

"I grieve to see the most advanced physical and social organization of the last century go down in shabby disgrace for lack of the same comprehensive imagination that built it up. [What is lacking is] the will of the companies to survive and to satisfy the public by inventiveness and skill."[1]

Shadow of Obsolescence

It is impossible to mention a single major industry that did not at one time qualify for the magic appellation of "growth industry." In each case its assumed strength lay in the apparently unchallenged superiority of its product. There appeared to be no effective substitute for it. It was itself a runaway substitute for the product it so triumphantly replaced. Yet one after another of these celebrated industries has come under a shadow. Let us look briefly at a few more of them, this time taking examples that have so far received a little less attention:

- *Dry cleaning*—This was once a growth industry with lavish prospects. In an age of wool garments, imagine being finally able to get them safely and easily clean. The boom was on.

  Yet here we are 30 years after the boom started and the industry is in trouble. Where has the competition come from? From a better way of cleaning? No. It has come from synthetic fibers and chemical additives that have cut the need for dry cleaning. But this is only the beginning. Lurking in the wings and ready to make chemical dry cleaning totally obsolescent is that powerful magician, ultrasonics.

- *Electric utilities*—This is another one of those supposedly "no-substitute" products that has been enthroned on a pedestal of invincible growth. When the incandescent lamp came along, kerosene lights were finished. Later the water wheel and the steam engine were cut to ribbons by the flexibility, reliability, simplicity, and just plain easy availability of electric motors. The prosperity of electric utilities continues to wax extravagant as the home is converted into a museum of electric gadgetry. How can anybody miss by investing in utilities, with no competition, nothing but growth ahead?

  But a second look is not quite so comforting. A score of nonutility companies are well advanced toward developing a powerful chemical fuel cell which could sit in some hidden closet of every home silently ticking off electric power. The electric lines that vulgarize so many neighborhoods will be eliminated. So will the endless demolition of streets and service interruptions during storms. Also on the horizon is solar energy, again pioneered by nonutility companies.

  Who says that the utilities have no competition? They may be natural monopolies now, but tomorrow they may be natural deaths. To avoid this prospect, they too will have to develop fuel cells, solar energy, and other power sources. To survive, they themselves will have to plot the obsolescence of what now produces their livelihood.

- *Grocery stores*—Many people find it hard to realize that there ever was a thriving establishment known as the "corner grocery store." The supermarket has taken over with a powerful effectiveness. Yet the big food chains of the 1930s narrowly escaped being completely wiped out by the aggressive expansion of independent supermarkets. The first genuine supermarket was opened in 1930, in Jamaica, Long Island. By 1933 supermarkets were thriving in California, Ohio, Pennsylvania, and elsewhere. Yet the established chains pompously ignored them. When they chose to notice them, it was with such derisive descriptions as "cheapy," "horse-and-buggy," "cracker-barrel storekeeping," and "unethical opportunists."

The executive of one big chain announced at the time that he found it "hard to believe that people will drive for miles to shop for foods and sacrifice the personal service chains have perfected and to which Mrs. Consumer is accustomed."[2] As late as 1936, the National Wholesale Grocers convention and the New Jersey Retail Grocers Association said there was nothing to fear. They said that the supers' narrow appeal to the price buyer limited the size of their market. They had to draw from miles around. When imitators came, there would be wholesale liquidations as volume fell. The current high sales of the supers was said to be partly due to their novelty. Basically people wanted convenient neighborhood grocers. If the neighborhood stores "cooperate with their suppliers, pay attention to their costs, and improve their service," they would be able to weather the competition until it blew over.[3]

It never blew over. The chains discovered that survival required going into the supermarket business. This meant the wholesale destruction of their huge investments in corner store sites and in established distribution and merchandising methods. The companies with "the courage of their convictions" resolutely stuck to the corner store philosophy. They kept their pride but lost their shirts.

Self-deceiving cycle: But memories are short. For example, it is hard for people who today confidently hail the twin messiahs of electronics and chemicals to see how things could possibly go wrong with these galloping industries. They probably also cannot see how a reasonably sensible businessman could have been as myopic as the famous Boston millionaire who 50 years ago unintentionally sentenced his heirs to poverty by stipulating that his entire estate be forever invested exclusively in electric streetcar securities. His posthumous declaration, "There will always be a big demand for efficient urban transportation," is no consolation to his heirs who sustain life by pumping gasoline at automobile filling stations.

Yet, in a casual survey I recently took among a group of intelligent business executives, nearly half agreed that it would be hard to hurt their heirs by tying their estates forever to the electronics industry. When I then confronted them with the Boston streetcar example, they chorused unanimously, "That's different!" But is it? Is not the basic situation identical?

In truth, *there is no such thing* as a growth industry, I believe. There are only companies organized and operated to create and capitalize on growth opportunities. Industries that assume themselves to be riding some automatic growth escalator invariably descend into stagnation. The history of every dead and dying "growth" industry shows a self-deceiving cycle of bountiful expansion and undetected decay. There are four conditions which usually guarantee this cycle:

1. The belief that growth is assured by an expanding and more affluent population.
2. The belief that there is no competitive substitute for the industry's major product.
3. Too much faith in mass production and in the advantages of rapidly declining unit costs as output rises.
4. Preoccupation with a product that lends itself to carefully controlled scientific experimentation, improvement, and manufacturing cost reduction.

I should like now to begin examining each of these conditions in some detail. To build my case as boldly as possible, I shall illustrate the points with reference to three industries—petroleum, automobiles, and electronics—particularly petroleum, because it spans more years and more vicissitudes. Not only do these three have excellent reputations with the general public and also enjoy the confidence of sophisticated investors, but their managements have become known for progressive thinking in areas like financial control, product research, and management training. If obsolescence can cripple even these industries, it can happen anywhere.

Population Myth ③

The belief that profits are assured by an expanding and more affluent population is dear to the heart of every industry. It takes the edge off the apprehensions everybody understandably feels about the future. If consumers are multiplying and also buying more of your product or service, you can face the future with considerably more comfort than if the market is shrinking. An expanding market keeps the manufacturer from having to think very hard or imaginatively. If thinking is an intellectual response to a problem, then the absence of a problem leads to the absence of thinking. If your product has an automatically expanding market, then you will not give much thought to how to expand it.

One of the most interesting examples of this is provided by the petroleum industry. Probably our oldest growth industry, it has an enviable record. While there are some current apprehensions about its growth rate, the industry itself tends to be optimistic.

But I believe it can be demonstrated that it is undergoing a fundamental yet typical change. It is not only ceasing to be a growth industry, but may actually be a declining one, relative to other business. Although there is widespread unawareness of it, I believe that within 25 years the oil industry may find itself in much the same position of retrospective glory that the railroads are now in. Despite its pioneering work in developing and applying the present-value method of investment evaluation, in employee relations, and in working with backward countries, the petroleum business is a distressing example of how complacency and wrongheadedness can stubbornly convert opportunity into near disaster.

One of the characteristics of this and other industries that have believed very strongly in the beneficial consequences of an expanding population, while at the same time being industries with a generic product for which there has appeared to be no competitive substitute, is that the individual companies have sought to outdo their competitors by improving on what they are already doing. This makes sense, of course, if one assumes that sales are tied to the country's population strings, because the customer can compare products only on a feature-by-feature basis. I believe it is significant, for example, that not since John D. Rockefeller sent free kerosene lamps to China has the oil industry done anything really outstanding to create a demand for its product. Not even in product improvement has it showered itself with eminence. The greatest single improvement—namely, the development of tetraethyl lead—came from outside the industry, specifically from General Motors and DuPont. The big contributions made by the industry itself are confined to the technology of oil exploration, production, and refining.

Asking for trouble: In other words, the industry's efforts have focused on improving the *efficiency* of getting and making its product, not really on improving the generic product or its marketing. Moreover, its chief product has continuously been defined in the narrowest possible terms, namely, gasoline, not energy, fuel, or transportation. This attitude has helped assure that:

• Major improvements in gasoline quality tend not to originate in the oil industry. Also, the development of superior alternative fuels comes from outside the oil industry, as will be shown later.

27

- Major innovations in automobile fuel marketing are originated by small new oil companies that are not primarily preoccupied with production or refining. These are the companies that have been responsible for the rapidly expanding multipump gasoline stations, with their successful emphasis on large and clean layouts, rapid and efficient driveway service, and quality gasoline at low prices.

Thus, the oil industry is asking for trouble from outsiders. Sooner or later, in this land of hungry inventors and entrepreneurs, a threat is sure to come. The possibilities of this will become more apparent when we turn to the next dangerous belief of many managements. For the sake of continuity, because this second belief is tied closely to the first, I shall continue with the same example.

Idea of indispensability: The petroleum industry is pretty much persuaded that there is no competitive substitute for its major product, gasoline—or if there is, that it will continue to be a derivative of crude oil, such as diesel fuel or kerosene jet fuel.

There is a lot of automatic wishful thinking in this assumption. The trouble is that most refining companies own huge amounts of crude oil reserves. These have value only if there is a market for products into which oil can be converted—hence the tenacious belief in the continuing competitive superiority of automobile fuels made from crude oil.

This idea persists despite all historic evidence against it. The evidence not only shows that oil has never been a superior product for any purpose for very long, but it also shows that the oil industry has never really been a growth industry. It has been a succession of different businesses that have gone through the usual historic cycles of growth, maturity, and decay. Its overall survival is owed to a series of miraculous escapes from total obsolescence, of last-minute and unexpected reprieves from total disaster reminiscent of the Perils of Pauline.

Perils of petroleum: I shall sketch in only the main episodes.

First, crude oil was largely a patent medicine. But even before that fad ran out, demand was greatly expanded by the use of oil in kerosene lamps. The prospect of lighting the world's lamps gave rise to an extravagant promise of growth. The prospects were similar to those the industry now holds for gasoline in other parts of the world. It can hardly wait for the underdeveloped nations to get a car in every garage.

In the days of the kerosene lamp, the oil companies competed with each other and against gaslight by trying to improve the illuminating characteristics of kerosene. Then suddenly the impossible happened. Edison invented a light which was totally nondependent on crude oil. Had it not been for the growing use of kerosene in space heaters, the incandescent lamp would have completely finished oil as a growth industry at that time. Oil would have been good for little else than axle grease.

Then disaster and reprieve struck again. Two great innovations occurred, neither originating in the oil industry. The successful development of coal-burning domestic central-heating systems made the space heater obsolete. While the industry reeled, along came its most magnificent boost yet—the internal combustion engine, also invented by outsiders. Then when the prodigious expansion for gasoline finally began to level off in the 1920s, along came the miraculous escape of a central oil heater. Once again, the escape was provided by an outsider's invention and development. And when that market weakened, wartime demand for aviation fuel came to the rescue. After the war the expansion of civilian aviation, the dieselization of railroads, and the explosive demand for cars and trucks kept the industry's growth in high gear.

Meanwhile, centralized oil heating—whose boom potential had only recently been proclaimed—ran into severe competition from natural gas. While the oil companies themselves owned the gas that now competed with their oil, the industry did not originate the natural gas revolution, nor has it to this day greatly profited from its gas ownership. The gas revolution was made by newly formed transmission companies that marketed the product with an aggressive ardor. They started a magnificent new industry, first against the advice and then against the resistance of the oil companies.

By all the logic of the situation, the oil companies themselves should have made the gas revolution. They not only owned the gas; they also were the only people experienced in handling, scrubbing, and using it, the only people experienced in pipeline technology and transmission, and they understood heating problems. But, partly because they knew that natural gas would compete with their own sale of heating oil, the oil companies pooh-poohed the potentials of gas.

The revolution was finally started by oil pipeline executives who, unable to persuade their own companies to go into gas, quit and organized the spectacularly successful gas transmission companies. Even after their success became painfully evident to the oil companies, the latter did not go into gas transmission. The multibillion dollar business which should have been theirs went to others. As in the past, the industry was blinded by its narrow preoccupation with a specific product and the value of its reserves. It paid little or no attention to its customers' basic needs and preferences.

The postwar years have not witnessed any change. Immediately after World War II the oil industry was greatly encouraged about its future by the rapid expansion of demand for its traditional line of products. In 1950 most companies projected annual rates of domestic expansion of around 6% through at least 1975. Though the ratio of crude oil reserves to demand in the Free World was about 20 to 1, with 10 to 1 being usually considered a reasonable working ratio in the United States, booming demand sent oil men searching for more without sufficient regard to what the future really promised. In 1952 they "hit" in the Middle East; the ratio skyrocketed to 42 to 1. If gross additions to reserves continue at the average rate of the past five years (37 billion barrels annually), then by 1970 the reserve ratio will be up to 45 to 1. This abundance of oil has weakened crude and product prices all over the world.

Uncertain future: Management cannot find much consolation today in the rapidly expanding petrochemical industry, another oil-using idea that did not originate in the leading firms. The total United States production of petrochemicals is equivalent to about 2% (by volume) of the demand for all petroleum products. Although the petrochemical industry is now expected to grow by about 10% per year, this will not offset other drains on the growth of crude oil consumption. Furthermore, while petrochemical products are many and growing, it is well to remember that there are nonpetroleum sources of the basic raw material, such as coal. Besides, a lot of plastics can be produced with relatively little oil. A 5,000-barrel-per-day oil refinery is now considered the absolute minimum size for efficiency. But a 5,000-barrel-per-day chemical plant is a giant operation.

Oil has never been a continuously strong growth industry. It has grown by fits and starts, always miraculously saved by innovations and developments not of its own making. The reason it has not grown in a smooth progression is that each time it thought it had a superior product safe from the possibility of competitive substitutes, the product turned out to be inferior and notoriously subject to obsolescence. Until now, gasoline (for motor fuel, anyhow) has escaped this fate. But, as we shall see later, it too may be on its last legs.

The point of all this is that there is no guarantee against product obsolescence. If a company's own research does not make it obsolete, another's will. Unless an industry is especially lucky, as oil has been until now, it can easily go down in a sea of red figures—just as the railroads have, as the buggy whip manufacturers have, as the corner grocery chains have, as most of the big movie companies have, and indeed as many other industries have.

The best way for a firm to be lucky is to make its own luck. That requires knowing what makes a business successful. One of the greatest enemies of this knowledge is mass production.

Production Pressures ④

Mass-production industries are impelled by a great drive to produce all they can. The prospect of steeply declining unit costs as output rises is more than most companies can usually resist. The profit possibilities look spectacular. All effort focuses on production. The result is that marketing gets neglected.

John Kenneth Galbraith contends that just the opposite occurs.[4] Output is so prodigious that all effort concentrates on trying to get rid of it. He says this accounts for singing commercials, desecration of the countryside with advertising signs, and other wasteful and vulgar practices. Galbraith has a finger on something real, but he misses the strategic point. Mass production does indeed generate great pressure to "move" the product. But what usually gets emphasized is selling, not marketing. Marketing, being a more sophisticated and complex process, gets ignored.

The difference between marketing and selling is more than semantic. Selling focuses on the needs of the seller, marketing on the needs of the buyer. Selling is preoccupied with the seller's need to convert his product into cash, marketing with the idea of satisfying the needs of the customer by means of the product and the whole cluster of things associated with creating, delivering, and finally consuming it.

In some industries the enticements of full mass production have been so powerful that for many years top management in effect has told the sales departments, "You get rid of it; we'll worry about profits." By contrast, a truly marketing-minded firm tries to create value-satisfying goods and services that consumers will want to buy. What it offers for sale includes not only the generic product or service, but also how it is made available to the customer, in what form, when, under what conditions, and at what terms of trade. Most important, what it offers for sale is determined not by the seller but by the buyer. The seller takes his cues from the buyer in such a way that the product becomes a consequence of the marketing effort, not vice versa.

Lag in Detroit: This may sound like an elementary rule of business, but that does not keep it from being violated wholesale. It is certainly more violated than honored. Take the automobile industry.

Here mass production is most famous, most honored, and has the greatest impact on the entire society. The industry has hitched its fortune to the relentless requirements of the annual model change, a policy that makes customer orientation an especially urgent necessity. Consequently the auto companies annually spend millions of dollars on consumer research. But the fact that the new compact cars are selling so well in their first year indicates that Detroit's vast researches have for a long time failed to reveal what the customer really wanted. Detroit was not persuaded that he wanted anything different from what he had been getting until it lost millions of customers to other small car manufacturers.

How could this unbelievable lag behind consumer wants have been perpetuated so long? Why did not research reveal consumer preferences before consumers' buying decisions themselves revealed the facts? Is that not what consumer research is for—to find out before the fact what is going to happen? The answer is that Detroit never really researched the customer's wants. It only researched his preferences between the kinds of things which it had already decided to offer him. For Detroit is mainly product-oriented, not customer-oriented. To the extent that the customer is recognized as having needs that the manufacturer should try to satisfy, Detroit usually acts as if the job can be done entirely by product changes. Occasionally attention gets paid to financing, too, but that is done more in order to sell than to enable the customer to buy.

As for taking care of other customer needs, there is not enough being done to write about. The areas of the greatest unsatisfied needs are ignored, or at best get stepchild attention. These are at the point of sale and on the matter of automotive repair and maintenance. Detroit views these problem areas as being of secondary importance. That is underscored by the fact that the retailing and servicing ends of this industry are neither owned and operated nor controlled by the manufacturers. Once the car is produced, things are pretty much in the dealer's inadequate hands. Illustrative of Detroit's arm's-length attitude is the fact that, while servicing holds enormous sales-stimulating, profit-building opportunities, only 57 of Chevrolet's 7,000 dealers provide night maintenance service.

Motorists repeatedly express their dissatisfaction with servicing and their apprehensions about buying cars under the present selling setup. The anxieties and problems they encounter during the auto buying and maintenance processes are probably more intense and widespread today than 30 years ago. Yet the automobile companies do not *seem* to listen to or take their cues from the anguished consumer. If they do listen, it must be through the filter of their own preoccupation with production.

The marketing effort is still viewed as a necessary consequence of the product, not vice versa, as it should be. That is the legacy of mass production, with its parochial view that profit resides essentially in low-cost full production.

What Ford put first: The profit lure of mass production obviously has a place in the plans and strategy of business management, but it must always *follow* hard thinking about the customer. This is one of the most important lessons that we can learn from the contradictory behavior of Henry Ford. In a sense, Ford was both the most brilliant and the most senseless marketer in American history. He was senseless because he refused to give the customer anything but a black car. He was brilliant because he fashioned a production system designed to fit market needs. We habitually celebrate him for the wrong reason, his production genius. His real genius was marketing. We think he was able to cut his selling price and therefore sell millions of $500 cars because his invention of the assembly line had reduced the costs. Actually he invented the assembly line because he had concluded that at $500 he could sell millions of cars. Mass production was the *result* not the cause of his low prices.

Ford repeatedly emphasized this point, but a nation of production-oriented business managers refuses to hear the great lesson he taught. Here is his operating philosophy as he expressed it succinctly:

"Our policy is to reduce the price, extend the operations, and improve the article. You will notice that the reduction of price comes first. We have never considered any costs as fixed. Therefore we first reduce the price to the point where we believe more sales will result. Then we go ahead and try to make the prices. We do not bother about the costs. The new price forces the costs down. The more usual way is to take the costs and then determine the price; and although that method may be scientific in the narrow sense, it is not scientific in the broad sense, because what earthly use is it to know the cost if it tells you that you cannot manufacture at a price at which the article can be sold? But more to the point is the fact that, although one may calculate what a cost is, and of course all of our costs are carefully calculated, no one knows what a cost ought to be. One of the ways of discovering . . . is to name a price so low as to force everybody in the place to the highest point of efficiency. The low price makes everybody dig for profits. We make more discoveries concerning manufacturing and selling under this forced method than by any method of leisurely investigation."[5]

Product provincialism: The tantalizing profit possibilities of low unit production costs may be the most seriously self-deceiving attitude that can afflict a company, particularly a "growth" company where an apparently assured expansion of demand already tends to undermine a proper concern for the importance of marketing and the customer.

The usual result of this narrow preoccupation with so-called concrete matters is that instead of growing, the industry declines. It usually means that the product fails to adapt to the constantly changing patterns of consumer needs and tastes, to new and modified marketing institutions and practices, or to product developments in competing or complementary industries. The industry has its eyes so firmly on its own specific product that it does not see how it is being made obsolete.

The classical example of this is the buggy whip industry. No amount of product improvement could stave off its death sentence. But had the industry defined itself as being in the transportation business rather than the buggy whip business, it might have survived. It would have done what survival always entails, that is, changing. Even if it had only defined its business as providing a stimulant or catalyst to an energy source, it might have survived by becoming a manufacturer of, say, fanbelts or air cleaners.

What may some day be a still more classical example is, again, the oil industry. Having let others steal marvelous opportunities from it (e.g., natural gas, as already mentioned, missile fuels, and jet engine lubricants), one would expect it to have taken steps never to let that happen again. But this is not the case. We are now getting extraordinary new developments in fuel systems specifically designed to power automobiles. Not only are these developments concentrated in firms outside the petroleum industry, but petroleum is almost systematically ignoring them, securely content in its wedded bliss to oil. It is the story of the kerosene lamp versus the incandescent lamp all over again. Oil is trying to improve hydrocarbon fuels rather than develop *any* fuels best suited to the needs of their users, whether or not made in different ways and with different raw materials from oil.

Here are some things which nonpetroleum companies are working on:

- Over a dozen such firms now have advanced working models of energy systems which, when perfected, will replace the internal combustion engine and eliminate the demand for gasoline. The superior merit of each of these systems is their elimination of frequent, time-consuming, and irritating refueling stops. Most of these systems are fuel cells designed to create electrical energy directly from chemicals without combustion. Most of them use chemicals that are not derived from oil, generally hydrogen and oxygen.

- Several other companies have advanced models of electric storage batteries designed to power automobiles. One of these is an aircraft producer that is working jointly with several electric utility companies. The latter hope to use off-peak generating capacity to supply overnight plug-in battery regeneration. Another company, also using the battery approach, is a medium-size electronics firm with extensive small-battery experience that it developed in connection with its work on hearing aids. It is collaborating with an automobile manufacturer. Recent improvements arising from the need for high-powered miniature power storage plants in rockets have put us within reach of a relatively small battery capable of withstanding great overloads or surges of power. Germanium diode applications and batteries using sintered-plate and nickel-cadmium techniques promise to make a revolution in our energy sources.

- Solar energy conversion systems are also getting increasing attention. One usually cautious Detroit auto executive recently ventured that solar-powered cars might be common by 1980.

As for the oil companies, they are more or less "watching developments," as one research director put it to me. A few are doing a bit of research on fuel cells, but almost always confined to developing cells powered by hydrocarbon chemicals. None of them are enthusiastically researching fuel cells, batteries, or solar power plants. None of them are spending a fraction as much on research in these profoundly important areas as they are on the usual run-of-the-mill things like reducing combustion chamber deposit in gasoline engines. One major integrated petroleum company recently took a tentative look at the fuel cell and concluded that although "the companies actively working on it indicate a belief in ultimate success . . . the timing and magnitude of its impact are too remote to warrant recognition in our forecasts."

One might, of course, ask: Why should the oil companies do anything different? Would not chemical fuel cells, batteries, or solar energy kill the present product lines? The answer is that they would indeed, and that is precisely the reason for the oil firms having to develop these power units before their competitors, so they will not be companies without an industry.

Management might be more likely to do what is needed for its own preservation if it thought of itself as being in the energy business. But even that would not be enough if it persists in imprisoning itself in the narrow grip of its tight product orientation. It has to think of itself as taking care of customer needs, not finding, refining, or even selling oil. Once it genuinely thinks of its business as taking care of people's transportation needs, nothing can stop it from creating its own extravagantly profitable growth.

'Creative destruction': Since words are cheap and deeds are dear, it may be appropriate to indicate what this kind of thinking involves and leads to. Let us start at the beginning—the customer. It can be shown that motorists strongly dislike the bother, delay, and experience of buying gasoline. People actually do not buy gasoline. They cannot see it, taste it, feel it, appreciate it, or really test it. What they buy is the right to continue driving their cars. The gas station is like a tax collector to whom people are compelled to pay a periodic toll as the price of using their cars. This makes the gas station a basically unpopular institution. It can never be made popular or pleasant, only less unpopular, less unpleasant.

To reduce its unpopularity completely means eliminating it. Nobody likes a tax collector, not even a pleasantly cheerful one. Nobody likes to interrupt a trip to buy a phantom product, not even from a handsome Adonis or a seductive Venus. Hence, companies that are working on exotic fuel substitutes which will eliminate the need for frequent refueling are heading directly into the outstretched arms of the irritated motorist. They are riding a wave of inevitability, not because they are creating something which is technologically superior or more sophisticated, but because they are satisfying a powerful customer need. They are also eliminating noxious odors and air pollution.

Once the petroleum companies recognize the customer-satisfying logic of what another power system can do they will see that they have no more choice about working on an efficient, long-lasting fuel (or some way of delivering present fuels without bothering the motorist) than the big food chains had a choice about going into the supermarket business, or the vacuum tube companies had a choice about making semiconductors. For their own good the oil firms will have to destroy their own highly profitable assets. No amount of wishful thinking can save them from the necessity of engaging in this form of "creative destruction."

I phrase the need as strongly as this because I think management must make quite an effort to break itself loose from conventional ways. It is all too easy in this day and age for a company or industry to let its sense of purpose become dominated by the economies of full production and to develop a dangerously lopsided product orientation. In short, if management lets itself drift, it invariably drifts in the direction of thinking of itself as producing goods and services, not customer satisfactions. While it probably will not descend to the depths of telling its salesmen, "You get rid of it; we'll worry about profits," it can, without knowing it, be practicing precisely that formula for withering decay. The historic fate of one growth industry after another has been its suicidal product provincialism.

Dangers of R&D

Another big danger to a firm's continued growth arises when top management is wholly transfixed by the profit possibilities of technical research and development. To illustrate I shall turn first to a new industry—electronics—and then return once more to the oil companies. By comparing a fresh example with a familiar one, I hope to emphasize the prevalence and insidiousness of a hazardous way of thinking.

Marketing shortchanged: In the case of electronics, the greatest danger which faces the glamorous new companies in this field is not that they do not pay enough attention to research and development, but that they pay *too much* attention to it. And the fact that the fastest growing electronics firms owe their eminence to their heavy emphasis on technical research is completely beside the point. They have vaulted to affluence on a sudden crest of unusually strong general receptiveness to new technical ideas. Also, their success has been shaped in the virtually guaranteed market of military subsidies and by military orders that in many cases actually preceded the existence of facilities to make the products. Their expansion has, in other words, been almost totally devoid of marketing effort.

Thus, they are growing up under conditions that come dangerously close to creating the illusion that a superior product will sell itself. Having created a successful company by making a superior product, it is not surprising that management continues to be oriented toward the product rather than the people who consume it. It develops the philosophy that continued growth is a matter of continued product innovation and improvement.

A number of other factors tend to strengthen and sustain this belief:

1. Because electronic products are highly complex and sophisticated, managements become top-heavy with engineers and scientists. This creates a selective bias in favor of research and production at the expense of marketing. The organization tends to view itself as

making things rather than satisfying customer needs. Marketing gets treated as a residual activity, "something else" that must be done once the vital job of product creation and production is completed.

2. To this bias in favor of product research, development, and production is added the bias in favor of dealing with controllable variables. Engineers and scientists are at home in the world of concrete things like machines, test tubes, production lines, and even balance sheets. The abstractions to which they feel kindly are those which are testable or manipulatable in the laboratory, or, if not testable, then functional, such as Euclid's axioms. In short, the managements of the new glamour-growth companies tend to favor those business activities which lend themselves to careful study, experimentation, and control—the hard, practical realities of the lab, the shop, the books.

What gets shortchanged are the realities of the *market*. Consumers are unpredictable, varied, fickle, stupid, shortsighted, stubborn, and generally bothersome. This is not what the engineer-managers say, but deep down in their consciousness it is what they believe. And this accounts for their concentrating on what they know and what they can control, namely, product research, engineering, and production. The emphasis on production becomes particularly attractive when the product can be made at declining unit costs. There is no more inviting way of making money than by running the plant full blast.

Today the top-heavy science-engineering-production orientation of so many electronics companies works reasonably well because they are pushing into new frontiers in which the armed services have pioneered virtually assured markets. The companies are in the felicitous position of having to fill, not find markets; of not having to discover what the customer needs and wants, but of having the customer voluntarily come forward with specific new product demands. If a team of consultants had been assigned specifically to design a business situation calculated to prevent the emergence and development of a customer-oriented marketing viewpoint, it could not have produced anything better than the conditions just described.

Stepchild treatment: The oil industry is a stunning example of how science, technology, and mass production can divert an entire group of companies from their main task. To the extent the consumer is studied at all (which is not much), the focus is forever on getting information which is designed to help the oil companies improve what they are now doing. They try to discover more convincing advertising themes, more effective sales promotional drives, what the market shares of the various companies are, what people like or dislike about service station dealers and oil companies, and so forth. Nobody seems as interested in probing deeply into the basic human needs that the industry might be trying to satisfy as in probing into the basic properties of the raw material that the companies work with in trying to deliver customer satisfactions.

Basic questions about customers and markets seldom get asked. The latter occupy a stepchild status. They are recognized as existing, as having to be taken care of, but not worth very much real thought or dedicated attention. Nobody gets as

excited about the customers in his own backyard as about the oil in the Sahara Desert. Nothing illustrates better the neglect of marketing than its treatment in the industry press.

The centennial issue of the *American Petroleum Institute Quarterly,* published in 1959 to celebrate the discovery of oil in Titusville, Pennsylvania, contained 21 feature articles proclaiming the industry's greatness. Only one of these talked about its achievements in marketing, and that was only a pictorial record of how service station architecture has changed. The issue also contained a special section on "New Horizons," which was devoted to showing the magnificent role oil would play in America's future. Every reference was ebulliently optimistic, never implying once that oil might have some hard competition. Even the reference to atomic energy was a cheerful catalogue of how oil would help make atomic energy a success. There was not a single apprehension that the oil industry's affluence might be threatened or a suggestion that one "new horizon" might include new and better ways of serving oil's present customers.

But the most revealing example of the stepchild treatment that marketing gets was still another special series of short articles on "The Revolutionary Potential of Electronics." Under that heading this list of articles appeared in the table of contents:

- "In the Search for Oil"
- "In Production Operations"
- "In Refinery Processes"
- "In Pipeline Operations"

Significantly, every one of the industry's major functional areas is listed, *except* marketing. Why? Either it is believed that electronics holds no revolutionary potential for petroleum marketing (which is palpably wrong), or the editors forgot to discuss marketing (which is more likely, and illustrates its stepchild status).

The order in which the four functional areas are listed also betrays the alienation of the oil industry from the consumer. The industry is implicitly defined as beginning with the search for oil and ending with its distribution from the refinery. But the truth is, it seems to me, that the industry begins with the needs of the customer for its products. From that primal position its definition moves steadily back-stream to areas of progressively lesser importance, until it finally comes to rest at the "search for oil."

Beginning & end: The view that an industry is a customer-satisfying process, not a goods-producing process, is vital for all businessmen to understand. An industry begins with the customer and his needs, not with a patent, a raw material, or a selling skill. Given the customer's needs, the industry develops backwards, first concerning itself with the physical *delivery* of customer satisfactions. Then it moves back further to *creating* the things by which these satisfactions are in part achieved. How these materials are created is a matter of indifference to the customer, hence the particular form of manufacturing, processing, or what-have-you cannot be considered as a vital aspect of the industry. Finally, the industry moves back still further to *finding* the raw materials necessary for making its products.

The irony of some industries oriented toward technical research and development is that the scientists who occupy the high executive positions are totally unscientific when it comes to defining their companies' overall needs and purposes. They violate the first two rules of the scientific method—being aware of and defining their companies' problems, and then developing testable hypotheses about solving them. They are scientific only about the convenient things, such as laboratory and product experiments.

The reason that the customer (and the satisfaction of his deepest needs) is not considered as being "the problem" is not because there is any certain belief that no such problem exists, but because an organizational lifetime has conditioned management to look in the opposite direction. Marketing is a stepchild.

I do not mean that selling is ignored. Far from it. But selling, again, is not marketing. As already pointed out, selling concerns itself with the tricks and techniques of getting people to exchange their cash for your product. It is not concerned with the values that the exchange is all about. And it does not, as marketing invariably does, view the entire business process as consisting of a tightly integrated effort to discover, create, arouse, and satisfy customer needs. The customer is somebody "out there" who, with proper cunning, can be separated from his loose change.

Actually, not even selling gets much attention in some technologically minded firms. Because there is a virtually guaranteed market for the abundant flow of their new products, they do not actually know what a real market is. It is as if they lived in a planned economy, moving their products routinely from factory to retail outlet. Their successful concentration on products tends to convince them of the soundness of what they have been doing, and they fail to see the gathering clouds over the market.

Conclusion

Less than 75 years ago American railroads enjoyed a fierce loyalty among astute Wall Streeters. European monarchs invested in them heavily. Eternal wealth was thought to be the benediction for anybody who could scrape a few thousand dollars together to put into rail stocks. No other form of transportation could compete with the railroads in speed, flexibility, durability, economy, and growth potentials.

As Jacques Barzun put it, "By the turn of the century it was an institution, an image of man, a tradition, a code of honor, a source of poetry, a nursery of boyhood desires, a sublimest of toys, and the most solemn machine—next to the funeral hearse—that marks the epochs in man's life."[6]

Even after the advent of automobiles, trucks, and airplanes, the railroad tycoons remained imperturbably self-confident. If you had told them 30 years ago that in 30 years they would be flat on their backs, broke, and pleading for government subsidies, they would have thought you totally demented. Such a future was simply not considered possible. It was not even a discussable subject, or an askable question, or a matter which any sane person would consider worth speculating about. The very thought was insane. Yet a lot of insane notions now have matter-of-fact acceptance—for example, the idea of 100-ton tubes of metal moving smoothly through the air 20,000 feet above the earth, loaded with 100 sane and solid citizens

casually drinking martinis—and they have dealt cruel blows to the railroads.

What specifically must other companies do to avoid this fate? What does customer orientation involve? These questions have in part been answered by the preceding examples and analysis. It would take another article to show in detail what is required for specific industries. In any case, it should be obvious that building an effective customer-oriented company involves far more than good intentions or promotional tricks; it involves profound matters of human organization and leadership. For the present, let me merely suggest what appear to be some general requirements.

Visceral feel of greatness: Obviously the company has to do what survival demands. It has to adapt to the requirements of the market, and it has to do it sooner rather than later. But mere survival is a so-so aspiration. Anybody can survive in some way or other, even the skid-row bum. The trick is to survive gallantly, to feel the surging impulse of commercial mastery; not just to experience the sweet smell of success, but to have the visceral feel of entrepreneurial greatness.

No organization can achieve greatness without a vigorous leader who is driven onward by his own pulsating *will to succeed.* He has to have a vision of grandeur, a vision that can produce eager followers in vast numbers. In business, the followers are the customers.

In order to produce these customers, the entire corporation must be viewed as a customer-creating and customer-satisfying organism. Management must think of itself not as producing products but as providing customer-creating value satisfactions. It must push this idea (and everything it means and requires) into every nook and cranny of the organization. It has to do this continuously and with the kind of flair that excites and stimulates the people in it. Otherwise, the company will be merely a series of pigeonholed parts, with no consolidating sense of purpose or direction.

In short, the organization must learn to think of itself not as producing goods or services but as *buying customers,* as doing the things that will make people *want* to do business with it. And the chief executive himself has the inescapable responsibility for creating this environment, this viewpoint, this attitude, this aspiration. He himself must set the company's style, its direction, and its goals. This means he has to know precisely where he himself wants to go, and to make sure the whole organization is enthusiastically aware of where that is. This is a first requisite of leadership, for *unless he knows where he is going, any road will take him there.*

If any road is okay, the chief executive might as well pack his attaché case and go fishing. If an organization does not know or care where it is going, it does not need to advertise that fact with a ceremonial figurehead. Everybody will notice it soon enough.

Retrospective Commentary

Amazed, finally, by his literary success, Isaac Bashevis Singer reconciled an attendant problem: "I think the moment you have published a book, it's not any more your private property. . . . If it has value, everybody can find in it what he finds, and I cannot tell the man I did not intend it to be so." Over the past 15 years,

"Marketing Myopia" has become a case in point. Remarkably, the article spawned a legion of loyal partisans—not to mention a host of unlikely bedfellows.

Its most common and, I believe, most influential consequence is the way certain companies for the first time gave serious thought to the question of what businesses they are really in.

The strategic consequences of this have in many cases been dramatic. The best-known case, of course, is the shift in thinking of oneself as being in the "oil business" to being in the "energy business." In some instances the payoff has been spectacular (getting into coal, for example) and in others dreadful (in terms of the time and money spent so far on fuel cell research). Another successful example is a company with a large chain of retail shoe stores that redefined itself as a retailer of moderately priced, frequently purchased, widely assorted consumer specialty products. The result was a dramatic growth in volume, earnings, and return on assets.

Some companies, again for the first time, asked themselves whether they wished to be masters of certain technologies for which they would seek markets, or be masters of markets for which they would seek customer-satisfying products and services.

Choosing the former, one company has declared, in effect, "We are experts in glass technology. We intend to improve and expand that expertise with the object of creating products that will attract customers." This decision has forced the company into a much more systematic and customer-sensitive look at possible markets and users, even though its stated strategic object has been to capitalize on glass technology.

Deciding to concentrate on markets, another company has determined that "we want to help people (primarily women) enhance their beauty and sense of youthfulness." This company has expanded its line of cosmetic products, but has also entered the fields of proprietary drugs and vitamin supplements.

All these examples illustrate the "policy" results of "Marketing Myopia." On the operating level, there has been, I think, an extraordinary heightening of sensitivity to customers and consumers. R&D departments have cultivated a greater "external" orientation toward uses, users, and markets—balancing thereby the previously one-sided "internal" focus on materials and methods; upper management has realized that marketing and sales departments should be somewhat more willingly accommodated than before, finance departments have become more receptive to the legitimacy of budgets for market research and experimentation in marketing, and salesmen have been better trained to listen to and understand customer needs and problems, rather than merely to "push" the product.

A Mirror, Not a Window

My impression is that the article has had more impact in industrial-products companies than in consumer-products companies—perhaps because the former had lagged most in customer orientation. There are at least two reasons for this lag: (1) industrial-products companies tend to be more capital intensive, and (2) in the past, at least, they have had to rely heavily on communicating face-to-face the technical character of what they made and sold. These points are worth explaining.

Capital-intensive businesses are understandably preoccupied with magnitudes, especially where the capital, once invested, cannot be easily moved, manipulated, or modified for the production of a variety of products—e.g., chemical plants, steel mills, airlines, and railroads. Understandably, they seek big volumes and operating efficiencies to pay off the equipment and meet the carrying costs.

At least one problem results: corporate power becomes disproportionately lodged with operating or financial executives. If you read the charter of one of the nation's largest companies, you will see that the chairman of the finance committee, not the chief executive officer, is the "chief." Executives with such backgrounds have an almost trained incapacity to see that getting "volume" may require understanding and serving many discrete and sometimes small market segments, rather than going after a perhaps mythical batch of big or homogeneous customers.

These executives also often fail to appreciate the competitive changes going on around them. They observe the changes, all right, but devalue their significance or underestimate their ability to nibble away at the company's markets.

Once dramatically alerted to the concept of segments, sectors, and customers, though, managers of capital-intensive businesses have become more responsive to the necessity of balancing their inescapable preoccupation with "paying the bills" or breaking even with the fact that the best way to accomplish this may be to pay more attention to segments, sectors, and customers.

The second reason industrial products companies have probably been more influenced by the article is that, in the case of the more technical industrial products or services, the necessity of clearly communicating product and service characteristics to prospects results in a lot of face-to-face "selling" effort. But precisely because the product is so complex, the situation produces salesmen who know the product more than they know the customer, who are more adept at explaining what they have and what it can do than learning what the customer's needs and problems are. The result has been a narrow product orientation rather than a liberating customer orientation, and "service" often suffered. To be sure, sellers said, "We have to provide service," but they tended to define service by looking into the mirror rather than out the window. They *thought* they were looking out the window at the customer, but it was actually a mirror—a reflection of their own product-oriented biases rather than a reflection of their customers' situations.

A Manifesto, Not a Prescription

Not everything has been rosy. A lot of bizarre things have happened as a result of the article:

- Some companies have developed what I call "marketing mania"—they've become obsessively responsive to every fleeting whim of the customer. Mass production operations have been converted to approximations of job shops, with cost and price consequences far exceeding the willingness of customers to buy the product.
- Management has expanded product lines and added new lines of business without first establishing adequate control systems to run more complex operations.

- Marketing staffs have suddenly and rapidly expanded themselves and their research budgets without either getting sufficient prior organizational support or, thereafter, producing sufficient results.
- Companies that are functionally organized have converted to product, brand, or market-based organizations with the expectation of instant and miraculous results. The outcome has been ambiguity, frustration, confusion, corporate infighting, losses, and finally a reversion to functional arrangements that only worsened the situation.
- Companies have attempted to "serve" customers by creating complex and beautifully efficient products or services that buyers are either too risk-averse to adopt or incapable of learning how to employ—in effect, there are now steam shovels for people who haven't yet learned to use spades. This problem has happened repeatedly in the so-called service industries (financial services, insurance, computer-based services) and with American companies selling in less-developed economies.

"Marketing Myopia" was not intended as analysis or even prescription; it was intended as manifesto. It did not pretend to take a balanced position. Nor was it a new idea—Peter F. Drucker, J. B. McKitterick, Wroe Alderson, John Howard, and Neil Borden had each done more original and balanced work on "the marketing concept." My scheme, however, tied marketing more closely to the inner orbit of business policy. Drucker—especially in *The Concept of the Corporation* and *The Practice of Management*—originally provided me with a great deal of insight.

My contribution, therefore, appears merely to have been a simple, brief, and useful way of communicating an existing way of thinking. I tried to do it in a very direct, but responsible fashion, knowing that few readers (customers), especially managers and leaders, could stand much equivocation or hesitation. I also knew that the colorful and lightly documented affirmation works better than the tortuously reasoned explanation.

But why the enormous popularity of what was actually such a simple preexisting idea? Why its appeal throughout the world to resolutely restrained scholars, implacably temperate managers, and high government officials, all accustomed to balanced and thoughtful calculation? Is it that concrete examples, joined to illustrate a simple idea and presented with some attention to literacy, communicate better than massive analytical reasoning that reads as though it were translated from the German? Is it that provocative assertions are more memorable and persuasive than restrained and balanced explanations, no matter who the audience? Is it that the character of the message is as much the message as its content? Or was mine not simply a different tune, but a new symphony? I don't know.

Of course, I'd do it again and in the same way, given my purposes, even with what more I now know—the good and the bad, the power of facts and the limits of rhetoric. If your mission is the moon, you don't use a car. Don Marquis's cockroach, Archy, provides some final consolation: "an idea is not responsible for who believes in it."

Critical Thinking

1. What are the main contributors to a company's decline? Do these contributors change with the times?
2. What are the basic, protective steps that companies can take to ward off their potential decline?

Notes

1. Jacques Barzun, "Trains and the Mind of Man," *Holiday*, February 1960, p. 21.
2. For more details see M. M. Zimmerman, *The Super Market: A Revolution in Distribution* (New York, McGraw-Hill Book Company, Inc., 1955), p. 48.
3. Ibid., pp. 45–47.
4. *The Affluent Society* (Boston, Houghton Mifflin Company, 1958), pp. 152–160.
5. Henry Ford, *My Life and* Work (New York, Doubleday, Page & Company, 1923), pp. 146–147.
6. Jacques Barzun, "Trains and the Mind of Man," *Holiday*, February 1960, p. 20.

At the time of the article's publication, **THEODORE LEVITT** was lecturer in business administration at the Harvard Business School. He is the author of several books, including *The Third Sector: New Tactics for a Responsive Society* (1973) and *Marketing for Business Growth* (1974).

Putting Customers First
Nine Surefire Ways to Increase Brand Loyalty

Kyle LaMalfa

"Customers first." It's the mantra of businesses everywhere. Yet the average company still loses 10% to 15% of customers each year. Most of them leave due to poor service or a disappointing product experience, yet only 4% of them will tell you about it. And once they've left, it's difficult (not to mention expensive) to get them back.

Fostering true loyalty and engagement with customers starts at a basic level, but here are nine techniques you can employ to make customer loyalty a powerful competitive advantage for your company. They can be broken down into three categories: loyalty basics (one through four), loyalty technologies (five through seven) and loyalty measurement (eight and nine).

1. Give Customers What They Expect

Knowing your customer's expectations and making sure your product or service meets them is Business 101, yet often ignored. At the basic level, business needs to be a balanced transaction where someone pays for something and expects a fair trade in return.

Expectations of product quality come from many sources, including previous quality levels set by your organization, what competitors are saying about you, and the media. Marketing and sales should work together to monitor customer expectations through feedback and surveys.

2. Go Beyond Simple Reward Programs

Points and rewards encourage repeat purchases, but don't actually build loyalty. This is demonstrated by a drop in sales when the rewards are no longer offered. True loyalty comes when customers purchase products without being bribed.

3. Turn Complaints into Opportunities

Managing questions, comments and concerns benefits your business in two important ways. First, research indicates that an upset customer whose problem is addressed with swiftness and certainty can be turned into a highly loyal customer. Second, unstructured feedback, gathered and managed appropriately, can be a rich source of ideas. To that end:

- Establish channels (electronic, phone and written) to build engagement, one customer at a time.
- Encourage customers to voice their thoughts.
- Create metrics to improve response to concerns (i.e., "time to first response," "time to resolution," etc.).
- Create metrics to measure loyalty before and after the problem.
- Use technology to help you centralize the information, create reports and structure drill-downs.

4. Build Opportunities for Repeat Business

Give your customers a chance to be loyal by offering products for repeat business. Monitor what customers request most and offer products or services that compliment other purchases. In addition, exceed expectations by driving product development to offer more value for less cost. Use technology to track, classify and categorize open-ended feedback.

5. Engage Customers in a Two-Way Dialogue

An engaged customer is more than satisfied and more than loyal. They support you during both good and bad times because they believe what you have to offer is superior to others.

Engagement takes your customer beyond passive loyalty to become an active participant and promoter of your product. Engaged customers will give you more feedback so you should be ready to handle it! All this translates into a customer who will spend more money with you over time. Accordingly:

- Listen to customer feedback from comment cards, letters, phone calls and surveys.
- Respond quickly and personally to concerns of high interest to your customers.
- Organize unstructured feedback for tracking and trending over time.
- Trust your customers to tell you what the problem is.
- Use statistical techniques to discover which action items will have the most impact on your business.

6. Survey Customers and Solicit Feedback

Actively soliciting information from a population of customers is a time-tested technique pioneered by Arthur Nielsen (creator of the Nielsen ratings) in the 1920s. Survey research can be used for problem identification or solving. Questions with simple scales such as "agree/disagree" deliver quantitative insight for problem identification. Open-ended follow-up questions can provide rich insight for solving problems. Some tips:

- Make sure your surveys are short, bias-free and well structured.
- Use random sampling to gather feedback continuously without over-surveying.
- Create summary survey indices that can be displayed graphically and tracked over time.

7. Create a Centralized System for Managing Feedback throughout the Enterprise

Technology such as enterprise feedback management (EFM) helps to centralize surveys and customer feedback and track both qualitative and quantitative information. EFM involves more than just collecting data, though; it adopts a strategic approach to building dialogs with your customers. Follow these steps:

- Empower customers to give feedback through common advertised channels.

- Centralize reporting for proactive surveys and complaint management solutions.
- Structure quantitative feedback into a drill-down or rollup report.
- Make open-ended feedback intuitively searchable.

8. Tie Customer Loyalty and Engagement to Business Outcomes

Orienting your organization to focus on satisfaction, loyalty and engagement is no panacea. But researchers have clearly documented evidence of short-term benefits to customer/employee retention and long-term benefits to profitability. Hence:

- Determine whether to measure your engagement outcome by satisfaction, likelihood to purchase again, likelihood to recommend, or another voice of the customer (VOC) metric.
- If necessary, create hybrid VOC measurements using more than one metric.
- Link your VOC metrics with business outcomes like shareholder returns, annual sales growth, gross margin, market share, cash flows, Tobin's Q or customer churn.
- Be aware that changes in loyalty/engagement scores generally precede changes in business outcomes.

9. Use Analysis to Predict Future Loyalty

Businesses use a variety of statistical techniques to make predictions about the potential for future events. Furthermore, predictive analytics may be used to ascertain the degree to which answers from a survey relate to particular goals (such as loyalty and engagement). Tactical knowledge of how action items impact an outcome discourages the wasting of resources on ineffective programs, and competent statistical modeling reveals which tactical options work. Consequently:

- Analyze data using a statistical technique to reveal the most important areas of focus.
- Ask your analyst about common statistical methods, including correlation and logit models.
- Recognize that the major areas of focus may change in response to changes in your economic, competitive and demographic environments.

Following these steps may not be the easiest process, but stay focused. Increasing your engagement and loyalty equals increasing profits and a competitive edge.

Critical Thinking

1. Discuss the importance of establishing two-way dialogue with customers and effectively responding to customer feedback.

2. With a small group of peers from your class, develop some ways that companies can achieve effective two-way dialogue with customers.

KYLE LAMALFA is the best practices manager and loyalty expert for Allegiance, Inc. He can be reached at kyle.lamalfa@allegiance.com. For more information about how to increase your loyalty and engagement, visit www.allegiance.com.

Making the Most of Customer Complaints

Dealing with service failures means a lot more than just fixing the immediate problem. Here's how to do it right.

STEFAN MICHEL, DAVID BOWEN, AND ROBERT JOHNSTON

Nobody's perfect. That's a fact, not an excuse.
Which is why it's crucial for companies to realize that the way they handle customer complaints is every bit as important as trying to provide great service in the first place. Because things happen.

Customers are constantly judging companies for service failures large and small, from a glitch-ridden business-software program to a hamburger served cold. They judge the company first on how it handles the problem, then on its willingness to make sure similar problems don't happen in the future. And they are far less forgiving when it comes to the latter. Fixing breakdowns in service—we call this service recovery—has enormous impact on customer satisfaction, repeat business, and, ultimately, profits and growth.

But unfortunately, most companies limit service recovery to the staff who deal directly with customers. All too often, companies have customer service sort out the immediate problem, offer an apology or some compensation, and then assume all is well. This approach is particularly damaging because it does nothing to address the underlying problem, practically guaranteeing similar failures and complaints.

What businesses should be doing is looking at service recovery as a mission that involves three stakeholders: customers who want their complaints resolved; managers in charge of the process of addressing those concerns; and the frontline employees who deal with the customers. All three need to be integrated into addressing and fixing service problems.

Tensions naturally arise in and among the groups. For example, customers can be left feeling that their problem wasn't addressed seriously, even when they've received some form of compensation. Service reps can start seeing complaining customers as the enemy, even though they point out flaws that need fixing.

Managers in charge of service recovery, meanwhile, can feel pressure to limit flows of critical customer comments, even though acting on the information will improve efficiency and profits.

However, successfully integrating these three perspectives is something that fewer than 8% of the 60 organizations in our study did well.

Based on our research and our own years of work in service management, here is a look at the three stakeholders in service recovery, focusing on their different perspectives and the tensions that arise among them. We then make recommendations on how to address these tensions and integrate the aims of all three to achieve better—if not perfect—service.

The Customer

Fairness is typically the biggest concern of customers who have lodged a service complaint. Because a service failure implies unfair treatment of the customer, service recovery has to re-establish justice from the customer's perspective.

Say a bank customer requests a deposit receipt from an ATM but the machine fails to print one. The customer becomes worried and goes to one of the bank tellers. The teller checks the account, and assures the customer that there is no problem, that the deposit was made. But if the teller only focuses on the fact that the account was credited, he or she has ignored what in the customer's view was the most severe and critical aspect of the service failure: the worry initially felt, and the extra time it took to verify the deposit.

Customers often want to know—within a reasonable time—not only that their problem has been resolved, but how the failure occurred and what the company is doing to make sure it doesn't happen again.

A customer's faith can be restored using this kind of approach—once. We have even noted something referred to as a "recovery paradox," in which customers can be more delighted by a skillful service recovery than they are by service that was failure-free to start with.

But there is a flip side to this as well: Customers have more tolerance for poor service than for poor service recovery. And if a customer experiences a second failure of the same service, there is no recovery strategy that can work well. In all likelihood, that customer will be lost forever.

Our research suggests that after a failed service recovery, what annoys—and even angers—customers is not that they weren't satisfied, but that they believe the system remains unchanged and likely to fail again.

The Manager

The chief aim of managers in service recovery is to help the company learn from service failures so it doesn't repeat them. Learning from failures is more important than simply fixing problems for individual customers, because process improvements increase overall customer satisfaction and thus have a direct impact on the bottom line.

But companies generally obtain and study only a fraction of the service-failure data that could be gathered from customers, employees and managers. Even when managers agree that customer feedback is essential, there is often poor information flow between the division that collects and deals with customer problems and the rest of the organization.

In some cases, one study revealed, the more negative feedback a customer-service department collects, the more isolated that department becomes, because it doesn't want to be seen by the company at large as a source of friction. Some companies even create specialist units that can soak up customer complaints and problems with no expectation of feeding this information back to the organization. Others actually impede service recovery by rewarding low complaint rates, and then assuming that a decline in the number of reports indicates customer satisfaction is improving.

Some managers in our study saw conflicts between providing great customer satisfaction and achieving high productivity. For instance, incentive structures sometimes placed equal values on sales and on customer service. But as one manager noted: "If you want to achieve 100% [satisfaction], you don't have time for selling. It's questionable whether you can score 100% on service quality and 100% on [sales] objectives."

In any kind of business, there comes a point at which a service recovery can become excessive in the company's eyes, and be seen as giving away the store. However, many customers don't want a payoff. They simply want to have their problem fixed and to be reassured that it won't happen to other people in the future.

The Employee

Frontline service employees have the greatest job satisfaction when they believe they can give customers what they expect.

These workers have the difficult task of dealing with customers who hold them responsible even when the failures in question are completely out of their control. The attitudes of customer-service workers, positive and negative, spill over onto customers.

Yet companies do surprisingly little to support them.

To be successful, these workers need to feel that management is providing the means to deliver successful service recovery on a continuing basis. Alternatively, when employees believe management doesn't support them, they tend to feel they are being unfairly treated and so treat customers unfairly. They display passive, maladaptive behaviors and can even sabotage service.

This alienation is compounded when the workers believe that management is not improving the service-delivery process, which keeps employees in recurring failure situations. Even though complaining customers represent an opportunity to fix problems and improve satisfaction, alienated employees often see them as the enemy. In a study of a major European bank, employees in Switzerland consistently indicated that they did not consider reports of missing account statements to be complaints. As one said: "These things happen. There is nothing we can do about that."

At companies that reward low complaint rates, frontline employees become tempted to send dissatisfied customers away instead of admitting a failure has occurred.

Resolving the Tensions

Our experience with managers interested in improving service recovery indicates that most hope for a quick fix of some specific tensions. But quick fixes only treat the symptoms of underlying problems. Real resolutions should involve closer integration among the three stakeholders, such as gathering more information from customers and sharing it throughout the company, and adopting new structures and practices that make it easier to spot problems and fix them.

We suggest the following five strategies:

- **Create a "service logic" that explains how everything fits together.** This should be a kind of mission statement or summary of how and why the business provides its services. It should integrate the perspectives of all three groups:

  What is the customer trying to accomplish, and why?
  How is the service produced, and why?
  What are employees doing to provide the service, and why?

The results should serve as a guide both for delivering service and for help with service recovery. It should include a detailed study of internal operations; map out how the company responds to customer complaints; and describe how the company uses that information to improve service-recovery processes. Similar mapping should detail every step of customer experiences, including those of real customers with complaints, highlighting their thoughts, reactions and emotions along the way. Highly skilled managers and employees who can think outside the box are a must.

TNT NV, a Netherlands-based global delivery company, developed a service logic to help it grow in a mature market.

Using a small, high-powered management team backed up by customer discussion forums, the company mapped its processes from a customer point of view, including a map of customer emotions during both regular processes and service recovery. The mapping exercise and the service logic that it produced led to a redesign of processes by managers and field staff that cut across traditional functional boundaries.

For example, previously a driver running late for a scheduled delivery had to call into the control center, which would then contact customer services, which would then contact the customer. Such calls often arrived after the delivery already had been made, thus further annoying the customer and embarrassing the driver. Since the process redesign, however, a driver running late is allowed to contact the customer directly. TNT drivers frequently visit the same customers almost every day, so their customers know them and appreciate the personal contact. The drivers also appreciate being able to make the calls directly.

- **Draw attention to the successes of customer-service groups.** Companies use in-house publications, intranets and training programs to share stories that emphasize their values and culture. Employees who come up with cost-saving ideas, for example, are often singled out for praise. But rewards and recognition also should flow to heroes in service-recovery stories. Such heroes can be on the operations side, helping to develop cost-efficient systems for handling complaints, and on the marketing side, giving a customer extraordinarily helpful treatment after a service failure.

Singapore Airlines Ltd., in its in-house magazines, frequently tells stories about employees who have provided not only outstanding service, but exceptional service recoveries. Senior managers, too, will not hesitate to swoop in anywhere there is an issue, creating more stories about internal vigilance.

Recovery Mode

The Issue: Every business can expect complaints from customers. It's how a business handles the complaints that matters most, and many do so poorly.

The Problem: When companies don't give upset customers a fair hearing or some assurance that the problem won't happen again, they are putting repeat business, profits and growth at risk.

The Solution: The key is to address tensions that arise among front-line employees who handle complaints, the managers of those employees, and the customers themselves. Steps include starting a complaints database that managers can analyze and use to improve service, and rewarding service employees not for reductions in complaints but for providing exceptional solutions to problems.

When customer-service employees believe that their goals are in line with the organization's values, they are more willing to exert the extra effort required in a failure-and-recovery situation.

- **Give customer-service staff as much freedom as your business strategy allows.** When a business has very few routines and its ties to customers are based on individual relations, service representatives should have more autonomy in resolving complaints. For such businesses, spending more time on service recovery—and retaining customers—has a clear effect on the bottom line. By contrast, in a highly standardized business with purely transactional customer relationships, such as a fast-food restaurant, employees should adhere to procedures in resolving complaints. Customer satisfaction in such businesses is closely aligned with high productivity, so there is less to be gained by customizing resolutions of complaints.

Ritz-Carlton, for example, the luxury brand of Marriott International Inc., authorizes personnel at the front desks of its hotels to credit unhappy customers up to $2,000 without asking a supervisor's approval. On the other hand, in one of our consulting projects, a client reacted very negatively to this approach, claiming that such a policy would be too expensive for his company. We replied that the high cost of poor service is exactly what makes this system work so well: It forces management to eliminate service failures in the first place.

- **Collect as much data as you can, and share it widely.** Companies must gather more feedback about poor service, record it and make it accessible. Managers and other employees have to be armed with strong information to be effective at resolving disputes.

It should be easy for customers to file complaints. One way to achieve this is by offering many communication channels. A regional airline in Asia, for example, uses annual passenger surveys, interviews with frequent fliers, focus-group discussions, customer hot lines, critical-incident surveys, onboard suggestion leaflets and even live call-in radio shows.

Software should be used that serves as a database for both positive and negative communications with customers. Employees and managers should be trained to mine the data and put it to use easily and quickly.

- **Use meaningful measures of employee performance—rewards and demerits.** Positive reinforcement and incentives should be offered for solving problems and pleasing customers. A system for measuring customer satisfaction should be devised to help rate employee performance. Salary increases and promotions then should be linked to an employee's achieving certain levels. There also should be disincentives or demerits for poor handling of customer complaints. Performance reviews thus may include a balanced scorecard—one that recognizes the need for both productivity and customer satisfaction.

Critical Thinking

1. Summarize the perspectives of the three stakeholders involved in service recovery.

2. In your opinion, why is it important to empower customer-service employees?

DR. MICHEL is associate professor of marketing at Thunderbird School of Global Management, Glendale, Ariz. **DR. BOWEN** is the Robert and Katherine Herberger chair in global management and a professor at Thunderbird. **DR. JOHNSTON** is professor of operations management at Warwick Business School, University of Warwick, Coventry, England. They can be reached at reports@wsj.com.

When Service Means Survival

Keeping customers happy is more critical than ever. Service champs economize on everything but TLC.

Jena McGregor

Hertz couldn't ask for a better customer than Richard M. Garber. The Cleveland-based business development manager typically rents cars from the chain 20 to 40 times a year when traveling on business for materials manufacturer FLEXcon. But now Garber is rethinking that loyalty. In the past month he has returned Hertz cars to the Boston and Minneapolis airports only to find nobody waiting with a handheld check-in device. In Minneapolis, Garber had to drag his bags to the counter to return his car; in Boston, he finally tracked down an employee who came out and explained that some colleagues had just been laid off. "When you're rushing for an airplane, every minute counts," says Garber. "The less convenient they are, the more likely I am to try someone else."

As the economy plunges deeper into recession, many companies are confronting the same brutal choices Hertz faced when it announced layoffs of some 4,000 people on Jan. 16. While businesses may feel forced to trim costs, cutting too deeply can drive away customers. Hertz spokesman Richard Broome says the company has reduced "instant return" hours at some smaller airports but is making adjustments to restore that service in locations where it "might have gone too far." Says Broome: "You try to create the right balance."

Across the business world, managers are trying to pull off the same perilous high-wire act. Just as companies are dealing with plummeting sales and sinking employee morale, skittish customers want more attention, better quality, and greater value for their money. Those same customers are also acutely aware that their patronage is of growing importance to companies as others decrease their spending. BMW Vice-President Alan Harris argues that in the current environment, consumers expect "that anyone who is in the market with money to spend is going to get treated like a king."

Keep the Front Lines Strong

The reality, of course, is that the opposite is often true. From retailers such as Talbots, which have stiffened their rules on returns, to airlines that now charge for checked bags, companies are stretching budgets in ways that can make things tougher for customers.

But the best performers are actually doing more to safeguard service in this recession. Bruce D. Temkin, principal analyst for customer experience at Forrester Research, says about half of the 90 large companies he recently surveyed are trying to avoid cuts to their customer service budgets. "There's some real resilience in spending," says Temkin.

That's especially true for many of the winners of our third annual ranking of Customer Service Champs. Top performers are treating their best customers better than ever, even if that means doing less to wow new ones. While cutting back-office expenses, they're trying to preserve front-line jobs and investing in cheap technology to improve service.

If anything, the tough economy has made starker the difference between companies that put customers first and those that sacrifice loyalty for short-term gain. In this year's ranking, based on data from J.D. Power & Associates, which, like *BusinessWeek,* is owned by The McGraw-Hill Companies, more than half of the top 25 brands showed improved customer service scores over last year. Among the bottom 25 of the more than 200 brands surveyed, scores mostly fell.

Cutting just four reps at a call center of three dozen can send the number of customers put on hold for four minutes from zero to 80.

Smart players have learned from previous downturns. Companies used to go after customer reps with the same blunt ax used elsewhere. Now managers are starting to understand the long-term damage created by such moves, from eroded market share to diminished brand value. The International Customer Management Institute, a call center consultant, has done studies that show eliminating just four reps in a call center of about three dozen agents can increase the number of customers put on hold for four minutes from zero to 80.

A better strategy is to get more out of the people you have. USAA, the insurance and financial services giant that caters to military families and ranks at No. 2 on our list, started cross-training its call center reps in 2007. Some 60% of the agents who answer investment queries can now respond to insurance-related calls. Not only did such training curb call transfers between agents, which drive up the cost of running a call center, but it also improved productivity. Even with Hurricane Ike and the stock market's financial crisis prompting a flood of calls to USAA's contact centers last year, the cross-training meant the company didn't have to expand its call center staff. Existing reps are more empowered to deal with customers, even if they may also have to do more work. No. 25 JW Marriott is training administrative assistants to step in as banquet servers when needed. And in November, brokerage Charles Schwab, No. 21 on our ranking, launched a "Flex Force" team of employees such as finance specialists and marketing managers at its San Francisco headquarters to handle calls on days of, say, rapid market fluctuations.

For those that slash costs, the challenge is keeping customers from noticing. Putting call center reps under one roof, for example, can eventually save as much as 35%, says Scott Casson, director of technology services at consultant Customer Operations Performance Center. On Feb. 12, USAA announced it will combine its six call centers into four; companies such as No. 11 KeyBank and Ace Hardware, No. 10, have also consolidated operations in the past year. Ace plowed the savings from that move into longer evening and weekend hours for customer calls. "During tough times there are plenty of other pressures customers face," says Ace Vice-President John Venhuizen. "We don't want a customer service issue to be what makes them blow their cork."

Pleasing Repeat Buyers

Hoteliers also are trying to trim in ways customers are unlikely to detect. They're increasingly combining purchasing power to get better deals across properties that are within the same chain but may have different owners. Some hotels in the Four Seasons chain, No. 12, are joining

Safeguarding Service

Times are unquestionably tough. But cutting too deeply may only make things worse. Here are four ideas for keeping costs down and customer service solid:

Flex Your Workforce

Cutbacks in staffing levels may be necessary as sales slow. But to keep service quality high, make the most of the workers you have. Cross-train employees so they can step up to fill a variety of needs—and you can avoid making new hires.

Spoil Surviving Staff

Slashing jobs and benefits can wreak havoc on morale. If you must cut back, keep the front lines happy with flexibility and other rewards. American Express, for example, now lets call center reps choose their own hours and swap shifts without supervisors' approval.

Invest in Simple Technology

It may not be the best time to upgrade your call center with pricey software. But easy self-serve solutions such as in-store Web cams that link customers with remote tech experts can serve multiple locations at minimal cost.

Baby Your Best Customers

Now is not the time for equal treatment. Keep your most active buyers coming back with faster service, extra attention, and flexible rules. As business travel slows, Marriott, for instance, is extending elite status to its best guests even if they don't qualify under normal rules.

up to buy goods and services such as coffee, valet parking agreements, and overnight cleaning contracts that each hotel once bought on its own. JW Marriott hotels are teaming up to buy landscaping services that would be costlier if contracted for separately. The Ritz-Carlton, No. 5, is doing laundry at night to save electricity and replacing fresh flowers at posh properties with potted plants. With occupancy rates falling, notes Ritz COO Simon F. Cooper, "you have to get better because you're forced to."

As the game changes from acquiring new customers to keeping old ones, companies are shifting more resources to their steady patrons. They're the ones who pay the bills. And while first-time guests may not miss the absence of fresh flowers, repeat customers probably will. "It's the little things that often got you in the crook of those loyal customers' arms," says Jeanne Bliss, a former Lands' End service chief who now coaches customer service execs. That has led to a renewed emphasis on "tiering"—routing elite-level customers to better agents, nicer surroundings, or faster service.

A Road Warrior's Story: Four Stars for the Four Seasons

Last April, I was visiting top tech companies in Austin, Tex., while working for the World Economic Forum. On the flight in, after the attendant said: "Please put your laptop away. This is the fifth time I've told you," I closed my laptop and put it down beside me. I was jet-lagged and super tired.

The next thing I know, I'm in my room unzipping my bag, thinking "Where's my laptop?" I was at the Four Seasons, so I call the concierge, Steven Beasley, and tell him what happened. Two seconds later, he calls back and says he has American Airlines on the phone. I explain the problem, and they say nothing has come up on the system. About five minutes later, the concierge phones me back and says he's called the San Francisco airport to alert them to check the plane when it arrives there.

By that time I've given up. I go down to have dinner, and I'm having a predinner drink when the concierge turns up at my table and says: "Mr. Mulcahy? I've got your laptop," and hands it to me. "Would you like me to take it to your room?" I'm like "what the—what?" He'd taken it upon himself to keep badgering American. They did another check, and in fact they still had the laptop in Austin.

The concierge could have just left a message. I was so grateful to him for having gone this obscenely extra mile.

A Social Networker's Story: The Zappos CEO and UPS Step In

I usually get packages sent to the office, but in December I ordered a big 110-pound storage unit from Target and needed it delivered to my house. I called UPS to check on it, and the rep said that sometimes during the Christmas season packages don't arrive until 9 P.M.

Getting agitated, I posted on Twitter about waiting for UPS and mentioned how I couldn't take my dog, Ridley, for a walk. After 9 P.M., I got a message from Tony Hsieh, CEO of Zappos, who started following my Tweets [comments on Twitter] after we met last year. He was having dinner with UPS's president for the Western region and sent a message saying the guy would call me. I got a call in the next five minutes. The UPS exec got me in touch with an operations manager to arrange for a delivery the next morning so I could make a scheduled client meeting.

At 9 A.M. on the dot, the doorbell rings. Not only do they have the package, but there's a UPS guy with flowers and chocolates and another with treats and toys for Ridley. They even offered to assemble the unit and listened to my suggestions for improving service. I now go out of my way to use UPS—and I bought shoes the next day at Zappos.

Consider No. 7, Zappos.com, the online shoe retailer whose devoted fans rave about its free shipping on both orders and returns. The retailer had typically upgraded both first-time and repeat customers to overnight shipping even though it wasn't advertising that perk. But starting in 2009, Zappos will no longer offer overnight upgrades to first-time visitors. Instead, CEO Tony Hsieh is moving those dollars into a new VIP service for Zappos' most loyal shoppers. Launched in December, the site, which for now can only be accessed by loyal customers who receive an invitation, promises overnight shipping and plans to offer earlier access to sales and new merchandise than the plain-vanilla site. (Repeat customers who aren't yet asked to join the VIP service will continue getting the overnight upgrade for now.) "We decided we wanted to invest more in repeat customers," says Hsieh. "We're shifting some of the costs that would have gone into new customers."

Some are also getting tougher on suppliers who serve their most frequent customers. No. 24 L.L. Bean dropped Bank of America as its vendor of store-branded credit cards in July 2008. The outdoor outfitter says the bank wasn't measuring up in terms of its vaunted customer support. Complaints about long hold times and call transfers between the bank's customer service agents were "endless," says Terry Sutton, L.L. Bean's vice-president for customer satisfaction. (Bank of America says it doesn't comment on specific relationships but is "focused on providing competitive products and exceptional customer service.") L.L. Bean switched to Barclays, which meant customers had to reapply. The risk that some might not take the time was high. "From a service standpoint, it was loaded with land mines," says Sutton. But she felt the move was worth it, especially since Barclays gave them a say on agents' scripts and set up its call center in the retailer's home state of Maine. Over 60% of cardholders have already switched.

Some companies are experimenting more with cheap technology, such as responding to customers via Twitter after they broadcast their complaints to the world. Other tech upgrades for customers can deliver unexpected cost savings. When No. 22 BMW rolled out Wi-Fi service at its dealerships last year, the move was intended to give customers a cheap way to pass the time while their cars were serviced. The cost was next to nothing since BMW just expanded the broadband dealers already used to run their businesses. But now that customers can use their waiting time productively, fewer are opting for free loaner cars, which are pricey for dealers to maintain. BMW's Alan

Harris says Wi-Fi, along with software that helps dealers better estimate loaner needs, has helped BMW cut its monthly loaner expenses by 10% to 15%.

When companies come up with simple, low-cost ways to trim costs while improving life for customers, they're likely to win in good times and bad. "I have a saying: 'Fix the customer before you fix the car,' " says Harris. "If you focus on fixing the customer's problem first, the rest is easy."

Critical Thinking

1. According to this article, why is it vital, in today's economy, for businesses to avoid cutting front-line service employees?

2. Describe some high and low satisfaction interactions you have personally had with service providers.

With Aili McConnon in New York and David Kiley in Detroit.

From *Bloomberg BusinessWeek*, March 2, 2009, pp. 26, 28–30. Copyright © Bloomberg 2009 by Bloomberg BusinessWeek. Reprinted by permission of Bloomberg LP via YGS Group.

Become the Main Attraction

**People go to summer events for music, food and fun—not for marketing materials.
Here's how you get them to pay attention to you.**

Piet Levy

There are hundreds, maybe thousands of people here. Many of them are just the types of customers you are looking for. But odds are that none of them are here to see you. Instead, the masses have gathered at this event to hear music, watch sports, eat food or, in the case of conferences, network and listen to keynote presentations.

The consumers are there for their reasons and you're there for yours: to market your brand and increase awareness and sales. In a sea of noise, surrounded by hordes of talking people, distracting attractions and numerous marketing booths and street teams competing for consumers' attention, you have to stand out. But in addition to turning heads, you have to open minds. Beyond handing out coupons or samples or tchotchkes, you must showcase the value of your product or service in an interactive and engaging way, which also means training the right people to serve as brand messengers. If you make sure you're memorable, when the event ends and the consumers go about their daily lives, they'll remember you, tell others about you and pay to experience your product or service.

Step Right Up

Event marketing is important because it "places your product or service face to face with your target audience," argues Brad Horowitz, vice president of marketing for Elite Marketing Group, an experiential agency with headquarters in New Hyde Park, N.Y. "Brands can have a conversation with consumers rather than delivering a monologue. Conversations allow for customized learning, which fosters purchasing behavior. Additionally, it allows for valuable feedback from consumers about the product or service and the perception out there in the real world."

To be the most effective event marketer, you have to go beyond just being at a popular event and set up shop in a premium position. "Juxtaposing your footprint to a high-traffic location at an event such as the entry or the food court will allow for the greatest reach and greatest amount of impressions," Horowitz says.

That's also where a lot of other marketing booths or street teams will be hanging out. But don't worry about them; worry about yourself, and calm those concerns by establishing a physical presence that pops.

Overland Park, Kan.-based Sprint Nextel Corp., which sponsors the National Association for Stock Car Auto Racing's (NASCAR) Sprint Cup Series, incorporates a jumbotron, trophy replica and NASCAR driver appearances at its display at races, says Tim Considine, general manager of the sponsorship. To attract mechanics to its travelling display last year, the U.S. Air Force showcased customized vehicles that incorporated Air Force technology, says Kristin Krajecki, director of experiential marketing at the Air Force's experiential agency, GSD&M Idea City in Austin, Texas. For its presence at the National Religious Broadcasters Convention and Exposition earlier this year, TV Magic Inc., a San Diego-based broadcast solutions provider, presented a cross designed out of televisions at its booth, the sort of visual element that conference-attending pastors may want at their churches, says Stephen Rosen, president and CEO of the company. "You've got to make an impressive impression and let [consumers] feel that spending a few minutes with you of their very precious time is worth it," Sprint's Considine says.

You may not have the budget to bring your own jumbotron, super car, or elaborate TV display to an event, but you can find creative ways to cut costs. TV Magic actually reduced its trade show budget by 50% this year and was still able to replace its "worse than blah" booth from last year with one featuring the TV display, Rosen says. Savings came from two areas: TV Magic reduced the number of company representatives at the booth from seven to three, and the company partnered with electronic suppliers such as Sony and Panasonic to provide equipment at no cost, says Jeff Symon, President and CEO of San Diego-based Aim Agency, TV Magic's agency. In some cases, you may even be able to find a company partner to participate with you at the event and subsidize expenses, he also suggests.

Whatever you put together, make sure the element is relevant to the audience and reflective of your brand. The cars at the Air Force display appealed to gear heads, but given the Air Force-inspired modifications, including an ejection seat, vertical doors, and aircraft style controls, the brand was even more reinforced. In addition to the church-friendly TV display at its convention booth, TV Magic put together a system where pastors could be filmed and the video edited and broadcast to a TV, online, and mobile device on the spot as a way to demonstrate the type of service the company provides, Symon says.

It's also a good idea to make your display interactive to increase the odds and length of time that consumers will stick around. Incentives are another way to draw people in. Sprint stages racing video games on its jumbotron that people can participate in and offers free gifts to customers, Considine says.

You should also try to design the space to allow for easier traffic flow. Symon suggests removing any table separating consumers from brand messengers to allow greater interactivity and openness. Considine says the Sprint layout features no walls or interiors to better increase impressions and interaction, and the jumbotron is in place to increase the possibility of engaging people from the periphery.

Razzle-Dazzle Them

The wow factor and selling points are crucial event marketing criteria, but Considine argues that "the hand you shake, the kindness that you show to someone in an [event] marketing environment, may be more powerful than the information you present."

In addition to head-turning displays, you have to rely on your brand representatives to present the brand properly, yet oftentimes marketers may have to outsource for those services, as Sprint does for its NASCAR display.

To find the right people for the job, Aim Agency first profiles what the brand stands for and the type of people who would best represent it. Then comes an online evaluation process that serves as a screener to see if candidates match brand objectives, Symon says.

If you don't have the budget to recruit an agency to help you with staffing, use the interview process to determine which candidates are extroverted, upbeat, articulate, and professional, Considine and Symon say. Jessica Fisher, Senior Manager of events for athletic apparel company Reebok International Ltd. in Canton, Mass., says that before an interview begins it's important to have a casual conversation about the candidate's perspective of the brand to gauge his enthusiasm and understanding. It also helps to recruit people who can relate to the target audience. For its M&M's supporting street team at NASCAR races, Mars Chocolate North America utilizes two employees from the company's PR agency, Weber Shandwick, who are actual fans of NASCAR so their interaction with fans will be authentic, says Suzanne Beaudoin, Vice President of sponsorship and sports marketing for the Hackettstown, N.J.-based company.

Once your team is in place, make sure staff members dress the part to not only physically represent the brand but also attract consumers. The M&M's street team stands out with NASCAR-style jumpsuits, Beaudoin argues, to help

---

By the Numbers

The Norwalk, Conn.-based Event Marketing Institute and Auburn Hills, Mich.-based experiential agency George P. Johnson Co. interviewed 108 sales and marketing management leaders for its EventView report, an annual study assessing the relevance of event marketing. Some key findings:

62% of respondents say their marketing budget for events has either remained constant or increased in 2010.

32% consider event marketing a "vital component" of their marketing plan.

64% cited event marketing as one of the top three elements for accelerating and deepening relationships, followed by social marketing (55%) and online marketing (54%).

Want a Ticket to Ride?

Follow These 10 Instructions for Successful Event Marketing:

1. Set up your booth or street team in highly trafficked areas.
2. Have a visual element that turns heads but connects back to your brand.
3. Find participating partners to subsidize costs.
4. Present an interactive element, like a game, so consumers stick around for a while.
5. Make your space as open as possible to maximize traffic and engagement.
6. Entice visitors with incentives like coupons or samples.
7. Find upbeat, extroverted, professional, articulate people to act as brand representatives.
8. Cast people who can relate with the target demographic, like employing NASCAR fans for booths at NASCAR events.
9. Train representatives with quizzes and run-throughs, but don't overwhelm them with details.
10. Dress your staff so they stand out, but make sure they look approachable.

---

communicate the brand's Most Colorful Fan website and Facebook page, which encourage NASCAR fans to submit photos displaying their love of the sport for a cash prize. Similarly, the Air Force tries to place its brand representatives in the most appropriate attire based on the event, says Captain Homero Martinez, the former chief of event marketing for the Air Force Recruiting Service. For a recent Memorial Day race, Martinez says, formal dress was appropriate given the holiday weekend's correlation with the Air Force. For more casual events like music festivals, staff wear more relaxed uniforms to reduce any consumer concern that they will be pressured to sign up.

The U.S. Air Force paraded customized cars equipped with jet-inspired technology at events last year in an effort to attract mechanics for the Air Force on the spot, he says.

Beyond looking the part, training must be done so that brand representatives can act the part. Training should include quizzing participants about the brand and business objectives in addition to on-site run-throughs, Symon says, and participants should be encouraged to ask questions for clarification's sake. Fisher recommends giving representatives the product when applicable, so that when they are on site, "they are not just giving out words, but talking from their own experiences." It's ideal to have people who work for the company on hand to help address consumer questions, but for those assigned with attracting people with their presence and interaction, it's important not to overwhelm them with instructions during the training process. Considine says his advice boils down to one simple philosophy: Treat passing consumers like guests at your home. If they feel welcome, there's a greater chance they'll welcome your product or service into their lives.

Critical Thinking

1. What makes event marketing an attractive promotion option for businesses?

2. With a small group of peers from your class, design an event marketing plan for any business of your choice.

How to Make Marketing Brilliance

An octogenarian's renaissance, a reinvention of the laptop and a bunch of irate birds—just a few examples of what grips the public's pop-culture consciousness. Some are the result of true innovation, some are examples of grace under pressure—and some things just go viral, because that's what happens now. Here's our look at the best marketing moves of the past year.

Jason Daley

Betty White

It's not like Betty White ever really went away. From radio dramas in the 1940s, TV variety shows in the '50s and '60s, a stint on *The Mary Tyler Moore Show* and, of course, her series-stealing turn as Rose Nylund on *The Golden Girls,* White has been a staple of popular entertainment since the cathode ray's beginning. But at the age of 88, White found herself in the middle of one of the strangest entertainment stories of 2010—a popular uprising.

In early 2010, David Mathews of San Antonio, Texas, launched a Facebook page asking for White to host *Saturday Night Live.* A successful Super Bowl Snickers commercial in which White takes a particularly brutal tackle, a surprise *Golden Girls* resurgence and a zany performance in the Sandra Bullock summer rom-com *The Proposal* all had whetted the public's appetite for White. The Facebook petition picked up several hundred thousand signers within a few months, and *SNL* producer Lorne Michaels offered White the Mother's Day edition of the show. She signed on, and White's digital dominance was complete.

White's performance was edgy and widely praised, and the grandmother with a blue streak finished out 2010 by agreeing to costar in the TV Land sitcom *Hot in Cleveland,* releasing a calendar and popping up in cameo roles on almost every self-respecting comedy in the fall.

The Betty White mania may be winding down, but that doesn't mean she'll ever fade away.

"In earlier days she probably had just as many fans," says Robert Lloyd, TV critic for the Los *Angeles Times.* "But not in the same way we can be a fan now. You can push a button and join a club, and be part of a movement.

The thing about Betty White is she belongs to a lot of generations. She's not just a cute old lady. The fact is, she's just funny."

The iPad

In the build-up to the iPad's release last April, Apple, the media and just about everyone else set their expectations pretty high, with claims that the tablet would change everything. It was never possible that the 3G-enabled tablet was going to make the laptop computer obsolete, save the publishing world, upend traditional marketing and buy everyone a Coke like the evangelizers claimed.

But almost a year later, it's hard not to be impressed by the iPad's accomplishments. It became the fastest-selling digital device in history; magazines and newspapers are slowly but surely redesigning themselves for a tablet-based world; and marketers have adopted the machine as fast as their industry will allow.

"Tablets are a real market that only Apple could have validated," says Eric Lai, mobile blogger for ZDNet. "A flood of Android tablets and RIM PlayBooks will follow, but it's all due to Apple's trailblazing. The iPad has really lived up to its hype—and more."

Lady Gaga

Stefani Germanotta who? Hit albums, viral videos, meat dresses and joy rides with Beyonce transformed this unknown NYC girl into the queen of pop.

Advertisers are impressed, too. According to a survey last November by Nielsen, iPad users are nearly twice as likely to respond to online ads—as long as the ads are new, interesting and use the unique capabilities of the iPad.

The market for the iPad and similar devices and, consequently, their ability to reach consumers, seems set for exponential growth, especially as universities, large businesses and government agencies begin figuring out how to use the tablets in their daily routines.

"Apple just knows how to cater to the technophile early-adopting consumer," Lai says.

"And now that the balance of power has shifted away from the IT department toward the end user, these consumers are forcing enterprises to support and deploy iPads."

JetBlue

Among the many gripes travelers have with airlines, the number one bugaboo is customer service. Weaving our way through labyrinthine phone menus and sending e-mails off into the ether with no guarantee of a reply is the modus operandi for most carriers.

But jetBlue, the low-cost carrier that has been slowly expanding across the country since 1999, decided in 2007 that it would be all about transparency and communication—an idea that led the company to set up a 24/7 Twitter account to answer customer questions and deal with complaints. It's a friendly, wide-ranging back-and-forth banter that covers everything from passengers onboard complaining about delays to people asking which NFL team jetBlue roots for. So far, the @JetBlue Twitter feed has collected 1.6 million followers, along with 150,000 more for its cheap deals feed and more than 440,000 friends on Facebook.

"When we first started, it was just me not sleeping a whole lot," says Morgan Johnston, the only guy fielding the questions at jetBlue when tweeting first began. Now a social media team of 17 supports Johnston, manager of corporate communications. JetBlue initially tried mainly to advertise deals on Twitter, he says, but that strategy fell flat.

"So we asked our customers what they wanted to hear. And we listened. That's how we built our following," he says

Not only has that following helped engender brand loyalty and trust, it also helped when crisis hit. When flight attendant Steven Slater cursed out passengers on the tarmac at Kennedy International Airport in New York before grabbing a couple of beers and exiting the aircraft via the evacuation slide, jetBlue took a few days before deciding on an appropriate response.

"We understood our reputation for being transparent, and it would have been the wrong action to try and ignore it," Johnston says.

Shake Weight

You know you've made it big when your awkward infomercials inspire an *SNL* parody.

Instead, the company came out with a short, tasteful and funny blog post mentioning the movie *Office Space* and praising its 2,300 other flight crew members who didn't wig out.

The first comment posted sums up the general reaction: "I love you jetBlue."

Angry Birds

Smartphones were pretty revolutionary when they first came out, but experts agree they were missing one key thing—testy little birds willing to fling themselves into concrete walls to destroy smirking green pigs.

Since Finland-based Rovio released the Angry Birds game in December 2009, 36 million gamers have downloaded the cute time-sink. Despite a brief partnership with publisher Chillingo at the app's release, Angry Birds has reached its dominance with a marketing budget close to zero.

"It really is intended for everybody. It's easy to pick up and start playing, even if you've never played any games before," says Ville Heijari, Rovio's vice president of public relations, explaining why the game has become so popular. "Not to forget the unique characters, wacky sound design and the seemingly absurd plotline. It really is the total sum of all its parts that makes it a great game."

Rovio is hoping 2010 was just the first of many years for its birds. This spring, the company plans to roll out Angry Birds versions for Facebook and the web, and it also hopes to launch versions for Xbox 360, Wii and PS3.

Merchandising of the game's cute birdies and pigs is underway with a plush toy collection, and rumors have been swirling that Angry Birds may get a feature film treatment as well.

In all, Rovio hopes that by the summer, the birds will reach 100 million players, both on and off the phone.

"Consider the Angry Birds like other loved characters, such as Mario," Heijari says. "There's a lot more to the story of Angry Birds than has been seen yet, and infinite possibilities for storytelling."

Conan O'Brien

The only way to describe the departure of late-night host Conan O'Brien from NBC's *The Tonight Show* is this: messy.

After seven months at the helm of the television show made legendary by Steve Allen, Jack Paar and Johnny Carson, O'Brien was given the choice to either move the show to a half hour later to make room for the return of Jay Leno, whose 10 P.M. experiment was a flop, or to hit the road. O'Brien decided that, instead of cheapening the *Tonight Show* brand by moving it later, he'd leave—taking with him $33 million and the status as a beloved underdog.

Though barred from discussing the debacle until last May or returning to television until last fall, O'Brien parlayed his troubles into marketing gold. Within 24 hours of launching his Twitter feed in February, he had more than 300,000 followers. His two-month "The Legally Prohibited From Being Funny on Television" tour launched in April and sold out quickly. Also in April, Conan told the world that he had signed on to begin a new late-night show on TBS starting in November.

Whether his TBS show will capture his old audience remains to be seen, but O'Brien's antics off the small screen were masterful.

"The important thing is he came out of this debacle looking like a folk hero, with a larger stature," says Troy Patterson, television critic for Slate.com and film critic at Spin. "He got to be an underdog that played into his persona as a gawky, aw-shucks type of guy."

The marketing for O'Brien's TBS show was equally inspired: His new logo simply played on the shock of red hair that has been his trademark since his television debut along with the name Team Coco. An orange blimp emblazoned with the word CONAN even traveled the East Coast, checking into Foursquare locations to advertise the show. All that had most of the country repeating the mantra spread by one of Conan's grassroots supporters: "I'm with Coco."

And 10 More…

Old Spice

When actor Isaiah Mustafa appeared as the "Old Spice Man" during last year's Super Bowl, the handsome towel-clad actor inaugurated the most creative advertising campaign of the year. But there was more to the

---

Glee

In addition to top ratings, singles from the hit musical comedy-drama series demolish the Beatles' record for most hit singles on the Billboard Charts. High school drama kids raise their spirit fingers in solidarity.

---

spots spearheaded by ad agency Wieden + Kennedy. In July, Mustafa and a crew of social media experts and production folks began creating and posting YouTube videos of the Old Spice Man answering real questions from the public. Over three days, Mustafa weighed in with 186 videos, advising everyone from Alyssa Milano to George Stephanopoulos. In all, the back and forth generated 34 million YouTube views in a week as well as countless mentions in Facebook, Twitter and the mainstream press.

Domino's Pizza

For years Domino's has been the pizza world's cleanup act. Its low cost and late hours appealed to after-hours partyers and college students. Anyone who cares how their pizza actually tastes abandoned the brand long ago. So when the company began acknowledging its status in the pizza pecking order in ads released early last year, the honesty was a shock.

After reworking its recipe, Domino's head chef brought the new pizzas to the homes of its harshest focus-group critics, where the new pies made their debut. Not only did the ads make customers sit up and listen, they also made them want to try the pizzas for themselves. In the first quarter of 2010, sales jumped 14 percent, and Domino's has recorded 11 percent to 12 percent growth each quarter since.

Heineken

Heineken's "Walk-in fridge" ad—in which a group of women goes nuts over their friend's walk-in closet, only to hear their husbands and boyfriends in the next room losing their minds over a walk-in refrigerator stocked with Heineken beer—garnered more than 4 million views on YouTube, not to mention the millions of impressions the ad made on the regular tube.

But instead of sitting back and waiting for their Clio, the ad company went guerilla. Soon after the ad's launch, groups of young men were spotted throughout Amsterdam trying to push giant cardboard boxes labeled "Walk-in fridge" into apartments and houses.

But Heineken's marketing coup de grâce last year was a video of a 2009 prank pulled on Champions League fans. That October, Heineken had enlisted wives, girlfriends, bosses and professors to sucker 1,136 Italian football fanatics in Milan into skipping the biggest match of the year—AC Milan vs. Real Madrid—to attend a classical music and poetry recital.

It recorded the forlorn men as they filed into the auditorium—then, 15 minutes into the unbearable concert, the game appeared on the screen. We're assuming they all got walk-in fridges as consolation prizes.

Groupon

Groupon, a web company whose name is a mashup of "group" and "coupon," introduced the world to its concept in late 2008. More than two years later, it's one of the marketing world's breakout stars.

The concept is simple: In each of Groupon's 150 North American and 100 international markets, a local deal is offered, say 50 percent off muffins at a bakery. If enough people sign up for the deal, it goes live and is available to everyone. The merchant drives traffic to the store, and Groupon takes a cut.

But last summer, Groupon showed its real muscle when it went national for the first time, with a Gap promotion promising $50 in merchandise for $25. The deal hit critical mass in a few hours, and Gap raked in $11 million in one day.

At press time, it was rumored that Groupon had rebuffed a $5 billion buyout offer from Google. That would have been quite a deal.

World Records

In the past three years, Guinness has seen world-record attempts spike 250 percent, but it's not because of crazy individuals growing out their fingernails or holding their breath. Instead, it's corporations trying to bring attention to their brands.

In 2009, Supercuts set the record for the most haircuts in a day (349). Last year, Sheraton Hotels & Resorts promoted a $120 million upgrade of its fitness facilities with a world-record resistance-band strength-training class (270 people). In November, Nike employees from around the world traveled to Las Vegas to break the record for the largest gathering of Elvis impersonators (645).

Those records may be a far cry from the most lightning strikes survived (7), but they're equally entertaining.

UNICEF

In the middle of Union Square in Manhattan last July, Unicef, the United Nation's Children's Fund, set up a bottled-water vending machine. But instead of spring-fed H20, the machine offered murky bottles labeled dysentery, cholera, dengue and malaria. The stunt was designed to call attention to the 4,200 children who die each day of water-borne diseases. No one actually drank the water, but the machine did accept donations, and the viral video featuring the stunt reached several hundred thousand people. Not bad for a video without Justin Bieber.

Volkswagen

Volkswagen's Fun Theory claims its mission is to inspire people to do good—and smile at the same time. The carmaker is behind the installation of slides and *Big*-inspired keyboards on subway steps—viral videos from years past.

But its mission for 2010 was finding a fun way to make drivers obey the speed limit.

After sifting through hundreds of entries, it chose The Speed Camera Lottery. In cooperation with Swedish authorities, it rigged a camera to photograph all the license plates that went by. Speeding drivers were fined, with the money going into a pot. Drivers who obeyed the speed limit were eligible to win the pot.

The experiment got drivers to drop their speed 22 percent—but, most of all, it gave Volkswagen another viral hit.

Sign Spinning

In an age where marketing seems to revolve around page views, retweets and audience share, a trend as old as, well, signs is making a mark. Sign spinning is a mashup of juggling, performance art and old-fashioned pavement pounding, and it is showing up at grand openings and special events around the country, bringing in foot traffic and attracting crowds.

The driving force and self-proclaimed inventors of sign spinning is AArrow Advertising, a San Diego-based franchise that has locations in 18 states, fielding an army of young spinners nationwide. And they're making waves off the street too. YouTube is full of sign-spinning videos, Ellen DeGeneres has featured sign spinners on her show, and spinners were in FX Network and Ford commercials.

Miracle Whip

In late 2009, Kraft's Miracle Whip began airing a spot showing hip twenty-somethings laughing and dancing around a pool on an urban rooftop while smearing their sandwiches with the distinctly unhip dressing. The monotone taglines, "Don't Be So Mayo" and "We Are Miracle Whip, and We Will Not Tone It Down," were youth-pandering at its worst, enough that Stephen Colbert ran a parody of the commercial, throwing his support behind regular mayonnaise on his Comedy Central show. But instead of taking it on the chin, Miracle Whip bought airtime during Colbert's show, running its rooftop ad with new voice-overs calling Colbert "So mayo," making fun of the silent "t" in his name and inviting him to the rooftop to dance. The stunt turned a marketing flop into a publicity juggernaut and icon of customer engagement.

Jersey

If you watched television in 2010, you were smacked in the face by the Garden State's bombardment of pop culture. At its height last October, MTV's "reality" show *Jersey Shore* boasted 6.7 million viewers, but its stars invaded more than the beach. Nicole "Snooki" Polizzi,

Mike "The Situation" Sorrentino and DJ Pauly D have parlayed their MTV hit into a minor media empire, creating workout videos, appearing on late-night talk shows, scoring endorsement deals for vodka, bronzer and pistachios—even writing a novel and getting a gig on *Dancing With the Stars*.

Other Jersey-based shows, including Bravo's *The Real Housewives of New Jersey* and the Style Network's *Jerseylicious,* a reality show about a salon in Green Brook, have kept the state's big hair and spray tans in the spotlight—despite Gov. Chris Christie's lament that *Jersey Shore* doesn't fairly represent his state. But locals don't seem to mind. According to the Seaside Heights Business Improvement District, the "gym, tan, laundry" lifestyle has boosted local revenues 38 percent in just one year.

Critical Thinking

1. Formulate your own definition for 'Marketing Brilliance.'
2. List some additional examples, beyond what's in the article, of marketing brilliance.

JASON DALEY is a freelance writer in "Madison, WI."

Imaginative Service

You need it more in tough times.

CHIP R. BELL AND JOHN R. PATTERSON

Take the Hertz shuttle bus at the Atlanta Airport, and you might meet *Archie Bostick.* Archie greets you with a welcoming grin. Instead of a tip jar, Archie paper-clips dollar bills across the front of his shirt. Nothing subtle about that ploy—it's an attention-getter that announces *this is a unique experience.* Once on the bus, Archie delivers a comedy routine and uses any excuse to break into song. As Archie pulls up to the terminal, he announces, "Now, I may never see you again, so I want us all to say together, 'I love Hertz!'" And everyone hollers, "I love Hertz!" You witness a service innovator at work—he takes your breath away.

Value-added has been the service solution for many service exemplars—take what the customer expects and add a little more. Nordstrom sales clerk escorts you to another department. Southwest Airlines gives you free peanuts with slapstick humor. And Rosie's Diner refills your ice tea glass without you being charged.

But value-added extras have gotten more expensive. That free snack on a flight is now $8, and service charges are standard fare on most bills. Pursuing the extras can also send a mixed message. What do employees think when told to "wow" customers in the morning and are later informed of staff cutbacks and expense reductions? Challenging financial times call for a new approach: *value-unique service.*

Value-unique is different than value-added. For most customers, value-added means taking the expected to a higher-level: "They gave me *more* than I anticipated." But, value-unique is not about addition—it's about an imaginative creation.

When service people are asked to *give more,* they think, "I'm already doing the best I can." But, if asked to *pleasantly surprise* more customers, they feel less like worker bees and more like fireflies. If employees are asked to create a big customer smile instead of work harder, they feel a part of an adventure. And, when they get to create, not just perform, they feel prized. Just ask a Southwest, Disney, or Lexus dealership employee what they think of their job, and you will get a smiling "It's awesome," not a shrugging "It's all right."

Imaginative service is sourced in joy and fun. It comes from the same part of the soul that plans a prank, organizes a party, or helps a friend. When that part is used regularly, it raises self-esteem, increases resilience, and improves morale. Take a look at *Fortune Magazine's* annual *100 Best Companies in America to Work For*—Nordstrom, Container Store, Marriott, eBay, Zappos.com, and FedEx—and you see the great service-high morale link. They boast the lowest turnover (a cost saver), the best recruits (an investment), the highest productivity (another positive) and the greatest profits.

Five Ways to Deliver Unique Value

Here are five ways to foster service that takes your customers' breath away:

1. *Project realness.* Imaginative service is about *realness,* not *roleness.* The stereotypical leader gets caught up with looking, sounding, and "acting" executive, and employees get a message of "plastic power"—which may engender *compliance* but never *commitment.* Great leaders are unimpressed with the trappings of supremacy and more interested in communicating an authentic spirit and egalitarian style.

Imaginative service leaders know they get from employees the attitude they project. Employees do not watch the leader's mouth; they watch the leader's moves. As all leaders move in the floodlight of employee observation, their actions can telegraph either optimism or gloom; excitement or despair. An animated attitude is contagious. When we are around happy, upbeat people, we more easily join in the spirit—especially if the invitation comes from someone who prefers we enroll. An unbridled spirit has magnetic power on both customers and employees.

2. *Protect customers.* Tasks are important; rules are essential. But, revenue comes from customers. Imaginative service leaders encourage and empower employees to put customers (not procedures) first. This is not about deliberately violating rules or putting anybody at risk.

Zappos.com was founded in 1999 with goal of doing to on-line shoe apparel what Amazon.com did to online books. In 2000 they had $1.6 million in sales; in 2008 their sales exceeded $1 billion! CEO **Tony Hsieh** explains their growth this way: "We're aligned around one mission—to provide the best customer service possible. Rather than focus on maximizing short-term profits, we focus on how we can maximize the service to our customers. We are a service company that happens to sell shoes." They protect customers from being taken for granted or subjected to discomfort.

3. **Proclaim joy.** In times of frugality, staff reductions, cost controls, and cutbacks, employees tend to be somber. Optimism is replaced with anxiety; hope is overshadowed by fear. The receiving end of such dower dispositions are customers with money to spend. When customers most need a shot of enthusiasm, they are served by sleepwalking employees who seem indifferent and bored. The antidote to such melancholy is a leader with unmistakable passion and irresistible joy. "The ultimate measure of a man," said Martin Luther King, "is not where he stands in moments of comfort and convenience, but where he stands at times of challenge and controversy."

"To succeed," says **Scott Cook,** founder of Intuit, "you need people with passion. You can't just order someone to be passionate about a business direction." Passion comes from a deep sense of purpose—not the "ought to" sense of obligation that drives duty, but the "can't wait to" enthusiasm that sets an employee on fire. As Federal Signal President **Alan Shaffer** said: "Our goal is not merely to get buy-in. I want to put a lump in their throats and a tear in their eyes. I want to take their breath away."

The number one impact on customer relations is employee relations—happy employees create happy customers.

4. **Provide trust.** Imaginative service happens in a climate of trust—where people are considerate and supportive. If people are given license to criticize colleagues behind their back, the setting turns to suspicion. If manipulative or unfair behavior is tolerated, the climate turns to protection. It requires leaders disciplined to model thoughtfulness and hold others accountable.

Trustful cultures nurture appropriate risk-taking that leads to novel solutions and refreshing customer experiences. Trusting leaders view *error* as a chance to learn and *failure* as an invitation to try another approach. They treat employees as valued gifts, not indentured slaves. They empower and encourage. They are open about their own foibles and upfront when they make mistakes. The word embedded in *trust* is *us*. Trustful leaders care for their employees with the same humanity they give their family. *Family-like* doesn't mean entitlement, paternalism, or nepotism. It means attention to fairness, justice, and compassionate conduct.

5. **Preserve integrity. S. Truett Cathy,** founder of Chick-Fil-A, has elected to remain closed on Sunday and gained favor for courageously remaining true and faithful to his values.

"I like dealing with an organization whose leaders stand for something!" comment customers when asked what they like most. Chick-Fil-A, Southwest Airlines, USAA, and The Container Store receive high marks. Stand-for-something leaders aren't the loud, flamboyant, publicity-seeking types. Instead, they are clear, focused, courageous, and committed to stay their course and stand their ground.

Imaginative service leaders are grounded in complete, no-exceptions integrity. They reek of integrity. As **Tom Peters** says, "There is no such thing as a *minor lapse of integrity.*" They show their nobility when they courageously tell the truth, relentlessly do what they say they will do, and gallantly turn their backs on all shady actions. They send signals through their character.

Customers seek more value for their money. As you scramble to shore up value, the time is ripe for service with inventiveness—not just service with generosity. Leaders must ensure that the elements they add to their leadership advance service innovation.

Critical Thinking

1. What do the authors of the article mean by a *value-unique* service?
2. With a small group of peers from your class, come up with a list of other imaginative services based on your own experiences and observations.

CHIP R. BELL and **JOHN R. PATTERSON** are customer loyalty consultants and authors of *Take Their Breath Away: How Imaginative Service Creates Devoted Customers.* www.taketheirbreathaway.com.

Walking the Talk

Eco-minded retailer, Patagonia caused a stir with its recent "conscious-consumption" holiday campaign that told consumers *not* to buy the featured product. Marketing VP Rob BonDurant discusses the strategy and shares some early results.

KATHERINE LING

Last fall on Cyber Monday, the busiest online shopping day of the year, Patagonia customers opened their e-mail inboxes to see these words in the outdoor apparel retailer's promotional message: "Don't Buy This Jacket."

The ensuing message read, in part: "Cyber Monday was created by the National Retail Federation in 2005 to focus media and public attention on online shopping. But Cyber Monday, and the culture of consumption it reflects, puts the economy of natural systems that support all life firmly in the red. . . .

"We ask you to buy less and to reflect before you spend a dime on this jacket or anything else. . . .

"The environmental cost of everything we make is astonishing. Consider the R2 Jacket shown, one of our best sellers. To make it required 135 liters of water, enough to meet the daily needs (three glasses a day) of 45 people. Its journey from its origin as 60 percent recycled polyester to our Reno warehouse generated nearly 20 pounds of carbon dioxide, 24 times the weight of the finished product. This jacket left behind, on its way to Reno, two-thirds its weight in waste.

"And this is a 60 percent recycled polyester jacket, knit and sewn to a high standard; it is exceptionally durable, so you won't have to replace it as often. . . . But, as is true of all the things we can make and you can buy, this jacket comes with an environmental cost higher than its price.

"There is much to be done and plenty for us all to do. Don't buy what you don't need. Think twice before you buy anything. Go to patagonia.com/CommonThreads, take the Common Threads Initiative pledge and join us in the fifth 'R,' to reimagine a world where we take only what nature can replace."

The e-mail message—and a related full-page ad that Patagonia ran in *The New York Times* for Black Friday—came on the heels of an ad campaign that told consumers to "Reduce what you buy," and prompted a whirlwind of media attention and online chatter about whether the message would hurt Patagonia's sales or help secure customer loyalty, or would simply be perceived as a marketing gimmick.

Rob BonDurant, vice president of marketing and communications at Ventura, Calif.-based Patagonia Inc., recently told *Marketing News* that the campaign has more than paid for itself with the amount of interest that it has generated for the brand and its Common Threads Initiative, a sustainability effort intended to prompt consumers to think twice about the environmental impact of buying any product and to encourage companies to be transparent about how their products are made.

If the "Don't Buy This Jacket" message boosts sales, that'd be an ancillary benefit, BonDurant says. The campaign's goal is to get consumers who aren't yet familiar with Patagonia and its sustainability-minded practices to take note of the company's culture and eco-minded business strategy, and to prompt more consumers to shop and live sustainably.

What follow are excerpts from *Marketing News'* interview with BonDurant. To see more of his insights, check out the March 1 issue of *Marketing News Exclusives* at MarketingPower.com/newsletters.

Q: What was the strategy behind this direct marketing effort?

A: It was really a comment on consumption for the sake of consumption. As a company, we have always been absolutely fascinated and committed to this idea of quality in place of consumption. We build our ethos around that because of where we came from. . . .

In 1972, before [Yvon Chouinard] founded the company, roughly, [mountain climbers] would pound nails into rocks that would leave marks and it would lead, ultimately, to degradation to the environment and against the very reason to go to these wild places. So he built these tools that you could pull out and remove and left no marks whatsoever. . . . He caused a disruption that changed the way we look at the rock climbing industry forever. . . .

Because we don't even consider ourselves a marketing company—we consider ourselves a company that makes products that solve problems—we are able to do things other companies can't. . . . When we began discussing this Black Friday/Cyber Monday thing . . . for Black Friday we are told to go out and consume a resource that is not renewable and we just couldn't really live with that. We decided to be exactly who we are and say: 'Hey, look: Only purchase what you need. We want you to be aware of what goes into the products that we make so you can make an educated choice about when you buy those products' . . .

That, in and of itself, was our counter to the myriad of discounts, offers, sweepstakes and tchotchkes, and traditional marketing tactics that are meant to pull us into retail stores and aren't necessarily going to improve the quality of our lives. They are temporary. . . . The message, 'Don't buy this jacket,' is obviously super counterintuitive to what a for-profit company would say, especially on a day like Black Friday, but honesty is what we really were after.

As a measurement tool, I needed to see that we created a dialogue. I mean, we only ran one ad in *The New York Times* and that one ad has actually generated so much PR that, literally, the interview process that we have been going through, that I have been going through since that very day, has gained steam. So it has more than paid for itself in value and it has gotten a dialogue going.

Q: Who were you targeting in this message?

A: This was a message that was meant to go out to a much broader constituency than ours alone. To that end, we expected that when we put something out on Black Friday in *The New York Times* and then backed that up with messaging in our retail stores, on our website and in a flight [of ads] on NYTimes.com, that we would have this very succinct, very sort of counterintuitive message out there.

For me personally, I knew it was effective when I went to visit my folks over Thanksgiving down in Florida, who live in a nice home on the golf course, and the next-door neighbor drove his golf cart over. I didn't tell anyone we were running this [campaign], and he had the ad in his hands and he looked at it and said, 'You Patagonia guys sure are different.' This is not one of our core customers. That is how I knew we had reached an audience that was very different than ours. And not that I was looking to acquire that particular customer: What I'm trying to do is to get the conversation and dialogue going to improve business [sustainability].

If there is a halo effect and it keeps Patagonia top of mind, we will take it. We are not a marketing company and I don't really consider myself to be a marketer. We very much don't use marketing as a vehicle to drive business. We use products

as a vehicle to drive business. We use word of mouth, recommendations, public relations and, only as a last resort, a little bit of advertising to get our messages out there, and to be opinionated and have a point of view and, hopefully, one that is positive in future thinking.

Q: Were you concerned at all about sounding preachy or people dismissing the ad as the luxury of a company that sells high-end goods?

A: Yes and no. The concern was that if we don't walk our talk, if we don't live our communication, then we are actually just a marketing company after all, that we are actually full of s*#t and ultimately doing what the naysayers would accuse us of, and certainly did accuse us of, which is using this message to drive sales.

It is the forbidden fruit message. I didn't read this, but this is what I garnered from some of the social media that I was reading that was negative. Once you say: 'Don't push the red button. Don't eat from the apple,' man, you can't resist that forbidden fruit. That wasn't our intention at all. Our intention was to stop you in the sea of ads that said, 'Discounts,' and, 'Off-price,' and, 'You can get more,' and do it in the headline. Then if you read the body copy, which is extremely long and counterintuitive to what you would want in a newspaper especially on this particular day, you get this fuller, deeper story. And that is what really moves people.

People who were far against us, I didn't expect them to move towards the middle. The people who love us, I expected would write us and tell us how brilliant this was. We got that. It's the people in the middle who are open to ideas about how we shift business through consumption, through this idea of evolving capitalism and conscious consumption that we wanted to affect.

Q: You were just certified as a 'B Corporation'—a type of for-profit corporation in which the company's governing body can consider social or environmental objectives ahead of profits—but you still need to make sales. Were you concerned about how this campaign could affect your sales, and how did you convince your CEO and CFO to do this?

A: Of course, we are always worried about sales for Black Friday, especially because we are largely a fourth-quarter business. We make products for cold weather and that's what we are most known for. It is an incredibly important period of time for us, in which we will do up to 40 percent of our annual volume in two months alone, so if we falter, then yes, we are concerned.

But what we said is bullet-proof because it is what we believe in. It is the way we run our business. Every aspect of how we run Patagonia is really speaking to that ethos and it's the heart of our culture, so it wasn't difficult for the CEO or CFO to get on board once we sort of outlined the stroke of the campaign, the expected results, the action plan, the post-campaign and then, ultimately, the return that we can get from the level of dialogue we create either via public relations or social media and, of course, the interviews we are doing now. Since Black Friday, there has been an interview request coming in every day, and that is just from one ad in one newspaper, so the messaging is absolutely of strength and relevance—an eyebrow raiser. People want to know more about it and they are sure to get into it. They can hopefully discover more about our company and the way that we run our business so that we can inspire the other businesses to choose sustainability and not feel that that is a choice against profit.

Q: Patagonia has different goals and is a different company. Could other companies replicate this campaign?

A: If it is a marketing campaign, no. If it is a way they live their lives and do their business, absolutely.

Since we have to put it in a box here, this was not a marketing campaign. This is a message that we had been sending for decades, I mean literally for decades. We just hadn't put it in an amplified voice and stuck it in *The New York Times* on Black Friday. . . .

The key to the whole effort [is]: Put your money where your mouth is, or where your marketing dollars are, and support a model that is built around the concept of sustainability. That means you can't just apply it to your messaging or to a particular window of time. It has to be done 24 hours a day, 365 days a week.

For me, it's a challenge of, OK, we are a direct marketing company. We send out six catalogs. We send them out, roughly, over 30 to 45 days. That is a tonnage of paper. How can I continue to deal with what direct marketing requires, which is direct communication in your mailbox, without increasing my paper count? How can I acquire more customers without increasing my paper count? That requires not just a catalog paper policy, but also a company-wide paper policy because if half the company is printing their horoscopes out on the printers and I am busting my hump trying to figure out how to increase our order base without actually increasing our paper, we are not walking the talk.

So again, it is putting everybody in the mix and having ownership not at the senior level, but at the staff level. At a company meeting, I want staff to stand up and say, 'This is how we made our department paperless.' That will inspire one other department to do that and that is what we are doing. As a result, we are getting much more refined in how we do our mailing and we work with 501(c)(3) nonprofits to ensure the paper we print is sustainably harvested. And to this day, we have not increased our paper usage by more than one pound in the last five years because this is what we focused on, but we have grown the company annually over the last few years by over 30 percent. . . .

It is not just enough to make good products anymore. There also has to be a message that people can buy into, that people feel they are a part of, that they can be solutions-based. That is what the communication efforts are really all about.

Q: What does your retail strategy look like—and given your environmental mindset, are you going to move away from catalogs?

A: We have going on about 100 retail stores on a global basis, a very robust e-commerce business and a website that has now shifted to become the centerpiece of what is going on at Patagonia anytime you want. The lights are always on at the website. It does not close like a retail store. You don't have to get it in your mailbox; it will come to you. You can get it via e-mail, RSS, however you want to get it.

We are shifting the catalog itself. The catalog can only represent, at any given time, maybe only 40 percent of what is available on the Patagonia line, so what we have done is we have shifted our thinking away from our catalog being the standalone vehicle—our soapbox, if you will—and stood up to say what was important to us: to the catalog being a push and offer vehicle to inspire you to go online or to go into brick-and-mortar stores.

So yes, our catalogs are shifting. Are they going to become extinct? Not in the next year, not in, maybe, the next two years. But we will slowly decrease our paper usage; we will slowly move people into the medium they are actually transacting on. Over 80 percent of people we send the paper catalog to buy online. If that is the way that people look at the catalog, we will build it along those models until the point that, hopefully, we can exit that arena completely. I am not sure we ever will. That is a little bit of a crystal ball I wouldn't feel comfortable pulling right now. But especially as a company that is known for their catalog, it is one of those things that I have to pay very close attention to and I have to honor how deeply the Patagonia catalog culture has been built.

Q: What percentage of your communication is direct marketing?

A: In terms of our distribution, we are 50 percent wholesale, so that is going to a reseller like REI, for instance, one of our bigger accounts, and 50 percent is direct. That would be through catalog, through social media, the e-mail program, e-commerce and what we do in terms of our retail stores. Probably 80 percent of our communication is direct marketing because of the fact that those businesses are mature and robust, and because we have such a big database of people that we can reach and a profound database of potential prospects. I have already got all the climbers I am going to get. . . . Now it is, How can I reach the people that we didn't reach previously through conventional mediums that are sport-specific, to find people who are aligned with our values, our goals of the company? . . .

[In our direct marketing,] 60 percent is product and 40 percent is messaging, environmental, photography and all the rest of it. I have got a lot of freedom to be fairly robust, to have a story unfold over a catalog or e-mail, or a video or a podcast or whatever you may choose for the media to view it on.

We have one customer. We don't have a wholesale customer or brick-and-mortar customer, or a catalog customer. We have a Patagonia customer. Wherever they want to consume Patagonia, learn about Patagonia and understand Patagonia, we want to be ready and waiting for them on their terms. That is not a catalog strategy anymore. A catalog shows up in your box once a month, at best, and is disposable. Nowadays, we demand that companies give us their information when we want it. If that means 2 A.M. on Tuesday morning, then fine. That is when we have to be ready and willing to say: 'How're you doing? Good morning. Let's talk.'

Critical Thinking

1. Formulate your own definition for 'conscious consumerism.'
2. Summarize Patagonia's Common Thread Initiative.
3. In your opinion, what effect(s) will this initiative have on Patagonia's existing customers and competitors' customers?

KATHERINE LING is a freelance writer based in Fairfax, Va.

Honest Innovation

Ethics issues in new product development could be stalling innovation growth.

CALVIN L. HODOCK

Product innovation is the fuel for America's growth. Two Harvard economists described its importance as follows: "Innovation is no mere vanity plate on the nation's economic engine. It trumps capital accumulation and allocation of resources as the most important contributor to growth."

Innovative initiatives are a high risk game; failures widely outnumber successes. While enthusiasm, conviction and creativity should flourish in the hearts and minds of the innovation team, judgments must remain totally, even brutally, objective. But unconscious and conscious marketing dishonesty may make this easier said than done.

Unconscious Marketing Dishonesty

People fall in love with what they create, including movies, television pilots, novels, art and new products. And all too often that love is blind: As objectivity eludes the creator, normally rational people become evangelical rather than practical, rational marketing executives.

The Coca-Cola executive suite was convinced that New Coke was the right thing to do. Procter & Gamble's research and development (R&D) believed that Citrus Hill was a better-tasting orange juice than Tropicana and Minute Maid. The spirited Pepsi Blue team overlooked the obvious knowledge that colas should be brown. Ford's MBA crowd believed in a "cheap Jag" strategy. And Motorola's engineers were misguided in their devotion to the Iridium satellite telephone system.

Crest Rejuvenating Effects was fake innovation: It basically was just regular Crest with a great cinnamon vanilla flavor and feminine packaging, positioned for the "nip and tuck" generation of women aged 30 to 45. Similar to Rice Krispies' famous "snap, crackle, and pop" campaign, it encountered a tepid reception, but the brand's custodians believed that America was ready for "his and hers" tubes of toothpaste in their medicine cabinets.

These were well-meaning people who wandered off course because they became enamored with what they created. But let's face it, optimism has limits. The marketplace disagreed, and that's the only vote that counts in any innovation effort.

Conscious Marketing Dishonesty

Conscious marketing dishonesty is more insidious. Blinded passion may still be part of the equation, but in this case the innovation team consciously pushes the envelope across the line of propriety. Before long, there are disquieting signs or signals that all is not well with the new product.

Unfavorable data or information might be ignored, perhaps even suppressed. There might be the blithe assumption that some miracle will surface, and make it all right. Successful innovation initiatives are not products of miracles, but simply take a good idea and execute all the basic steps that are part of the discovery process. The reward goes to those who excel in executing the thousands of details associated with the dirt of doing.

Either way, conscious or unconscious, marketing dishonesty means resources are wasted, valuable time and energy are lost forever and shareholder value may be diminished (depending on the magnitude of the mistake). Often, nobody takes the blame—and many get promoted, because activity gets rewarded over achievement.

There's often no accountability, even though the new product blueprint is peppered with the fingerprints of many. New product assignments are similar to a NASCAR pit stop. The players are constantly moved around the chess board. The brand manager working on a new product for six to nine months moves to mouthwash. The mouthwash brand manager moves to shampoos. And what we have is a game of musical chairs, with no accountability. It is understandable why innovation teams are willing to "run bad ideas up the flag pole" in lassiez-faire-type innovation environments.

While there are supposed to be security checkpoints in the development process, the marketing "id" finds ways to maneuver around them. When important marketing research findings are ignored or rationalized away, because the innovation team is racing toward a launch date promised to management, the spigot of objectivity is turned off because reality might get in the way. Innovation initiatives build momentum to the point where nothing will stop the new product from being launched—not even dire news.

Marketing Dishonesty

There are eight recurring errors associated with flawed innovation. The most disingenuous is marketing dishonesty, where the innovation team consciously engages in deception—even though there is a red flag flapping in the breeze, indicating that a new product is ill. Six marketing dishonesty scenarios are outlined here.

Campbell's Souper Combo

Souper Combo was a combination frozen soup and sandwich for microwave heating; it tested extremely well as a concept. The product was test marketed, and national introduction was recommended.

Two forecasts surfaced. The new product team estimated that Souper Combo would be a $68 million business. The marketing research department viewed it differently: It would be a $40 million to $45 million business, due to weak repeat purchase rates. Nobody challenged the optimistic forecast. Senior management trusted what they heard, while being fed a bouillabaisse of marketing dishonesty. The national introduction was a disaster, and Souper Combo died on the altar of blemished innovation in nine months.

Crystal Pepsi

Pepsi's innovation team ignored focus group participants who hated the taste of this clear cola. It was forced through the Pepsi distribution system on its journey to failure. When was the last time you saw Crystal Pepsi on the store shelves?

Apple Newton

The Newton was the first (but flawed) PDA rushed to market, because then-CEO John Scully viewed it as his signature product—knowing that Apple loyalists were dismayed that a "Pepsi guy" was running the company. Scully wanted to establish a technical legacy that endured long after he left the Apple campus.

The first Newtons were shipped to market with more than a thousand documented bugs. Nobody had the courage to tell Scully and the Apple board about this.

Arthritis Foundation Pain Relievers

This was a line of parity analgesics, involving a licensing agreement where the company paid the Atlanta-based Arthritis Foundation $1 million annually for trademark use. This analgesic line was a positioning gimmick destined for a law and order encounter, and that doesn't mean the NBC television program. Nineteen states attorney generals said the proposition was deceptive. The drugs contained analgesics common to other pain relievers, and were developed without assistance from the Arthritis Foundation. The Foundation was paid handsomely for the use of its name.

Although McNeil Consumer Healthcare admitted no wrong doing, the case was settled for close to $2 million.

Pontiac Aztek

This was considered the ugliest car ever, and the research verified this. While the research predicted that the Aztek was a hopeless cause, the project team sanitized the research sent to senior management to make the situation look better than it was. Decisions about the Aztek's fate were based on intelligence that was heavily modified and edited. Get it out became more important than "get it right."

Aztek-type decisions became regrettably common in the General Motors culture. John Scully never heard the bad news about the Newton, and the General Motors executive suite didn't want to hear any bad news about their cars. It is a heck of way to run one of America's largest corporations and a bad deal for General Motors shareholders, when a culture of intimidation fuels marketing dishonesty. No wonder things are grim at GM these days.

Polaroid Captiva

This camera was similar to Polaroid's original goldmine product the SX 70, but with a smaller film format. It was priced at $120, although marketing research indicated it would not sell if priced over $60. In this scenario, marketing sold a bad idea supported with a specious assumption; marketing research couldn't sell the truth.

Captiva's potential sales were inflated with an assumption about high levels of repeat purchases after introduction. Selling cameras is different than selling cookies or shampoo, products that need replacement. Captiva perished in the marketplace, as the company violated its cardinal principle: Make the cash register ring selling film, while offering the cameras at cost.

Ethics Issues

While these new products had varied product deficiencies, they all share a common denominator: an optimistic sales forecast. An innovation team can manipulate the numbers to get any sales level it wants. It's easy to do, use optimistic assumptions. New product teams can, and do, cook the books with creative number crunching.

Most new product failures are heavily researched. It is used to justify moving a bad new product forward. In a recent *Advertising Age* article, Bob Barocci, the CEO of the Advertising Research Foundation, remarked, "There is a general belief

---

Executive Briefing

Jeffery Garten, former dean of the Yale School of Management and *BusinessWeek* columnist, graded briefing business schools with a C+ in teaching ethics. Sweeping bad news about new product initiatives under the rug can be more costly than embezzlement, and it is just as unethical. A *USA Today* survey says that 52% of students working on their master's of business administration degrees would buy stock illegally on inside information. Business schools need to emphasize ethics training far more than they do now, particularly since unethical behavior can be an underlying dynamic in new product failures.

that over 50% of the research done at companies is wasted." He attributed this to the desire to "support decisions already made." All too often, innovation teams push questionable new products through the pipeline with the support of "justification research."

Another ethical issue is targeting. It is difficult to imagine that ad agencies and their clients did not know Vioxx and Celebrex were overprescribed drugs, sold to consumers with minor aches and pains who could have used less expensive alternatives like Advil and Aleve. Both clients and agencies mutually formulated target strategies with Celebrex and Vioxx as examples. These drugs were developed for senior citizens with chronic pain. But the target segment was too small, so the focus shifted to aging baby boomers with clients and agencies in agreement on the reconfiguration.

Prescriptives

Here are seven recommendations:

1. **Innovation committee.** Boards have finance, audit, nominating and compensation committees. Why not an innovation committee composed of outsiders who are not board members? Their role is to assist the board in assessing innovation initiatives. The board can then decide what action should be taken, including pressing the "kill button."

   Companies sometimes do postmortems after failure. The innovation committee should perform pre-mortems early in the development process, before bad ideas soak up lots of money. There is a rich reservoir of people resources to serve on innovation committees (e.g., academics, retired senior executives, industrial designers, and product and industry specialists). But one thing that they should not be is cronies of professional management.

2. **Find a value-added marketing research department.** The prior case histories illustrate that bad research news often is ignored or rationalized away. Hire a research director who knows how to develop and steward a value-added research department, and that has senior management's respect. The respect factor will protect the function from retribution, should the news be bad. Such a person will not be easy to find. One company's solution was to hire a consultant from McKinsey & Company to steward their research department.

   In the early days, pioneer researchers such as Alfred Politz and Ernest Dichter presented their findings to boards of directors. Marketing research lost it status on its journey from infancy to maturity. Today's market research is frequently unseen by the board. The right person in the function—think one with management respect—gives marketing research an influential voice in the innovation process that it currently does not have.

3. **Reinforce the unvarnished truth.** Senior management needs to embrace skeptics, rather than surround themselves with "yes people." Before management reviews a new product plan, key players—manufacturing, finance, marketing, and marketing research—should sign off that the plan's assumptions, the underlying source for rosy sales forecasts, are truthful.

4. **Ethics boot camp.** Corporations spend millions on employee training, but how much is focused on ethics to help marketers navigate through gray areas? The innovation team should attend an ethics boot camp early in the development process. This should include everybody, including the ad agencies. Manipulating the forecast for a new product is unethical. It cheats the shareholders even more than it cheats the public.

5. **Teaching new product development.** In academia, new product courses are taught with a focus on best practices; a different perspective is required. The abysmal failure rate is due to worst practices. Classroom discussions of best practices aren't doing much to reduce failure. Class lectures should focus on ethics issues, like manipulating forecasts and justification research used to keep bad ideas afloat.

6. **Ethics test.** Business schools screen candidates based on their graduate management admission test (GMAT) scores. But there is another much-needed test that business schools should implement: an ethics test. Ethics scores should carry equal weight with GMATs. This demonstrates to candidates that ethics are important, and represent a significant prerequisite for admission. As evidenced in new product cases, ethics is more than simply the despicable acts of WorldCom's Bernie Ebbers and Enron Corporation's Andrew Fastow. And, most important, this should help business schools turn out students with a stronger moral compass—ones who don't feed management a duplicitous forecast for a flawed new product.

7. **Corporate endowments.** Corporations interact with business schools on many different levels. They make sizable donations, fund basic research and send their executives to workshops and seminars. They also need to endow ethics chairs with dedicated academics who are interested in ethics scholarship. Corporations should not hesitate to open up their vaults of information to these academics. What are the ethical patterns that underscore an endless stream of new product failures?

Final Thoughts

Failure is inevitable in product innovation. Perfect success is impossible, even undesirable, because it impedes reaching for the stars like Apple did with iPhone or Toyota with the Prius. Perfect success would be a dull agenda of safe bets like a new fragrance or a new flavor. This means the company has elected to play small ball.

This was the trap that Procter & Gamble fell into for close to three decades, despite having 1,250 PhD scientists churning out a treasure chest of patents—leading to 250 proprietary technologies. Despite all this patent activity, very few marketplace hits that made the company famous—think Tide or Pampers as examples—had surfaced from this scientific capability. The innovation focus had drifted to minor product improvements, until the newly anointed CEO A. G. Lafley came along to change all that.

Lafley mandated that P&G be more aggressive, expect failures, and shoot for an innovation success rate in the range of 50% to 60%. And that means having only 4 out of 10 new products fail at Procter & Gamble, well below the industry norm.

The statistic—nine out of 10 new products fail—has hovered over the marketing landscape for six decades. It is estimated that the food industry loses $20 billion to $30 billion annually on failed new products. Would it not be refreshing to attempt to scale this back with a healthy dose of marketing honesty?

Critical Thinking

1. Define *unconscious marketing dishonesty*. Do you agree with the author's distinction between unconscious and conscious marketing dishonesty?

2. List some additional examples, beyond what's in the articles, of conscious and unconscious marketing dishonesty.

CALVIN L. HODOCK is former chairperson of the American Marketing Association board, author of *Why Smart Companies Do Dumb Things* (Prometheus Books, 2007), and professor of marketing at Berkeley College, based in West Paterson, N.J. He may be reached at calhodock@hotmail.com.

It's Hard to Be Good

But it's worth it. Here are five companies whose success is built on responsible business practices.

ALISON BEARD AND RICHARD HORNIK

On the following pages, HBR profiles five "good" companies that do more than just pay lip service to community engagement, labor relations, environmental protection, corporate governance, and supply chain accountability. Neither our editors nor the academics we consulted have voted them the world's most socially responsible corporations. But each excels in one or more of the areas just listed, and does so by making them part of its internal corporate logic—something that Rosabeth Moss Kanter argues, that all businesses should do.

These firms have also succeeded commercially—hard evidence that doing the right thing as a company doesn't conflict with bottom-line imperatives. As Zhang Yue, the founding chairman of Broad Group, says, "The survival and growth of a company is the same thing as its social responsibility."

The Experts

Pamela Hartigan is the director of the Skoll Centre for Social Entrepreneurship at the University of Oxford's Said Business School. She is also a founding partner of Volans.

Thomas Kochan is the George Maverick Bunker Professor of Management and a codirector of the Institute for Work and Employment Research at the MIT Sloan School of Management.

Christopher Marquis is an associate professor in the organizational behavior unit at Harvard Business School.

Roger Martin is the dean of the Rotman School of Management at the University of Toronto.

Dan Esty is the Hillhouse Professor of Environmental Law and Policy at Yale University. He is also the director of the Yale Center for Environmental Law and Policy and the Center for Business and the Environment at Yale, and the commissioner of the Connecticut Department of Energy and Environmental Protection.

Royal DSM

A decade ago, Royal DSM's core offerings were petrochemicals, plastics, and base chemicals and materials. Today the Dutch firm is in the same sector, but its output is very different: nutritional supplements, pharmaceutical ingredients, and energy-efficient building materials.

If the company's first step on the path to being a good corporate citizen was to develop and sell more-sustainable, health-enhancing technologies and products, the second step is even bolder—and less obviously commercial: giving them away to those who need them most.

But both moves are strategic and designed to promote long-term corporate success in an increasingly complex global economy. The biggest initiative is a partnership with the World Food Programme to distribute DSM's vitamins, nutrient mixes, and fortified food to malnourished people in Nepal, Kenya, Bangladesh, and Afghanistan; 10 million will be served by the end of this year. But the company, which has 250 sites in 50 countries, also participates in many smaller initiatives. For instance, it has contributed lightweight composite modules to a new school in Pune, India, which reduced the costs, time, and

---

Notable Strength

Community Engagement

- **CORE BUSINESS** Chemicals
- **COUNTRY** Netherlands
- **YEAR FOUNDED** 1902
- **EMPLOYEES** 22,000

2010 Revenue

€8.2 billion

- **10-YEAR ANNUALIZED**
- **TOTAL SHAREHOLDER RETURN** 9.6 percent
- **FACT** A group of South African primary school children who ate porridge fortified with MixMe, a DSM multi-micronutrient powder, saw their mean store of body iron double over the course of a 23-week company-sponsored clinical study.

environmental impact of construction; the school's students will also be given access to a DSM nutrition program. Elsewhere in India, one of DSM's anti-infectives units offers free medical services to nearby villagers. And in Mexico, DSM employees hold monthly seminars on safety, health, and the environment for local schoolchildren.

> "A lot of companies' CSR initiatives have nothing to do with their core business. DSM, by contrast, has used its savoir faire, its expertise, and mobilized staff to improve the nutrients in the food given in situations of famine or hunger. If we could clone Feike Sijbesma, the CEO, the world would be a better place."
>
> —Pamela Hartigan, Saïd Business School

Fokko Wientjes, the director of sustainability at DSM, says the company believes that providing aid is both the right thing to do and critical to the future growth of the business. "The benefit isn't difficult to explain," he says.

"First, in the war for talent, this way of thinking makes DSM an attractive employer. This is a company that's doing more than just working for shareholders. We have extremely low turnover.

"Second, it helps us understand what the needs are in the different countries where an organization like the World Food Programme operates, which helps us innovate.

"And third, when you work with these groups you really get the message out on issues like the importance of nutrients. And in the end that will lead to interventions and investments that could be profitable."

The service mentality starts at the top with CEO Feike Sijbesma, who spearheaded the sustainability-focused rebalancing of DSM's product portfolio. Rank-and-file employees participate by nominating small projects for the company to fund. In the middle, local managers are encouraged to budget for outreach and engagement in their communities.

"You look at your environment and think, What can I contribute here?" says Wientjes, whose stints with DSM's South American and Egyptian operations involved work on safer house construction and environmental cleanup. There's just one rule: "It needs to be linked to our strategy, to our expertise. We wouldn't do language lessons for children. But chemistry and math? That suits our company. That's what we know.

"With big projects, you have to find the right partner and the right cause. You have to think, What more can I do with these competencies to build something both for society and for the company?"

It's not just donations. In India, one of DSM's most important growth markets, the company has a subsidiary tasked with helping local base-of-the-pyramid businesses move toward more-sustainable production, primarily in agriculture (for example, by using better cow feed to improve milk yields) and energy (by providing enzymes to improve the efficiency of gas plants powered by animal manure).

Wientjes acknowledges that DSM's return on its social investment is hard to quantify. "We don't really put a value on it right now, and maybe we should to have the investor community better understand," he says. "But shareholders haven't ever called me and said, 'Please stop.'"

Southwest Airlines

Southwest's first newspaper ad, published in 1971, promised that its flight attendants—then called air hostesses—would serve from the heart. (Later commercials made it clear they would also wear hot pants.) But what the marketing campaigns didn't explain was how the company planned to create its energetic corps of customer-loving, costume-wearing employees. The strategy was simple: Southwest would make its staff happy. Customer satisfaction and profits would follow.

Today that doesn't sound new. But back then it was. And the philosophy has paid off. Southwest is now the largest United States domestic air carrier and has been profitable for 38 consecutive years, during which many competitors declared bankruptcy or operated in the red.

Last May, on the day the company finalized its $3.2 billion merger with AirTran, Southwest's management team flew to AirTran's Atlanta headquarters to throw an air-hangar barbecue for the 6,000 acquired employees based there. CEO Gary Kelly helped serve brisket. The next day the executive group went back to work on a plan that will merge seniority lists in 16 collective bargaining agreements and preserve the job of every manager below the C-suite, though some might be required to relocate. This approach highlights two key elements of Southwest's employees-first strategy: meaningful interaction between staff and management, and good relationships with organized labor.

The company also champions a corporate culture—"warrior spirit, servant's heart, fun-loving attitude"—that promotes collaboration. There is a "culture committee," which is made up of 200 employees from all levels and meets quarterly to plan activities. One favorite initiative is "Delight and Surprise," when committee members unexpectedly greet the crew of an arriving flight with food and drink and relieve them of plane-cleaning duties.

Employee development starts with intense onboarding and continues through the company's six-week MIT (managers-in-training) program. Two poster children for career advancement at Southwest are Mike Ryan, a VP of labor relations who started in the mail room, and Teresa Laraba, senior VP of customer services, who began as a part-time agent in the El Paso airport.

Notable Strength

Labor Relations

- **CORE BUSINESS** Airline
- **COUNTRY** United States
- **YEAR FOUNDED** 1967
- **EMPLOYEES** 35,000

2010 REVENUE

$12.1 billion

- **10-YEAR ANNUALIZED**
- **TOTAL SHAREHOLDER RETURN**−6.9 percent
- **FACT** Southwest consistently has the lowest ratio of complaints per passengers boarded of all major United States carriers reporting statistics to the United States Department of Transportation.

Southwest's pay and benefits are above the industry average. In 1973 it was the first airline to establish profit sharing, and employees now own 5 percent of company stock. Diversity is a priority, and HR policies allow for small but critical concessions like letting flight attendants trade hours.

Much of this is negotiated with the unions, with which Southwest has always worked well. Senior labor relations counsel Joe Harris, who has represented the company since 1972, remembers the initial thinking of founder and CEO Lamar Muse and his legendary successor, Herb Kelleher. "They simply adopted the position that our employees needed an effective voice so we would partner with these organizations," Harris recalls. Of course, "we've had very contentious negotiations over the years. But we're not like the Hatfields and the Mc-Coys, where we keep fighting after the fight is over. At the end of the day we have a common objective to keep the company healthy and prosperous."

> **"Southwest has been consistently successful by staying true to its values. Other airlines have said, 'We know we should improve labor relations, but we have 9/11, Asian flu, gas prices . . .' It's always, 'We'll get to that.' Southwest has said, 'The only way we can turn these planes around quickly is by having committed, problem-solving employees that work together. So what kind of HR practices promote that?'"**
>
> —Thomas Kochan, MIT Sloan School of Management

Southwest reinforces the employee ownership mentality through aggressive internal communication at live events like Kelly's annual "message to the field" speaking tour and through new technologies. The company offers text alerts for corporate news and has a smartphone app for its intranet, where Kelly posts a weekly audio update and senior managers blog and respond to comments.

Will Southwest be able to keep it going and remain a profit leader among airlines even as the economy stagnates, margins tighten, and competitors cotton on to the employees-customers-shareholder continuum? "It's a tremendous challenge," Harris acknowledges. "But this philosophy really does still permeate the entire organization."

Broad Group

"Responsibility is more important than growth." "Protecting the environment is more important than profit." "Love is more important than anything else."

You might expect to find those lines in the values statement of a company that makes energy-efficient air conditioners. But would you expect them from one based in hypercompetitive, high-pollution China? From one with industrial customers in more than 70 countries and more than $500 million in sales? From one led by a man worth an estimated $850 million? From one that might soon go public?

Broad Group, the Changsha-based business we've just described, doesn't see a trade-off between responsibility and growth. Instead, the company—which makes not only air conditioners but also air

filtration systems and prefabricated energy-efficient buildings—is proof that the two can go hand in hand.

"Being good itself is competitive," says Zhang Yue, who founded the company with $3,000 in 1988 and is now its chairman. "A bad company may be competitive in a market for a while, but it won't last long. If you offer something of social value, you will survive, and you will prosper."

Of course that wasn't clear in the 1990s or even the early 2000s, when Broad was trying to persuade industrial customers to switch to its air conditioners. Its technology, which counterintuitively uses natural gas or waste heat to cool, is better for the environment—it avoids the ozone-depleting refrigerants used in electric cooling, reduces the load on power grids, and requires less energy overall. But the up-front costs are still significantly higher than those of less environmentally friendly options, making it a harder sell.

> **"Broad Group continually pushes forward new ideas, products, and services that not only help them meet bottom-line objectives but also satisfy their core mission—solving environmental problems in a way that connects to their existing business."**
>
> —Christopher Marquis, Harvard Business School

The company's earliest successes were in locales with unstable electric systems. Now Broad Group exports to developed markets around the world, supplying airports from Madrid to Bangkok as well as military bases in the United States. It claims to triple the energy efficiency of facilities while dramatically reducing emissions.

The company's other "good" products were developed partly as a response to social and environmental crises: Its air purification systems were designed after the 2002–2003 SARS outbreak in Asia (a cell phone that monitors air quality is on the way); its prefab building

---

Notable Strength

Environmental Protection

- **CORE BUSINESS** Industrial Products
- **COUNTRY** China
- **YEAR FOUNDED** 1988
- **EMPLOYEES** 2,600

2010 Revenue

RMB 3.6 billion

- **10-YEAR ANNUALIZED**
- **TOTAL SHAREHOLDER RETURN** Undisclosed
- **FACT** Broad Town, the company's one-square-kilometer headquarters, comprises 28 buildings made of recycled packing crates and shipping pallets. Three times a day, employees there are served meals sourced from an on-site organic farm.

system—which allows for fast, zero-pollution construction of sturdy, well-insulated structures—followed the 2008 Sichuan earthquake.

Zhang sees that system, the BSB (Broad Sustainable Building), as the company's future. "Buildings consume 40 percent of the world's energy," he explains. As soon as the BSB standards are verified by the Chinese government, the company will tackle its goal of producing 700 million square feet of energy-conserving space by 2020. Working through 100 franchised distributors, it hopes to win a 30 percent share of the global construction market. "We boldly dream that one day the whole world will cut CO_2 emissions by 40 percent using this technology," Zhang says.

Observers have been impressed by a video showing a prototype 15-story hotel built in 90 hours. But it's a long way to world domination—hence the desire to raise more capital by taking the company public.

A stock market listing will bring new stakeholders, but Zhang thinks he can hold fast to the company's ethos and culture. Indeed, investors will know exactly what they're buying into: a company with environmental protection at its core, led by an outspoken tycoon who recently renounced his private jet and who refuses to contribute to overpopulation by having a second child.

Zhang really does seem to think he can build a global business on love. "If everybody and every business becomes socially responsible," he says, "then the earth will become a beautiful hometown for us all."

Potash Corporation

A decade ago, after the grand corporate frauds at Enron and WorldCom unleashed a wave of scandal-inspired regulation, the executives and directors of Potash Corporation made a decision. The Canadian fertilizer producer wouldn't just follow the new rules. It would get ahead of them.

"There was this groundswell around governance in the academic, shareholder, and regulatory communities, and that made us stop and

---

Notable Strength

Corporate Governance

- **CORE BUSINESS** Fertilizers
- **COUNTRY** Canada
- **YEAR FOUNDED** 1975
- **EMPLOYEES** 5,500

2010 Revenue

US$6.5 billion

- **10-YEAR ANNUALIZED**
- **TOTAL SHAREHOLDER RETURN** 27.4 percent
- **FACT** After BHP Billiton launched a hostile takeover of PotashCorp last year, the company's board of directors met 35 times (compared with eight times in a typical year), with an attendance record of 97 percent. The bid was eventually quashed by the Canadian government.

---

take a comprehensive look at what we were doing," says Joe Podwika, general counsel. "We had established a sustainability committee, and we realized one of the pillars had to be good corporate governance. Instead of adhering to the minimum requirements, we could implement best-practice programs that in the long run would be good for the company."

What started with a core values statement and code of conduct has grown to include a host of shareholder-friendly initiatives, from directors elected by majority vote to "say on pay" for executives—all before such measures were customary or mandated. Most initiatives—such as the stock-option plan based on three-year performance that covers 220 managers and goes up for shareholder vote each year—are taken proactively. But PotashCorp also reacts to outside pressures. Not long ago a big Canadian investor group requested direct contact with board members about executive pay, without management or counsel listening in. "The instinct is to say, 'We can't do that,'" Podwika says. "But we looked at it and decided we ought to"—even at a time when CEO William Doyle's annual package of about $10 million (he also held roughly $400 million in stock and options) was generating controversy.

PotashCorp is not without critics. As recently as 1989 it was a debt-burdened government entity. Its mining operations create serious short-term environmental damage, even if it invests heavily in land reclamation. The company also still places "maximize long-term shareholder value" at the top of its key goals, followed by ones related to customers, communities, employees, and the environment (in that order).

> **"Potash shows leadership in the clarity and forthrightness of its compensation disclosure. Rather than giving the minimum required and forcing the investor to try to figure out what the compensation really is, it voluntarily reports how much its executives earn from exercising stock options—even though in recent years it has been an embarrassingly high number. And it does so with a very user-friendly and transparent chart."**
>
> —Roger Martin, Rotman School of Management

But when it comes to governance, PotashCorp is by all accounts doing the right thing. What benefit does the company get as a result? "One way to think about the ROI is that it's like an insurance policy," says Podwika. "There's a generally understood principle that the real value of the company is our reputation. I'd say that everybody has it on their consciousness—our CEO, our CFO, and certainly our board. People in every part of the company. We talk about it all the time."

Unilever

To understand the challenge of making Unilever's supply chain sustainable, consider this: Each year, the company sells 170 billion products across 180 countries, sourcing materials from 150,000 suppliers and operating more than 250 factories. It's hard to manage that network, much less improve its performance on sustainability. But, according to Pier Luigi Sigismondi, Unilever's chief supply chain officer, doing better in that area is a strategic imperative. "We have to do business this way to sustain our long-term business goals," he says. After all, the maker of Lipton tea, Knorr soup, and Dove soap can't ignore farmland degradation or threats to the world's water supply. And a leading consumer goods company must respond to consumer demand for sustainably sourced products.

Execution rests on a "prioritize and conquer" approach. For agricultural sourcing, Unilever identified its top 10 raw materials (as measured by volume, strategic importance, and consumer interest in sustainability) and set out goals for moving to sustainable supply (as measured by 11 factors from soil quality to labor practices). For example, it buys 1.4 million tons of palm oil annually, or 3 percent of the global yield, but this year more than half of that will come from growers certified by the Roundtable on Sustainable Palm Oil, a group it helped establish. By 2015 the company intends to use sustainable palm oil exclusively.

> **"Unilever has developed a pathbreaking framework for looking at products in a cradle-to-grave, value-chain-wide way. That represents a real step forward in companies' taking on a higher burden."**
>
> —Dan Esty, Yale Law School

In manufacturing and logistics, the company has set goals for reducing its environmental impact both directly (in factories, distribution centers, and transport) and indirectly (via better packaging and consumer education). Factories are required to submit monthly scorecards on their waste disposal and energy and water use. "We monitor it just as we monitor cost and sales," Sigismondi says. By 2020 the company aims to reduce CO2 emissions from manufacturing and logistics by more than 40 percent from a 1995 baseline. So "we know we need to do 4 percent or 5 percent a year."

Unilever typically works with governments and NGOs to ensure that its supply chain is following best practices. Though Sigismondi was recently in India visiting vegetable farms, he admits "it's impossible to do it all on a one-to-one basis." Suppliers in markets with no certification bodies are told to "self-certify" against Unilever's Sustainable Agriculture Code; their progress is monitored with software tools and audits. And when activist groups unearth problems, as Greenpeace did in some of Unilever's Southeast Asian palm plantations, the company responds (in the plantations' case by revoking their contracts).

All this requires investment, and the return is variable. Tea growers certified by the Rainforest Alliance offer higher yields, which reduce product costs, but for sustainable palm oil the balance-sheet defense has yet to materialize. Still, "we're big enough to afford the premiums, and we believe this is the future of the industry," Sigismondi says. "Today we're investing. We'll see the return in years to come."

There's more to do. Unilever has not set targets for sustainable sourcing of chemicals, minerals, and packaging other than paper and

---

Notable Strength

Supply Chain Accountability

- **CORE BUSINESS** Consumer products
- **COUNTRY** UK/Netherlands
- **YEAR FOUNDED** 1930
- **EMPLOYEES** 167,000

2010 Revenue

€44.3 billion

- **10-YEAR ANNUALIZED**
- **TOTAL SHAREHOLDER RETURN** 4.2 percent
- **FACT** It takes 3.5 million pounds of eggs from 125,000 cage-free hens to make the 30 million jars of Hellmann's Light mayonnaise sold in North America.

---

board. It continues to explore ways to convince customers that they must behave responsibly, too. "Sixty-five percent of our environmental footprint is related to how consumers use our products," Sigismondi says. "We have to lead beyond our own four walls."

Critical Thinking

1. In your opinion, what are the direct and indirect consequences of corporate social responsibility for the organization and the consumer?

2. With a small group of peers from your class, identify three corporations (besides the ones mentioned in the article) that have excelled at corporate social responsibility and have also succeeded commercially.

ALISON BEARD is a senior editor, and **RICHARD HORNIK** is a contributing editor, at HBR. **HEATHER WANG, MEGHAN ENNES, ERIN RUSH,** and **SAMANTHA PRESNAL** provided additional reporting for this article.

Acknowledgements—Harvard Business Review and Harvard Business Publishing Newsletter content on EBSCOhost is licensed for the private individual use of authorized EBSCOhost users. It is not intended for use as assigned course material in academic institutions nor as corporate learning or training materials in businesses. Academic licensees may not use this content in electronic reserves, electronic course packs, persistent linking from syllabi or by any other means of incorporating the content into course resources. Business licensees may not host this content on learning management systems or use persistent linking or other means to incorporate the content into learning management systems. Harvard Business Publishing will be pleased to grant permission to make this content available through such means. For rates and permission, contact permissions@harvardbusiness.org.

From *Harvard Business Review,* November 2011, pp. 88–96. Copyright © 2011 by Harvard Business School Publishing. Reprinted by permission.

UNIT 2

Research, Markets, and Consumer Behavior

Unit Selections

17. **A Step-by-Step Guide to Smart Business Experiments,** Eric T. Anderson and Duncan Simester
18. **Know What Your Customers Want before They Do,** Thomas H. Davenport, Leandro Dalle Mule, and John Lucker
19. **Respect Your Elders,** Tom Stein and Tim Devaney
20. **Marketing to Kids Gets More Savvy with New Technologies,** Bruce Horovitz
21. **It's Cooler than Ever to Be a Tween,** Sharon Jayson
22. **Segmenting the Base of the Pyramid,** V. Kasturi Rangan
23. **Can More Information Be a Bad Thing?** Robert S. Duboff
24. **The Tyranny of Choice: You Choose,** *The Economist*
25. **Tapping the Untapped,** Diana Derval

Learning Outcomes

After reading this Unit, you will be able to:

- As marketing research techniques become more and more advanced, and as psychographic analysis leads to more and more sophisticated models of consumer behavior, do you believe marketing will become more capable of predicting consumer behavior? Explain.

- Where the target population lives, its age, and its ethnicity are demographic factors of importance to marketers. What other demographic factors must be taken into account in long-range market planning?

- Psychographic segmentation is the process whereby consumer markets are divided up into segments based upon similarities in lifestyles, attitudes, personality type, social class, and buying behavior. In what specific ways do you envision psychographic research and findings helping marketing planning and strategy in the next decade?

Student Website
www.mhhe.com/cls

Internet References

Canadian Innovation Centre
www.innovationcentre.ca

BizMiner—Industry Analysis and Trends
www.bizminer.com/market_research.asp

Small Business Center—Articles & Insights
www.bcentral.com/articles/krotz/123.asp

Maritz Marketing Research
www.maritzresearch.com

USADATA
www.usadata.com

WWW Virtual Library: Demography & Population Studies
http://demography.anu.edu.au/VirtualLibrary

"It's hard to target a message to a generic 35-year-old middle-class working mother of two. It's much easier to target a message to Jennifer, who has two children under four, works as a paralegal, and is always looking for quick but healthy dinners and ways to spend more time with her kids and less time on housework."

—Elizabeth Gardner, Internet Retailer

If marketing activities were all we knew about an individual, we would know a great deal. By tracing these daily activities over only a short period of time, we could probably guess rather accurately that person's tastes, understand much of his or her system of personal values, and learn quite a bit about how he or she deals with the world.

In a sense, this is a key to successful marketing management: tracing a market's activities and understanding its behavior. However, in spite of the increasing sophistication of market research techniques, this task is not easy. Today, a new society is evolving out of the changing lifestyles of Americans, and these divergent lifestyles have put great pressure on the marketer who hopes to identify and profitably reach a target market. At the same time, however, each change in consumer behavior leads to new marketing opportunities.

The writings in this unit were selected to provide information and insight into the effect that lifestyle changes and demographic trends are having on American industry.

The first article in the *Market Research* subsection argues that every company can profit from testing customers' reactions to change. The authors provide step-by-step guidance to companies on how to start. The second article, "Know What Your Customers Want Before They Do," suggests that retailers need to target customers with the right deal, "the next best offer" at the right time.

The articles in the *Markets and Demographics* subsection examine the importance of demographic and psychographic data, economic forces, and age considerations in making marketing decisions. "Respect Your Elders" argues that the ideal marketing mix should make room for both digital and

Steve Cole/Getty Images

conventional marketing techniques. In "Marketing to Kids Gets More Savvy with New Technologies," Bruce Horovitz tackles the controversial issue of the increased practice of targeted advertising to tech-savvy children. In her *USA Today* article, Jayson argues that tweens are an attractive, yet very complicated market segment, and finally, "Segmenting the Base of the Pyramid" establishes that, if companies link their own financial success with that of their constituencies, marketing to the base of the pyramid can be quite profitable.

The articles in the final subsection analyze how consumer behavior, social attitudes, cues, and quality considerations will have an impact on the evaluation and purchase of various products and services for different consumers. Duboff tackles the subjective components of consumer choice and problem solving. *The Economist* presents an entertaining look at how variety in choices can hinder the consumer decision-making process. The final article, "Tapping the Untapped" proposes that preferences and purchases may be linked to consumers' physiology and perception.

A Step-by-Step Guide to Smart Business Experiments

Every company can profit from testing customers' reactions to changes. Here's how to get started.

ERIC T. ANDERSON AND DUNCAN SIMESTER

Over the past decade, managers have awakened to the power of analytics. Sophisticated computers and software have given companies access to immense troves of data: According to one estimate, businesses collected more customer information in 2010 than in all prior years combined. This avalanche of data presents companies with big opportunities to increase profits—if they can find a way to use it effectively.

The reality is that most firms can't. Analytics, which focuses on dissecting past data, is a complicated task. Few firms have the technical skills to implement a full-scale analytics program. Even companies that make big investments in analytics often find the results difficult to interpret, subject to limitations, or difficult to use to immediately improve the bottom line.

Most companies will get more value from simple business experiments. That's because it's easier to draw the right conclusions using data generated through experiments than by studying historical transactions. Managers need to become adept at using basic research techniques. Specifically, they need to embrace the "test and learn" approach: Take one action with one group of customers, take a different action (or often no action at all) with a control group, and then compare the results. The outcomes are simple to analyze, the data are easily interpreted, and causality is usually clear. The test-and-learn approach is also remarkably powerful. Feedback from even a handful of experiments can yield immediate and dramatic improvements in profits. (See the sidebar "How One Retailer Tested Its Discount Strategy.") And unlike analytics, experimentation is a skill that nearly any manager can acquire.

Admittedly, it can be hard to know where to start. In this article, we provide a step-by-step guide to conducting smart business experiments.

It's All about Testing Customers' Responses

In some industries, experimentation is already a way of life. The J. Crew or Pottery Barn catalog that arrives in your mailbox is almost certainly part of an experiment—testing products, prices, or even the weight of the paper. Charitable solicitations and credit card offers are usually part of marketing tests, too. Capital One conducts tens of thousands of experiments each year to improve the way it acquires customers, maximizes their lifetime value, and even terminates unprofitable ones. In doing so, Capital One has grown from a small division of Signet Bank to an independent company with a market capitalization of $19 billion.

The ease with which companies can experiment depends on how easily they can observe outcomes. Direct-mail houses, catalog companies, and online retailers can accurately target individuals with different actions and gauge the responses. But many companies engage in activities or reach customers through channels that make it impossible to obtain reliable feedback. The classic example is television advertising. Coke can only guess at how viewers responded to its advertising during the last Olympics, a limitation recognized by John Wanamaker's famous axiom, "Half the money I spend on advertising is wasted; the trouble is, I don't know which half." Without an effective feedback mechanism, the basis for decision making reverts to intuition.

In practice, most companies fall somewhere between these two extremes. Many are capable of conducting tests only at an aggregate level, and they're forced to compare nonequivalent treatment and control groups to evaluate the response. If Apple wants to experiment with the prices of a new iPhone, it may be limited to charging different prices in different countries and observing the response. In general, it's easier to experiment with pricing and product decisions than with channel management or advertising decisions. It's also easier to experiment in consumer settings than in business-to-business settings, because B2C markets typically have far more potential customers to serve as subjects.

Think Like a Scientist

Running a business experiment requires two things: a control group and a feedback mechanism.

Overcoming Reluctance to Experiment

A large bank we worked with decided to use experiments to improve the way it advertised its certificates of deposit, a core product. In the past, decisions on ads had been made largely by a single manager, whose extensive experience endowed him with power and status within the organization—and a big salary.

The possibility that the bank would use experiments to supplant his intuitive decision making was a threat to the manager. Not surprisingly, he obstructed the process, arguing that planning lead times were too long and decisions had already been made. A senior leader whose P&L was directly affected by the advertising decisions had to intervene. He allowed the experiments to go forward—and reassured his team that any missteps resulting from the experiments would not affect their year-end bonuses.

Organizational recalcitrance is one of the key hurdles companies encounter when trying to create a culture of experimentation. The main obstacle to establishing the new usual is the old usual. Organizations have their ways of making decisions, and changing them can be a formidable challenge.

One mistake some firms make is to delegate experimentation to a customer intelligence group. This group has to lobby each business unit for the authority to conduct experiments. That's the wrong approach: Experiments are designed to improve decision making, and so responsibility for them must occur where those decisions are made—in the business units themselves.

It is also important to set the right expectations. It's a mistake to expect every experiment to discover a more profitable approach—perhaps only 5 percent of them will do that. Those odds mean that taking eight months to implement a single large-scale experiment is a bad strategy. Productive experimentation requires an infrastructure to support dozens of small-scale experiments. Of perhaps 100 experiments, only five to 10 will look promising and can be replicated, yielding one to two actions that are almost certain to be profitable. Focus your organization on these and scale them hard. Your goal, at least initially, is to find the golden ticket—you're not looking for lots of small wins.

Golden tickets can be hard to find, but that's largely because most organizations lack the perseverance to overcome the institutional resistance that stands in the way of discovering them.

Though most managers understand the purpose of control groups in experimentation, many companies neglect to use them, rolling out tests of new offerings across their entire customer base. A company that wants to evaluate the effect of exclusivity on its dealer network, for instance, is missing an opportunity if it offers all its dealers exclusivity. It should maintain nonexclusivity in certain regions to make it easier to evaluate how exclusivity affects outcomes.

Ideally, control groups are selected through randomization. When Capital One wanted to test the effectiveness of free transfers of balances from other credit cards (the innovation that initially launched its success), it offered the promotion to a random sample of prospective customers, while a different random sample (the control group) received a standard offer. Often it makes sense for a company to set up a treatment group and then use the remainder of the customer base as a control group, as one bank did when it wanted to experiment with its online retail trading platform. That approach gave bank managers a very large sample of equivalent customers against which to evaluate the response to the new platform.

The key to success with treatment and control groups is to ensure separation between them so that the actions taken with one group do not spill over to the other. That can be difficult to achieve in an online setting where customers may visit your website repeatedly, making it challenging to track which versions of the site they were exposed to. Separation can also be hard to achieve in traditional settings, where varying treatments across stores may lead to spillovers for customers who visit multiple stores. If you cannot achieve geographic separation, one solution may be to vary your actions over time. If there is concern that changes in underlying demand may confound the comparisons across time, consider repeating the different actions in multiple short time periods.

The second requirement is a feedback mechanism that allows you to observe how customers respond to different treatments. There are two types of feedback metrics: behavioral and perceptual. Behavioral metrics measure actions—ideally, actual purchases. However, even intermediate steps in the purchasing

Idea in Brief

Companies today understand the power of analytics, but dissecting past data is a complicated task that few firms have the technical skills to master. Most companies will get more value from simple business experiments.

To grow profits, managers need to become adept at techniques used by lab scientists and medical researchers: They should establish control and treatment groups to test the effects of changes in price, promotion, or product variation. They should also grasp the opportunities provided by general changes in the business—like store openings—that constitute natural experiments in consumer behavior.

Creating a culture of experimentation requires companies to overcome internal political and organizational obstacles. And not every experiment will succeed. But over time, companies that embrace a test-and-learn approach are more apt to find the golden tickets that will drive growth.

Much of what companies learn from mammoth experiments can be gleaned from smaller tests that involve fewer variables, saving resources for follow-up tests.

process provide useful data, as Google's success illustrates. One reason Google is so valuable to advertisers is that it enables them to observe behavioral expressions of interest—such as clicking on ads. If Google could measure purchases rather than mere clicks, it would be even more valuable. Of course, Google and its competitors realize this and are actively exploring ways to measure the effects of advertising on purchasing decisions in online and traditional channels.

Perceptual measures indicate how customers think they will respond to your actions. This speculative form of feedback is most often obtained via surveys, focus groups, conjoint studies, and other traditional forms of market research. These measures are useful in diagnosing intermediate changes in customers' decision processes.

Given that the goal of most firms is to influence customers' behavior rather than just their perceptions, experiments that measure behavior provide a more direct link to profit, particularly when they measure purchasing behavior.

Seven Rules for Running Experiments

As with many endeavors, the best experimentation programs start with the low-hanging fruit—experiments that are easy to implement and yield quick, clear insights. A company takes an action—such as raising or lowering a price or sending out a direct-mail offer—and observes customers' reactions.

You can identify opportunities for quick-hit experiments at your company using these criteria.

1. **Focus on individuals and think short term.** The most accurate experiments involve actions to individual customers, rather than segments or geographies, and observations of their responses. The tests measure purchasing behavior (rather than perceptions) and reveal whether changes lead to higher profits. Focus your experiments on settings in which customers respond immediately. When UBS was considering how to use experiments to improve its wealth management business, it recognized that the place to start was customer acquisition, not improving lifetime customer value. The effects of experiments on customer acquisitions can be measured immediately, while the impact on customer lifetime value could take 25 years to assess.

2. **Keep it simple.** Look for experiments that are easy to execute using existing resources and staff. When a bank wanted to run a customer experiment, it didn't start with actions that required retraining of retail tellers. Instead, it focused on actions that could be automated through the bank's information systems. Experiments that require

extensive manipulation of store layout, product offerings, or employee responsibilities may be prohibitively costly. We know one retailer that ran a pricing experiment involving thousands of items across a large number of stores—a labor-intensive action that cost more than $1 million. Much of what the retailer learned from that mammoth experiment could have been gleaned from a smaller test that used fewer stores and fewer products and preserved resources for follow-up tests.

3. **Start with a proof-of-concept test.** In academic experiments, researchers change one variable at a time so that they know what caused the outcome. In a business setting, it's important to first establish proof of concept. Change as many variables in whatever combination you believe is most likely to get the result you want. When a chain of convenience stores wanted to test the best way to shift demand from national brands to its private-label brands, it increased the prices of the national brands and decreased the private-label brand prices. Once it established that shifting demand was feasible, the retailer then refined its strategy by varying each of the prices individually.

4. **When the results come in, slice the data.** When customers are randomly assigned to treatment and control groups, and there are many customers in each group, then you may effectively have multiple experiments to analyze. For example, if your sample includes both men and women, you can evaluate the outcome with men and women separately. Most actions affect some customers more than others. So when the data arrive, look for subgroups within your control and treatment groups. If you examine only aggregate data, you may incorrectly conclude that there no effects on any customers. (See the exhibit "Slicing an Experiment.")

The characteristics that you use to group customers, such as gender or historical purchasing patterns, must be independent of the action itself. For example, if you want to analyze how a store opening affects catalog demand, you cannot simply compare customers who made a purchase at the store with customers who did not. The results will reflect existing customer differences rather than the impact of opening the store. Consider instead comparing purchases by customers who live close to the new store versus customers who live far away. As long as the two groups are roughly equivalent, the differences in their behavior can be attributed to the store opening.

5. **Try out-of-the-box thinking.** A common mistake companies make is running experiments that only incrementally adjust current policies. For example, IBM may experiment with sales revenues by varying the wholesale prices that it offers to resellers. However, it may be more profitable to experiment with completely different sales approaches—perhaps involving exclusive territories or cooperative advertising programs. If you never engage in "what-if" thinking, your experiments are

How One Retailer Tested Its Discount Strategy

Walk into any large retail store, and you'll find price promotions being offered on big national brands—discounts that are funded by the manufacturer. For retailers, these promotions can be a mixed bag: Although the lower prices may increase sales of the item, the promotion may hurt sales of competing private-label products, which offer higher margins. We worked with one national retailer that decided to conduct experiments to determine how it might shield its private-label market share by promoting these products while the national brands were on sale.

The retailer designed six experimental conditions—a control and five discount levels that ranged from zero to 35 percent for the private-label items. The retailer divided its stores into six groups, and the treatments were randomized across the groups. This meant each store had a mixture of the experimental conditions distributed across the different products in the study. For example, in Store A private-label sugar was discounted 20 percent, and private-label mascara was full price, whereas in Store B mascara was discounted, but sugar was not. This experimental design allowed the retailer to control for variations in sales that occurred because the store groups were not identical.

The test revealed that matching the national brand promotions with moderate discounts on the private-label products generated 10 percent more profits than not promoting the private-label items. As a result, the retailer now automatically discounts private-label items when the competing national brands are under promotion. After establishing proof of concept, it refined its shielding policies by testing responses to various types of national brand promotions. For example, it discovered that a "Buy One, Get One for 50 percent Off" promotion on a national brand should also be matched with the same offer on the private label, rather than just a straight discount.

These experiments were successful for two main reasons: The actions were easy to implement, and the results were easy to measure. Each set of experiments lasted just one week. There were few enough products involved that stores did not require any additional labor. The experiments piggybacked on the standard procedures for promoting an item—indeed, the store employees were unaware that they were helping to implement an experiment.

In previous experiments the retailer had learned that if it changed too many things at once, the stores could not handle the implementation without long delays and a lot of additional cost. In some cases temporary labor had to be trained to go into the stores, find the products, and change the prices and shelf signage. Moreover, if the experiment extended beyond a week, problems arose as shelves were constantly rearranged and new signs applied. A maintenance program was required to monitor store compliance. In effect the retailer experimented on experimentation itself—it learned how to design studies that it could analyze more quickly and implement more easily.

---

unlikely to yield breakthrough improvements. A good illustration is provided by Tesco, the UK supermarket chain. It reportedly discovered that it was profitable to send coupons for organic food to customers who bought wild birdseed. This is out-of-the-box thinking. Tesco allows relatively junior analysts at its corporate headquarters to conduct experiments on small numbers of customers. These employees deliver something that the senior managers generally don't: a steady stream of creative new ideas that are relevant to younger customers.

6. **Measure everything that matters.** A caution about feedback measures: They must capture all the relevant effects. A large national apparel retailer recently conducted a large-scale test to decide how often to mail catalogs and other promotions to different groups of customers. Some customers received 17 catalogs over nine months, whereas another randomly selected group received 12 catalogs over the same time period. The retailer discovered that for its best customers the additional catalogs increased sales during the test period, but lowered sales in subsequent months. When the retailer compared sales across its channels, it found that its best customers purchased more often through the catalog channel (via mail and telephone) but less from its online stores. When the firm aggregated sales across the different time periods and across its retail channels, it concluded that it could mail a lot less frequently to its best customers without sacrificing sales. Viewing results in context is critical whenever actions in one channel affect sales in other channels or when short-term actions can lead to long-run outcomes. This is the reason that we recommend starting with actions that have only short-run outcomes, such as actions that drive customer acquisition.

7. **Look for natural experiments.** The Norwegian economist Trygve Haavelmo, who won the 1989 Nobel Prize, observed that there are two types of experiments: "those we should like to make" and "the stream of experiments that nature is steadily turning out from her own enormous laboratory, and which we merely watch as passive observers." If firms can recognize when natural experiments occur, they can learn from them at little or no additional expense. For example, when an apparel retailer opened its first store in a state, it was required by law to start charging sales tax on online and catalog orders shipped to that state, whereas previously those purchases had been tax-free. This provided an opportunity to discover how sales taxes affected online and catalog demand. The retailer compared online and catalog sales before and after the store opening for customers who lived on either side of the state's southern border, which was a long way from the new

Slicing an Experiment

When you're conducting an experiment, it's important to remember that initial results may be deceiving. Consider a publishing company that tried to assess how discounts affect customers' future shopping behavior. It mailed a control group of customers a catalog containing a shallow discount—its standard practice. The treatment group of customers received catalogs with deep discounts on certain items. For two years, the company tracked purchases at an aggregate level, and the difference between the two groups was negligible:

ALL CUSTOMERS	PER CUSTOMER
Customers who received the catalog with shallow discounts spent:	**$159** CONTROL
Customers who received the catalog with deep discounts spent:	**$157** TEST
	$(2) CHANGE

But that view of the data did not tell the whole story. Further analysis revealed a disturbing outcome among customers who had recently purchased a high-priced item and then received a catalog offering the same item at a 70 percent discount. Apparently upset by this perceived overcharge, these customers (some of them long-standing ones) cut future spending by 18 percent:

CUSTOMERS WHO RECENTLY BOUGHT A HIGH-PRICED ITEM	PER CUSTOMER
Customers who received the catalog with shallow discounts spent:	**$506** CONTROL
Customers who received the catalog with deep discounts spent:	**$415** TEST
	$(91) CHANGE

Upon learning these results, the publishing firm modified its direct-mail approach to avoid inadvertently antagonizing its best customers.

store. None of the customers were likely to shop in the new store, so its opening would have no effect on demand—the only change was the taxation of online and catalog purchases, which affected consumers only on one side of the border. The comparison revealed that the introduction of sales taxes led to a large drop in online sales but had essentially no impact on catalog demand.

The key to identifying and analyzing natural experiments is to find treatment and control groups that were created by some outside factor, not specifically gathered for an experiment. Geographic segmentation is one common approach for natural experiments, but it will not always be a distinguishing characteristic. For example, when GM, Ford, and Chrysler offered the public the opportunity to purchase new cars at employee discount levels, there was no natural geographic separation—all customers were offered the deal. Instead, to evaluate the outcome of these promotions, researchers compared transactions in the weeks immediately before and after the promotions were introduced. Interestingly, they discovered that the jump in sales levels was accompanied by a sharp increase in prices. Customers thought they were getting a good deal, but in reality prices on many models were actually lower before the promotion than with the employee discount prices. Customers responded to the promotion itself rather than to the actual prices, with the result that many customers were happy with the deal, even though they were paying higher prices.

Avoid Obstacles

Companies that want to tap into the power of experimentation need to be aware of the obstacles—both external and internal ones. In some cases, there are legal obstacles: Firms must be careful when charging different prices to distributors and retailers, particularly firms competing with one another. Although there are fewer legal ramifications when charging consumers different prices (the person sitting next to you on your airline flight has usually paid more or less than you), the threat of an adverse consumer reaction is a sufficient deterrent for some firms. No one likes to be treated less favorably than others. This is particularly true when it comes to prices, and the widespread availability of price information online means that variations are often easily discovered.

The internal obstacles to experimentation are often larger than the external barriers. In an organization with a culture of decision making by intuition, shifting to an experimentation culture requires a fundamental change in management outlook. Management-by-intuition is often rooted in an individual's desire to make decisions quickly and a culture that frowns upon failure. In contrast, experimentation requires a more measured decision-making style and a willingness to try many approaches, some of which will not succeed.

Some companies mistakenly believe that the only useful experiments are successful ones. But the goal is not to conduct perfect experiments; rather, the goal is to learn and make better decisions than you are making right now. Without experimentation, managers generally base decisions on gut instinct. What's surprising is not just how bad those decisions typically are, but how good managers feel about them. They shouldn't—there's usually a lot of room for improvement. Organizations that cultivate a culture of experimentation are often led by senior managers who have a clear understanding of the opportunities and include experimentation as a strategic goal of the firm. This is true of Gary Loveman, the CEO of Harrah's, now called Caesars Entertainment, who transformed the culture of a 35,000-employee organization to eventually enshrine experimentation as a core value. He invested in the people and infrastructure required to support experimentation and also enforced a governance mechanism that rewarded this approach. Decisions based solely upon intuition were censured, even if the hunch was subsequently proved correct.

The goal is not to conduct perfect experiments; it is to make better decisions.

There is generally a practical limit on the number of experiments managers can run. Because of that, analytics can play an important role, even at companies in which experiments drive decision making. When Capital One solicits new cardholders by mail, it can run thousands of experiments; there's no need to pretest the experiments by analyzing historical data. But other companies' business models may allow for only a few experiments; in such cases, managers should carefully plan and pretest experiments using analytics. For example, conducting experiments in channel settings is difficult because changes involve confrontation and disruption of existing relationships. This means that most firms will be limited in how many channel experiments they can run. In these situations, analyzing historic data, including competitors' actions and outcomes in related industries, can offer valuable initial insights that help focus your experiments.

Whether the experiments are small or large, natural or created, your goal as a manager is the same: to shift your organization from a culture of decision making by intuition to one of experimentation. Intuition will continue to serve an important role in innovation. However, it must be validated through experimentation before ideas see widespread implementation. In the long run, companies that truly embrace this data-driven approach will be able to delegate authority to run small-scale experiments to even low levels of management. This will encourage the out-of-the-box innovations that lead to real transformation.

Critical Thinking

1. List and summarize the seven rules for running experiments proposed in this article.

2. Discuss the example—provided in the article—of the retailer that conducted experiments on promotion and pricing. Suggest similar examples of other retailers that utilize experimentation as a basis for decision-making.

3. With a small group of peers from your class, debate the following paragraph from the article: "your goal as a manager is . . . to shift your organization from a culture of decision making by intuition to one of experimentation. Intuition will continue to serve an important role in innovation. However, it must be validated through experimentation before ideas see widespread implementation."

ERIC T. ANDERSON is the Hartmarx Professor of Marketing at Northwestern's Kellogg School of Management. DUNCAN SIMESTER is the NTU Professor of Management Science at MIT's Sloan School of Management.

Acknowledgements—Harvard Business Review and Harvard Business Publishing Newsletter content on EBSCOhost is licensed for the private individual use of authorized EBSCOhost users. It is not intended for use as assigned course material in academic institutions nor as corporate learning or training materials in businesses. Academic licensees may not use this content in electronic reserves, electronic course packs, persistent linking from syllabi or by any other means of incorporating the content into course resources. Business licensees may not host this content on learning management systems or use persistent linking or other means to incorporate the content into learning management systems. Harvard Business Publishing will be pleased to grant permission to make this content available through such means. For rates and permission, contact permissions@harvardbusiness.org.

Know What Your Customers Want before They Do

Retailers need to target customers with the right deal at the right time. Here's how to nail the "next best offer."

THOMAS H. DAVENPORT, LEANDRO DALLE MULE, AND JOHN LUCKER

Shoppers once relied on a familiar salesperson—such as the proprietor of their neighborhood general store—to help them find just what they wanted. Drawing on what he knew or could quickly deduce about the customer, he would locate the perfect product and, often, suggest additional items the customer hadn't even thought of. It's a quaint scenario. Today's distracted consumers, bombarded with information and options, often struggle to find the products or services that will best meet their needs. The shorthanded and often poorly informed floor staff at many retailing sites can't begin to replicate the personal touch that shoppers once depended on—and consumers are still largely on their own when they shop online.

This sorry state of affairs is changing. Advances in information technology, data gathering, and analytics are making it possible to deliver something like—or perhaps even better than—the proprietor's advice. Using increasingly granular data, from detailed demographics and psychographics to consumers' clickstreams on the web, businesses are starting to create highly customized offers that steer consumers to the "right" merchandise or services—at the right moment, at the right price, and in the right channel. These are called "next best offers." Consider Microsoft's success with e-mail offers for its search engine Bing. Those e-mails are tailored to the recipient at the moment they're opened. In 200 milliseconds—a lag imperceptible to the recipient—advanced analytics software assembles an offer based on real-time information about him or her: data including location, age, gender, and online activity both historical and immediately preceding, along with the most recent responses of other customers. These ads have lifted conversion rates by as much as 70 percent—dramatically more than similar but uncustomized marketing efforts.

The technologies and strategies for crafting next best offers are evolving, but businesses that wait to exploit them will see their customers defect to competitors that take the lead. Microsoft is just one example; other companies, too, are revealing the business potential of well-crafted NBOs. But in our research on NBO strategies in dozens of retail, software, financial services,

and other companies, which included interviews with executives at 15 firms in the vanguard, we found that if NBOs are done at all, they're often done poorly. Most are indiscriminate or ill-targeted—pitches to customers who have already bought the offering, for example. One retail bank discovered that its NBOs were more likely to create ill will than to increase sales.

Companies can pursue myriad good goals using customer analytics, but NBO programs provide perhaps the greatest value in terms of both potential ROI and enhanced competitiveness. In this article we provide a framework for crafting NBOs. You may not be able to undertake all the steps right away, but progress on each will be necessary at some point to improve your offers.

Define Objectives

Many organizations flounder in their NBO efforts not because they lack analytics capability but because they lack clear objectives. So the first question is, What do you want to achieve? Increased revenues? Increased customer loyalty? A greater share of wallet? New customers?

The UK-based retailer Tesco has focused its NBO strategy on increasing sales to regular customers and enhancing loyalty with targeted coupon offers delivered through its Clubcard program. As Roland Rust and colleagues have described ("Rethinking Marketing," HBR January-February 2010), Tesco uses Clubcard to track which stores customers visit, what they buy, and how they pay. This has enabled the retailer to adjust merchandise for local tastes and to customize offerings at the individual level across a variety of store formats, from hypermarts to neighborhood shops. For example, Clubcard shoppers who buy diapers for the first time at a Tesco store are mailed coupons not only for baby wipes and toys but also for beer. (Data analysis revealed that new fathers tend to buy more beer, because they are spending less time at the pub.) More recently, Tesco has experimented with "flash sales" that as much as triple the redemption value of certain Clubcard coupons—in

What Makes an NBO?

"Next best offer" is increasingly used to refer to a proposal customized on the basis of

- THE CONSUMER'S ATTRIBUTES AND BEHAVIORS (demographics, shopping history)

- THE PURCHASE CONTEXT (bricks and mortar, online)

- PRODUCT OR SERVICE CHARACTERISTICS (shoe style, type of mortgage)

- THE ORGANIZATION'S STRATEGIC GOALS (increase sales, build customer loyalty)

NBOs are most often designed to inspire a purchase, drive loyalty, or both. They can consist of

- PRODUCTS (a coupon for diapers)

- SERVICES (a discount on a spa visit)

- INFORMATION (Google ads to click on)

- RELATIONSHIPS (LinkedIn and Facebook recommendations)

Despite the name, an NBO may in fact be an initial engagement. And whether the customer relationship is new or ongoing, the NBO is intended to be a "best offer."

Gather Data

To create an effective NBO, you must collect and integrate detailed data about your customers, your offerings, and the circumstances in which purchases are made.

Know Your Customers

Information valuable for tailoring NBOs can be relatively basic and easily acquired or derived: age, gender, number of children, residential address, income or assets, and psychographic lifestyle and behavior data. Previous purchases are often the single best guide to what a customer will buy next, but that information may be harder to capture, particularly from offline channels. Loyalty programs like Tesco's can be a powerful tool for tracking consumers' buying patterns.

Even as companies work (and sometimes struggle) to acquire these familiar kinds of customer data, the growing availability of social, mobile, and location (SoMoLo) information creates major new data sets to be mined. Companies are beginning to craft offers based on where a customer is at any given moment, what his social media posts say about his interests, and even what his friends are buying or discussing online.

One example is Foursquare, which makes customized offers according to how many times consumers have "checked in" to a certain retail store. Another is Walmart, which acquired the social media technology start-up Kosmix to join its newly formed digital strategy unit, @WalmartLabs, in capitalizing on consumer SoMoLo data for its offers. Among the unit's projects is finding ways to predict shoppers' Walmart.com purchases on the basis of their social media interests. Walmart is also looking into location-based technologies that will help customers find products in its cavernous stores. The apparel retailer H&M has partnered with the online game MyTown to gather and use information on customer location. If potential

essence making its best offer even better for selected customers. A countdown mechanism shows how quickly time or products are running out, building tension and driving responses. Some of these offers have sold out in 90 minutes.

Tesco's NBO strategy seeks to expand the range of customers' purchases, but it also targets regular customers with deals on products they usually buy. As a result of its carefully crafted, creatively executed offers, Tesco and its in-house consultant dunnhumby achieve redemption rates ranging from 8 percent to 14 percent—far higher than the 1 percent or 2 percent seen elsewhere in the grocery industry. Microsoft had a very different set of objectives for its Bing NBO: getting new customers to try the service, download it to their smartphones, install the Bing search bar in their browsers, and make it their default search engine.

Starting with a clear objective is essential. So is being flexible about modifying it as needed. The low-cost DVD rental company Redbox initially made e-mail and internet coupon site offers intended to familiarize consumers with its kiosks. Redbox kiosks were a new retail concept, but in time people became accustomed to automated movie rentals. As the business grew, the company's executives realized that to increase profits while maintaining the low-cost model, they needed to persuade customers to rent more than one DVD per visit. So they shifted the emphasis of their NBO strategy from attracting new customers to discounting multiple rentals.

Idea in Brief

Targeting individuals with perfectly customized offers at the right moment across the right channel is marketing's holy grail. As companies' ability to capture and analyze highly granular customer data improves, such offers are possible—yet most companies make them poorly, if at all.

Perfecting these "next best offers" (NBOs) involves four steps: defining objectives; gathering data about your customers, your offerings, and the contexts in which customers buy; using data analytics and business rules to devise and execute offers; and, finally, applying lessons learned.

It's hard to perfect all four steps at once, but progress on each is essential to competitiveness. As the amount of data that can be captured grows and the number of channels for interaction proliferates, companies that are not rapidly improving their offers will only fall further behind.

customers are playing the game on a mobile device near an H&M store and check in, H&M rewards them with virtual clothing and points; if they scan promoted products in the store, it enters them in a sweepstakes. Early results show that of 700,000 customers who checked in online, 300,000 went into the store and scanned an item.

Many retailers focus on how to use customers' location information in real time; where the customers have been can also reveal a lot about them. In the United States alone, mobile devices send about 600 billion geospatially tagged data feeds back to telecommunications providers every day. An application developed by the software analytics company Sense Networks can compare a consumer's movements with billions of data points on the movements and attributes of others. Using this location history, it can estimate the consumer's age, travel style, level of wealth, and next likely location, among other things. The implications for creating highly customized NBOs are clear.

Know Your Offerings

Unless a company has detailed information about its own products or services, it will have trouble determining which offerings might appeal most to a customer. For some products, such as movies, third-party databases supply product attributes, and companies that rent or sell movies can surmise that if you liked one movie with a particular actor or plot type, you will probably like another. But in other retail industries, such as apparel and groceries, compiling product attributes is much more difficult. Manufacturers don't uniformly classify a sweater as "fashion forward" or "traditional," for example. They don't even have clear and standardized color categories. So retailers must spend a lot of time and effort capturing product attributes on their own. Zappos has three departments working to optimize customers' searches and create the most effective offers for its shoes. Even when the attributes are narrowed down to product type, style, color, brand, and price, a shoe might have any of more than 40 material patterns—pearlized, patchwork, pebbled, pinstripe, paisley, polka dot, or plaid, to name just those beginning with "p." Without a system for such detailed classification of product attributes, Zappos wouldn't know that a customer had often bought paisley in the past, so it wouldn't know that it should include paisley products in NBOs to that customer.

Similarly, without good classification systems, grocers can't easily determine what products will lure adventurous, health-conscious, or penny-pinching customers. When Tesco wants to identify products that appeal to adventurous palates, it will start with something that is widely agreed to be a daring choice in a given country—Thai green curry paste in the UK, perhaps—and then analyze the other purchases that buyers of the daring choice make. If customers who buy curry paste also frequently buy squid or wild rocket (arugula) pesto, these products have a high relationship coefficient.

Know the Purchase Context

Finally, NBOs must take into account factors such as the channel through which a customer is making contact with a business (face-to-face, on the phone, by e-mail, on the web), the reason for contact and its circumstances, and even voice volume

Building the Next Best Offer

Exemplary companies build or sharpen an NBO strategy through four broad activities:

1. **Defining Objectives** Craft NBOs to achieve specific goals, such as attracting new customers or increasing sales, loyalty, or share of wallet. Be ready to modify your objectives to exploit changing circumstances.

2. **Gathering Data** Collect detailed data about customers (demographics and psycho-graphics; purchase history; social, mobile, and location information), your offerings (product attributes, profitability, availability), and purchase context (customer's contact channel, proximity, the time of day or week).

3. **Analyzing and Executing** Use statistical analysis, predictive modeling, and other tools to match customers and offers. Use business rules to guide what offers are made under what circumstances. Carefully match offers and channels. Make offers sparingly, time them deliberately, and monitor contact frequency.

4. **Learning and Evolving** Think of every offer as a test. Incorporate data on customers' responses in follow-on offers. Formulate rules of thumb for designing new offers that are based on the performance of previous ones.

and pitch, indicating whether the customer is calm or upset. (Emotion-detection software is proving valuable for the last factor.) Bank of America has learned that mortgage offers presented through an ATM at the moment of customer contact don't work well because customers have neither the time nor the inclination to engage with them, whereas they might be receptive to the same offers during a walk-in. Likewise, someone who calls customer service with a complaint is unlikely to respond to a product offer, though he or she might welcome it by e-mail at another time.

Other contextual factors that may affect the design of an NBO—and a consumer's response to it—include the weather, the time of day or the day of the week, and whether a customer is alone or accompanied. Although clickstream or recent online purchase data are often the most relevant in guiding an online NBO strategy, in some cases, such as air-travel ticket pricing, time and day are important: Airlines can hike prices on a Sunday evening, because more people search then than, say, midday during the week. A Chinese shoe retailer we studied is testing offers that target primary buyers' companions. When a woman walks into one of its stores with her husband, she is usually the primary buyer, and the retailer's NBO is usually a relatively inexpensive item for the husband. The choice of what to offer him arises from the insight that men who accompany their wives shopping but are not actively shopping themselves are more price sensitive than solo husbands who are searching for a specific product.

The weather, the time of day or day of the week, and whether or not a customer is accompanied may affect the design of an offer.

Of course, countless other contextual factors depend on the nature of the business and its customers.

Analyze and Execute

The earliest predictive NBOs were created by Amazon and other online companies that developed "people who bought this also bought that" offers based on relatively simple cross-purchase correlations; they didn't depend on substantial knowledge of the customer or product attributes, and thus were rather a blunt instrument. Somewhat more targeted offers are based on a customer's own past purchase behavior, but even those are famously indiscriminate. If you buy a book or a CD for a friend who doesn't share your tastes, that can easily skew the future offers you receive.

Companies that have systematically gathered information about their customers, product attributes, and purchase contexts can make much more sophisticated and effective offers. Statistical analysis and predictive modeling can create a treasure trove of synthetic data from these raw information sources to, for example, gauge a customer's likelihood of responding to a discounted cross-sell offer delivered on her mobile device. Behavioral segmentation and other advanced data analytics that simultaneously account for customer demographics, attitudes, buying patterns, and related factors can help identify those customers who are most likely to defect. Armed with this information and a customer's expected customer lifetime value, an organization can determine whether its NBO to that customer should encourage or discourage defection. (A detailed discussion of marketing data analytics is beyond the scope of this article, but the 2002 book *Marketing Engineering,* by Gary L. Lilien and Arvind Rangaswamy, offers a robust overview of key analytical, quantitative, and computer modeling techniques.)

Although such analytics can yield a profusion of potentially effective offers, business rules govern the next step. When an analysis shows that a customer is equally likely to purchase any of several products, a rule might determine which offer is made. Or it might limit the overall contact frequency for a customer if analyses have shown that too much contact reduces response rates. These rules tend to go beyond the logic of predictive models to serve broad strategic goals—such as putting increasing customer loyalty above maximizing purchases.

A carefully crafted NBO is only as good as its delivery. Put another way, a brilliant e-mail NBO that never gets opened might as well not exist. Should the NBO be delivered face-to-face? Presented at an in-store kiosk? Sent to a mobile device? Printed on a register receipt? Often the answer is relatively straightforward: The channel through which the customer made contact is the appropriate channel for delivering the NBO. For example, a CVS customer who scans her ExtraCare loyalty card at an in-store kiosk can instantly receive customized coupons.

There are times, however, when the inbound and outbound channels should differ. A complex offer shouldn't be delivered through a simple channel. Recall Bank of America's experience with mortgage offers: The inbound channel—the ATM—was quickly found to be a poor outbound channel, because mortgages are just too complicated for that setting. Similarly, many call-center reps don't understand customer needs and product details well enough to make effective offers—particularly when the reps' primary purpose is to complete simple sales or service transactions.

Companies often test offers through multiple channels to find the most efficient one. At CVS, ExtraCare offers are delivered not only through kiosks but also on register receipts, by e-mail and targeted circulars, and, recently, via coupons sent directly to customers' mobile phones. Qdoba Mexican Grill, a quick-serve franchise, is expanding its loyalty program by delivering coupons to customers' smart-phones at certain times of the day or week to increase sales and smooth demand. Late-night campaigns near universities have seen a nearly 40 percent redemption rate, whereas redemption rates average 16 percent for Qdoba's overall program. Starbucks uses at least 10 online channels to deliver targeted offers, gauge customer satisfaction and reaction, develop products, and enhance brand advocacy. For example, its smartphone app allows customers to receive tailored promotions for food, drinks, and merchandise based on their SoLoMo information.

Upscale retailers and financial services firms find that a human being is often the best channel for delivering offers.

Nordstrom and other upscale retailers, and financial services firms with wealthy clients, invest heavily in their salespeople's product knowledge and ability to understand customers' needs and build relationships. For these businesses, a human being is often the best channel for delivering offers. Many organizations devise multiple offers and sort them according to predictive models that rank a customer's propensity to accept them on the basis of previous purchases or other data. Salespeople or customer service reps can select from among these offers in real time, guided by their dialogue with the customer, the customer's perceived appetite for a given offer, and even the comfort level between the customer and the salesperson. Combining human judgment with predictive models can be more effective than simply following a model's recommendations. For example, insisting that a rep deliver a specific offer in every case may actually reduce both customers' likelihood of accepting the offer and their postpurchase satisfaction. The investment firm T. Rowe Price provides call-center representatives with targeted offers, but it has concluded that if a rep delivers the offers in more than 50 percent of interactions, he or she probably isn't tuning in to customers' needs.

Learn and Evolve

Creating NBOs is an inexact but constantly improving science. Like any science, it requires experimentation. Some offers will work better than others; companies must measure the performance of each and apply the resulting lessons. As one CVS executive said to us, "Think of every offer as a test."

Companies can develop rules of thumb from their NBOs' performance to guide the creation of future offers—until new data require a modification of the rules. These rules will differ from one company to the next. In our research we identified some that leading companies use:

- **Footlocker:** Promote only fashion-forward shoes through social media.
- **CVS:** Provide discounts on things a customer has bought previously.
- **Sam's Club:** Provide individually relevant offers for categories in which a customer has not yet purchased, and reward customer loyalty.
- **Nordstrom:** Provide offers through sales associates in face-to-face customer interactions.

Rules of thumb should be derived from data-driven and fact-based analyses, not convention or lore. The rules above have been tested, but they will need to be challenged and retested over time to ensure continued effectiveness.

Meanwhile, legal, ethical, and regulatory issues associated with NBO strategies are evolving fast, as the collection and use of customer data become increasingly sophisticated. When companies enthusiastically experiment with NBOs, they should be wary of unwittingly crossing legal or ethical boundaries.

It would be hard for any company to incorporate every possible customer, product, and context variable into an NBO model, but no retailer should fail to gather basic demographics, psychographics, and customer purchase histories. Most retailers need to accelerate their work in this area: Their customers are not impressed by the quality or the value of offers thus far. Variables and available delivery channels will only grow in number; companies that aren't rapidly improving their offers will just fall further behind.

Critical Thinking

1. Explain the concept of "Next Best Offer" (NBO) as defined by the authors.
2. List and summarize the steps in the framework for crafting NBOs proposed in the article.

THOMAS H. DAVENPORT is the President's Distinguished Professor of Information Technology and Management at Babson College, a senior adviser to Deloitte Analytics, and the research director of the International Institute for Analytics. **LEANDRO DALLE MULE** is the global analytics director at Citibank. **JOHN LUCKER** is a principal at Deloitte Consulting LLP, where he is a leader of Deloitte Analytics in the United States and of advanced analytics and modeling globally.

Acknowledgements—Harvard Business Review and Harvard Business Publishing Newsletter content on EBSCOhost is licensed for the private individual use of authorized EBSCOhost users. It is not intended for use as assigned course material in academic institutions nor as corporate learning or training materials in businesses. Academic licensees may not use this content in electronic reserves, electronic course packs, persistent linking from syllabi or by any other means of incorporating the content into course resources. Business licensees may not host this content on learning management systems or use persistent linking or other means to incorporate the content into learning management systems. Harvard Business Publishing will be pleased to grant permission to make this content available through such means. For rates and permission, contact permissions@harvardbusiness.org.

Respect Your Elders

Digital marketing techniques might be flashy and young, but conventional marketing strategies haven't lost their impact. The ideal modern marketing mix makes room for both.

TOM STEIN AND TIM DEVANEY

Once the cool but unnecessary add-on to most companies' marketing strategies, digital marketing now leads the charge, and offline strategies, tactics and channels often complement marketers' increasingly Web- and mobile-focused efforts. The tide has officially turned, and if you're not incorporating blogs, social networks, search advertising, QR codes, geo-targeted promotions and the like into your marketing strategy, you're unapologetically behind the times and at risk of generating ineffective marketing initiatives—or so it would seem.

As the American Marketing Association and countless trade groups and business publications the world over have reported, all companies should at least have an online presence and invest in regular search marketing and social marketing efforts, but the demise of conventional, offline marketing strategies and tactics has been greatly exaggerated. Traditional techniques such as print advertising and direct mail still work—and work well—and many successful marketing strategies today have found the right balance between those traditional techniques and their flashier digital counterparts.

Face Time Beats Facebook

A November 2011 survey by Constant Contact Inc., a Waltham, Mass.-based firm that specializes in helping small businesses with their e-mail marketing, online surveys and events, shows that while most small businesses now market online and many are embracing social media, they also remain committed to more conventional methods. Eighty-one percent of small-business executives who responded to the survey said that they use Facebook and other social sites for marketing, and the same percentage reported that they also use good, old-fashioned face time. And while 66 percent invest in online advertising, 71 percent still invest in print ads.

Meanwhile, on the receiving end, customers say that social media is one of the least effective ways for a business to gain their loyalty, according to a November 2011 survey by Stamford, Conn.-based customer communications management firm Pitney Bowes Inc. that polled customers in the United States

and United Kingdom. Just 18 percent of survey respondents said that interaction with a business via Facebook, Twitter or some other social network would make them more likely to buy from the business again, and for small businesses, that number drops to 15 percent. The most effective ways to engender customer loyalty, according to the survey, are offering customers home delivery options and arming them with the ability to choose which communication channel through which they'd prefer to connect with your company.

In with the Old

Old-school methods are still a vital tool in marketers' kits—and might be even more effective now. Mike Sprouse, president and CEO of Sprouse Marketing Group, a full-service firm with clients such as Salesforce.com and Yahoo, and author of *The Greatness Gap,* says that if the herd is zigging to social marketing, savvy businesses should zag toward traditional media such as TV and print. "If 95 percent of marketers go one way, I want to be among the 5 percent going the other," he says. "Mail volume is down, but people still get—and open—mail, so why wouldn't I want to have my mail piece in someone's mailbox with, say, three other pieces, as opposed to years ago when it was with 10 other pieces? The old-school channels haven't disappeared; they're just not in vogue. But smart marketers know how to leverage that."

David Langton, principal and co-founder of New York-based communications design firm Langton Cherubino Group Ltd. and co-author of *Visual Marketing: 99 Proven Ways for Small Businesses to Market with Images and Design,* says that there's a story in his book about a building contractor who mailed postcards of his work to a list of prospects. Years later, his card was still generating new business. "People held onto that postcard," Langton says. "They put it on the fridge or stuck it in a book. Traditional marketing has stronger staying power than the ephemeral digital work we're bombarded with. It's easier to keep a postcard and view it multiple times than the e-mails and banner ads we swat away every day."

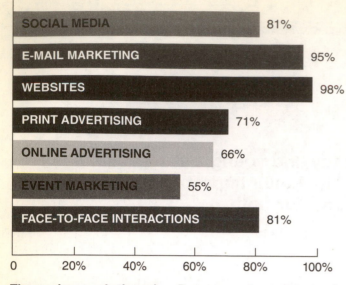

The modern marketing mix. Percentage of respondents who report using the tactic/channel

Source: The Fall 2011 Attitudes and Outlook Survey by Constant Contact Inc. polled 1,972 mostly United States-based respondents across a range of small businesses in both business-to-business and business-to-consumer industries.

In fact, one survey found that consumers consider online advertising to be twice as annoying as offline ads. In a survey for the 2010 digital marketing show ad:tech London, respondents called traditional advertising more informative, entertaining and necessary than online, with 69 percent saying that traditional advertising was relevant to them, compared with just 45 percent for online.

It's All about Balance

Of course, any business that relies too heavily on old-school marketing tactics risks looking, well, old-school. Coupled with the fact that online marketing has proven to be effective, this means that marketers should find a balance between new and old.

Most small businesses know this. The aforementioned survey by Constant Contact reports that 65 percent of small businesses use social media tools in conjunction with other forms of marketing. Offline campaigns that might otherwise look stodgy—a door hanger, a windshield flyer—can be energized with a QR code and URLs for your Facebook and Twitter accounts. Word of mouth, widely considered to be the most powerful form of advertising, gets a digital boost when satisfied customers share their experiences online in consumer-generated reviews and blog posts.

Even some businesses that operate entirely online are rediscovering the power of offline marketing. Fan Bi, co-founder of Blank Label, a Boston-based e-commerce retailer that lets customers design their own dress shirts, says that his company tried Facebook—and he wasn't impressed.

"We spent an hour a day thinking up engaging messages to post on our page," he says. "We were getting thousands of likes, but we weren't really seeing any customers come through Facebook."

Traditional marketing tactics have been much more effective, Bi says. He and his partners call and write to reporters and editors to pitch their story directly, and Blank Label has so far been featured in *The New York Times, Bloomberg Businessweek, Fast Company* and *Forbes*. Each time a story has run in a print publication, Blank Label has experienced a jump in sales.

"It's funny," Bi says. "Most people think old-school marketing is dying and social media is the wave of the future. In reality, without old-fashioned media relations and PR, we'd never have been able to grow our business so quickly."

Critical Thinking

1. The United States Baby Boomer cohort is significant in size and purchasing power. With a small group of peers, conduct some research on baby boomers and generate a profile of this cohort.

2. Summarize the article's main premise in regards to digital marketing techniques.

TOM STEIN and TIM DEVANEY are freelance writers based in Palo Alto, Calif.

Marketing to Kids Gets More Savvy with New Technologies

Ads come in tricky, fun-loving new forms.

BRUCE HOROVITZ

Isabella Sweet doesn't wear a target on her chest. But kid marketers covet this 9-year-old as if she does. Perhaps it's because she's a techie. The fourth-grader from Davis, Calif., spends almost an hour a day on the Webkinz website. The site charms kids by linking Webkinz plush animals—of which she owns 18—with online games that encourage kids to earn and spend virtual money so they can create elaborate rooms for virtual versions of their Webkinz pets.

The site does one more thing: It posts ads that reward kids with virtual currency when they click. Every time a kid clicks on an ad, there's a virtual ka-ching at the other end for Ganz, which owns Webkinz.

At issue: With the use of new, kid-enchanting technologies, are savvy marketers gaining the upper hand on parents? Are toy marketers such as Ganz, food marketers such as McDonald's and kid-coddling apparel retailers such as 77kids by American Eagle too eager to target kids?

At stake: $1.12 trillion. That's the amount that kids influenced last year in overall family spending, says James McNeal, a kid marketing consultant and author of *Kids as Consumers: A Handbook of Marketing to Children*. "Up to age 16, kids are determining most expenditures in the household," he says. "This is very attractive to marketers."

It used to be so simple. A well-placed TV spot on a Saturday-morning cartoon show or a kid-friendly image on a cereal box was all it took. No longer. The world of marketing to kids has grown extremely complex and tech-heavy. Marketers that seek new ways to target kids are aware of new calls for federal action—including voluntary marketing guidelines that would affect food marketers. Kids, who are spending less time watching TV and more time on computers or smartphones, are becoming targets online.

"Marketers are getting more and more devious," says Susan Linn, director of Campaign for a Commercial-Free Childhood, a watchdog group. With the growing use of smartphones and social media, she says, "They have new avenues for targeting children" that parents might miss.

Even ad-savvy parents are sometimes unaware how marketers are reaching out to their children.

Getting around Ad Blockers

While on the Webkinz site, Sweet recently clicked once a day for seven days on an ad for a film trailer that was posted for *Judy Moody and the NOT Bummer Summer*. She says that she wasn't really interested in the movie. But each day that she clicked it and answered three questions, she earned a virtual lime-green dresser and bulletin board for the rooms she created online for her Webkinz.

"I've got five dressers and seven bulletin boards," says the girl. "I don't have enough rooms to fit them all in."

This kind of marketing to kids drives Isabella's mother crazy. "They're doing this right under the noses of parents," says Elizabeth Sweet, a doctoral student at University of California-Davis doing her dissertation on the marketing of kids' toys. Even so, she says, she had no idea about the video ads on Webkinz until her daughter told her.

"This whole planting of movie videos in the online game experience is new to me," Sweet says. "What bothers me most is that when she first signed up for the site, I thought it was OK."

Sweet has an ad-blocker app on her browser. These movie ads are woven into the site content in such a way that her daughter sees—and responds to them—anyway, she says.

"We occasionally introduce limited-time promotions so that our Webkinz World members can enjoy fun, unique activities and events," says Susan McVeigh, a Ganz spokeswoman, in an e-mail.

But Elizabeth Sweet isn't the only parent who's unhappy with how and what Webkinz markets to kids.

Last month, Christina Cunningham, a full-time mother from Port St. Lucie, Fla., happened to look over as two of her daughters—ages 9 and 7—were signing onto the Webkinz website. On the log-in screen, an ad flashed for BabyPictureMaker.com, which nudges consumers to download pictures of two people—promising to send back a picture of what a baby they might have together would look like.

"This is not acceptable," says Cunningham, who shooed her kids away from the site and fired off an e-mail to Webkinz. When she didn't hear back, she sent another. Again, she says, she received no response. But McVeigh says Webkinz e-mailed Cunningham responses, twice. A frustrated Cunningham contacted Campaign for a Commercial-Free Childhood. The group contacted Webkinz, which removed the ad. "We will make sure to open an investigation into the matter and take the appropriate steps," spokeswoman McVeigh assured the group in a letter.

The Fast-Food Connection

Webkinz declined to share the outcome of this investigation with *USA TODAY*—nor would it explain how the ad got on the site. "We're fully committed to a responsible approach regarding advertising and the advertisers we allow on the site," says McVeigh, in an e-mail.

But in the eyes of some parents, no one goes more over the top in marketing to kids than the big food sellers—particularly sellers of high-sugar cereals and high-fat, high-calorie fast food.

That's one reason the Obama administration is proposing that food-makers adopt voluntary limits on the way they market to kids.

These proposed voluntary guidelines, to be written by a team from four federal agencies, have set the food and ad industries howling—even before they've been completed.

"I can't imagine any mom in America who thinks stripping tigers and toucans off cereal boxes will do anything to address obesity," said Scott Faber, a spokesman for the Grocery Manufacturers Association, at a May hearing.

But Wayne Altman thinks the voluntary guidelines are critical.

He's a family physician in the Boston area who has three sons ages 13, 5 and 4. He's particularly concerned about Ronald McDonald. "We know that children under 8 have no ability to establish between truth and advertising," he says. "So, to have this clown get a new generation hooked on a bad product just isn't right."

Because of the obesity, heart disease and food-related illnesses fed partly by savvy food marketers such as McDonald's, Altman says, "We have a generation of children that is the first to have a life expectancy less than its parents."

Plenty of others think as Altman does, even though Ronald is regularly used to promote Ronald McDonald House Charities. Ronald also shows up in schools. He's got his own website, Ronald.com, where the clown promises that kids can "learn, play and create while having fun." And he's the focal point of a new social-media campaign that nudges kids to download their own photos with images of Ronald and share them with friends.

More than 1,000 doctors, including Altman, recently signed a petition that asked McDonald's to stop using Ronald to market to kids. "People have a right to sell and advertise," he says. "But where do we draw the line?"

McDonald's—which recently announced it will modify its Happy Meals in September by reducing the number of fries and adding apple slices—has no plans to dump Ronald. "Ronald McDonald is an ambassador for McDonald's and an ambassador for good," CEO Jim Skinner told shareholders in May at the company's annual meeting. "Ronald McDonald is going nowhere."

77kids Entertains Shoppers

But American Eagle is going somewhere. And if any retailer exemplifies the techie new world of marketing to kids, it may be 77kids by American Eagle.

The outside-the-box store that it just opened at New York's Times Square sells midpriced clothing targeting boys and girls from toddler to 12. But the heart of the target is the 10-year-old.

Getting a 10-year-old's attention is all about whiz-bang technology—like the chain's virtual ticket to rock stardom.

In the center of the Times Square store sits a "Be a Rock Star" photo booth. It's all about music and tech. The booth has a big-screen TV that shows a video of a rock band composed of 10- to 12-year-old kids singing *I Wanna Rock* by Twisted Sister. Any tween, with parental permission, can download his or her photo and substitute it on the screen for one of the rock stars.

"Our brand ideology is: Think like a mom, see like a kid," explains Betsy Schumacher, chief merchandising officer at 77kids. "It made sense to us to have technology in the store that speaks to a kid's experience—and how they play."

Each 77kids store also has two iPad-like touch-screens that allow kids to virtually try on most of the clothing in the store. Who needs a dressing room when you can download your own photo and have it instantly matched online with that cool motorcycle vest or hip pair of distressed jeans? The same touch-screen also allows kids to play instant DJ, where they can mess online with the very same music that's being played in the store—slowing it down, speeding it up or even voting it off the playlist.

Nearly nine in 10 kids who shop at 77kids try one of these technologies while visiting the store, Schumacher estimates.

The company makes no bones about laser-targeting 10-year-olds. "The point is to keep a kid engaged so that shopping is enjoyable," Schumacher says. "Kids are looking for entertainment when they come to the mall."

Ex-adman Wants Change

Marketers, in turn, are looking for kids. And profits.

It isn't just advertising watchdogs who think it's time for a change. So does the guy who two years ago was arguably the ad world's top creative executive, Alex Bogusky. The agency that he has since left, Crispin Porter + Bogusky, has created campaigns for such kid-craving companies as Burger King and Domino's. Now, with the ad biz in his rearview mirror, Bogusky suggests it may be time for marketers to rethink.

"So what if we stopped it?" he recently posed on his personal blog. "What if we decided that advertising to children was something none of us would engage in anymore? What would happen? A lot of things would happen, and almost all seem to be for the good of society."

Babies as young as 6 months old can form mental images of logos and mascots—and brand loyalties can be established as early as 2, says the watchdog group Center for a New American Dream. McNeal, the kids marketing guru, says he consults with companies that are constantly trying to figure out how to get inside day care centers and bore their images inside the minds of preschoolers.

Back at Isabella Sweet's Webkinz-filled home, she's still saving her weekly $1 allowance to buy yet more. She can't help it, she says, even though each one costs $5 to $13. Even the family cats drag out her Webkinz to play.

"I wish I had a favorite Webkinz, but I don't," says Isabella. "I love them all."

Critical Thinking

1. With a small group of peers from your class, debate the ethical implications of marketing directly to children and teens.

2. The article states that "Marketers are getting more and more devious. . . . They have new avenues for targeting children." Present current marketing examples that support this premise. Do you agree with this statement?

From *USA Today Newspaper*, August 2011. Copyright © 2011 by USA Today, a division of Gannett Satellite Information Network, Inc. Reprinted by permission via PARS International.

It's Cooler than Ever to Be a Tween

They're a hot market, they're complicated, and there are two in the White House.

SHARON JAYSON

The prepubescent children of days gone by have given way to a cooler kid—the tween—who aspires to teenhood but is not quite there yet.

Tweens are in-between—generally the 8-to-12 set. The U.S. Census estimates that in 2009, tweens are about 20 million strong and projected to hit almost 23 million by 2020.

Among them now are Malia Obama, at 10 already a tween, and sister Sasha, who turns 8 this year. With the Obama daughters in the White House, the nation's attention will focus even more on this emerging group—and the new "first tweens" will likely be high-profile representatives of their generation.

"My daughter is really excited that there's a girl in the White House the same age she is," says Courtney Pineau, 31, of Bellingham, Wash., mother of fifth-grader Sophia, age 10.

Retailers know tweens are a hot market for clothes, music and entertainment. But now psychologists and behavioral researchers are beginning to study tweens, too. They say tweens are a complicated lot, still forming their personalities, and are torn between family and BFFs, between fitting in and learning how to be an individual.

Tweens have "their own sense of fashion in a way we didn't have before and their own parts of the popular culture targeted toward them," says child and adolescent psychologist Dave Verhaagen of Charlotte. How will this shape their personalities? "Time will tell. We don't know."

Research has shown that middle school is where some troubles, particularly academic, first appear. Also, a 2007 review of surveys in the journal *Prevention Science* found that the percentage of children who use alcohol doubles between grades four and six; the largest jump comes between fifth and sixth grades.

"They're kids for a shorter period of time," adds psychologist Frank Gaskill, who also works with tweens

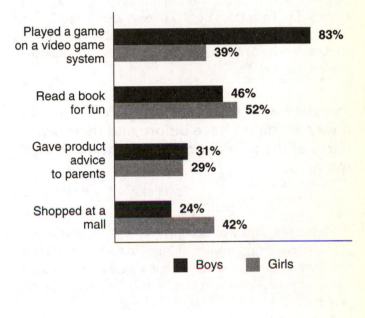

In the past week:

	Boys	Girls
Played a game on a video game system	83%	39%
Read a book for fun	46%	52%
Gave product advice to parents	31%	29%
Shopped at a mall	24%	42%

What tweens are doing.

Source: Youth Trends (based on in-person interviews with 1,223 8-12-year-olds in December. Margin of error ±2.8 percentage points).

in Charlotte. "More is expected of them academically, responsibility-wise."

Many parents, including Beth Harpaz, 48, of Brooklyn, are well aware of this short-lived time. Her older son is 16 and a high school junior; her younger son is 11 and in fifth grade.

"I'm trying really hard to save his childhood. I want him to enjoy little-boy things and don't want him to feel that he has to put on that big hoodie and wear the $100 sneakers and have that iPod in his ear listening to what somebody has told him is cool music," says Harpaz, author of *13 is the New 18.*

Gender Differences

Boys haven't been the main target of marketers hawking all things tween, from clothes and makeup to TV shows and music. But Disney wants to change that with its launch Feb. 13 of Disney XD, a "boy-focused" cable brand that includes TV and a website with themes of adventure, accomplishment, gaming, music and sports.

Until now, Disney has been "a tween-girl machine," Verhaagen says. "It may be that teen idols and celebrities are more inherently appealing to girls because it's all about personality and music and relational things that girls are more interested in. Boys at that age are more interested in sports and adventure and are not as easily marketed to by personalities and pop stars."

The Disney Channel and Nickelodeon are favorites, according to an online survey this summer for the 2008–09 GfK Roper Youth Report. The data, released to *USA Today,* found that of 500 tweens ages 8 to 12 asked about activities within the past week, 82% had watched Nickelodeon and 69% had watched Disney; 92% said they had played outside.

Tweens have "their own sense of fashion in a way we didn't have before and their own parts of the popular culture targeted toward them."

—Psychologist Dave Verhaagen

Verhaagen, father of two girls, 11 and 13, says tweens are "immersed in consumer culture" and seek connections and identity through social networking and shared entertainment experiences, but they're still "aligned with their parents."

New data from in-person interviews in December by Youth Trends, a marketing services company based in Ramsey, N.J., found 85% of the 1,223 respondents ages 8–12 agreed that "my family is the most important part of my life" and 70% said "I consider my Mom and/or Dad to be one of my best friends."

Elizabeth Hartley-Brewer, a parenting expert in London and author of *Talking to Tweens,* says the tween years are when young people begin to realize the wider world, and to see themselves as separate from their families. That's why the peer group is so crucial, she says.

Jade Jacobs, 12, of North Potomac, Md., is active in soccer, basketball, gymnastics and two cheerleading teams. "The main reason I do most of my sports is to hang out with my friends and to get exercise," she says.

She also loves to shop with friends. "It's not always about buy, buy, buy," she says. But, "if we have a little money, we'll find a cute accessory."

Her mother, Christina Jacobs, 43, says the idea of "mean girls" is part of the tween years, which is one reason girls worry about clothes. "Girls are looking at each other and seeing who is wearing what. They're harder on each other," she says. "Girls are looking at each other at 9 and 10, and boys are in la-la land."

Music Is Cool

Eleven-year-old Campbell Shelhoss, a fifth-grader in Towson, Md., says he's not in a hurry to be a teenager, even though he says he has outgrown some childhood pastimes.

"I feel like Pokémon is a little young," he says, and he puts cartoon toys and handheld video games in the same category.

He plays baseball and golf. He wanted a cellphone "for a few weeks" and then decided it wasn't that important to him.

Almost two-thirds (63%) of kids 8 to 12 do not have a cellphone, the Youth Trends study finds. It also finds that tweens spend 12.1 hours a week watching TV and 7.3 hours online.

The Roper report also asked tweens to rate 17 items as "cool or not cool." Music was at the top of the cool list, followed by going to the movies. "Being smart" ranked third—tied with video games—followed by electronics, sports, fashion and protecting the environment.

The "First Tweens"

"Right now, their friends and their status is everything to them," says Marissa Aranki, 41, of Fullerton, Calif. She is a fifth-grade teacher and has two daughters, 18 and 12.

"It's universal for the age, but they show it in different ways. For boys, the whole friendship thing is through technology and through sports," she says. "Girls like to talk, either about other girls or about boys. A lot of the girls are really boy-crazy. And some of the boys are not really girl-crazy yet. They're really out of the loop in that case. They've got their little guy friends and they're trying to be athletic, and that's what they care about."

Tweens are part of the larger generational group sometimes called Millennials or Generation Y. Those in their late teens through mid-20s are "first-wave" Millennials because they're the ones who set the trends that this later wave (born between the early 1990s and about 2003 or 2004) continues to follow, suggests historian and demographer Neil Howe, co-author of several books on the generations.

Verhaagen, author of *Parenting the Millennial Generation,* says older and younger Millennials share certain traits, such as comfort with technology and diversity, and being family-oriented.

He believes the struggling economy also will leave an imprint on both groups of Millennials; the younger ones could become less materialistic and consumer-driven.

Howe says tweens are even more interested in being protected and sheltered than their older Millennial siblings; he says this is because the parents of older Millennials tend to be Baby Boomers while parents of the younger group are often part of Generation X, in their 30s to mid-40s.

"These Xers are concerned about such things as safety and protection," he says. "They're not as worried as Boomers were about making their children paragons of perfection. Xers care less about that and try to do less. They're more pragmatic."

Howe counts Barack and Michelle Obama as Gen Xers, those born between 1961 and 1981. But many view the president and first lady as post-Boomers who are part of "Generation Jones," a term coined by cultural historian Jonathan Pontell for people born between 1954 and 1965.

Either way, it may be tough for the Obama girls to stay out of the spotlight, suggests Denise Restauri, founder of a research and consulting firm called AK Tweens and the tween social networking site AllyKatzz.com.

"They're in nirvana," she says. "Right now, (Malia and Sasha) are the most popular girls in school. It doesn't get much better than that when you're a tween."

Critical Thinking

1. Summarize the purchasing attitudes and habits of Tweens in the United States.

2. In your opinion, what current lifestyle shifts explain Tweens' purchasing patterns?

Segmenting the Base of the Pyramid

**To succeed, you'll need to link your commercial
interests with your constituencies' well-being.**

V. KASTURI RANGAN, MICHAEL CHU, AND DJORDJIJA PETKOSKI

Cross the invisible line into the base of the economic pyramid in emerging markets and you enter a world of pitfalls. If a company embarks on an initiative that focuses solely on commercial gain, civil society and governments are likely to oppose it intensely, as the international water utility company Aguas del Tunari discovered in Bolivia. If a company tries to stay under the radar by keeping its base-of-the-pyramid operations small, profits are likely to be meager, as Procter & Gamble found out with its water-purification product in Latin America and Asia. Even if you focus mainly on social impact and consider profits secondary, the base of the pyramid is a risky place: Projects that fail to make money will eventually be relegated to companies' corporate social responsibility departments, as Microsoft discovered.

Our research has shown a way to traverse this difficult landscape. Indeed, decent profits can be made at the base of the pyramid if companies link their own financial success with that of their constituencies. In other words, as companies make money, the communities in which they operate must benefit by, for example, acquiring basic services or growing more affluent. This leads to more income and consumption—and triggers more demand within the communities, which in turn allows the companies' businesses to keep growing. A corollary of that principle is that from the very beginning, scale is critical: Tentative forays into the base of the pyramid do not yield success.

Business models that call for creating private and public value while aiming for scale are gradually becoming more prevalent. Hindustan Unilever has succeeded by training tens of thousands of sales and distribution agents. The Afghan mobile network operator Roshan has succeeded by doing the same for small retailers. The local communities' growing economic health boosts profits and prosperity for everyone along the value chain.

In studying dozens of companies over many years, we have found that those with skill at simultaneously building private and public value tend to have a nuanced understanding of their constituencies. The 4 billion people at the base of the pyramid—whose output represents one-third of the world's economy—are not a monolith. To emulate the most effective pioneers, companies must commit to learning what constitutes value for the various components of this population. The way to start is to divide the 4 billion people into three basic segments.

Segmenting by Living Standard

The simplest way to analyze the base of the pyramid is to recognize that the income level of $1 a day separates the extremely poor from everyone else, and that people above that demarcation can be roughly divided into those earning $1 to $3 a day and those earning $3 to $5 a day. It's not the only way to categorize this tier of the pyramid, but it's a useful one.

Low Income

The adults among the roughly 1.4 billion people who live on $3 to $5 a day typically have a couple of years of secondary education and the skills needed to enter the job market. Many earn semi-regular incomes as construction workers, petty traders, drivers, or low-level staff in public and commercial establishments. They conduct their transactions in both formal and informal markets, and they tend to live near or among the people who occupy the next layer up in the pyramid—those with incomes of just over $5 a day. Families in the $3 to $5 segment often own such consumer goods as bicycles, televisions, and cell phones. As they strive for higher education and steadier, better-paying work, they need good housing and access to credit and to health care specialists. Many of them have a reasonable hope that they or their children will achieve a modestly higher living standard.

Subsistence

The bulk of the roughly 1.6 billion people who live on $1 to $3 a day are poorly educated and low skilled. Although they typically have some income as day laborers or temporary workers, their earnings are not steady. Many need improved sanitation, health care, and education. They can typically afford one square meal a day, but the nutritional content is often substandard. If they live in slums or shantytowns, they might work as helpers or assistants in petty trade. In rural areas, they are likely to be

Which Value-Creation Strategies Work Best at the Base of the Pyramid?

		1 Providing appropriate and affordable products and services directly to consumers	2 Enlisting individuals or small businesses to provide efficient reach and coverage	3 Engaging the community to coproduce value— for example, in the supply chain	4 Forming commercial partnerships with governments and NGOs
LOW INCOME **$3-$5 a day** 1.4 billion people	All four of these strategies can be applied throughout the base of the pyramid, but each has a sweet spot in one of the income segments.				
SUBSISTENCE **$1-$3 a day** 1.6 billion people					
EXTREME POVERTY Below $1 a day 1 billion people		Sweet spot: **LOW INCOME**	Sweet spot: **SUBSISTENCE**	Sweet spot: **SUBSISTENCE**	Sweet spot: **EXTREME POVERTY**

temporary, migratory farmhands during sowing or harvesting seasons. As both consumers and producers, they conduct transactions in informal markets, which often bustle with activity but are inefficient because they lack infrastructure and supportive institutions. Without bank accounts or access to formal credit, they turn to moneylenders for loans at exorbitant rates and are vulnerable to exploitation by middlemen. Unlikely to reach a $5-a-day standard of living, they nonetheless strive to improve their circumstances. They need gainful employment and inexpensive items for day-to-day living.

Extreme Poverty

The bottom 1 billion lack basic necessities: sufficient food, clean water, and adequate shelter. War, civil strife, and natural disasters have displaced many from their homes. They are forced into transactions that are irregular even by the standards of informal markets. Some live in barter economies; others are bonded laborers. Women often have to walk long distances along nonsecure pathways to fetch water. Poor health, lack of nutrition, financial vulnerability, limited education, and a dearth of marketable skills shut them out of the organized economy. The precariousness of their daily existence precludes participation in the market as consumers or producers. The lucky ones receive aid from nonprofit and international agencies or government relief programs.

Segmenting by Value-Creation Role

In addition to segmenting the people at the base of the pyramid by standard of living, businesses need to understand the roles those people can play in the value-creation relationship: as consumers, coproducers, or clients.

Consumers

Companies can provide value to consumers by directly addressing their needs for services such as clean water, better sanitation, education, and credit. A more indirect way is to introduce

innovations that enable people to devote fewer resources to basic activities and more to other pursuits. If all their costs and hours are fully taken into account, people at the base of the pyramid often turn out to be paying premiums for, and wasting a great deal of time on, products and services that are shoddy at best. So there's significant room for innovative businesses to provide good-quality offerings with lower overall usage costs and greater convenience than those of present alternatives. The result: a profound effect on productivity.

Before 1997, for example, many people in eastern Manila, in the Philippines, were not connected to the water system and were paying six times the municipal rates to buy low-quality water from informal dealers. Delivery costs drove the high prices: The municipal system was being tapped illegally, and the water was transferred to trucks, passed to intermediaries, and sold door-to-door in jerry cans, leaving it vulnerable to contamination. Manila Water, a private consortium, found ways to connect more people to the city system, reduce the trade in pilfered water, and bring costs down for millions of people. The company benefits economically from the increased volumes being used, but it also has created public value by improving people's access to clean, less expensive water.

Casting the people in the role of consumers is often most appropriate in the low-income segment, where individuals have the greatest resources for making purchases and a business can shape a profitable value proposition on the demand side alone. People in the subsistence segment also have consumer potential, but considerably less of it. (See the exhibit "Which Value-Creation Strategies Work Best at the Base of the Pyramid?")

Coproducers

When a company views base-of-the-pyramid residents as coproducers, it provides them with work and income. A multinational might, for instance, give farmers technical knowledge to upgrade the quality of their output and reward them with greater monetary returns, as Nestlé has done with the sourcing of milk from small dairy farmers in Asia and Mars has done with cocoa farmers in West Africa. With a little training, people at the base of the pyramid can also take part in basic production and assembly jobs or in activities such as transportation, distribution, and retailing—bridging the "last mile" to the customer. For example, Hindustan Unilever has helped to create entrepreneurs by training 50,000 women to go door-to-door educating consumers and selling soap, toothpaste, and other products. These women in turn nourish the local economic ecosystem by borrowing from local banks and microfinance institutions.

Companies may find that engaging people as coproducers is most appropriate in the subsistence segment because earning some additional income is their primary need. With this extra income, they can try to improve the quality of their consumption. However, businesses also can and do engage people in the low-income segment as coproducers—for example, by employing them to make products for consumers who are higher up in the pyramid. Individuals in the extreme-poverty segment are not potential coproducers because they are too difficult to access or don't have the necessary skills.

Clients

A significant portion of the people at the base of the pyramid, primarily in the extreme-poverty segment, are most appropriately treated as clients. The reality is that they need "agents," so to speak, to garner resources on their behalf. The government can serve as an agent, as can a civil society institution, a community organization, or a commercial enterprise. For example, Devi Shetty's advocacy for farmers and other workers in Karnataka, India, engendered the Yeshasvini Health Insurance plan, which started with government subsidies. Patients covered by Yeshasvini are eligible for free care, but bureaucracy and poor management in the public health system too often prevent people from getting acceptable levels of service. The insurer became an advocate for the poor, negotiating for better service from public hospitals. Those hospitals also benefited, by receiving payments from Yeshasvini.

Missteps at the Base of the Pyramid

Numerous companies have blundered by failing to understand the importance of bolstering the success of the base-of-the-pyramid communities where they do business. Too often they assume that their responsibilities end once they have provided a needed product or service, or have engaged people as suppliers or workers.

Companies too often assume that their responsibilities end once they have provided a needed product or service.

That attitude leaves companies vulnerable to criticism. In 2000, when the Bechtel-led water consortium Aguas del Tunari tried to raise water tariffs and collect rents on private wells in Bolivia, all within the purview of its privatization agreement with the local government, violent protests erupted, forcing the company to abandon its business. In essence, it had failed to recognize how people in the region defined success for themselves and, therefore, failed to contribute to that success.

The same trap has ensnared micro-finance. The industry is periodically threatened with shutdowns, especially in India, because of outcries over interest rates, even though the average rate charged by Indian microfinance institutions is among the lowest in the world: 25 percent to 27 percent. The real problem is that microfinanciers have sometimes appeared to be profiting on the backs of the poor, less because of their interest rates than because of policies that ignore social value. Many microfinance firms assume they are doing the poor a service just by offering lower rates than moneylenders do. They appear not to recognize that many of their clients, despite getting loans, have been unable to achieve a higher standard of living. As a result, the companies become scapegoats when customers face tough economic times.

Equitas is one Indian microfinancier that hasn't been targeted. It has shown a commitment to social value by earmarking 5 percent of its profits for clients' health care, skills development, and children's education, and it has placed a cap on its profits.

In many instances, profits have been so hard to come by in the low-margin environment at the base of the pyramid that companies' commercial initiatives have been quietly absorbed into their CSR efforts. That's what happened with Procter & Gamble's PUR water-purification packets after the company was unable to find a profitable distribution strategy and price. Microsoft's Unlimited Potential program also met that fate. After trying for a few years to eke out a profit by providing refurbished computers, internet cafes, and a scaled-down version of the Windows operating system to developing countries, the company passed some of these initiatives to its corporate citizenship group.

How to Entwine Commercial and Social Value

Many companies have simultaneously created private and public value in part through innovative business models that enlist community members or other organizations in distribution, access, payment, and even security activities. Ensuring that such a model is both commercially feasible and sustainable over the long term involves streamlining operations and designing appropriate incentives for the people who are brought into the economic ecosystems that the companies have created. Let's look at some of these segment by segment.

In the Low-Income Segment

Examples of innovative, large-scale distribution strategies include M-Pesa's reliance on nearly 18,000 mom-and-pop retail operators to deliver its mobile money-transfer service in Kenya; Novartis's mobilization of more than 20,000 volunteer doctors to visit villages, examine patients, and provide medicines as part of its Arogya Parivar ("healthy family") program in India; and Hindustan Unilever's investment in its army of

Where Private and Public Value Intersect

The Opportunity

Two decades ago, many of the poor in eastern Manila, the Philippines, were paying six times the municipal rates to buy their water in metal jerry cans from vendors who had illegally tapped into the water system.

The Execution

In 1997 Manila Water, a private consortium, won the concession for providing water. It improved access to clean, less-expensive water and gained consumers' trust by partnering with public authorities, local communities, and contractors. Exclusivity rights and other government guarantees gave the company an incentive to rapidly build infrastructure, if it met certain thresholds for service in poor communities. Manila Water has managed to invest more than $1 billion in capital improvements and to install several thousand miles of its distinctive blue PVC pipes.

The Results

A greater than 15 percent return on equity each year for the past 10 years.

Safer Water

- 1997 **0.3** M
- 2009 **1.1** M

1.1 M Households receiving safe municipal water

Greater Access to Water

- 1997 **2.6** percent
- 2009 **99** percent

99 percent of areas with 24-hour access to water

More Billing for Services

- 1997 **37** percent
- 2009 **84** percent

84 percent increased billings to cover a greater percentage of water outflow

The California-based biopharmaceuticals manufacturer Gilead Sciences uses an innovative access strategy to produce powerful results. Of the estimated 35 million people with HIV/AIDS in sub-Saharan Africa and South Asia in 2003, nearly 10 million were candidates for antiretroviral drugs. The medications were scarce in developing countries, but not primarily because of affordability—pharmaceutical companies were selling to poor countries at cost. The main stumbling block was a lack of access: Regulations governing registration, licensing, and importation of medicines were limiting availabilty.

Gilead, one of the world's leading suppliers of antiretrovirals, made the patents for two of its top products, Viread and Truvada, available to 12 generic-drug manufacturers in India and South Africa—companies that could have copied the drugs under their governments' licenses to make them affordable to patients. Gilead didn't charge a fee for the technology transfer. It asked only that the manufacturers pay a royalty of 5 percent of the selling price on the generic versions of Gilead's drugs. These makers were able to produce the drugs much more cheaply than Gilead and to quickly break into markets in Asia and Africa.

Not surprisingly, Gilead's licensing program broke even in 2009, and by 2010 it had generated a $5 million surplus and reached more than 1.4 million patients in low-income countries. In addition, Gilead has helped to create an ecosystem that will aid these countries as they produce and distribute other essential drugs.

In the Subsistence Segment

People often lack essential information about new products or methods and are reluctant to adopt them. Companies must create demand for entire categories of products. A good example is the water purifier: Hindustan Unilever's Pureit can bring international water-purity standards to millions of homes that have neither running water nor continuous electricity. But many consumers aren't fully aware of the health benefits of purification, and those who are aware have a ready alternative-boiling their water—that seems a lot more affordable than a $22 purifier. As is often the case in the subsistence segment, the access channel must play a role in generating demand. Hindustan Unilever relies on NGOs to both educate consumers and sell its purifiers.

Telecommunications companies such as Safaricom in Africa provide examples of community-based strategies for aggregating millions of small payments. Because consumers lack the cash to buy in bulk or pay a monthly fee, these companies provide airtime for cash up front and sell additional airtime through their networks of agents, usually small retailers. Instead of dealing with millions of consumers with millions of small payments, the companies rely on the agents to aggregate the financial transactions, thereby keeping operations economical and bolstering the economic ecosystem of the small retailers.

The mobile network operator Roshan provides an example of integrating community members into security operations. Before Roshan's founding, in 2003, only about 80,000 of Afghanistan's 34 million people had access to phones. The company established its presence by building eight stores and encouraging Afghans to form distribution networks that supply

door-to-door saleswomen. All three strategies depend on the companies' ability to provide incentives and support for the small retailers, doctors, and saleswomen who are integral to the distribution channels and, by extension, to the companies' business models and newly created economic ecosystems.

Commercial and social value are like the two blades of a pair of scissors, and scale is like the tailor's deft hand.

SIM cards and handsets to other consumers. The network has grown to more than 3,500 outlets, the subscriber base to 3.5 million users, and the pool of people directly or indirectly employed to more than 30,000. Roshan has recruited community leaders to monitor the security of its towers, which the Taliban threatens. The community leaders have multiple incentives to protect the towers: A functioning network provides jobs, training, and security fees. Roshan says this approach has saved it more than $15 million a year.

Other companies, even while selling products and services to customers higher up in the pyramid, create tremendous value by extensively engaging the subsistence segment in their supply chains. Nestle does it with dairy, Mars with chocolate, and Unilever with cooking and bath oils.

In the Extreme-Poverty Segment

Where delivering basic services such as water, sanitation, health care, and education requires heavy investments, companies have little choice but to enter into public-private partnerships that provide guarantees on cost recovery, subsidies, and market exclusivity. Without the partnerships, opportunities for profits are few, even in the long run. Because the needs of the extreme-poverty segment are for the basics (many people consider them fundamental human rights), a company should be careful to earn the community's trust by providing outstanding value, and that value should be the engine of profitability. (See the exhibit "Where Private and Public Value Intersect.")

Businesses also should not overlook the advantages of teaming up with locally established NGOs. The Geneva-based Global Alliance for Improved Nutrition, for example, has worked with some of the world's leading food companies to tackle hunger and malnutrition. Because of a lack of interest from commercial enterprises, GAIN took on the role of venture capitalist, providing seed money to facilitate businesses' development of products and markets for this segment. Among GAIN's partners are Unilever, Cargill, and Akzo Nobel. By providing both financial support and technical expertise, GAIN has ensured that staple grains in China and South Africa are fortified with essential vitamins and minerals. Building on pilot projects financed by GAIN, companies such as Britannia Industries have launched fully commercial product lines as part of their regular businesses.

We don't mean to make this sound easy. The base of the pyramid is a risky place for companies. Indeed, well-meaning, well-financed ones have failed, as Microsoft did with Unlimited Potential. That, unfortunately, has been the fate of many such corporate forays as shareholders become impatient with money-losing ventures. But a strategy of creating private and public value while aiming for scale gives companies their best chance to succeed. Commercial and social value are like the two blades of a pair of scissors, and scale is like the tailor's deft hand. You must have all three elements to slice through the knotty obstacles at the base of the pyramid.

Critical Thinking

1. Explain 'Base of the Pyramid' (BOP) as defined by the authors.

2. What are the different segmentation bases for BOP suggested by the article?

3. With a small group of peers from your class, debate the following paragraph from the article: "Commercial and social values are like the two blades of a pair of scissors, and scale is like the tailor's deft hand. You must have all three elements to slice through the knotty obstacles at the base of the pyramid."

V. Kasturi Rangan is the Malcolm P. McNair Professor of Marketing and cochair of the Social Enterprise Initiative at Harvard Business School. **Michael Chu** is a senior lecturer at Harvard Business School. **Djordjija Petkoski** is a lead specialist at the World Bank.

Acknowledgements—Harvard Business Review and Harvard Business Publishing Newsletter content on EBSCOhost is licensed for the private individual use of authorized EBSCOhost users. It is not intended for use as assigned course material in academic institutions nor as corporate learning or training materials in businesses. Academic licensees may not use this content in electronic reserves, electronic course packs, persistent linking from syllabi or by any other means of incorporating the content into course resources. Business licensees may not host this content on learning management systems or use persistent linking or other means to incorporate the content into learning management systems. Harvard Business Publishing will be pleased to grant permission to make this content available through such means. For rates and permission, contact permissions@harvardbusiness.org.

Can More Information Be a Bad Thing?

Despite the best efforts of researchers, consumer decisions will always have subjective components.

Robert S. Duboff

The basic paradigm is so engrained in our business culture that it is rarely even stated explicitly: To make marketing decisions, we amass facts and, using our best judgment and experience, we opt for the alternative that the available information favors. This is implicit in every market research brief and proposal; it is a given for any task force charged with deciding on a path forward on an issue.

The "facts lead us to the best option" approach can also be easily inferred from every press release or other explanation of a decision. Only Steve Jobs (and a few others) have had the temerity to explain a course of action as being based on his or her own instinct. And even he, while eschewing much market research with consumers, often alluded to data that supported Apple's decision.

It has not always been so. In Plato's days, there was the Philosopher King, who, uniquely, could discern reality in the mists and make decisions based on judgment and, perhaps, his own experience.

Most people likely feel our evolved model is a better one: Use all our resources to gather as much information as possible, and then (perhaps using a decision tree or a set of criteria) go where the data lead. And yet a growing set of discoveries is now calling this very left-brain, logical approach into question.

A New Paradigm

Before discussing the evidence that threatens the rule of reason for decisions, I want to clarify the focus. "Decision-making" is an extremely broad term of reference, including the trivial and the personal, as well as the life-changing and bet-your-company calls. I will focus here on business marketing decisions of some importance made by an individual or small team.

Also, there are decisions that clearly depend on future acts/reactions of humans (e.g., hiring, new product launch) vs. those more focused on inanimate objects (e.g., where to locate a plant or to invest capital). The latter are more about mathematics, so the former will be the focus here. For our purposes, we will be thinking in the context of important marketing decisions that involve future human actions. The core thesis is that the assumed, if not stated, paradigm is flawed in practice, except for a very few cases. While good decision-making means deliberating and selecting the best option after gathering sufficient information is a Platonic ideal, I believe that better decisions can be made by embracing these facts:

- "Information" is rarely truly factual and, where it purports to predict the future actions of people, is never valid, even if produced with skill and objectivity (neither of which is always present).
- Regardless of how they may feel or describe themselves, decision makers are not objective beings willing to rationally choose whatever option the information might indicate.

My thesis is supported with evidence from behavioral economics, neurophysiology and, I hope, common sense. Of course, I accept that a reader who firmly believes in the sanctity of well-developed numbers and his or her own objectivity will never fully accept this and might well stop reading here.

For those still open to thinking about the best ways to make marketing decisions, let me suggest a new paradigm and then provide the evidence indicating that this may be a better route than current practice, which is to say and act as we are following the ideal rational paradigm.

Preconceptions Play a Role

Assume we have to decide whether to introduce a new brand, one in a category that already exists.

We have invested a great deal based on research that depicted an unmet need in this mass market. We have 12 months or so before we need to decide to go ahead or not.

Let us further assume that the payoff will be in the tens of millions of profit per year if we can become the second or third in market share.

Before we commission market research, we get the three decision makers together and ask each one what he or she would decide today if they had to decide, and why. If they all agree, we ask them to name a key lieutenant or two that they trust to play the other side—to marshal the best arguments against the current choice.

At the same time, we question them about their degree of confidence and their concerns. We ask them about what information might change their minds. We probe them about how their current preferred decision would make them feel. Do they have any qualms? We ask how they feel about the investment made so far.

At this point, we might conclude that it is highly unlikely that their minds will change and make the decision today, thereby getting a head start and saving all the money that would have been spent producing information. In my experience, if the decision maker(s) on the go/no go launch are the same as those who authorized the spending on development so far, it is likely they will go ahead. I have always read the new Coke launch decision this way, despite all the ex post facto justification that (flawed) consumer taste tests drove the decision.

Or, if it seems there is really an openness to going in a different direction, we might launch the "best arguments against" and/or gather (only) any information that could hit at their concerns and qualms.

In this case, we would likely engage third parties respected by these decision makers, in essence, a mutually agreed upon arbiter.

There are other concepts that might help, but the key prescription is to get the decision maker(s) to acknowledge the role of their preconceptions and preferences rather than the current practice of (intentionally or not) pretending there is a totally fact-based decision to be made.

Why is this approach better?

First and foremost, there is now voluminous evidence that all of us are influenced by non-rational factors when we make decisions. Too often, decision makers use information only for affirmation.

Even worse, we are often not aware that we are doing is or being influenced. *Thinking, Fast and Slow* by Daniel Kahneman is the latest of a long line of research-based books that show the impact of factors such as anchoring, selective perception, cognitive dissonance and the like. [See sidebar on page 97 for definitions.]

Second, a related, pernicious mental factor is frame of reference. Too often, people do not position their product broadly enough, the classic marketing myopia. Most recently, this has seen RIM ignore the iPhone to its peril.

The Innovator's Dilemma is a subset of this. Companies, especially first-mover technology companies, see their core product and customer base as the key universe. They

Briefly

- Recognize the influence of non-objective factors when designing research.
- Acknowledge the right brain's important function in consumer decision-making.
- Remember that information is not always truly factual.

focus so heavily on meeting short-term enhancements (versions 2.0, etc.) that they miss someone else redefining the category.

Third, the information that decision makers receive is often filtered, if not tainted, in an attempt to support the views of the decision maker and often to seek his/her favor. The *now known to be erroneous information* given to President George W. Bush that indicated there were weapons of mass destruction in Iraq is a prime example of this.

Fourth, even without a filter, the most common source of information about how the market will likely react to a new product is market research. This information is increasingly suspect because of at least three factors:

- It is nigh impossible to get a sample representative of any large universe (except one's own customers if a business is lucky enough that customers need or want to register with them).
- There are simply no good lists of all the cell phone numbers from which to randomly select.
- There is no online panel with a truly representative group of members who can be selected (vs. them opting in) for a given study.

These factors add to the age-old problem that consumers will often lie about key issues (their past purchasing behavior, for example).

Even with a representative sample telling the truth as they know it, there are still erroneous responses due to the same factors that influence decision makers. What people were doing before the survey, what words they were hearing, whom they last talked to about the topic, etc., could all influence responses such that the answers do not represent how that respondent really feels or thinks, much less how they will act.

Related to this is that, unless the survey picks up their knowledge about the topic, it cannot allow researchers to play out scenarios as new facts or factors emerge or current ones become known between the time of the survey and the time the respondents are able to buy the new product.

Even with a good sample and truthful respondents and no unconscious influences, there is a fundamental flaw that decision makers and researchers have accepted only by suspending disbelief. As Steve Jobs stated, consumers simply cannot reliably tell us how they will respond to something they don't readily recognize. In our example, we are not talking about an iPod in MP3 days or an iPad before tablets.

But any new brand that purports to be different/better in a new way cannot really be understood by a consumer, can it? At some level we know this, and yet research is still the most accepted and likely best way to get some estimate, some number to grasp. If we like the number, we allow our disbelief to dissipate. If we don't like the number, maybe we rejigger it or simply reject the research.

Research shows that playing French music correlates with boosted sales of French wine in the same store where, during the playing of German music, German wine sales increase. Could you capture this in a survey? The point is not to stop doing surveys, but rather to focus any research on questions that (1) respondents can answer accurately and (2) might have an impact on the actual decision maker.

When Research Works

In the hypothetical new product launch mentioned earlier, if decision makers are truly concerned about whether enough people will buy the new product, the research could focus on what the "ideal" product in the category would do and measure each existing product against the ideal on the specific attributes. The research could also talk to retailers and distributors to get their expert perspective on the category. This would make it easier to understand the market and how best to promote the new brands. Other options exist as well.

How does the ad agency feel? Would they rather have the account of the current leader in the category or this new brand? Do they have ideas about how to message about it?

Finally, it is always good practice to run reaction tests—focus groups with valued customers to pilot the decision to learn if there are dramatic and, especially, unanticipated reactions to the favored decision.

If nothing else, this kind of testing would protect against a decision from the gut that flies in the face of customers.

There are also techniques such as Delphi panels and lead users that have proven far more prescient than more normal surveys, no matter how well-crafted. [See sidebar below for further explanation.] Delphis and lead users research don't pretend to be "reliable" in the statistical sense; they are not projectable to the marketplace.

However, they may be more "valid," the other test of research, in that they can portray a picture of the evolving marketplace that is likely to be more true than surveys representative of the current consumers.

To summarize, most decisions are not made in a truly objective, information-based manner. While decisions can be based on data, they all have subjective components. Where the gut lines up with the brain, the decision is relatively easy. Where it doesn't, emotion often rules.

Ways Decision Makers May Be Subconsciously (or Not) Biased

- **Anchoring:** Influence of initial information on the topic
- **Cognitive Dissonance:** Tendency to eliminate/lessen any possible contradictions by rationalizing toward the stronger feeling (e.g., explaining away statements of or charges against a favored politician)
- **Recency:** Relying more on the latest or last information received
- **Priming:** Influence of even disconnected words or other input heard before a decision (i.e., French music in a liquor store correlates with heightened purchase of French wines)
- **Selective Perception:** Accepting information that comes from a source you deem reliable and/or confirms instinct, while filtering out contradictory data

---

Research Techniques That Work

Some research methods are not based on the simplest paradigm of asking direct questions about what respondents will do in the future and then projecting their responses to the universe of interest.

Lead user analysis, developed by Professor Von Hippel of MIT, is predicated on the assumption that people who are most in need of the product or service (e.g., in B-to-B, the buyers for whom your product is essential; in B-to-C, airline travel or alarm clocks for a frequent business flyer) will provide the most valid and thoughtful information. Even more valid data can be gathered by observing how they use the product because often they will have made adaptations that could presage what other people or companies might want to do if you offered those enhancements.

This core concept has been amended by others to extend into early adopters as, literally, "lead users" whose decision about whether to buy or recommend your product will determine whether others will see it and/or think enough of it to try it.

Another premise is akin to the wisdom of crowds. The Delphi research technique utilizes a set of experts in diverse fields who are asked the likelihood of various well-thought-out and researched scenarios (or more simply, the likelihood of X people buying Y product). The results are tabulated and then the experts, after seeing how others voted, opine again. If consensus grows, the marketer's confidence grows.

This technique was invented by the Rand Corporation in the wake of World War II and is credited with the development of the Marshall Plan. It has since been successfully used to help several companies decide whether or not to invest in emerging technologies.

My final argument is the most fact-based. The track record on marketing decisions is pretty poor, particularly in the area of new products. Estimates of the failure rate range from 60 percent to 90 percent. Think of all the wasted time and money. Wouldn't it be better to acknowledge the role of the right brain on decisions and, rather than hiding it and seeming to use bad research and/or filtering it, legitimize the gut instinct and the influences of the past and use that as the starting point for more focused research and discussions?

Even if that only works half the time, it's better than our current decision-making performance.

Critical Thinking

1. According to the article, is decision-making a rational and scientific process?

2. List some reasons why decision-makers may be subconsciously biased.

3. Discuss a recent decision-making experience that had subjective components.

ROBERT S. DUBOFF is CEO of HawkPartners, a Cambridge, Mass., consultancy that works at the intersection of marketing and marketing research. He may be reached at Rob.Duboff@hawkpartners.com.

Reprinted with permission from *Marketing Management,* Summer 2012, pp. 25–29, published by the American Marketing Association. Copyright © 2012 by American Marketing Association.

The Tyranny of Choice

You Choose

If you can have everything in 57 varieties, making decisions becomes hard work.

THE ECONOMIST

These are momentous times for the British potato crisp. Little over a generation ago the humble snack came in just a trio of flavours: ready salted, cheese and onion, or salt and vinegar. Today the choice is tongue-tingling: Thai sweet chilli, balsamic vinegar and caramelised onion, Oriental red curry, lime and coriander chutney, vintage cheddar and onion chutney, buffalo mozzarella and herbs, chicken tikka masala. And those are merely the varieties confected by a single crispmaker, Walkers, a division of PepsiCo, which turns out 10m bags of crisps every day for the British market alone. Venture towards the gourmet fringes of the crisp offering, and the choice and exoticism multiply: jalapeño pepper, roast ox, horseradish and sour cream, Ludlow sausage with wholegrain mustard. Crisps these days can be crinkle-cut, thick-cut, ridge-cut, square-cut, hand-fried, reduced fat, sold in six-packs, grab bags, party size or family packs.

Wheel a trolley down the aisle of any modern Western hypermarket, and the choice of all sorts is dazzling. The average American supermarket now carries 48,750 items, according to the Food Marketing Institute, more than five times the number in 1975. Britain's Tesco stocks 91 different shampoos, 93 varieties of toothpaste and 115 of household cleaner. Carrefour's hypermarket in the Paris suburb of Montesson, a hangar-like place filled with everything from mountain bikes to foie gras, is so vast that staff circulate on rollerblades.

Choice seduces the modern consumer at every turn. Lattes come tall, short, skinny, decaf, flavoured, iced, spiced or frappé. Jeans come flared, bootlegged, skinny, cropped, straight, low-rise, bleach-rinsed, dark-washed or distressed. Moisturiser nourishes, lifts, smooths, revitalises, conditions, firms, refreshes and rejuvenates. Tropicana, another part of PepsiCo, turns out freshly pulped juice in more than 20 different varieties, up from just six in 2004; it says there could be as many as 30 in the next decade.

Thanks to a mix of modern medicine, technology and social change, choice has expanded from the grocery shelf to areas that once had few or none. Faces, noses, wrinkles, breasts and bellies can be remodelled, plumped or tucked. America in 2008 alone saw 2.5m Botox injections, 355,671 breast implants, 341,144 liposuction treatments, 195,104 eyelid lifts and 147,392 stomach tucks, according to the American Society for Aesthetic Plastic Surgery.

Teenagers can choose to surf, chat, tweet, zap or poke in ways that their parents can barely fathom. Moving pictures and music can be viewed, recorded, downloaded or streamed on all manner of screens or devices. The internet has handed huge power to the consumer to research options, whether of medical procedures or weekend breaks. Even the choice of price-comparison sites to help people choose is expanding.

Offline choices have multiplied too. European Union citizens can move, study, work and live wherever they like within the union. Vouchers and other school reforms in many countries give parents increasing choice over where to send their children. Modular university courses offer students endless combinations. The University of California, Berkeley, has over 350 degree programmes, including Buddhist Studies and Lesbian, Gay, Bisexual and Transgender Studies, each made up of scores of courses.

Choice has come to some of life's biggest personal decisions as well. In many countries couples can decide whether and where to marry, cohabit, divorce or remarry. Internet dating promises to find a match from a database of potential partners. Women in the rich world can choose when, and whether, to reproduce. "Do I want a baby? Will I find love again? Is this it?" screams the front cover of one recent women's magazine. Mothers (and sometimes fathers) can choose to work, or not, or take time off to raise children and then go back to their jobs. New life can be created against the odds. For sufferers from many chronic illnesses, life in old age can be prolonged—or ended.

Too Much of a Good Thing

Many of these options have improved life immeasurably in the rich world, and to a lesser extent in poorer parts. They are testimony to human ingenuity and innovation. Free choice is the basis on which markets work, driving competition and generating economic growth. It is the cornerstone of liberal democracy. The 20th century bears the scars of too many failed experiments in which people had no choice. But amid all the dizzying possibilities, a nagging question lurks: is so much extra choice unambiguously a good thing?

Over the past decade behavioural scientists have come up with some intriguing insights. In one landmark experiment, conducted in an upmarket grocery store in California, researchers set up a sampling table with a display of jams. In the first test they offered a tempting array of 24 different jams to taste; on a different day they displayed just six. Shoppers who took part in the sampling were rewarded with a discount voucher to buy any jam of the same brand in the store. It turned out that more shoppers stopped at the display when there were 24 jams. But when it came to buying afterwards, fully 30% of those who stopped at the six-jam table went on to purchase a pot, against merely 3% of those who were faced with the selection of 24.

The researchers repeated the experiment with chocolate as well as student essay topics and found similar results. Too much choice, concluded Sheena Iyengar of Columbia University and Mark Lepper of Stanford, is demotivating. Others have since come up with similar results from experiments with writing pens, gift boxes, coffee and even American 401(k) pension plans. (It is not all that way: German researchers, by contrast, found that shoppers were not put off by too much choice, whether of jams, chocolates or jelly beans—though this may be down to Germany's price-conscious shoppers and the sheer dreariness of the country's supermarkets.)

Expectations have been inflated to such an extent that people think the perfect choice exists.

As options multiply, there may be a point at which the effort required to obtain enough information to be able to distinguish sensibly between alternatives outweighs the benefit to the consumer of the extra choice. "At this point," writes Barry Schwartz in "The Paradox of Choice," "choice no longer liberates, but debilitates. It might even be said to tyrannise." In other words, as Mr Schwartz puts it, "the fact that *some* choice is good doesn't necessarily mean that *more* choice is better."

Daniel McFadden, an economist at the University of California, Berkeley, says that consumers find too many options troubling because of the "risk of misperception and miscalculation, of misunderstanding the available alternatives, of misreading one's own tastes, of yielding to a moment's whim and regretting it afterwards," combined with "the stress of information acquisition." Indeed, the expectation of indecision can prompt panic and a failure to choose at all. Too many options means too much effort to make a sensible decision: better to bury your head under a pillow, or have somebody else pick for you. The vast majority of shoppers in the Californian grocery store faced with 24 jam varieties simply chose not to buy any. The more expensive an item—a car, say—the more daunting the decision. As the French saying has it: "Trop de choix tue le choix" (too much choice kills the choice).

Surely, though, knowing that lots of choice is out there still feels good? The thrill is in the anticipation of falling upon the perfect Tuscan hotel, or shade of duck-egg blue with which to repaint the kitchen. Or the reassurance that competition to supply all that choice of electricity or telephony is keeping prices down and pushing service up. But not, according to psychologists, if more choice raises expectations too high, which may make even a good decision feel bad. The potential for regret about the options not taken—the faster car, the hotel with the better view—seems to be greater in the face of multiple choices.

Expectations have been inflated to such an extent that people think the perfect choice exists, argues Renata Salecl in her book "Choice." Consider seduction. Bookshops are crowded with self-help guides and self-improvement manuals with titles such as "How to Choose & Keep Your Partner" or "Love is a Choice." Internet dating sites promise to find the perfect match with just a few clicks of the mouse. This nourishes the hope of making the ideal choice, she says, as well as the fanciful idea that there are "quick, rational solutions to the complicated question of seduction."

Confusion, indecision, panic, regret, anxiety: choice seems to come at a price. In one episode of "The Simpsons," Marge takes Apu shopping in a new supermarket, Monstromart, whose cheery advertising slogan is "where shopping is a baffling ordeal." "How is it," muses Ms Salecl, "that in the developed world this increase in choice, through which we can supposedly customise our lives and make them perfect leads not to more satisfaction but rather to greater anxiety, and greater feelings of inadequacy and guilt?" A 2010 study by researchers at the University of Bristol found that 47% of respondents thought life was more confusing than it was ten years ago, and 42% reported lying awake at night trying to resolve problems.

It could be that today's children, growing up in a world of abundant choice, will find decisions even harder to make when they grow up. Their lives may be packed with instant choices as they zap from one site to another while texting a friend and listening to music on YouTube. But much of this is reflexive activity. The digital generation is doing what Mr Schwartz calls "picking," not "choosing:" "With a world of choices rushing by like a music video," he says, "all a picker can do is grab this or that and hope for the best." Young people have grown up with masses of choice, says Dan O'Neil, a British life coach who helps people overcome indecision, "but they have never learned to make a choice and run with it. In adult life, they aren't equipped to cope."

Following the Crowd

Ever since the 19th century, when Levi Strauss began to stitch denim jeans for Americans and Abram Lyle started to sell tins of golden syrup to the English, brand managers have made it their business to offer shoppers an easier life. Brands simplify choices. They are a guarantee of quality or consistency in a confusing market, and a badge of trust. Companies spend heavily on marketing and legal advice to protect or reinvent their brands and keep customers loyal, exploiting customers' aversion to choice.

The more that options multiply, the more important brands become. Today, when paralysed by bewildering choice, a consumer will often turn to a brand that is cleverly marketed to appear to be one that others trust.

In Italo Calvino's novel "Mr Palomar," the eponymous hero is dazzled by the mouth-watering variety of cheese he comes across at a fine Parisian *fromagerie*. "Mr Palomar's spirit vacillates between contrasting urges: the one that aims at complete, exhaustive knowledge and could be satisfied only by tasting all the varieties; and the one that tends toward an absolute choice, the identification of the cheese that is his alone," writes Mr Calvino. In the end, "he stammers; he falls back on the most obvious, the most banal, the most advertised, as if the automatons of mass civilisation were waiting only for this moment of uncertainty on his part in order to seize him again and have him at their mercy."

The anti-globalisation and green movements have stirred a consumer backlash against a surfeit of choice

---

Despite the crisp flavourologists' best efforts, there is a limit to how many packs can be stacked on a supermarket shelf. What of stuff that is distributed digitally, however, where choice is almost limitless? Technology has cut media distribution costs and made available a vast new array of material that caters to specialised or obscure tastes, in music, video or the written word. In this universe of proliferating choice, demand is said to be shifting from a few mass products (at the head of the distribution curve) towards a great many niche interests (at the tail end), as argued by Chris Anderson in "The Long Tail."

It turns out, however, that despite the availability of all the extra stuff the hits are as important as ever. In 2009 there were 558 films released in America, up from 479 in 2000, not to mention the gigabytes of videos and film uploaded or shared online. Yet it was also the year in which one film, James Cameron's "Avatar," broke all box-office records to become the highest-grossing film ever, beating the director's own 1997 blockbuster, "Titanic." However many niches there are, in other words, filmgoers or TV viewers still want to watch what everybody else is watching, and musicians still manage to release mega-hits. Indeed, in a world that celebrates individualism and freedom, many people decide to watch, wear or listen to exactly the same things as everybody else.

When Less Is More

In small corners of the temples of consumption, business has begun to wake up to the perils of excess choice. Some firms employ "choice architects" to help guide consumers' decision-making and curb confusion. Tropicana's extra fruit-juice varieties boosted sales by 23% in Britain in 2009. But now the company puts colour-coded bottletops on sub-categories of juice to help customers "navigate what can be a difficult range," says Patrick Kalotis, its marketing director in Britain. In "Nudge," Richard Thaler and Cass Sunstein, two American academics, cite a study of company retirement plans. When a default option automatically selected an investment portfolio, saving employees the chore of picking their own mix of assets, participation shot up from 9% to 34%.

Some firms have pruned their ranges to avoid confusing shoppers. For example, Glidden, an American paint brand, decided in 2009 to reduce its palette of wall colours from an eye-dazzling 1,000 to a mere 282 because of a change in "Americans' priorities from 'more is better' to 'less is more.'" L'Astrance, a three-star Michelin restaurant in Paris's swanky 16th arrondissement, offers no choice at all on its menu: Pascal Barbot, the chef, concocts what he fancies from produce picked up in the market that day. And sometimes less really is more. When Procter & Gamble, an American consumer-products company, thinned its range of Head & Shoulders shampoos from 26 to 15, sales increased by 10%, according to Sheena Iyengar in "The Art of Choosing."

"Traditionally, companies said that it's all about the customer, and therefore give them everything they want," says Glen Williams of Bain, a consultancy. "In reality, this can make it difficult to identify which products the customer really wants, and can create problems for managing the business." Offering too many jazzy options for new cars, say, may not only confuse consumers but add to production costs and increase the potential for factory-floor bungles. A 2006 Bain study suggested that reducing complexity and narrowing choice can boost revenues by 5–40% and cut costs by 10–35%.

At the same time the anti-globalisation and green movements have stirred a consumer backlash against a surfeit of choice. Campaigns urge shoppers to buy locally grown fruit in season, and to shun cherries in winter or green beans flown in from Kenya. A "voluntary simplicity" movement calls on households to do away with excess consumer choice and lead a low-consumption, eco-friendly life. Courses promise to help people shed the distractions and stresses of the consumerist world and journey towards their inner wholeness. Short of turning the lawn over to organic vegetables and selling the car, books with such titles as "The Power of Less: The fine art of limiting yourself to the essential . . . in business and in life" or "Living Simply: Choosing less in a world of more" suggest practical ideas for cutting down on the effort of decision-making. The advice seems to boil down to shopping less often, keeping less stuff, watching less TV and sending fewer e-mails.

Life coaches offer to help with the perplexity of bigger choices. As recently as the early 1960s, in the world elegantly portrayed by a TV series, "Mad Men," society gave both women and men far fewer options. Dealing with the strains and expectations of choice is today's payback. "At a certain age, my clients have this sudden realisation that life hasn't gone quite the way they intended, and they feel stuck," says Mr O'Neil, who runs life-coaching classes. In the past they would have just got on with it. Today, he says, "they are paralysed by having too much choice."

Fifty years after the contraceptive pill was first licensed in America and 37 years after the Supreme Court legalised abortion, women seem to agonise more than ever about breeding. "We've grown up with a lot more choice than our mothers or grandmothers; for them, being child-free wasn't a choice, it was pitied," says Beth Follini, an American life coach who specialises in the "maybe baby" dilemma. "The anxiety comes from worrying about making the wrong choice." Having options seems to make people think they can have control over outcomes too. Sometimes, says Ms Follini, choosing is about learning to live without control.

Those in the business of helping people choose offer various tips. Mr O'Neil says the key is taking a decision: "The truth is that it doesn't matter what we choose, only that we do choose." Stick to the choices that matter and eliminate the rest, suggests one advocate of simple living, who supplies no fewer than 72 steps to choose from in order to simplify life. Another helpfully explains that "when you approach simple living, sometimes the decision is clear-cut. Sometimes it's not." The trouble with simplifying your life, it turns out, is that it involves too many choices.

Critical Thinking

1. With a small group of peers from your class, debate the following paragraph from the article: "As options multiply, there may be a point at which the effort required to obtain enough information to be able to distinguish sensibly between alternatives outweighs the benefit to the consumer of the extra choice. 'At this point . . . choice no longer liberates, but debilitates. . . . the fact that *some* choice is good doesn't necessarily mean that *more* choice is better.' "

2. Relate a personal choice (decision making) experience that either supports or negates the above statement.

Tapping the Untapped

**Marketers can learn from product preferences
that are simply linked to consumers' physiology.**

DIANA DERVAL

Product preferences are closely linked to our physiology: Nearsighted people are relaxed by blue, and testosterone-driven women prefer fruity scents, for example. Brands, therefore, can use physiological knowledge to predict consumers' preferences and design the right sensory mix.

Sensory Perception

Sensory perception is an untapped strategic resource that has a direct impact on purchasing decisions. Everything from shape, color, texture, smell and taste can attract or repulse consumers. Variations in sensory perception are huge among individuals: Some people hear the same sound four-times louder, or feel the same fabric 12-times softer than others do. The success stories of beauty retailer Sephora, Domino's Pizza and Pleo pet dinosaurs illustrate how grabbing the opportunity of sensory perception analysis at an early stage can help marketers with:

- increasing the innovation hit rate,
- identifying local and emerging markets and
- increasing sales.

Pleo Reborn

Pleo is an example of using scientific market research to win new markets. After the International Consumer Electronics Show in Las Vegas, Innvo Labs Corp. took the show at the Gulf Information Technology Exhibition consumer electronics shopping extravaganza in Dubai with the new Pleo RB (reborn). The robotic companion pet is back with more sensors to interact with the environment: shaking when it's too cold, answering to its name, asking for food and appreciating hugs.

The original Pleo, launched in green for the U.S. and European markets, didn't appeal as much to the Chinese and Hong Kong markets. Innvo Labs wondered about which color to choose for Pleo Reborn.

Derek Dotson, CEO of Innvo Labs, confirms that traditional market research gives little help: "When we asked our customer base which color they prefer, many of them said red, others blue and some green."

Luckily, scientific research can help. You might wonder what science has to do with attractive colors. Well, according to the laws of physics, each color has a different refraction: blue and violet, for instance, will hit the front of our eyeball, whereas red and yellow will hit the back of our eyeball. The focal point of the eye [is] where all color waves meet after passing the lens.

The twist is that the exact location of the focal point varies depending on an individual's physiology, and determines his or her favorite colors:

- Nearsighted people focus light in front of the retina; viewing blue is effortless for them. To perceive red, they must tense their ocular muscles.
- Farsighted people have a shorter eyeball, and the F point is beyond the retina. Viewing red is effortless for them. To perceive blue, they must tense their ocular muscles.

China, including Hong Kong, happens to have the largest population of nearsighted people in the world, with 400 million individuals—33 percent of the Chinese population and more than 60 percent of the Chinese youth. So brands targeting young Chinese shoppers can use blue as a relaxing color and red as an exciting one. When targeting Australians, the vast majority of whom are farsighted, it is the contrary: Blue will be an exciting color and red a relaxing one.

Innvo Labs successfully introduced to Hong Kong its Pleo Reborn—in blue, of course.

The Hormonal Quotient®

As we saw from the Pleo case, segmenting consumers based on their sensory perception makes a lot more sense than grouping them by revenue or age. And it enables brands to

Briefly

- Product preferences are directly linked to the millions of sensors monitoring our bodies and brains.
- Segmenting consumers based on their sensory perception is more powerful than grouping them by revenue or age.
- When in the same context, consumers who have an identical Hormonal Quotient® make the same purchasing decisions.

design the right products and services for each target group and local market.

An interesting finding is that product preferences are directly linked to the millions of sensors monitoring our bodies and brains. The number and distribution of these sensors are greatly influenced by prenatal hormones so that it is possible to predict favorite colors, tastes, scents, shapes, textures and sounds—almost from the womb.

Some people, for instance, hear high-pitch sounds four times louder than others. If they switch to an electric car, these super-amplifiers are more likely to enjoy a Chevrolet Volt than a Nissan Leaf, just because noise diagrams confirm that the Nissan Leaf engine generates high frequency noises that are extremely annoying to sensitive super-amplifiers' ears.

In many animal species, there are several types of males and several types of females with specific behaviors and preferences. These gender polymorphisms are directly linked to the influence of prenatal hormones.

Among side-blotched lizards, for instance, orange-throated males—exposed to higher levels of prenatal testosterone—are dating several females at the same time and do not perceive stress. Meanwhile, blue-throated males have a smaller territory and are monogamous.

Based on thousands of measurements in more than 25 countries, Chicago-based DervalResearch identified eight gender polymorphisms in humans—the Hormonal Quotient®—so that shoppers with the same HQ profile show very similar preferences in terms of colors, shapes, scents, tastes, textures, and sounds. For instance, women with a testosterone-driven HQ are more likely to prefer fruity to floral scents—always good to know for a beauty retailer like Sephora, or for men who haven't given up on offering perfumes.

Furthermore, women with a testosterone-driven HQ are also more likely to be sensitive to chemicals, so the safe areas for these super-inhalers would be air, food and mates' scents. That's good to know if you are a hotel planning to spread synthetic fragrances in the lobby, or a shop intending to burn incense throughout the day. If these women are in your target, you might end up repulsing the consumers you wanted to attract.

The Domino's Pizza Case

Domino's Pizza and Pizza Hut decided to penetrate a complex market with many local disparities (a bit like in the United States): France. Both brands have a very strong network of outlets, but the distribution on the map is very different, with Pizza Hut concentrated on the biggest cities and Domino's Pizza present also toward the Atlantic coast. So which of these pizza brands is the No. 1 in France, and why?

Interestingly, when referencing more research, it's found that consumers more likely to eat pizza are concentrated in the big cities and toward the Atlantic coast. Domino's Pizza clearly became the No. 1 pizza player in France by opening outlets in the right catchment areas, taste-wise.

Integrating a sensory approach at an early stage of a business plan is highly beneficial, but the initiative can come from research and development, product marketing, process innovation, brand management, business development or the consumer experience teams. What really matters is to be ready to look at one's own products from a new and more scientific angle.

Sensory perception can be used to:

- design the ideal consumer experience for a given target group (a fruity scent for testosterone-driven women) or geographical area (a blue Pleo for the Chinese market); or
- identify the most profitable market opportunity or geographical area for a given product or service—like the French Atlantic coast for Domino's Pizzas.

An Exact Science

The promise of this scientific approach to marketing is huge: No more gambling, endless surveys, evening focus groups or pricey brain scans. Brands just need to identify the sensory profiles of their target consumers once.

Marketers can then make decisions for each new product and service, based on reliable scientific observations. The time and budget saver is that people with the same sensory profile, in the same context, behave in the same way. Brands can team up with experts in behavioral neuro-endocrinology, who understand the impact of hormones on the body and the brain, to develop the products and services that consumers want. This field of research is growing fast: More than 500 scientific articles have been published over the past two years about hormones and behavior, with marketing applications from segmentation to positioning. Consumers will greatly benefit from a sensory-friendly brand experience.

SENSORY QUIZ PROPOSED BY DERVALRESEARCH

Are You More Into?

		(a)	(b)
1.	**TASTE**	(a) strong black coffee	(b) tea or coffee with milk
2.	**SMELL**	(a) flower scent	(b) fruit scent
3.	**SOUND**	(a) pop music	(b) other music genres
4.	**VISION**	(a) ▮▮▮▮▮▮	(b) ▮▮▮▮▮▮
5.	**TOUCH**	(a) cotton	(b) silk

Your Sensory Profile:

		Answer (A)	Answer (B)
1.	**TASTE**	You are not very sensitive to bitterness and can eat almost anything.	You are sensitive to bitterness and more picky on food.
2.	**SMELL**	You enjoy most scents and essential oils.	You are sensitive to synthetic fragrances and prefer natural scents.
3.	**SOUND**	You struggle following a conversation with background noise.	You prefer bass sounds to high pitch noises.
4.	**VISION**	You see well far away and are relaxed by colors like red or orange.	You see better close-up and are relaxed by colors like blue or purple.
5.	**TOUCH**	You are irritated by certain fabrics and very sensitive to temperature changes.	You enjoy all sorts of fabrics and pay more attention to the clothing style.

Critical Thinking

1. Define the term "Sensory Perception."
2. Discuss how the Pleo Reborn is a good example of effective scientific market research.
3. Do you agree with the premise that "segmenting consumers based on their sensory perceptions is more powerful than grouping them by revenue or age"?

DIANA DERVAL is president and research director of DervalResearch, an international market research firm specializing in human perception and behavior, inventor of the Hormonal Quotient® and author of *The Right Sensory Mix: Targeting Consumer Product Development Scientifically* (Springer, 2010), a finalist of the Berry-AMA award for best marketing book 2011. She may be reached at Diana@ derval-research.com.

UNIT 3

Developing and Implementing Marketing Strategies

Unit Selections

26. **The CMO and the Future of Marketing,** George S. Day and Robert Malcolm
27. **Innovate or Die,** Stephen C. Harper and Thomas W. Porter
28. **Brand Integrity,** Tom Peters and Valarie Willis
29. **Brand Apathy Calls for New Methods: Turn Customer Preference from "No Brand" to "Some Brand",** Don E. Schultz
30. **Branding's Big Guns,** Paula Andruss
31. **Playing Well Together,** Jason Daley
32. **Competing against Free,** David J. Bryce, Jeffrey H. Dyer, and Nile W. Hatch
33. **Ditch the Discounts,** Rafi Mohammed
34. **The Devolution of Marketing: Is America's Marketing Model Fighting Hard Enough to Keep Up?** Andrew R. Thomas and Timothy J. Wilkinson
35. **In Lean Times, Retailers Shop for Survival Strategies,** Jayne O'Donnell
36. **The Rebirth of Retail,** Jason Ankeny
37. **Marketing Communication in a Digital Era: Marketers Should Focus Efforts on Emerging Social, Mobile and Local Trends,** Donna L. Hoffman and Thomas P. Novak
38. **Selling Green,** Matt Villano
39. **What's Your Social Media Strategy?** H. James Wilson et al.
40. **Advertising's New Campaign,** Jennifer Wang

Learning Outcomes

After reading this Unit, you will be able to:

- Most ethical questions seem to arise in regard to the promotional component of the marketing mix. How fair is the general public's criticism of some forms of personal selling and advertising? Give some examples.

- What role, if any, do you think the quality of a product plays in making a business competitive in consumer markets? What role does price play? Would you rather market a higher-priced, better-quality product or one that was the lowest priced? Why?

- What do you envision will be the major problems or challenges retailers will face in the next decade? Explain.

- Given the rapidly increasing costs of personal selling, what role do you think it will play as a strategy in the marketing mix in the future? What other promotion strategies will play increased or decreased roles in the next decade?

Student Website

www.mhhe.com/cls

Internet References

American Marketing Association Homepage
    www.marketingpower.com
Consumer Buying Behavior
    www.courses.psu.edu/mktg/mktg220_rso3/sls_cons.htm

"Strategy and timing are the Himalayas of marketing. Everything else is the Catskills."

—Al Ries

"Marketing management objectives," the late Wroe Alderson once wrote, "are very simple in essence. The firm wants to expand its volume of sales, or it wants to handle the volume it has more efficiently." Although the essential objectives of marketing might be stated this simply, the development and implementation of strategies to accomplish them is considerably more complex. Many of these complexities are due to changes in the environment within which managers must operate. Strategies that fail to heed the social, political, and economic forces of society have little chance of success over the long run. The lead article in this section examines how the roles, responsibilities and influence of the chief marketing officer have and will continue to evolve in the future. The selections in this unit provide a wide-ranging discussion of how marketing professionals and U.S. companies interpret and employ various marketing strategies today. The readings also include specific examples from industry to illustrate their points. The articles are grouped in four sections, each dealing with one of the main strategy areas: product, pricing, distribution (place), and promotion. Because each selection discusses more than one of these areas, it is important that you read them broadly. For example, many of the articles covered in the distribution section discuss important aspects of personal selling and advertising.

Purestock/SuperStock

Product Strategy

The essence of the marketing concept is to begin with what consumers want and need. After determining a need, an enterprise must respond by providing the product or service demanded. Successful marketing managers recognize the need for continuous product improvement and/or new product introduction.

The articles in this subsection focus on various facets of product strategy. The first article stresses the importance of innovation, and examines why many companies are not as innovative as they could be. "Brand Integrity" reflects that excellence is achieved when the brand, the talent, and the customer experience are all in alignment. In "Brand Apathy Calls for New Methods," Schultz argues that building market share requires a new set of tools and brand strategies designed to shift consumer preference away from competitive brands. The next article, "Branding's Big Guns?" chronicles the success of the 10 most trusted U.S. brands that have become household names. The last article under product strategy highlights the various strategic benefits associated with franchise cobranding efforts.

Pricing Strategy

Few elements of the total strategy of the "marketing mix" demand so much managerial and social attention as pricing. There is a good deal of public misunderstanding about the ability of

marketing managers to control prices and even greater misunderstanding about how pricing policies are determined. New products present especially difficult problems in terms of both costs and pricing. The costs for developing a new product are usually very high, and if a product is truly new, it cannot be priced competitively, for it has no competitors. In his review piece on pricing and value exchange, Smith describes how managers should deal with the qualitative and quantitative issues in setting prices.

The *HBR* article, "Competing against Free," documents how free offerings are rapidly spreading beyond online markets to the physical, brick and mortar world. The authors give pointers on how incumbents can effectively fight back. Finally, Rafi Mohamad's "Ditch the Discounts," discusses pricing strategies and tactics that are more appropriate for economic recovery than the adaptive pricing companies adopted during the recent recession.

Distribution Strategy

For many enterprises, the largest marketing costs result from closing the gap in space and time between producer and consumer. In no other area of marketing is efficiency so eagerly sought after. Physical distribution seems to be the one area where significant cost savings can be achieved. The costs of physical distribution are tied closely with decisions made about the number, the size, and the diversity of marketing intermediaries between producer and consumer. The articles in this subsection scrutinize ways retailers can create value for their customers and be very competitive in the marketplace. "The Devolution of Marketing" is a thought-provoking article that argues that the current American marketing distribution model is dysfunctional, and small and medium-sized businesses operate under a misconceived ideology of producing and selling. Jayne O'Donnell's USA Today article describes how retailers are in search of tenable survival strategies during recent difficult economic times. "The Rebirth of Retail" discusses the inspiration and vision behind Shopkick, a new shopping application.

Promotion Strategy

The basic objectives of promotion are to inform, persuade, or remind the consumer to buy a firm's product or pay for the firm's service. Advertising is the most obvious promotional activity. However, in total dollars spent and in cost per person reached, advertising takes second place to personal selling. Sales promotion supports either personal selling and advertising, or both. Such media as point-of-purchase displays, catalogs, and direct mail place the sales promotion specialist closer to the advertising agency than to the salesperson. "Selling Green" presents a five-step guide to correctly market a business as environmentally conscious. The remaining articles in this final unit subsection cover such topics as social and digital media. "What's Your Social Media Strategy?" describes four ways companies are using technology to form connections, and "Advertising's New Campaign" discusses the power of blogging and brand-sponsored communities.

The CMO and the Future of Marketing

Tomorrow's CMOs will need a broader skill set to survive and thrive.

GEORGE S. DAY AND ROBERT MALCOLM

How will the roles, responsibilities and influence of the chief marketing officer evolve in the future? The answers will emerge from the interplay of three driving forces and the unique features of each company's strategy and legacy. These three driving forces are: the predictable trends in the marketplaces, the changing role of the C-suite, and uncertainty about the economic climate and organizational design in the future.

The impact of the three driving forces on the job of the CMO will be amplified by the unrealistic expectations of the chief executive officer and the rest of the leadership team about what a CMO can accomplish . . . and the lack of preparation of a majority of candidates for this job.

The average tenure of a CMO is about three years, and is unlikely to be much longer in the future. Yet some CMOs will rise to the intensifying challenge, and earn a "seat at the table." These "whole-brain" marketing leaders will ground their decisions in analytic realities, while painting a realistic vision for the company that bridges today and the future. They will excel at the five priority actions needed to navigate escalating complexity and uncertainty:

- act as the visionary for the future of the company;
- build adaptive marketing capabilities;
- win the war for marketing talent;
- tighten the alignment with sales; and
- take accountability for the returns on marketing spending.

Forces Shaping Marketing's Future

When thinking about the future in an era of accelerating change, five years is a long time. To appreciate how much can happen in five years, think back to 2007. Facebook and Twitter were barely on the horizon, e-books hardly existed, clouds were still something in the sky and the credit bubble that triggered the financial meltdown was still expanding. We can be sure that five years from now in 2017 there will be equally dramatic surprises; we are uncertain about these shocks and events. At the same time, there are a number of predictable trends that CMOs can prepare for with some confidence.

The Evolving C-Level

A recent analysis of C-level jobs concluded that once people reached the C-level, the skills and functional mastery that got them there matter less than their leadership skills and general business acumen. The chief information officer, chief technology officer or CMO who thrives as a member of the senior leadership team will be a team player who can lead without rank and has built an organization that earns the respect of the rest of the business. The skills that are increasingly in favor are strong communication, willingness to partner and strategic thinking. Successful members of the management team will advise the CEO on key decisions and strategic choices, but offer their own well-informed insights.

For CMOs to thrive and survive in a collaborative C-suite, they will have to adopt a general management mindset and earn the respect of the others with fact-based analyses. They will be accountable for the brand strategy, driving the organic growth agenda and positioning the business for the future. As the acknowledged voice of the customer and consumer, they will ensure the strategy is built and executed from the outside in. They can no longer be passive service providers, content to oversee market insight activities, coordinate relationships with key marketing partners and ensure compliance "reasonably" with brand guidelines.

Predictable Marketplace Trends

The second set of driving forces has been the subject of many analyses in Our purpose here is to highlight a few trends to make the basic point that marketing in the future will be increasingly complex, and will change at a faster rate than most companies can handle. Consider the interplay of the following trends:

- demographic shifts;
- connected and empowered consumers;

- new technologies enabling micro-targeting;
- the rise of global markets in China, India, Brazil and Indonesia;
- new media (cinema, video, sponsorship, direct mail, SMS, Internet, social, etc.); and
- channels of distribution becoming complex ecosystems of networked partners.

> **"The best possible solutions come only from a combination of rational analysis based on the nature of things, and imaginative reintegration of all the different items into a new pattern, using non-linear brain power."**
>
> —*Kenichi Ohmae* "The Mind of the Strategist"

The predictable consequences of these trends, which we have already experienced, will surely accelerate to make markets more complex and fragmented. There will be a continuing shift in power to consumers and a proliferation of media and channels—all at the same time that plummeting communication costs and diffused manufacturing technologies enable new, low-cost competitors to enter from anywhere in the world. These trends have exciting (and scary) prospects for marketers who will be expected to be creative and tech-savvy global thinkers and results-oriented leaders.

Living with Uncertainty

What will the future bring? This question is hard to answer because of many uncertainties where the outcome is not known with any confidence. What will the price of oil be? The geopolitical climate? The regulatory requirements? These are material, but to a group of CMOs brought together by the American Marketing Association, the two uncertainties that were most informative and potentially influential were the system-wide resources available to marketing and the dominant organizational models. These two critical uncertainties were each reduced to a single spectrum with the credible extreme states at each pole (as seen in Figure 1).

These two axes were crossed to form a 2 × 2 matrix, with four different quadrants of uncertainty. Each quadrant portrays a plausible, alternative hypothesis or scenario about how the environment might unfold, and highlights the risks and

opportunities to the organization—or, in this case, to the function of marketing within the firm.

These scenarios let marketers "learn from the future." They can rehearse the future to avoid surprises by breaking through the illusion of certainty. Unlike traditional strategic planning, which presumes there is a likely answer to a strategic issue, scenario learning considers multiple futures. It meets the needs of marketers for plans, capabilities and organization models that are robust across the scenarios, so the organization is prepared for whatever the future will bring.

The "best-case" scenario is that system-wide resources are plentiful and we stay with the traditional closed model. The most challenging scenario for marketers is scarce resources and open network, because this is likely to subordinate the role and influence of marketing.

The reason for uncertainty is that the traditional organization model has shown an amazing level of adaptability. On the other hand, there is considerable evidence that companies that have a network structure are more nimble and will win the market battle. Companies such as Cisco Systems Inc. or Li & Fung Ltd. are organizing as a network structure to leverage and gain more resources. The best place to see open networks in action is the area of open innovation or innovation networks. However, at this stage, we cannot be certain whether this model will prevail or will be another management fad, because alliances and joint ventures have not had a very successful track record.

The second area of uncertainty relates to the availability of resources. Will they be abundant or scarce? If you read The *Wall Street Journal*, the *Financial Times*, or *The New York Times*, the mood swings are quite abrupt. It could well be that we are going to face a persistently weak economic climate with shrinking profits. One of the consequences is that there will be many more price wars, intense competition and people will manage for the short run. In that environment, marketing almost invariably is on the defensive. However, if resources are perceived to be abundant, the marketers can take the offensive and partner with sales—and there is grounds for optimism.

CMO Challenges

How will the "whole-brain" marketing leader become an influential member of the C-suite and ensure the organization stays ahead of the myriad driving forces that shape the future? First and foremost, they will advocate outside-in thinking that starts with the market when designing strategies, rather than the other way around. Winning strategies will be viewed through

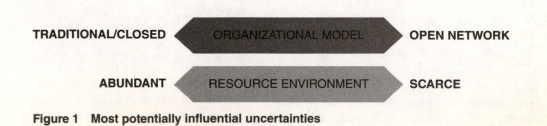

Figure 1 Most potentially influential uncertainties

a customer value lens and illuminated by deep market insights. Second, they will embrace the dual challenge of building a world-class marketing function that can anticipate and act on the driving forces of change. From our CMO experience and work with dozens of CMOs, there are five priority actions that stand out.

"Winning strategies will be viewed through a customer value lens and illuminated by deep market insights"

Acting as the Visionary for the Future of the Organization

Adaptive organizations continuously scan for opportunities in markets, competitive white spaces and changing customer needs. They win by seeing sooner than their rivals. This will take an experimental mindset, a willingness to learn quickly from mistakes, and identifying, testing and deploying new models.

Increasingly, the CMO will be the person leading a function that is adept at monitoring markets and extracting insights for future growth. When Kim Feil, Walgreens CMO, learned from her research group that some consumers viewed the retailer as a convenience store with a pharmacy on the back wall, she saw both a problem and an opportunity. At her urging, the company began to reposition itself as a premium healthcare brand, by showcasing its wellness offerings and walk-in clinic.

Building Adaptive Marketing Capabilities

The CMO of the future must wear many hats and embrace sometimes competing, even contradictory, forces both within and outside the organization. Among the most challenging is the need to deliver business results today, while "creating" the business of tomorrow. Both are essential to a healthy business (and a successful CMO), but require very different marketing processes, skills and capabilities

---

Briefly

- The CMO's future role will be determined by the interplay of three driving forces: the predictable trends in their marketplaces, the changing role of the C-suite, and uncertainty about the economic climate and organizational design in the future.
- For CMOs to thrive and survive in a collaborative C-suite, they will have to adopt a general management mindset and earn the respect of the others with fact-based analyses.
- It is the job of the CMO to continue finding ways to make the organization more efficient—not just the marketing spend.

Delivering today requires more proven, predictable and repeatable tools, skills and processes. It is a bit more left- than right-brained. You are in delivery mode more than planning mode. The marketing capabilities required are developing and executing repeatable models, simplification, executional discipline, rigorous measurement and decisive action. Convergence, focus and delivery with a more short-term mindset is required. The CMO who does not master these capabilities and build them in the organization will not likely get the chance to spend much time on the longer-term challenges and opportunities.

"Creating" the business of tomorrow is equally critical and, longer term, the CMOs who do not master these primary sources of knowledge, expertise and ultimate success. With the digital-technology-led transformation in communication, it is the "future generation" who has the great knowledge, understanding and comfort of the new digital and social-marketing applications. Indeed, they are the digital "natives" for whom Facebook, social networks, tweets and blogs are "just the way we live."

The adaptive organization will recognize the value in getting the best out of the "immigrant and native" digital marketers, and will neither be stuck in the past, nor discard all the institutional knowledge and experience in jumping to a completely new model of marketing. Despite what many pundits would have us believe, the fundamentals of marketing strategy and consumer behavior have not been repealed. The adaptive organization will study the changes, understand how the consumer "consumes influence" with the new marketing technologies, will challenge old models and tactics and experiment with new ones. They will figure out what works in the new digital environment for their business and customer and evolve their models and practices. They will neither totally abandon the past, nor completely adopt the latest digital fad.

Tightening the Alignment with Sales

Too often, there is an adversarial Mars vs. Venus coloration to the relationship of sales and marketing. It has historically been rooted in mutual incomprehension of the other's role, different time horizons and divergent goals and incentives. Typically the two functions occupied separate silos, and one function had more power than the other, depending on the industry.

The traditional lines between marketing and sales are blurring. Key account managers serving large, powerful customers are engaged in long-run marketing strategy and brand development. Meanwhile, the number of possible points of contact with customers and consumers has been increasing exponentially, with social media, interactivity and mobility demanding closer coordination. Increasingly, CEOs are looking for a single point of contact with all market-facing activities, who can take responsibility for the value proposition, innovation, marketing and sales across all platforms. Many companies have responded with a new combined role of chief commercial officer. This combined function ensures closer internal and external alignment, by using the Internet to coordinate all marketing and sales activities—from customer-service reps responding to complaints on blogs to systems for tracking sales calls and consumer Web behavior.

Q/A
Robert Malcolm Elaborates on His Article with George S. Day, Discussing the Role and Expectations of CMOs Today

Q. What is the background of the incoming CMOs? Is their experience appropriate? What kind of experience would be appropriate?

A. The background of incoming CMOs is as varied as the role and responsibilities of CMOs: There is no standard CMO role profile and the educational and work experience preparation of CMOs varies wildly.

Not surprisingly, a critical issue at the root of the relatively low success rate and short tenure of CMOs is the mismatch between expectations and the ability to deliver the expectations. Sometimes, this is a function of misalignment of expectations and resources within the business and sometimes, it is a misalignment in the expectations and the capability of the CMO. David Aaker, vice chairman of the global marketing consultancy Prophet, has identified five broad classifications of CMO roles: facilitator, consultant, service provider, strategic partner and strategic captain. For the CMO whose job expectation lies primarily in the area of providing marketing services, specific experience in this area—but not necessarily in [profit-and-loss] management, cross-functional leadership, strategy or business transformation—would be sufficient. For the strategic captain—who leads the strategic direction of the entity, has a core responsibility to deliver profitable growth, drives the resource allocation decisions, and owns the effectiveness and return on marketing spending—there is a very different set of experiences and capabilities required. The key is to match the role and the experiences/capabilities, and this is too often done poorly.

Today's CMOs, unlike their CFO counterparts for the most part, come from a wide experience and educational base. Some have an educational background in marketing, many, if not most, do not. Some come out of marketing functional roles, but many also come from sales or strategy roles. Some even come from the agency side. Some have grown up in very strong marketing functional training companies, where marketing has a central role and is dedicated to the training of future marketing leaders—companies like Procter & Gamble, Coca-Cola, Unilever, Diageo, General Mills, etc. Many come from companies in which there is minimal training, and where marketing plays a secondary or supportive role. By contrast, most CFOs have a strong finance education and functional training track record. As the role is similar, and many of the deliverables are determined by strict financial and accounting reporting and regulations, there is more homogeneity in experience and preparation than for CMOs.

Q. Do companies discourage the needed working style (e.g., collaboration) by the way they operate and promote people into other C-level roles?

A. In my experience, silos exist more as a result of historical organizational and reward structures—rather than as a conscious effort to discourage collaboration. Oftentimes, functional structures and rewards inadvertently create conflict, even competition. For marketing, this is most often the case vis-à-vis the sales function. But it can also show up in the relationship with the finance function. Every effective CMO I know works diligently to build understanding of and confidence in the marketing function, what it does and how it contributes to creating enterprise value. They open up the function, rather than close it down or protect it. Less-successful CMOs do not always recognize the broader leadership and collaboration imperative, and thus stay more isolated within the function.

Q. Do the kind of people that are needed actually exist in large enough numbers? If the average tenure of CMOs is due to this problem, then should companies keep trying the same tactics and expect a different outcome? Maybe the role needs to be redesigned.

A. The answer lies in that last statement: Each company needs to design the right role for their business; these will not be uniform. The CMO needs to have the right skills, experience and culture fit for the properly scoped role. Critically, the role needs to be set up for success, and this is not often done. In many cases, a CEO will have an expectation for the CMO to achieve things that the organization is not structured, resourced or culturally aligned to achieve. CMOs who finds themselves in this situation and cannot change these things to allow for success, are set up for failure—and failure pretty quickly. Turning to the first question, my experience is there are not enough CMOs who have the combination of talent, experience and leadership skills to do many of the large transformational CMO roles in the largest corporations. The key challenge is to develop the functional mastery and the "total business leadership" pedigree that cannot only deliver the needed marketing outputs, but influence the broader organization so that it gets the best results out of its marketing. More CMOs fail on the "total business leadership" dimension than another.

Taking Accountability for the Returns on Marketing Spending

There is no foreseeable future where marketing won't have to demonstrate that it can earn acceptable returns on marketing investments. While there is admittedly a fair amount of craft (even art) in effective marketing, the discipline at its core, exists to create value for the enterprise. The CMO who doesn't understand this, embrace it and build marketing culture and capability around value creation through the performance of its marketing investment, will not survive. Key to this is recognizing that this is not a contradiction with the creative side of marketing. As Bill Bernbach, one of the agency creative giants of the 20th century put it: "Properly practiced creativity MUST result in greater sales more economically achieved."

In our experience, once a CMO has embraced the dual responsibilities of creative and accountable delivery, there are several core priorities. The first is the mindset—adopting the mindset of the general manager or CEO, not the creative CMO. The marketing function exists to deliver increased enterprise value in the short-, medium- and long-term. And it does so by owning both the numerator and denominator of the "value equation"—optimizing the ability of marketing to generate top-line growth (the numerator) and reducing the cost of delivering that growth (the denominator). The CMO needs to adopt this mindset and create a marketing culture that fully embraces it. He or she needs to role model the desired values and behavior, and embrace the core metrics and measurements—not avoid them.

Second is the importance of building a strong relationship with the chief financial officer and the financial function. The successful CMO understands the financial model for the business, how economic profits are generated and the expectations of the CFO. More importantly, the CFO and finance function have resources that every CMO should use to improve the marketing value equation. Finally, a CFO who knows and trusts his CMO is an indispensable ally when there are tough judgment calls to be made.

Third, in order to deliver improved enterprise value, you need to know how marketing "works" for your business. How does it create value? What are the specific growth levers and how do you best employ them? Here, you must get past the assumptions or general marketing beliefs and truly know your business. You have to be ready to pull the plug on things that don't work, and consistently reallocate funds to the drivers of more value. This also means an obsession with the efficiency of marketing—and the entire organization.

Fourth, be obsessed with improving the efficiency of marketing, eliminating the "dogs" and making the "stars" more efficient. This is not the job of the procurement department, although they can certainly help. It is the job of the CMO. And, it includes always finding how to make the organization more efficient—not just the marketing spend.

Critical Thinking

1. With a small group of peers from your class, draft a job description for a CMO.
2. List and summarize the three driving forces, discussed in the article, that shape the role of an organization's CMO.

GEORGE S. DAY is the Geoffrey T. Boisi Professor, professor of marketing and co-director of the Mack Center for Technological Innovation at the Wharton School of the University of Pennsylvania. ROBERT MALCOLM is a lecturer in marketing at The Wharton School at the University of Pennsylvania, has held senior marketing and general management positions at Procter & Gamble, and was the chief marketing and sales officer at Diageo. They may be reached at DayG@wharton.upenn.edu and RMalc@wharton.upenn.edu, respectively.

Innovate or Die

STEPHEN C. HARPER AND THOMAS W. PORTER

The below quote from Theodore Levitt's classic article, "Marketing Myopia," which appeared in *Harvard Business Review* years ago, has considerable applicability today. Among other things, it stressed the need for businesses to broaden how they define themselves and to explore the marketplace for opportunities. Peter Drucker provided great advice about how to identify opportunities when he said, "Within every problem lies at least one disguised business opportunity." Today, the list of "Why can't anyone develop a product that . . . ?" questions is almost endless. In a world where companies are desperate to find ways to increase their total sales revenue—which often includes reckless expansion and acquisitions—an almost infinite number of problems remain to be solved.

> **"It is constant watchfulness for opportunities to apply their technical know-how to the creation of customer-satisfying uses which accounts for their prodigious output of successful new products."**
>
> —*Theodore Levitt,* Economist and Educator

For example, why did it take so long for someone to develop a plastic paint can that will not rust and that has a pourable spout and a screw cap for easy opening and closing? Why did it take so long to develop a ceiling paint that looks pink when applied so you can see where you have painted, and then it turns white as it dries? Why did it take so long to come up with a vacuum cleaner that has a ball instead of wheels to enhance maneuverability?

For years, the United States has prided itself on innovation. United States businesses have operated with the philosophy, "China-based manufacturers may have an edge in the cost of manufacturing products, but the Americans are coming up with great product ideas." Therefore, it is troubling that after decades of being the world's leading manufacturer, some sources say China has passed the United States. While United States manufacturers have made considerable progress in improving competitiveness via new technology, processes and equipment, the Chinese clearly are improving their competitiveness—and not just in making relatively inexpensive items. In the manufacturing horse race, the United States has not been looking over its shoulder to see that people in China, India, South Korea and other countries are narrowing the innovation gap.

> **"The best way to predict the future is to invent it."**
>
> —*Alan Kay,* Computer Scientist

Reducing Innovation Myopia

Too many companies are not as innovative as they could be because their search for market and innovation opportunities is too narrow and too shortsighted. They are so involved in their daily business activities that they fail to install mechanisms for creating, capturing and funneling innovative ideas into their product development and process development pipelines.

> **"Discovery consists of seeing what everybody has seen and thinking what nobody has thought."**
>
> — *Albert von Szent-Gyorgy,* Biochemist, Discoverer of Vitamin C

Warning: Continuous improvement is not enough. While building upon existing product platforms and processes can create value, competitors can match such incremental innovation. Products at the maturity stage of their life cycles have a relatively consistent feature set across competitors. This means incremental innovation cannot produce a sustainable competitive advantage. Management author Tom Peters echoes this point when he notes that companies that are 100 percent into continuous improvement are thus 0 percent into innovation.

Breakthrough innovation requires new insights, new ideas and new solutions to solving customer problems and satisfying customer needs. According to Peters, you need to set improvement goals of 10 times rather than 10 percent. To become 10 times faster at one-tenth the cost, people must look at the situation from new perspectives. If the goal is 10 percent better, faster or cheaper, then people will be prone to "tweak" what they are doing. Even though you may not improve tenfold or even twofold, such efforts surely will beat the 10 percent better goal by a mile. This is necessary to gain a true competitive edge.

Organizations have many ways to become more innovative. But the best approach is a two-step process that identifies opportunities and then capitalizes on them. Corporate success and economic growth occur when preparation meets opportunity. Going back to Drucker's observation, the key is a constant flow of innovative products, services and processes that solve customer problems.

Thoroughly Understand the Customer

Winning in the marketplace means you have to be better than your competitors on the things that truly matter to your target market. Being customer-centric involves offering superior solutions to customer problems. In short, the business that offers the most customer-centric solution wins. In all the years we have been teaching and working with engineers, it is clear that they take pride in their ability to solve problems. Solving problems and finding a better way of doing things are the shots of adrenaline that drive them. This includes designing products and developing processes that enhance their organization's efficiency, quality, speed and so forth.

A note of caution: Companies need to make sure they do not over-engineer products by adding whistles and bells when customers only want something that will get the job done. Features and benefits are different things. Features are added to the basic product. Benefits are features that consumers value and are willing to pay for. When products are being designed and developed, what the targeted customers consider "must haves" need to be distinguished from the "nice to have" and "I don't care about that" features. As someone once noted, few consumers want a $29.95 fly evaporator. They just want a fly swatter for a dollar. The issue is not about being different; it is about being different on the things that matter to targeted customers. Being different does not automatically mean you are better. But to be better, you must be different, and that involves innovation. Companies that are not better than their competitors are like commodities. Commodities without cost and price advantages quickly become irrelevant in the marketplace.

Don't Be Too Customer-Centric

The tricky part is not becoming too customer-centric. For years, marketing researchers have stressed the need for mall intercepts, focus groups and surveys to find out what customers want. Yet it turns out that these techniques do not provide failsafe insights. Guy Kawasaki, a key player in Apple's evolution, noted in his "Rules for Revolutionaries" presentation at Stanford University that when you ask customers what they want, they often tell you what they think is the right answer. He stresses the need to observe what people actually do rather than what they say. Glenn Reid, who was an engineer at Apple,

noted in a recent *Fast Company* article about Apple that people cannot envision what they really want—especially things that don't exist.

> **"To raise new questions, new possibilities, to regard old problems from a new angle, requires creative imagination and marks real advance in science."**
>
> —*Albert Einstein*, Physicist

In *Competing for the Future*, Gary Hamel and C.K. Prahalad note that businesses need to pay attention to consumers' "unarticulated needs," rather than the articulated needs. Probe customers to find out what they need but are not actively trying to address.

They note that unarticulated needs may represent significant opportunities. They encourage firms to ask their customers, "What, if it is changed, would change everything?" This is like exploring what it will take to make the impossible possible. Remember, nearly a century ago Henry Ford said, "If I'd asked people what they wanted, they would have told me, 'A faster horse.'"

> **"Creativity is thinking up new things. Innovation is doing new things."**
>
> —*Theodore Levitt*, Economist and Professor

Improve the Value Equation

When Jack Welch took over General Electric in the 1980s, he stressed the need to improve quality and reduce costs. He was one of the first executives to break the mental model that assumed higher quality and lower costs were a zero-sum formula. He recognized that GE may not be able to be the lowest-cost provider, but the optimal quality/price ratio would increase GE's competitiveness.

Blue Ocean Strategy by W. Chan Kim and Renee Mauborgne represents the next stage in this line of thinking. They emphasize finding ways to pursue product differentiation and low cost rather than increasing product differentiation with a higher cost and price. Kim and Mauborgne provide guidelines for creating uncontested market space and making your competition irrelevant through "value innovation." Their guidelines combine the ability of United States companies to come up with better product and service ideas (product differentiation) with their need to drive the cost down. That is the sweet spot for creating value, attracting customers and transforming noncustomers into customers. The strategy of providing inferior products at bargain basement prices may work in some markets. But exploring the marketplace for "value gaps" and then developing and launching superior products in a timely fashion with a lower-than-expected price is more compelling for United States businesses.

Look Beyond your Products

While most think about the need to innovate their company's products and/ or services, innovation applies outside that core. Look at new processes, platforms, business techniques and business models. Innovation can include packaging (Pringles), making it possible for the customer to have the product serviced/fixed without having to take it back to the seller (Dell direct access to your computer while online), or even Zappos' free shipping both ways and one-year return policy.

Howard Schultz's latest book, *Onward,* profiles how he transformed Starbucks in the last few years. He wrote that he takes pride in how Starbucks chases the unexpected, gives people license to be disruptive, seeks game-changing opportunities, and tries to reinvent product categories by being unequivocally original.

Blending Varied Perspectives

All products, processes, patents and profits come from people. There are two ways to approach the people and innovation challenge. The first approach is to bring in people who have various perspectives. Breakthrough ideas and radical innovation usually come from outsiders. Most innovation springs from a diverse set of people. Looking at a problem, situation or challenge from multiple perspectives increases the probability that you will gain true insights and develop an innovative solution, product, service or process.

Bureaucracy, mental mindsets, risk aversion and other factors will inhibit innovation. Therefore, make an effort to identify and reduce or eliminate such factors. Establish processes and systems that enhance innovation. Consider setting up an idea review committee, an innovation seed fund, or an incubator so ideas can be nurtured. Couple this with a system for recognizing and rewarding people and teams that devise value-added ideas.

Recognize that innovation will not occur with a flip of the switch. People who don't innovate will not become innovative overnight. When he was president of IBM, Thomas Watson noted, "You can tame a wild duck, but you cannot make a tame duck wild." It may take a while for people to share ideas openly, try new ways to do things and look for new things to do. Expect some resistance from your people because today each person is expected to do more—including the jobs of people who were laid off—with less. Learning how to be more innovative in addition to dealing with ongoing hardware and software changes will be taxing. Expect some setbacks because innovation is an evolutionary process that involves learning, experimentation and improvisation. As you begin to see more innovation, raise the bar by seeking greater challenges. Keep in mind, however, that innovation has a short shelf life. What is innovative today may be obsolete tomorrow. And when your organization becomes more innovative, do not spend too much time celebrating; keep innovating instead.

"If you're not failing every now and again, it's a sign you're not doing anything very innovative."

—*Woody Allen,* Filmmaker

New Generations from All

While hiring innovative people has merit, the second approach is to engage all your people. Charge everyone, not just the inventors or research and development labs, with the task of generating new ideas. If given training and opportunity, most people are capable of coming up with innovative ideas, solutions, products and processes. John Gardner wrote years ago in his essay "The Life and Death of Institutions" that "The still untapped source of human vitality, the unmined load of talent, is in those people already hired and thereafter neglected." He further observed, "There is usually no shortage of ideas; the problem is getting a hearing for them."

"The uncreative mind can spot wrong answers, but it takes a very creative mind to spot wrong questions."

—*Anthony Jay,* Journalist and Writer

If you want innovation, then you need to create an environment that fosters innovation. This means people need to have the opportunity to explore and experiment. They also need to have the freedom to fail.

Most companies are myopic when it comes to seeking ideas from people not on their payroll, although a few businesses have benefited from being open to those sources. Some are experimenting with crowdsourcing to solicit innovative ideas. Some are tapping social media to become more aware of what frustrates their customers, along with consumer suggestions on how businesses can improve their operations and offerings. Schultz noted in *Onward* that since Starbucks set up MyStarbucksIdea.com, it has received more than 100,000 ideas.

The following tips also can help.

- Make time for innovation. Hamel and Prahalad's research found that senior executives spend less than 3 percent of their time thinking seriously about the future. Organizations that want to foster significant innovation must direct more time, attention, best people and other resources to the future.
- Adopt a portfolio approach to innovation that balances time horizons, funding and risk. Seek an optimal balance between incremental and breakthrough innovation. Develop a balanced portfolio so your company has a steady pipeline of new products, services and processes.
- Business process re-engineering starts with a clean sheet of paper. Innovation also should start with a clean sheet of paper so people analyze every facet of operations, including product development, thus minimizing innovation myopia.
- To introduce the new, be willing to discontinue the current. Invest your limited resources from today's breadwinners to make tomorrow's breadwinners. This includes processes as well as products.

- Apply the 80/20 rule to innovation. Focus on the few things that will make the biggest difference from a strategic ROI perspective.
- Do not get too caught up in what your competitors are doing. Compete against yourself in your ability to delight customers.
- Don't offer a solution where there isn't a problem unless the problem is certain to arise.
- Welch noted that revolutions begin with ideas. Encourage your people to look for things others cannot see, to think thoughts others do not think, to develop ideas no one has developed, and to have the guts to do what no one has ever done.
- Always believe that there has to be a better way. Unleash the "inner engineer" in every employee so they can search for and develop better ways to do things. Encourage your people to challenge the status quo, conventional thinking and accepted business practices.
- Foster and capture the irreverence found in entrepreneurs who seek market gaps where people's needs are not being met well or at all. Encourage your people to search the marketplace for points of frustration and pain. Every time they hear, "I wish there was a business that could . . ." that is the voice of a customer in search of a business. Schultz noted that most people ask "why?" Entrepreneurs ask "why not?" Entrepreneurs find ways to break the code.

> **"It ought to be remembered that there is nothing more difficult to take in hand, more perilous to conduct, or more uncertain in its success, than to take the lead in the introduction of a new order of things."**
>
> —*Niccolò Machiavelli,* Italian Writer and Philosopher

- Look for problems other companies cannot solve.
- Look for "Wow, why didn't I think of that?" problems/ opportunities/markets.
- Look for ways to simplify the product. Be like Nintendo, which developed the hand-held wand so playing computer games is a lot easier. And then be like Microsoft, which developed Kinect, which eliminates the need for a hand-held device.

> **"Nothing is so embarrassing as watching someone do something that you said could not be done."**
>
> —*Steve Jobs,* CEO, Apple

- Last but not least, remember that ideas are worthless without effective implementation.

This Won't Be Easy

Creating an environment that fosters continuous and profitable innovation will be difficult. Learning and adopting quality principles and practices was a major challenge, but now United States companies are competitive with some of the best organizations in the global marketplace. Learning and adopting innovation principles and practices will be far more difficult. Enhancing quality was more of a science than an art. Enhancing innovation is more of an art than a science. Yes, consultants will tell you they have their own "systems" for fostering innovation, but the truth of the matter is that innovation is as multifaceted as a diamond. When it comes to innovation, there is no silver bullet or quick fix. Statistical techniques, step-by-step processes and certifications are possible with quality. They can be taught, learned and implemented more easily than the various facets associated with innovation.

Quality issues are far easier to deal with because many causes are quantitative in nature and can be measured. Innovation is like advertising, where only half of the money you spend produces the desired results. The problem is that you do not know in advance which half will work. Innovation has only one guarantee; if you aren't innovative, then you won't be competitive, and before long you won't be in business. The marketplace has many alternatives and shows no mercy. People used to say, "You have to lead, follow, or get out of the way." In the race for competitiveness, it's "Innovate or get blown away."

Three additional points are worth noting. First, for the last couple of decades more people in China have been learning to speak English each year than people speak English in the United States. Second, the percentage of people pursuing PhD in the United States who are from foreign countries—including those in Asia—is significant. Even more significant is that more of them choose to return to their home countries. China is making a deliberate effort to entice them back to their homeland by building research and development centers. Third, it was not that long ago that American companies developed new product ideas and fleshed them out here. Now businesses can send their concepts to China and other countries and get a complete set of drawings, and in some cases prototypes, in a matter of days. How long will it be before China-based companies become the developers of innovative products and do the whole cycle in China?

Someone once noted, "Firms succeed to the extent they improve the quality of people's lives and increase their corporate customers' profitability." Companies looking for growth opportunities should look for the sources of frustration and pain in the marketplace and develop solutions that reduce the frustration and/or pain. To be more innovative, corporations must break down the walls that insulate them from problems that may be all around.

Don't wait until your company is gasping for revenue or for opportunity to knock. Don't define your business by the products and services it offers, the customers and geographic markets it serves, and the technology and processes it uses. Adopt the following non-myopic definition: We are an ever-evolving, problem seeking firm that transforms problems into opportunities by developing innovative processes and solutions for current and future problems for our current and future customers.

> "Every act of creation is first of all an
> act of destruction."
>
> —*Pablo Picasso,* Artist

STEPHEN C. HARPER is Progress Energy/Betty Cameron Distinguished Professor of Entrepreneurship at the University of North Carolina Wilmington. He earned his PhD from Arizona State University. He is the author of numerous books on leadership and entrepreneurship. His latest book, *The Ever-Evolving Enterprise: Guidelines for Creating Your Company's Future,* was published in January. He has conducted hundreds of seminars on how to create exceptional enterprises. THOMAS W. PORTER is associate professor of marketing at the University of North Carolina Wilmington. He received his BS in industrial engineering from Purdue University and his PhD in marketing from Indiana University. His research focuses on the areas of marketing strategy implementation and Internet marketing.

Critical Thinking

1. In your perspective, what is innovation myopia?

2. What recommendations do the authors propose to prevent innovation myopia? Do you agree with these recommendations, and can you offer any others?

From *Industrial Engineer,* September 2011, pp. 34–39. Copyright © 2011 by Institute of Industrial Engineers. Reprinted by permission.

Brand Integrity

It starts with internal focus.

TOM PETERS AND VALARIE WILLIS

After the layoffs and budget cuts, now what do you do? Are you living up to your brand promises, or are you falling short on customer experiences? How can you sustain your brand and the power of your values? When you focus only on the bottom line and ignore people, your brand suffers—as your customers lose sight of what you stand for, and they no longer trust what you can deliver.

What about Your Brand?

The news is full of stories about downsizing, job evaporations, and budgets being slashed to shreds. So, what happens to your brand? Does it survive? Or is it bruised and battered? As a leader, you are responsible for the integrity of your brand. You need to pull your head out of the financial data long enough to assess the current state of your brand and of your talent.

When you experience a strong economic shift, your brand can easily become diluted, especially if no one is asking, "What about the brand?"

In the hub of your organization is your talent, and your talent is your brand. It is the talent that brings your brand to life. If your people (talent) are no longer happy, if they are concerned about their own welfare, or they are hunkered down to stay out of sight, your brand may be on its last breath as well. And when the brand is struggling, the customer experience is compromised. Talent can become non-caring and cynical, and these attitudes permeate into how customers experience the brand.

Whenever you experience a strong shift, you must recalibrate and set the organization back on course. As a leader, you can best do this by taking these five steps: 1) revisit the ambition or goal of the organization and connect people to it; 2) spend time on the front lines talking to people and getting a handle on the issues; 3) re-state the brand promise and ensure that everyone knows how his or her job affects the promise; 4) look at the changes and assess the impact on the brand and the impact on the customer experience; and 5) design a course of action to put the brand back on track.

If your brand is bruised and battered, your customers may be headed to the competition—the exact opposite of your aims. In tough economic times, focus on keeping your current loyal customers and clients. Now is the time to re-think how to make the brand truly distinctive in the marketplace.

Excellence is achieved when the brand, the talent, and the customer experience are all in alignment.

Excellence Audit

To learn how your organization is doing, and if it needs recalibration, take our *Excellence Audit*. The 50 characteristics in the *Excellence Audit* describe the seven elements that interact in the *Future Shape of the Winner* model. As a mini-audit, answer these five questions:

- How can you keep focused on excellence in these tough economic times?
- Have you modified your ambitions in light of today's operating context?
- Are your team members fully committed to pursuing the agreed direction?
- Are your people totally focused on creating value for their customers?
- Is everyone on the payroll making their optimum contribution?

The *Excellence Audit* demystifies *excellence* for you by generating quantitative data on excellence. It identifies the most promising places to target improvement; reveals whether people agree about the priorities for improvement; exposes barriers to progress; helps you compile optimum improvement agendas that fit your context; generates joint agendas for management and professional teams determined to pursue excellence locally; helps you get your area focused and moving forward; and provides clarity and focus amid baffling complexity and conflicting demands.

Brand Inside's Effect on Brand

A cornerstone of our message about brand is that *your employees are also your customers*. We call this *Brand Inside*. We stirred up controversy over this notion by posting a PPT entitled *The Customer Comes Second*. The message is this: Since the customers in the firm serve the customers in the marketplace, put your employees first.

Matthew Kelly states: "Your employees are your first customers, and your most important customers."

Let me, Tom, get personal about all this. I *love* great customer or "end user" feedback! I am competitive to a fault in that regard and a slave to the market—after all these years.

At a higher level of marketplace engagement, I *love* a hearty business backlog, especially if it's based on repeat business—and I carefully measure it against the year-to-date of previous years. And I *love* a fee-per-event yield that exceeds last year, the year before, and so on. And yet, in an important way, I put the customer or end user second or third to employees.

It's simple and crystal clear to me: To give a high-impact, well-regarded, occasionally life-changing speech "to customers," I first, second, and third have to focus all my restless energy on "satisfying" *myself.* I must be physically, emotionally, and intellectually agitated and excited and desperate beyond measure to communicate, connect, compel, and grab people by the collar and say my piece about a few things, often contentious and not "crowd-pleasers," that, at the moment, are literally a matter of personal *life and death.*

I crave great customer feedback—but in no way, shape, or form am I trying to "satisfy my customer." I am, instead, trying to satisfy *me*—my own deep need to reach out and grab my customer and connect with my customer over ideas that consume me.

Hence, my "Job One" is purely *selfish and internally focused*—to be completely captivated by the subject matter at hand. That is Job One: *self-motivation.*

Warren Bennis, my primo mentor, said, "No leader sets out to be a leader *per se,* but rather to express him- or herself freely and fully. That is, leaders have no interest in proving themselves, but an abiding interest in expressing themselves."

So I'm back to my somewhat disingenuous message: To put the marketplace customer first, I must put the person serving the customer "more first." Excitement and self-stimulation first. Customer service second. That's my cause-and-effect scheme.

My message is that in order to *put the marketplace customer first, I must put the person serving the customer "more first."*

There is no great external focus unless a great internal focus is in place. I contend that finding and keeping and co-creating with great folks is not about clever tools to induce prospective "thems" to "shop with us," but a 99 percent internal effort to create such an exciting, spirited, entrepreneurial, diverse, humane "professional home" that people will line up by the gazillions (physically or electronically) to try and get a chance to come and live in our house and become what they'd never imagined they could become!

If you are serious about developing leaders, I suggest that you construct small leadership opportunities for people within days of their start on the job. *Everybody a leader* is entirely possible. So give you folks leadership responsibility from the outset, if not day #1 then within the first month. Hence, leadership development becomes a theme activity from stem to stern.

Boost Your Brand

Take this quick quiz (only 10 questions) for assessing your organization. Ask team members to rate themselves and the team against each question.

1. I know what my organization does to provide value to our customers.
2. I understand our products and services well enough to explain them.
3. I see how my job contributes to the value our organization creates.
4. I understand what a brand is.
5. I can tell the story of our brand.
6. I believe our brand is valuable.
7. We continually improve how we deliver products/services to customers.
8. I understand how my job brings our brand promise to life.
9. I can develop my talent while contributing to this organization's success.
10. I'm passionate about my work.

These questions investigate how connected you and your team feel to your *Purpose* and *Brand Promise.* The consolidated results can be used in a team discussion to identify the most promising targets for development.

Critical Thinking

1. In your perspective, what do the authors mean by "excellence is achieved when the brand, the talent, and the customer experience are all in alignment"?
2. Do you agree with the following statement: "Your employees are your first customers, and your most important customers"? Justify your answer.

TOM PETERS is CEO of The Tom Peters Company, and VALARIE WILLIS is a Keynote Speaker, Facilitator, and Consultant. Visit www.tompeters.com.

Brand Apathy Calls for New Methods

Turn Customer Preference from "No Brand" to "Some Brand"

DON E. SCHULTZ

Brand managers are accustomed to seeing challenging numbers. Faltering economies around the world guarantee that. Yet management plows ahead—setting double-digit internal sales objectives, increasing market share and expanding retail shelf space—doing all the things that mollify shareholders and prop up stock prices.

There's increasing evidence that organic sales improvement, line extensions and acquisitions just don't do it today.

Some brands have tried more focused sales efforts on specific segments, expanded their online and interactive promotional tools, and adjusted prices through coupons and other promotions. Still, major national brands are challenged as never before.

Unfortunately, the news I have to deliver in this column isn't very encouraging. However, if brand managers understand the new competitive landscape and refocus their efforts on differentiated initiatives while adjusting their competitive mindset, all is not lost. A rainbow and pot of gold may not be just around the corner, but there may be an improved opportunity for national brands.

Brand managers historically have focused on the general marketplace (i.e., sales volume compared with a year ago, incremental distribution increases and the like). While paying attention to competitive brands, they've often been willing to give up short-term share points to generate sales volume. The result has been more market knowledge than competitive knowledge. Share has been important, just not that important, primarily because they've been incented to grow volume.

That game is changing. Following four quarters of profit declines, Procter & Gamble (P&G) has declared "no more market share losses." Moving from valuing sales volume (in the case of P&G, the base was organic sales growth) to market share doesn't sound like a big deal—but it is. Brand managers cut their teeth driving short-term, quarter-to-quarter sales increases.

Building share is a different ball game, requiring a new set of tools and techniques. Finely tuned brand strategies designed to shift ongoing consumer preference and purchase from competitive brands to yours on an ongoing basis are the orders of the day—long-term, not short-term, returns.

Not so difficult, one would think—only it is. Getting consumers to change brands and maintain that change through ongoing preference is much more difficult than simply getting short-term sales volume from in-and-out, deal-prone consumers.

Most fast-moving consumer goods markets consist of (a) a limited number of brand loyal buyers, (b) a large group of brand switchers and (c) a growing bunch of unknowns or in-and-out buyers. That is, they only purchase when the price or promotion or communication is right. Promote to the switchers and sales often go up.

Observing this new emphasis on brand share growth, a Northwestern colleague and I decided to take a fresh look at brands, brand preferences and brand shares. That's where we found the scary numbers.

A rainbow and pot of gold may not be just around the corner, but there may be an improved opportunity for national brands.

While one could argue that preference doesn't really reflect actual purchases, a person must be favorably inclined if a brand purchase is to be made. In addition, brand preference is forward-looking, while actual measured brand shares are historical. Thus, we believe preference is a relevant measure for most brands and their managers.

Using monthly online consumer reported preference information from the BIGresearch Consumer Intentions and Actions (CIA) panel, the consumer reported brand preferences were calculated for two product categories: breakfast products and salty snacks. (The data used was for August 2010 with a base of 8,000-plus U.S. respondents. See www.bigresearch.com for details.) Consumers also reported their retail grocery/mass merchandiser preferences. This dual retailer/brand combination is important. From previous research, we've found consumer retail store loyalty impacts national brand sales. If the preferred retailer doesn't stock the national brand, sales don't occur.

From the CIA data, a modified "Net Promoter" calculation, similar to the one Fredrick Reichheld of Boston-based Bain & Company developed, was calculated. Using a scale of 1 to 10 (1 being detractors or non-recommenders and 10 being promoters or people who favorably recommend), a Net Promoter Score was calculated first for the retail food store.

The store chain with the top Net Promoter Score was Publix, followed by Aldi and then HEB. Far down the list were some of the retailing giants, such as Wal-Mart and Safeway.

While these retail calculations were interesting, the brand results were even more so. For this, the brand preference rating in two product categories (using the same 1-to-10 system) was determined. That was then combined with the retail chain preference.

In the breakfast product category, when the chain and brand were indexed, the top brand was Cheerios, followed by Special K. The only brand with an index greater than 100 was Kashi. This simply means that Kashi brand preference is stronger than the retail store preference.

In the salty snack category, Frito-Lay (no specific product name) was the top indexing brand, followed by Tostitos. None of the national brands indexed more than 100, signifying to us that the retail chain store choice was stronger than the brand choice.

The really scary numbers in both categories, however, were the large numbers of "no preference" consumers. In the breakfast product category, 30 percent reported no preference. In salty snacks, 36.7 percent had no preference. Store brands (private label) registered a 4.1 share in breakfast products and a 6.8 share in salty snacks.

These scary figures seem to indicate that the share battle going forward isn't going to be getting consumers to prefer General Mills products over Kellogg's. The challenge is getting them to prefer "some brand" over "no brand." The national brand battle isn't between the leading national brands—or even the national brands against store brands or private label. It's against brand apathy.

Preference apathy is a tough task for a brand manager. If consumers don't care about the brand or don't perceive that it is even worth their time to learn about the category or the brand, most traditional marketing tools and concepts go right out the window.

When 30 percent or more of your product category consumers say their top choice is no preference, major rethinking needs to be done. Maybe P&G is right in shifting its performance evaluation to share-of-peer brand market, but how relevant is that when there is such a preponderance of customers who just don't care?

Critical Thinking

1. In your perspective, has the competitive landscape changed for businesses operating today? If yes, then discuss these changes.

2. With a small group of peers from your class, develop a list of DOs and DON'Ts to help businesses compete more effectively and enhance their market shares.

DON E. SCHULTZ is professor emeritus-in-service of integrated marketing communications at The Medill School, Northwestern University. He also is president of the Agora Inc. consulting firm in Evanston, Ill. He may be reached at dschultz@northwestern.edu.

Branding's Big Guns

**Dreaming of the day your business becomes a household name?
Follow the examples of the 10 most trusted United States brands.**

PAULA ANDRUSS

There's no better way to dissect the how-tos of branding than to dig deep into the companies everybody knows and trusts. To accomplish this, *Entrepreneur* teamed with The Values Institute at DGWB, a Santa Ana, Calif-based think tank that focuses on brand relationships, on a consumer survey that explored the reasons some brands manage to stay on top.

What became clear: Though they may not have the biggest sales or market share in their categories, today's most trustworthy brands have created relationships with consumers through experiences that trigger a visceral response.

"We're seeing more of an emphasis on brands building emotional relationships with consumers because it's powerful and it works," says branding consultant Jim Stengel, former global marketing officer of Procter & Gamble and author of *Grow: How Ideals Power Growth and Profit at the World's Greatest Companies*. "When you do it, you have a much stronger affinity, a much stronger business, much stronger growth and much stronger results.

"When we looked at brands [at P&G] that had a very, very strong emotional benefit vs. our competition," Stengel adds, "our shares were much, much higher. And the margin of growth vs. our competitor was much higher than those that had just a functional superiority."

Here, a look at the tactics used by America's most trustworthy brands to connect with consumers—and ways you can put them to work for your business.

1. Get Personal: Amazon

The online retailer of, well, just about everything, ran away with the list, posting the highest scores not just in overall brand trust but in every individual trust value.

That's no surprise to Brad VanAuken, chief brand strategist for The Blake Project consultancy. He says Amazon's exceptional product accessibility, functionality and customer experience all converge to create a strong brand that consumers trust.

"With millions of products, 24/7 access, superior search and browse technology, user reviews and many other sources of in-depth product information, Amazon.com offers a superior purchase experience," VanAuken says.

He adds that the brand—with its low prices and free shipping on orders over a minimum total—is seen as offering value, while its one-click ordering and quick-shipping options help shoppers save time. Consumers also rely on Amazon to have all the products they're looking for, thanks to partnerships with other selling channels such as Partner Count merchandise.

While such a vast array of offerings could be perceived as impersonal, VanAuken says Amazon does an exemplary job of fostering relationships with consumers by helping them make decisions through recommendations of items based on past purchases, user reviews and ratings and suggested complementary purchases. Consumers also have many options for forging a personal bond with the brand, including user profiles, reviews and ratings, wish lists and Listmania lists for recommending favorite products.

2. Sell Happiness: Coca-Cola

Ice-cold Sunshine. The Pause That Refreshes. Life Tastes Good. Since its inception, the promise of the world's largest beverage-maker has been to delight consumers. "Everything they do is inspired by this idea of, How do we promote, develop and create happiness?" author Stengel says. Coca-Cola pushes this message across all points of customer contact, from Facebook to its custom vending machines, which allow consumers to concoct their favorite combinations of flavors. "They take the ideas of spontaneity and delight and infuse [them] into everything," Stengel says.

Putting aside the '80s branding debacle that was New Coke, Stengel adds that the company backs up its focus on happiness with a consistently strong corporate identity based on longevity and heritage. "They have a deep and healthy respect for their past and for the people who have gone before them," he says. "They never forget why they started and where they came from, which means a lot to consumers."

> **"[Coca-Cola has] a deep and healthy respect for their past and for the people who have gone before them. They never forget why they started and where they came from, which means a lot to consumers."**
>
> —*Jim Stengel*, Branding Consultant

That trust is evident among respondents to our survey, who did not give Coca-Cola a single negative remark.

3. Live Up to Your Promise: Fedex

With a straightforward passion for the task at hand, FedEx has created a strong corporate identity. Not surprisingly, the company received its strongest ratings in ability, specifically for being able to achieve what it promises and for the efficiency of its operations.

In addition to providing what is seen as a reliable service, the brand has engendered trust through initiatives such as its "We Understand" campaign, says Kari Blanchard, senior director of strategy in the New York office of Future-Brand. "They've elevated the brand by recognizing that it's not just about the logistics of moving packages and boxes," Blanchard says. "They appreciate that it's people's treasures, livelihoods and futures, and that the contents of those packages mean a lot to people."

To further deliver that message, FedEx engages with consumers through its personalized rewards program and by interacting on social media channels. "When you've already nailed attributes like trustworthiness and reliability—things that are essential to the business but don't exactly make you fall in love with a brand—that's where thinking of your customer as a person and not just a number becomes crucial," Blanchard says.

4. Keep It Cool (And Fun): Apple

What other company has the public and the press waiting breathlessly for each new product release? The bottom line is whatever that new Apple product is, consumers trust that it will be smart and sleek and that it will improve the way they communicate, work or spend their leisure time. What's more, they'll enjoy the experience of making the purchase.

While Apple has always been about creativity and expression, the brand has kicked up the emotional quotient by creating retail stores that foster a sense of collaboration and transparency between customers and sales staff. "They hire empathetic people, and they don't measure their sales associates on sales," Stengel says. He calls Apple's approach to its stores "the best retail endeavor in history. They really want people to come in and be inspired, build confidence and really feel better about themselves from the experience they had in the store."

Apple uses its retail outlets to show, not tell, consumers its brand philosophy, from the large tables, open spaces and walls of windows to its well-trained associates (Apple's biggest brand advocates), who are armed with handheld checkout scanners that enable shoppers to make purchases without having to stand in line.

> **Apple uses its retail outlets to show, not tell, consumers its brand philosophy.**

Some sour bits: The brand got lower than average scores for a sense of connection to Apple's corporate side, as well as for the perception that the company doesn't value customers' business or reward them for their loyalty. Those sentiments may simply be the result of Apple focusing on its core functions.

"Steve Jobs just thought about what was right for the brand and the consumer," Stengel says. "That focus is part of the reason they've done such a good job of creating new categories and products that continue to distance themselves from their competitors."

5. Design an Experience: Target

It's easy to forget that Target is a discount store. With its sleek, stylish ad campaigns and collaborations with high-end designers who create limited-edition merchandise that sends fashionistas into a frenzy, Target's public face often belies its mass-merchant status.

Further distinguishing it from its superstore brethren, Target consistently delivers an exceptional retail experience—from store design to merchandise selection to price and customer service.

"Target makes a real effort to provide an enjoyable shopper experience, but you still get quality merchandise at a good price," says branding consultant Rob Frankel. "As part of their brand persona, they make an effort to be warm and human, and that resonates with people and drives them to embrace it."

Thanks to easy-to-maneuver layouts and a consistent design, Target's retail outlets are easy and intuitive places to shop, giving customers confidence they will be able to find what they want, even on a vast selling floor. "It's not only more pleasant than their competitors; people actually enjoy being there," Frankel says.

Target customers also appreciate the brand's ability to design attractive yet affordable merchandise—most notably, an ever-changing array of trendy clothing and home accessories. "Target says [it's] going to give you a decent alternative that can hold up against more expensive fashion brands," Frankel says.

Customer service is friendly and consistent, as several survey respondents noted, from the way "cashiers look for people in line and direct them to a less crowded line," to the perceptions that "they, always have enough employees in the store at one time" and that "their customers are considered guests."

Frankel says businesses should recognize that providing a warm, human experience will foster the kind of trust that lets them command higher margins, drive traffic and enjoy better brand perception than their competitors. "No matter what you sell, if you don't give people a reason to go, they're not going to figure it out by themselves, because price alone just doesn't do it," he says.

6. Stay Consistent: Ford

In an era when the only thing that seems certain is change, Ford's consistent branding has established the company as a beacon of reliability.

The Blake Project's VanAuken points out that from its simple, one-syllable name to its iconic logo and emphasis on founding father Henry Ford, the company's brand identity stands the test of time.

"Everyone knows and admires the Ford story" he says. "Of the three Detroit-based automakers, Ford has the most consistent brand, product strategy and execution."

Ford also listens to and acts on its customers' needs, VanAuken adds, noting that CEO Alan Mulally is actively involved in interacting with customers through social media.

Those attributes forge a strong connection: The brand ranked high for stability and dependability, and respondents gave it the strongest average ratings for concern, specifically for behaving responsibly and caring about the well-being of employees and customers. Several respondents cited Ford's refusal to take government bailout money as evidence of the company's integrity.

"Once you have developed a unique and compelling value proposition for your brand, repeat it again and again."

—*Brad VanAuken*, The Blake Project

VanAuken emphasizes that consistency needs to reach all corners of any business. "Changing the logo, tag line and messaging on a frequent basis will ensure that nothing about your brand sticks in your intended customers' heads," he says. "Once you have developed a unique and compelling value proposition for your brand, repeat it again and again."

7. Can-Do Attitude: Nike

On its website, Nike declares its mission to "bring inspiration and innovation to every athlete in the world," adding, "If you have a body, you are an athlete."

It's that aspirational message and mainstream appeal that connects the athletic apparel company to consumers worldwide, according to branding consultant Kevin Lane Keller, professor of marketing at the Tuck School of Business at Dartmouth College. "Nike's always been extremely customer-focused, with a broad access point that makes the brand relevant to elite athletes as well as the everyday person," Keller says. "It's about self-empowerment and being your best, and the brand really does invite everyone to 'Just Do It.'"

Nike's constant product development, including introducing technologies such as Nike Air cushioning and Dri-Fit fabrics, is one of its biggest strengths, according to Keller, who says that consumers tend to equate innovation with expertise.

"When you're innovative, consumers are more trusting, because they think you really know what you're doing," he says. "Nike's first product was just the first step on this journey that's allowed them to completely transcend their roots as a quality running shoe to be everything athletic, all over the world, in all kinds of sports."

Keller says Nike gains trust points because celebrated co-founder Phil Knight is still involved with operations, a fact noted by one survey respondent who claimed to be "confident that [Knight's] company would always behave responsibly."

Notes Keller, "When the founder is still there, people respect the brand in a way that doesn't happen when the reins have been handed down over and over. Having his voice and persona still associated with the company keeps it closely connected to the consumer."

8. Forge Connections: Starbucks

After suffering a slump a few years back, the world's leading specialty coffee retailer has perked up its business and its brand by getting back to its original promise of bringing people together. "Starbucks has gotten much more in touch with the reason they're here, and that's to help create connections," author Stengel says.

From the free Wi-Fi to the in-store music to the large tables with room for groups and meetings, the company's stores are designed to help customers interact. "Go into any Starbucks, and business is happening and people are sharing, and the company understands that," Stengel says. "Everything in there is about connection, discovery inspiration and creation."

Startups would do well to note the company's innovative approach, which has enabled it to set the agenda in a category that has been around for centuries. "They carved out this dynamic niche with their brand and became very successful/and there's still nobody else like them," Stengel says.

The key, he says, is to thoroughly understand category norms and competitors' strategies, and determine how to direct those toward your advantage. "If you're an entrepreneur entering a category, maybe you can't set the agenda, but if you can redirect that agenda, that's how you win," he says. "If you're going to enter a category and be a 'me too,' don't bother."

9. Serve up the Quirky: Southwest Airlines

This low-cost carrier has consistently set its own route in the airline industry creating a distinct personality through everything from open passenger seating to flight attendants who sing the safety demonstrations.

"Southwest has always been a very independent brand that's quick to break the norms of the airline industry" says Tim Calkins, clinical professor of marketing at Northwestern University's Kellogg School of Management. "From the seating assignments to the fact that it doesn't list in many of the big online reservation systems, it has always prided itself on being very different."

Calkins says much of Southwest's brand success comes from the fact that although its operations and corporate culture are idiosyncratic, those differences support the company's central function.

Although its operations and corporate culture are idiosyncratic, those differences support Southwest's central function.

"Southwest has a fun, energetic corporate culture that's unique in the airline industry but at the core they are a very proficient operation that gets travelers from point to point in an efficient, affordable manner," he says.

While the airline received low ratings for not sharing information on decision-making, those protective measures may be among the reasons it continues to thrive. Several of the big carriers have tried to follow Southwest's model with low-cost subsidiaries (think Delta's Song and United's Ted), but none have been able to maintain them.

"You can see what [Southwest] does—they fly one kind of airplane, they don't charge for baggage and they have friendly employees—so you'd think someone could replicate that, but they can't," Calkins says. "The magic of Southwest is that even though the brand has many unique elements, all of the different pieces work together to serve its customers in a unique way."

10. Focus on the Customer: Nordstrom

When mythic stories circulate about your company's awesome customer service, you know you're doing something right. That's the hallmark of this upscale department store, which is rumored to have once graciously accepted the return of a set of tires, even though the store has never sold tires.

"Nordstrom is all about the power of delivering exceptional customer service that goes above and beyond a typical service experience," Northwestern's Calkins says.

Nordstrom scored strongly among respondents for concern for the customer, as well as for the quality of the products in its nearly 230 stores. Attentive service—which includes a liberal return policy, e-mailing digital photos of new items to regular customers and sending thank-you notes after purchases—frees the Seattle-based retailer from having to focus on competitive pricing, which helps keeps profit margins higher.

"They don't pretend to have the lowest prices, but they don't have to," Calkins says. "When people go there they know they may pay a little more, but the service is so good that it makes it worthwhile."

Respondents criticized Nordstrom for not providing consumers with much information about its corporate decision-making policies, but Calkins contends that when building a brand identity, it's OK for your proposition to focus on one principal element, as long as you do it right.

"What makes this brand tick is the service experience, not the approach," he says. "Nordstrom has never focused on its company or its people; all of that positive energy is directed at the customer and the retail experience, and it's the secret to their success."

Cincinnati-based Paula Andruss has written for *Usa Today, Woman's Day* and numerous marketing publications.

[About the survey] The Values Institute, which conducted the study, identified five values that influence trust in a brand: **ability** [company performance]; **concern** [care for consumers, employees and community]; **connection** [sharing consumers' values]; **consistency** [dependability of products/services]; and **sincerity** [openness and honesty].

A total of 1,220 United States consumers were asked to rate each trust value on a five-point scale, from "very unimportant" to "very important." Additionally, five consumer perceptions were measured for each value; these included statements such as "They respond to feedback, about their products and services," and "They value my business and reward me for the loyalty." Each respondent rated two randomly selected brands; those who felt strongly were also asked to provide individual comments. The result is the "Trust Index," a composite score that indicates the level of trust respondents had with each individual brand in relation to the other studied brands.

Critical Thinking

1. By reading over the examples of successful companies presented in this article, what are some tactics a brand can use to build an 'emotional relationship' with its customers?

2. With a small group of peers in your class, develop your own list of 3 brands that have successfully connected with their target markets. Justify your choices.

Playing Well Together

CO-BRANDING among franchises appeared to have lost its luster in recent years. But new concepts are emerging to prove that strategic combinations of businesses can cut costs and broaden the customer base.

JASON DALEY

If you flip through annual reports from Yum Brands, you'll notice an increasing frenzy starting in 1992 around "multibranding." A decade later, Yum—the holding company that owns and operates Taco Bell, KFC, Pizza Hut and, until last year, A&W and Long John Silver's—hailed the concept as "potentially the biggest sales and profit driver for the restaurant industry since the advent of the drive-thru window."

Co-branding (also known as piggyback franchising and dual or combination franchising) is, at face value, a brilliant idea: Take two franchise concepts, stick them in the same building and watch the revenue roll in. Not only does co-branding promise to save on operational costs like leasing, staff, kitchen equipment, building maintenance and advertising, it can even out customer flow, especially if one concept appeals to the breakfast and lunch crowd and the other is destined for dinner. But franchise systems have touted co-branding's biggest advantage as providing a one-stop option for groups of people with different cravings. Tommy and Sally want chicken fingers but Mom and Dad want pizza? Come on in to our pizza parlor/chicken shack, and everyone will be happy.

In 2002, co-branded outlets accounted for $2 billion in sales for Yum. But just a decade later, Yum is quietly stripping down many of its co-branded locations, and in its 2010 annual report, hidden in the black-and-white financial section many pages beyond the color photos of smiling kids and well-groomed employees, the company admits it has suspended co-branding as a long-term strategy.

The last few years have been littered with corporate co-branding marriages that bit the dust. Wendy's asked Tim Hortons to the dance, but they broke up in 2006. Dunkin' Donuts tried to make it work with Togo's sandwiches, and Arby's fooled around with everyone on the block for almost a decade before deciding to stay single.

While co-branding does have some benefits, especially in airports and other specialized locations, the "something for everyone" model has not proved its worth. Yum found that adding A&W and Long John Silver's to other concepts did not add to unit revenue—co-branding those concepts just created headaches and increased costs. Co-branding can increase operational complexity, which can lead to substandard products and poor customer service. More important, the concepts need to mesh on the most basic level, drawing from the same customer base and making intuitive sense: Franchises have found that skeptical consumers will pass up a baffling lobster-and-hot-wings merger for a single brand they understand—every time.

Many well-established brands have difficulty bending their strict operations rules to accommodate a partner, and they may run the risk of diluting their image if they sticker over their core concept with less-trusted brands. For example, Yum found that the limited menus at A&W and Long John Silver's were perceived as old-fashioned and boring, especially when paired with those at Taco Bell and KFC. Adding those smaller brands to an existing unit achieved little except to pull the focus from the more popular brand.

While the great co-branding experiment has more or less fizzled, the idea is not completely dead. Co-branding can be successful if it's done strategically between complementary brands, like salads and smoothies or pizza and another savory impulse snack. Many companies that have thought through their co-branding are finding the economies of scale the strategy produces are worth it.

"There are definitely some clear challenges in co-branding," says Steve Beagelman, president of SMB Franchise Advisors, who has worked with co-branded franchises over the last 25 years. "But if you can make it work, there are a lot of synergies and benefits, especially in making sure franchisees can make money. And that's ultimately what small business is about, especially in franchising. Let's say a franchisee has found a great location, but the costs are just too high. Co-branding gives you a real good opportunity to make that location work."

Selective Salons Bonnie

Vas Maniatis built his Seva salon chain almost exclusively through co-branding, though his model is a bit different than putting two food concepts together. Instead, his small salons, which focus primarily on eyebrow threading, lash extensions and nails, are found exclusively in Walmart stores. While Seva is completely independent from Walmart, the salon chain's convenience, value pricing and speed make it appealing to the mass merchant's shoppers, according to Maniatis.

"Our customer is the Walmart customer, so co-branding to me has been huge," he says. "We're all about enhancing the one-stop shopping experience [that] Sam Walton built." Maniatis has opened 25 units in eight states since 2010 and hopes to double growth in 2012.

Seva didn't start out as a co-branded franchise. In fact, it didn't start out as "Seva" at all. For the first several years, the Chicago-based salon was called Simply Eyebrows and performed only eyebrow threading—a quick, less-painful alternative to waxing. Most threading takes place in malls at open-air kiosks; Maniatis hoped to improve the experience by offering a private session in a spa atmosphere. He was also focused on convenience and value, so a friend suggested he talk to Walmart about opening in a new development in Indianapolis.

A skeptical Walmart initially gave Maniatis the brushoff, but unbeknownst to him, a regional manager had been pushing for the concept, and when another tenant dropped out a year later, the space was offered for the salon. That first store was a hit, and in late 2009, two Walmart executives flew to Chicago to talk to Maniatis about a partnership.

"They basically said, 'Look, we love your concept,'" he recalls. But, he says, the execs thought it needed to be "bigger" and suggested adding other salon services and positioning the company as a Walmart exclusive.

Maniatis agreed, found a more appealing name and hasn't looked back. Co-branding with Walmart has not only given Seva huge traffic flow, it has freed up resources to develop other aspects of the business. "Our franchisees start with built-in traffic of 30,000 to 50,000 customers per week, with no marketing costs. That's given us an opportunity to do things that are state of the art in customer engagement," Maniatis says. "We've built an iPad-based paperless system . . . We have remote monitoring capabilities and can see our stores in real time and see what type of customer transactions work."

The only drawback to the co-branding relationship is that Seva can grow only as quickly as Walmart does, and the salon doesn't have a guaranteed spot in every development; it has to be chosen from a shortlist of approved tenants that include McDonald's, Subway and other elite franchises.

"It's been hard for us to open in as many spaces as we'd like," Maniatis admits. But, he adds, partnering with Walmart, takes the guesswork out of site selection. "The marketing's done by Walmart. The due diligence on where to locate is done by Walmart. We just need to focus on our core, which is our service, and engaging both the active and potential customer."

Sweet Spot Jenna

Sevas partnership is a dream scenario for co-branding. Other companies have more complex relationships, though they can be just as rewarding. Ted Milburn, vice president of franchise development for Nestle Tollhouse Cafe, which sells baked goods, coffee and frozen yogurt, has worked at other concepts that have co-branded—some successfully and others not. When he was approached with an opportunity to team Tollhouse with Haagen-Dazs, he thought the synergy would be perfect, evening out year-round customer flow and complementing both products. In 2011, the companies began opening co-branded locations across the country.

Not only do the co-branded stores smooth out the annual sales calendar, they appeal to the public with their synergistic offerings. "We eliminate the deal-breaker," Milburn says. "We cover the gamut, from cookies to frozen coffee beverages to smoothies to ice cream creations. Whatever people want, we can cover it. It would

be different if we were co-branded with a pizza concept. People come in to a pizza place for pizza; we would be just an afterthought."

Dan Ogiba, director of development for Haagen-Dazs, agrees. "We're a complete dessert cafe," he says. "We looked at this as an opportunity to grow and for our franchisees to increase their revenues. We think serving larger groups outweighs any competition between our sweet products."

Focus Brands, which owns Schlotzsky's deli, Cinnabon and Carvel Ice Cream, thinks putting sweet treats together with sandwiches is a winning concept. Schlotzsky's and Cinnabon both bake their products daily; this appeals to franchisees, whose employees already have experience running ovens, according to Schlotzsky's president Kelly Roddy. Adding a Carvel element for a tri-branded store is a little more expensive, but Roddy thinks it complements the other offerings nicely.

"One of our concerns was that selling Cinnabon products would cannibalize purchases from our core Schlotzsky's menu," he says. "We found it didn't, and that it actually brought additional customers into stores and grew revenues with no additional labor costs, no rent, no managers or any of the things that come up with a separate unit."

Already, 165 Schlotzsky's have retrofitted Cinnabon ovens into their stores; Roddy projects that by year's end, more than 200 of the brand's 350 units will be selling cinnamon rolls. In 2011, 90 percent of new-store sales were tri-branded locations; in 2012, plans are to include Cinnabon and Carvel elements in all new Schlotzsky's units. So far, the co-branded stores are drawing in more customers in the 18 to 25 demographic, and more women.

"It has really worked out to be a home run for franchisees," Roddy says. He insists the co-branding isn't about shoe-horning Focus Brands concepts together willy-nilly, pointing out that significant testing and research indicated that the concepts would make a good partnership. "I haven't seen many co-branded concepts recently that work well and make sense as these do," he says.

Co-branding is not nearly as prevalent or hyped as it was a decade ago, but impressive numbers of franchises are giving it another shot. Hot dog chain Nathan's Famous is committed to growing almost exclusively through co-branding. Cold Stone Creamery has partnerships with Tim Hortons and the Rocky Mountain Chocolate Factory; Tasti D-Lite, which purchased Planet Smoothie, plans to give co-branding a test-drive.

While it's doubtful that co-branding will prove as revolutionary as the drivethru window, it may turn out to be a profitable strategy after all. "There is definitely a part of co-branding that really makes a lot of sense," SMB's Beagelman says. "It can help a franchisor grow quicker. It can help make sure franchisees make money. And for smaller franchisors, you can learn how more successful chains do things. It's not for every brand, but if you're flexible and are willing to listen, it can work."

Critical Thinking

1. In your opinion, what are the potential advantages of co-branding for organizations and their customers?

2. With a small group of peers in your class, develop your own list of successful franchise co-branding. Justify your choices.

Competing against Free

Free offerings are rapidly spreading beyond online markets to the physical world. Here's how incumbents can fight back.

DAVID J. BRYCE, JEFFREY H. DYER, AND NILE W. HATCH

A new competitor enters your market and offers a product very similar to yours but with one key difference: It's free. Do you ignore it, hoping that your customers won't defect or the free product won't last? Or do you rapidly introduce a free product of your own in an attempt to quash the threat? These are questions faced by an increasing number of companies—and not just in the digital realm. The "free" business models popularized by companies such as Google, Adobe, and Mozilla are spreading to markets in the physical world, from pharmaceuticals to airlines to automobiles.

How should established companies respond? Clearly, managers are having difficulty figuring this out. For the past five years, we have been studying how incumbents have dealt with competitors employing free business models in a variety of product markets. (See the sidebar "About the Research.") We have found no examples of companies in the non-digital realm that have prevailed against rivals with free offerings. In fact, in two-thirds of the battles that have progressed far enough to be judged, incumbents (both digital and physical) made the wrong choice. In a handful of instances, companies that should not have taken action did so immediately by introducing their own free offering—hurting their revenues and profitability. They should have either waited and allowed the attacker to self-destruct or recognized that the two could peacefully coexist.

More commonly, companies that should have taken action didn't do so quickly enough or at all. Surprisingly, these included incumbents that had identified a genuine threat from a new entrant and had all the weapons they needed to win a head-to-head battle: an established customer base, superior product features, a strong reputation, and abundant financial resources.

Even companies with formidable assets are slow to fend off free-product competitors. The reason: the ubiquity of the profit-center structure and mind-set.

Why didn't these companies use their formidable assets to fend off free-product competitors? The answer is so obvious that you've probably guessed it: Managers were reluctant to abandon an existing business model that was generating healthy revenues and profits. But if the answer is obvious, why did managers make this mistake? The reason is the ubiquity of the profit-center structure and mind-set. Drawing from our research on free offerings in online and physical markets, we explore in this article how to assess whether the introduction of a free product or service in your market is a threat and how to overcome the profit-center challenge.

Assessing the Threat

The seriousness of the threat posed by a new entrant hinges on three factors: the entrant's ability to cover its costs quickly enough, the rate at which the number of users of the free offering is growing, and the speed with which your paying customers are defecting.

Some new competitors self-destruct because they can't convert nonpaying customers into paying ones fast enough to cover costs or because they can't find a third party that will pay for access to their users. So it's crucial to determine if the competitor's free offering is generating revenue in some way. Of course, some companies may have enough funding to wait a year or more before they need to monetize their user base. (For example, Skype offered its free phone service for a year before it introduced SkypeOut, a paid service for calling landlines from a computer.) But this scenario can actually benefit an incumbent by giving it time to assess the potential of the model and decide whether to launch its own free product.

We learned that an entrant will usually find a way to turn users into revenue-generating customers if its user base is growing rapidly or if the incumbent's paying customers are defecting to the free offering at a high rate. What rates signal danger? Our examination of the dynamics in a number of markets suggests that if the free offering's user base is growing by 40 percent or more a year (meaning that it will at least double every two years) or your customer defection rate is 5 percent or

Idea in Brief

Business models that involve offering a product or service for free and making money in other ways are spreading beyond the digital realm. But managers of threatened companies are having difficulty figuring out how to respond: An ongoing study has found that some companies respond too quickly but most don't do so quickly enough—even when they have sufficient resources.

To assess the threat, incumbents should consider the entrant's ability to cover its costs quickly enough, the rate at which the number of users of the free offering is growing, and the speed with which paying customers are defecting.

A bigger challenge is overcoming the ubiquitous profit-center structure, which discourages managers from giving away offerings. The remedy is to move P&L responsibility to a senior management group and to assign revenue stream and cost management oversight to separate lower-level groups.

more a year (meaning that you stand to lose at least 25 percent of your customers within five years), serious trouble may be looming. As the matrix "How Big a Threat Is 'Free' Competition?" shows, assessing those rates (or reasonable estimates of them) helps a company determine the level of threat from the free product and respond accordingly.

Choosing Whether and When to Respond

When both rates mentioned above are high, the entrant represents a *business model* threat. Most established companies must not only respond with a free offering but also radically change their business model to survive. And they need to do so pretty quickly—within two or three years. Many newspapers competing against online rivals that offer free classified advertising or editorial content are in this quadrant. They will continue to deteriorate sharply without a fundamental rethinking of their business model.

Fortunately for incumbents, most threats wind up in one of the other quadrants, which means there may be more time to respond. When the entrant's users are multiplying rapidly but the established firm's customers are defecting slowly, the entrant represents a *delayed* threat. This means the free product or service is attracting either customers from other established competitors or brand-new users. In such cases, your offering can coexist with the free one for at least a few years—especially if yours is targeting premium segments. This is the situation that Microsoft finds itself in with its Office software: Because of the high switching costs, most current enterprise users aren't defecting, but new users—college students, small businesses, and educational institutions—are increasingly using Google Docs and Oracle's Open Office, both of which are free. (See the sidebar "Why Microsoft Should Take Its 'Free' Competition More Seriously.")

The trick for incumbents facing delayed threats is figuring out exactly when to respond with either a free version of the existing offering or a new free product that appeals to new users. Responding sooner rather than later allows an incumbent to beat back the entrant and probably won't significantly hurt existing sales (because established customers are switching slowly). As soon as the entrant's users are in the millions, however, the incumbent must respond—as Intuit did when it acquired upstart Mint.com for $170 million in 2009, eliminating a threat to its Quicken personal finance software and gaining a free online product. (Mint.com had attracted more than 2 million users in just three years.)

When the defection rate among your paying customers is high and the growth rate of the entrant's users is low, the threat is obviously *immediate* because your revenues are rapidly eroding. Even though the free offering has not yet attracted a large following, it's a problem for you and demands a prompt response. It also suggests that you are overserving your customers and thereby inviting disruption. You must quickly figure out a way to launch a free offering.

Finally, when both rates are low, the threat is *minor*. In these cases, the incumbent should continue to monitor the situation.

Offer a Better Free

If you've established that free offerings are a threat to your business and have considered the timing of your response, the next step is to figure out *how* to respond. Most incumbents can successfully counterattack by unleashing their arsenal of weapons, which typically includes a large base of users or customers who have made investments in learning how to use the product, advanced technical know-how, substantial brand equity, significant financial resources, knowledge of the market, and access to important distribution and marketing channels. Incumbents can use those assets to introduce a better free product and to employ some tried-and-true sales and pricing strategies to generate revenues and profits: up-selling, cross-selling, selling access to customers, and bundling the free product with paid offerings. (See the sidebar "Four Tried-and-True Strategies.")

Yet, as we mentioned above, incumbents often fail to counterattack. A widely known case in point is the reluctance of almost all major newspapers in the United States to embrace a free business model when Craigslist attacked their profitable classified-ads business. According to our research, Salt Lake City is the only top 50 U.S. metropolitan market for classified ads that is not dominated by Craigslist. The reason? Deseret Media (which includes the *Deseret News,* KSL TV, and KSL NewsRadio) responded quickly to the business model threat by launching its own free classifieds site and making other significant changes. The site, ksl.com, is better developed and easier to navigate than Craigslist, and it leveraged the established KSL brand to attract classified ads.

Deseret Media quickly benefited from network effects: More buyers went to ksl.com than to Craigslist because more sellers were posting there. The site generates revenue by charging

How Big a Threat Is "Free" Competition?

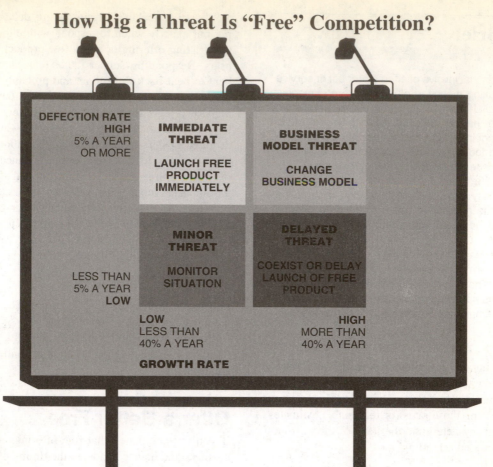

Companies That Prevailed

Personal finance software company **Intuit** responded to the threat from free rival Mint.com by purchasing the company. Mint.com, which makes money by selling access to its user base, lets Intuit maintain a free offering separate from its popular Quicken product.

Yahoo, the leading provider of free e-mail, responded to Google's entry by matching, and then exceeding, Gmail's free storage offer.

Companies That Ignored the Threat

The major airlines in Europe have been slow to respond to **Ryanair,** which offers free or deeply discounted tickets and charges for other services. Ryanair has made impressive gains in Europe; its share now exceeds that of Air France.

Satellite radio company **SiriusXM,** which offers subscription packages for its more than 180 channels, has done nothing to stem the loss of share to Pandora, which provides free radio over the internet and generates revenue by charging for ad-free service and selling access to its user base to third parties.

advertisers that want to post regular ads as well as classified sellers who want preferred positions. The site's profits now exceed those of the traditional businesses, including the newspaper.

Meanwhile, Deseret Media has changed the newspaper's business model by cutting nearly half its staff and crowdsourcing some of its content. In 2010, the paper increased its print and online audience by 15 percent, the second-highest growth rate in the industry. Overall, Deseret Media is thriving.

Yahoo is another example of an incumbent that prevailed by introducing a better free product. In 2004, Google launched its free Gmail service, which provided 10 times more storage than Yahoo, the leading provider of free e-mail at the time. As a new

entrant, Google could afford to offer significantly more storage because it had relatively few users. A Google executive told us, "We don't do something unless it is an order of magnitude better—maybe five to 10 times better—than what others are offering, particularly if we have to get users to switch from another free product to ours."

Google's entry created a dilemma for Yahoo, which generated some revenue from up-selling (persuading users to pay for more storage or other add-ons) but much more from advertisers

Four Tried-and-True Strategies

1. Up-Sell

Introduce a free basic offering to gain widespread use and then charge for a premium version.

Requirements

- A free product that appeals to a very large user base so that even a low conversion rate of users to paying customers will generate substantial revenues **or**
- A high percentage of users willing to pay for the premium version

Examples

Virtually every iPhone app uses this strategy. One tactic is to offer a free version of the product to consumers and a premium version to the business market, as Adobe does with its Reader software.

Skype, which offers free computer-to-computer calls and charges for add-ons, succeeds with up-selling because it has more than 400 million users, many of whom become paying customers. Flickr, the free photo-sharing site, has a much smaller user base and a low conversion rate. That explains why eBay paid $2.6 billion for Skype, and Yahoo paid less than $30 million for Flickr.

2. Cross-Sell

Sell other products that are not directly tied to the free product.

Requirements

- A broad product line—preferably one that complements the free product—**or**
- The ability through partnerships to sell a broad line of products to users of the free product

Examples

Ryanair offers roughly 25 percent of its airline seats free but cross-sells a variety of add-on services, such as seat reservations and priority boarding. Once on the plane, the customer is sold food, scratch-card games, perfume, digital cameras, MP3 players, and other products. (Ryanair employs a second strategy: charging third parties for in-flight advertisements.) Specialty pharmaceuticals company Galderma rebates out-of-pocket costs for Epiduo, a prescription acne gel, and cross-sells other skin care products.

3. Charge Third Parties

Provide a free product to users and then charge a third party for access to them.

Requirements

- A free offering that attracts either many users who can be segmented for advertisers or a targeted group that makes up a customer segment **and**
- Third parties willing to pay to reach these users

Examples

Google, which charges companies to advertise to its millions of users, is the poster child for this strategy. Another example is Finnish telecommunications company Blyk, which offers 200 free cell-phone minutes a month to 16-to-24-year-olds who fill out a survey and agree to receive ads. Blyk then sells access to and information about them. Blyk was recently acquired by Orange, the largest brand of France Telecom.

Generating users does not guarantee success. Xmarks offered web-browser add-on tools that attracted more than 2 million users—and plenty of venture capital. But the company recently shut down because it couldn't deliver a clear segment to advertisers.

4. Bundle

Offer a free product or service with a paid offering.

Requirements

- Products or services that can be bundled with the free offering **or**
- A free product that needs regular maintenance or a complementary offering

Examples

Here the "free" effect is largely psychological—the customer must buy the bundle to get the free product. Think of Hewlett-Packard, which often gives away a printer with the purchase of a computer.

Better Place plans to lease electric cars in Israel by bundling a free lease with a service contract. Customers would pay to swap out their battery packs.

Banks are increasingly bundling free services, such as accounts and stock trades, with paid services, such as investment accounts that require minimum balances. But the bundled product doesn't have to be related to the free one. Banks also give away iPods, iPads, and other products to customers opening accounts.

(its real customers). To match Google's offer, Yahoo would have had to buy warehouses of servers to provide storage for its 125 million e-mail users—an investment that would have generated no additional revenues.

Yahoo decided to respond in a way that sent a message to Google and to its own e-mail users and advertisers: It immediately announced that it would match Google's offer of one gigabyte of free storage. A couple of years later, it began to offer unlimited storage. Those moves left Yahoo users with no reason to switch to Google—and left Google with few options for offering a better free product. Although the increased costs hurt Yahoo's profits in the short term, the company's share of the e-mail market continues to be several times larger than Google's. But Google has not given up: Gmail now serves as a platform for the company's other free products, such as Google Docs and Calendar. In the long run, this could make Gmail the better free product.

The most important lesson from these cases? If your user base is vital to your revenue stream, you must quickly offer a free product that is comparable or superior to the new competitor's. If you can, you should try to crush that competitor or at least prevent it from becoming powerful enough to mount a serious challenge.

Rethink Profit Centers

Two obstacles prevent managers at established companies from making the leap to free strategies. The first is the deeply rooted belief that products must generate a respectable level of revenues and profits on their own. The second is the profit-center structure and the accounting system it employs, which both reflect and reinforce this mind-set.

In stable competitive environments, profit centers are a godsend: They push P&L accountability down, usually to the product level; they place revenue and cost streams in the hands of an individual, clearly identifying where the buck stops; and they provide a career ladder for those hoping to oversee units with larger budgets. But profit centers have a dark side: They make it impossible for an organization to consider a product's revenues and costs separately—a perspective that's essential for conceiving and implementing a free-product strategy.

To fix this problem, profit responsibility must be pushed up to a management group that oversees revenue and cost streams from a much wider variety of sources than traditional profit centers do. Clearly, a company that relies primarily on free-product strategies, such as Google, will place this responsibility much higher in the organization than one that uses free offerings as a small part of a more comprehensive strategy.

In addition to moving profit responsibility higher, companies with free business models generally place responsibility for revenue streams and cost management at lower levels, and in separate hands. *Revenue managers* in these companies pursue all possible ways to increase revenues—except product price. Clearly, the job requires creativity, but revenue is typically generated in the four ways mentioned up-selling, cross-selling, selling access to users, and bundling.

A separate set of *product development managers* is responsible for overseeing costs and building in product features that will expand the user base as rapidly as possible. On the basis of conversations with current executives at Google, we estimate that only the CEO and three or four senior vice presidents have P&L responsibility there.

Clearly, tensions can arise between the revenue group and the product development group, and it pays to spell out how they will be resolved. For example, Google's product development group can nix revenue models it believes would damage the user experience. When the two groups can't resolve disagreements, the senior managers with P&L responsibility—and sometimes even the CEO—arbitrate.

Why Microsoft Should Take Its "Free" Competition More Seriously

For the past four years, Microsoft's Office software has been under attack from free alternatives: Google Docs and Oracle's Open Office. Although Microsoft finally responded in 2010 with Microsoft Live, a free "cloud" version of Office, it waited too long and was not forceful enough to contain what could become a serious threat.

Microsoft's reluctance to embrace a free-product strategy is not surprising. Its office applications business has long enjoyed a near monopoly and has been highly profitable. And except for price-sensitive users such as college students and public entities, its customers have not flocked to the free products. Indeed, concerns about file incompatibility, the lack of functions in competing products, and the need to teach employees how to use new applications have kept the vast majority of Microsoft's target corporate customers in the fold.

But in our view, Microsoft has erred in not taking the defection among price-sensitive customers more seriously. Our survey of college students suggests that nearly 20 percent now exclusively use free alternatives, up from about 4 percent five years ago. According to a competitor, the number of students in the United States using Google Apps has increased from 7 million to 10 million in the past two years, and about 3 million small-business users and some large institutions (including Brown, the California State University system, Gonzaga, the University of Minnesota, the University of Virginia, Vanderbilt, Villanova, and William & Mary) have adopted it as well. This is a big problem for Microsoft: Open Office and Google Docs will continue to improve, becoming more attractive to younger and newer users as well as price-sensitive institutions—especially those overserved by the function-laden Office suite.

So far, Microsoft Live doesn't seem to be effective in countering the free offerings of its competitors. There are several possible reasons. One is that Microsoft, unlike Open Office, doesn't offer a version that can be downloaded to and operated from an individual computer. Another is that Microsoft has not promoted its free product aggressively enough, and, as a result, it is not as well-known as Google Docs.

Judging from Microsoft's half-hearted response to date, the company doesn't want customers switching to its free product. This is a mistake. By sacrificing a portion of revenues from price-sensitive or overserved customers, Microsoft could prevent free-product competitors from expanding their foothold and give itself a better shot at retaining its most valuable customers: the business and power home users who are loyal today but could ultimately defect.

Another culprit that undermines many companies' ability to offer free products is the cost accounting system, which is excellent for averaging costs across large numbers of products and then allocating overhead but not for identifying the *actual* cost of the last product or service sold. The distinction between average cost (what some call variable cost or total cost) and actual cost (what some call marginal cost) is important because the latter is almost always lower than the former, often dramatically so. Think of what it costs an airline to fly an empty seat on an otherwise full or mostly full airplane: essentially nothing. This principle applies in nearly every industry. Once an operation is up and running and costs are largely incurred, generating additional products or services adds very little to total costs. Company leaders can use this notion to their advantage as they consider alternative pricing approaches, such as free offerings. By stepping back from the cost accounting system, they may find flexibility they didn't realize they had.

An example from the pharmaceutical industry illustrates how the profit-center structure and mind-set and the cost accounting system make it difficult for established companies to react when rivals offer free products or services. In 2008, specialty pharmaceuticals manufacturer Galderma (a joint venture of Nestlé and L'Oréal) launched Epiduo, a prescription acne lotion, in the United States. Because Benzac, its other acne product, was about to lose U.S. patent protection, Galderma felt tremendous pressure to build Epiduo's U.S. market share as quickly as possible. But in Europe, the product had met stiff competition from Duac, an acne gel made by GlaxoSmithKline (GSK). Expecting more of the same in the United States, Galderma decided to implement a program to reimburse a patient's out-of-pocket costs for the product for as long as a year. In exchange for rebate coupons, customers gave the company their e-mail addresses. Galderma then sent them skin care tips, acne information, and special offers for its non-prescription products, such as cleansing bars.

Heavily rebating new drugs in the early days to build market share is a common strategy in the pharmaceutical industry. The hope is that once the company has won a substantial share, health insurance companies will agree to cover the drug, allowing the company to offset its development costs and make a profit before its patents expire.

But incumbents selling established drugs are generally unwilling to take risks with pricing. Their cost accounting systems and P&L structures make them feel that they must cover their substantial product costs—which explains why GSK and other incumbents seemed paralyzed when Galderma launched the rebate program for Epiduo. One GSK executive told us, "We can't afford to match them, and we can scarcely afford to discount. So we're losing share."

In reality, the marginal cost—the material and labor—of a tube of lotion or gel is small (from a few pennies to a few dollars). Therefore, in the short run incumbents would have lost almost nothing if they had deeply discounted their products or matched Galderma's rebate. Moreover, like Galderma,

About the Research

For five years, we have been studying companies that face competition from rivals offering free products and services. The 34 incumbents we've been following are in 26 product markets representing the digital and physical realms as well as the intersection of the two. The markets include airlines, automobiles, classified advertising, dermatology pharmaceuticals, internet services, music, office applications, operating systems, personal finance software, radio, and telecommunications. Twenty-four of the battles between incumbents and free-product rivals have progressed far enough for us to judge the incumbents' actions. In two-thirds of those cases, the incumbents made the wrong choice: They introduced their own free offering too quickly, responded too slowly, or did nothing at all.

they could have cross-sold products and, by breaking down the walls around P&L centers, used profits from other highly successful products to subsidize short-term losses in dermatology. This would have forced Galderma into the untenable position of giving away its product without growing share. The battle is ongoing, but so far Galderma's strategy has allowed it to gain customers and profitably cross-sell products.

Because free-product strategies entail experimentation and, admittedly, some risk taking, embracing them may require a cultural shift. Strong executive leadership will be needed to build the case for mounting a competitive response, revamping organizational structures, and questioning cost accounting information. When a free offering is a threat, few strategies are available besides meeting free with free. Incumbents that spend too much time looking for some other killer strategy often only defer the inevitable. By taking decisive action as soon as the threat is clear, incumbents can survive and thrive.

Critical Thinking

1. Discuss how consumer defection rate and growth rate impact the seriousness of the threat posed by a new market entrant.

2. In your opinion, what do the authors mean by a "better free"? Do you agree with their recommended strategies?

DAVID J. BRYCE (dbryce@byu.edu) is an associate professor of strategy, JEFFREY H. DYER (jdyer@byu.edu) is the Horace Beesley Professor of Strategy, and NILE W. HATCH (nile@byu.edu) is an associate professor of entrepreneurship at Brigham Young University's Marriott School of Management. Dyer is also an adjunct professor at the University of Pennsylvania's Wharton School.

From *Harvard Business Review*, June 2011, pp. 104–111. Copyright © 2011 by Harvard Business School Publishing. Reprinted by permission.

Ditch the Discounts

Smart companies used adaptive pricing to ride out the recession. Now it's time to reprice for recovery.

RAFI MOHAMMED

The first shot in what historians may someday commemorate as the Great Pizza War was fired by Domino's in late 2009. The chain had been charging about $9 for a medium two-topping pizza, but to boost sales it began offering recession-weary consumers two of its two-topping pies for $5.99 each. Several weeks later Papa John's and Pizza Hut fired back, offering large three-topping pizzas for just $10—at least a third less than the usual price. Soon they improved the deal, so that customers could buy a large pizza with unlimited toppings for $10. Sure enough, sales at all three chains rose—and even now many chains are offering discounted pizzas.

On the surface, this type of price-cutting makes sense: How else to bolster sales in a time of weak demand? But even though the recession has been officially over for 18 months, its effects are likely to linger; GDP has been growing at a sluggish pace. In this environment, few companies have much pricing power—and in many industries, discounts will remain the norm.

That's unfortunate, because across-the-board price cuts unnecessarily reduce profits. Consider a company that held the line on prices during the recession and saw a 20 percent drop in sales. That means it made 80 percent of its usual sales, even at full price—so why give discounts to all those customers? More important, deep discounts devalue a product or service, limiting companies' ability to raise prices as the economy improves. If people get used to paying $10 for a large pizza with lots of toppings, it's hard to restore a price of, say, $16.99 when demand picks back up.

Some companies have avoided this trap by using adaptive pricing, which capitalizes on the fact that different customers have different needs and therefore place different values on a given product or service. As we wait for the economy to return to full speed, managers have a good opportunity to learn from companies that weathered the recession by employing adaptive-pricing strategies—and to develop plans that could help their own businesses regain lost ground in the recovery.

The key to adaptive pricing is realizing that price, like color or style, is simply one of a product's attributes. And companies routinely vary colors and styles to appeal to different kinds of customers. They sell through different channels (online, direct sales, brick-and-mortar stores) and sometimes charge vastly different prices based on the channel. (A box of cereal typically costs much more in a convenience store than it does in a big-box store.) By using adaptive pricing, companies can adjust a product's attributes to better appeal to customers' sense of value without necessarily dropping the price.

The simplest adaptive-pricing method is called "versioning"—offering "good," "better," and "best" varieties of the same product. A lower-priced version (poorer quality, smaller quantity, fewer features) can be a powerful magnet for price-sensitive customers. The method worked well for consumer product companies during the recession and should be considered by all companies, especially those in markets with weak demand. P&G has had great success with it. In 2005 the company created "Basic" lines of Charmin toilet tissue and Bounty paper towels, aimed at low- and middle-income consumers who wanted quality but didn't want to pay premium prices. The Basic products utilized one-ply sheets and cost 15 percent to 25 percent less than the regular ones. A.G. Lafley, P&G's former CEO, noted that brands that had used versioning outperformed the company's other products during the recession. (The strategy has its downsides, though; see "Should You Launch a Fighter Brand?" HBR October 2009.)

Hyundai let buyers who lost their jobs return their vehicles. It thus avoided further price cuts—and in nine months, fewer than 50 vehicles were returned.

Let's look at two very different approaches to recession pricing in the fast food industry. Subway won acclaim and saw sales jump by 17 percent in 2008, when it dropped the price of its foot-long sandwiches to $5—thus taking a traditional tack. But customers have become conditioned to paying that amount, and the chain is continuing to offer some foot-long sandwiches at that low-margin price. In contrast, Quiznos created entirely

How to Price

IN A RECESSION

Introduce Lower-Priced Versions

To defend the price of existing offerings while attracting budget shoppers, create bargain versions. For its 2011 lineup, Harley-Davidson is introducing the SuperLow. The aim: to allow "even the most budget conscious rider to own a Harley-Davidson."

Use Promotions to Avoid Price Drops

Instead of reducing nightly rates, Disney resorts offered promotions such as "Buy 4 Nights, Get 3 Free." This type of deal lowers the effective cost without changing the advertised nightly rate—a form of discounting that avoids devaluing the brand in consumers' minds.

Adapt Products to Maintain Affordability

Companies in many categories, including peanut butter, juice, cereal, and soap, faced higher costs and so decreased product size or volume. This strategy increases the price per unit but maintains the overall sticker price—the one consumers are more apt to notice.

Unbundle Services and Add Extra Fees

As travel demand dropped, airlines added fees for telephone reservations, luggage, meals, and preferred seats. This allowed them to advertise low prices and attract price-sensitive customers while earning higher profits from travelers willing to pay a premium.

IN A RECOVERY

Withdraw Recession-Pricing Tactics

Tide Basic, launched in 2009, cost 20 percent less than regular Tide. P&G withdrew it in 2010 as regular Tide began regaining market share in the United States. Similarly, restaurants like Ruby Tuesday have begun cutting back on price promotions and are maintaining growth.

Introduce New Premium Products

As the economy picks up, take advantage of consumers' willingness to splurge. Panera recently sold a lobster roll for $16.99. Concert promoters are offering VIP packages with more features; for example, last year one Bon Jovi package sold for $1,875.

Increase the Price of Regular Products

When you raise prices, it's important to tell customers why. Some common reasons: "Our costs are rising" and "During the recession, we lowered margins to help customers." Last fall Kraft, General Mills, and McDonald's all announced price increases.

Offer New Ways to Experience Luxury

JetSuite customers can now take a four-person private plane from Van Nuys, California, to Las Vegas for $999. Ritz-Carlton has a "Resort Reconnect" promotion targeted at couples who are feeing flush enough to resume vacationing at upscale resorts.

new inexpensive sandwiches: $2 Sammies, $3 Bullets, and $4 Torpedoes. This adaptive-pricing technique allowed it to continue charging full price for its signature items and avoid Subway's dilemma when the economy started to improve.

Some of the most successful adaptive-pricing innovations may not even seem, on the surface, like pricing innovations. One of the boldest was Hyundai's Assurance program, which the company introduced in January 2009. Despite steep price cuts, automobile sales had dropped sharply the previous fall as customers reacted to the continuing economic crisis. "What we heard consistently was, 'I know the deals are good, but I'm worried that if I lose my job, then I'll lose the car,'" Hyundai's top United States executive, John Krafcik, has said. So the company came up with a way of assuaging this fear. The Assurance program let buyers who lost their jobs stop making payments and return their vehicles. By providing this safety net, Hyundai was able to prosper without making further price cuts. While the United States market for auto sales dropped by more than 20 percent in 2009, Hyundai's United States sales increased by 8 percent. And the cost to the company was minimal: During the first nine months of the Assurance program, fewer than 50 cars were returned.

Sometimes creative financing is the best way to hold the line on prices. This is far from a new technique; carmakers and consumer appliance companies have used credit policies to boost sales since the 1920s, and General Motors came out with a highly touted 0 percent financing offer after the September 11 attacks. But some marketers deployed especially creative financing strategies during the latest recession. For instance, in 2008 Best Buy offered two-year, no-interest financing for purchases totaling at least $999—far more than the average person spends at one time in a consumer electronics store. "Some customers [were] literally adding items to their shopping cart so they would hit the $999 minimum," Best Buy executive vice president Mike Vitelli later said. The same year Best Buy's main rival, Circuit City, filed for bankruptcy and shut down.

Adaptive pricing is such an effective tool, in fact, that sometimes it works *too* well. In 2009 Tony Maws, the owner of a high-end restaurant in Cambridge, Massachusetts, called Craigie on Main, wanted to boost evening business during the week without cutting into profits on the weekend, when the restaurant was typically full. So he instituted a midweek special—a drink and two appetizers for $29.99—available to customers seated at the bar from 5:30 to 6:00. Soon the bar was not just full but overflowing with standing-room-only customers who also wanted, and were given, the special deal. After a month Maws decided to end the promotion—it had created too much demand.

A Better Way to Make Deals On Meals

When it comes to adaptive pricing, it's tough to beat the airline and hotel industries, which have used "yield management" systems for many years. But another industry is becoming smarter about pricing: restaurants.

As the economy recovers, some high-end restaurants are trying more-innovative pricing models. Star chef Grant Achatz plans to open a restaurant called Next in Chicago. It will sell tickets online for meals at specific dates and times, basing the price on the popularity of the slot reserved. A five-course meal might cost $75 at 8 on Saturday; the identical meal might cost only $45 at 6 on Tuesday.

This strategy has risks. Customers might simply go elsewhere on Saturdays. They might devalue Next's food, thinking, "I can get the same meal for half the price on Tuesday."

Here's a better idea: Keep the prices of entrees the same, but set minimum customer spending levels, varying them according to demand. A high-end restaurant might require a diner to spend $150 on a Saturday night but only $75 on a week-night. This arrangement would allow free-spending customers to choose the popular night (and spend more on high-margin items like cocktails and desserts), while letting frugal diners ("Just an entree and tap water, please") find a seat on a slower night. It avoids charging different prices for the same food and also has the advantage of flexibility: If a given Saturday is slow to book, the restaurant could lower the minimum in its reservation system. And the strategy could work for restaurants at all pricing levels, not just upscale places serving five-course meals.

One of the biggest advantages of adaptive pricing is increased flexibility as the economy begins to rebound. For instance, P&G simply withdrew Tide Basic from the market in June 2010; it didn't have to wean customers off any recessionary discount on the regular brand. Other companies are courting newly flush consumers by introducing higher-quality, higher-priced versions of some items. In the summer of 2010 Burger King began selling premium fire-grilled ribs for $7.19 an order. Customers quickly bought up the entire supply— 10 million ribs.

Although the anemic recovery may have you wondering whether consumer demand will ever return in full force, rest assured that it will—and when it does, you need to be ready. For companies that view pricing as just an "increase or decrease" strategy, readiness is primarily a matter of deciding when it's time to flip the switch. But such companies will be missing an opportunity. If you implement a creative, constantly evolving array of pricing strategies, you can more effectively reach new customers— and transfer more of their money to your bottom line.

Critical Thinking

1. List and summarize the pricing tactics that are appropriate in a recession and in a recovery.

2. Do you agree that marketers should utilize different pricing strategies and tactics in a recovery and in a recession? Justify your response.

RAFI MOHAMMED (rafi@cultureofprofit.com) is the founder of the consulting company Culture of Profit and the author of *The 1 % Windfall: How Successful Companies Use Price to Profit and Grow* (Harper Business, 2010).

Acknowledgements—Harvard Business Review and Harvard Business Publishing Newsletter content on EBSCOhost is licensed for the private individual use of authorized EBSCOhost users. It is not intended for use as assigned course material in academic institutions nor as corporate learning or training materials in businesses. Academic licensees may not use this content in electronic reserves, electronic course packs, persistent linking from syllabi or by any other means of incorporating the content into course resources. Business licensees may not host this content on learning management systems or use persistent linking or other means to incorporate the content into learning management systems. Harvard Business Publishing will be pleased to grant permission to make this content available through such means. For rates and permission, contact permissions@harvardbusiness.org.

The Devolution of Marketing

Is America's Marketing Model Fighting Hard Enough to Keep Up?

Andrew R. Thomas and Timothy J. Wilkinson

The American marketing model is dysfunctional. Small and medium-sized companies, as well as large multinational firms, have been lured into a misconceived form of producing and selling. It goes like this:

- Invest blood, sweat, tears and money to innovate a new product or service.
- Sell it through the largest distributor possible.
- Maximize the volume of sales through that distributor.
- Deal with the inevitable cost-cutting demands.
- Compromise brand integrity.
- Export capital, jobs, quality control and pollution to developing markets.
- Watch the innovation become a commodity.
- Lose money.
- Begin to develop new innovations.
- And then, start all over again . . .

A large portion of what drove us into the Great Recession is rooted in this dysfunctional pattern of distribution. Sell more and more through a mega-distributor—with much of the profit split by distributors and overseas manufacturers. Earnings obtained by the latter are reinvested into the United States, and then are lent to consumers so they can continue to spend beyond their means—thereby propping up the global economy.

Discussions are abundant about out-of-control lending, consumer spending, the impact of outsourcing and the lack of sustainability. But little attention is paid to the harmful impact that the distribution strategies employed by mega-distributors have played—not only on innovators, but on the overall economy. As we talk to business leaders around the world, it is clear that many of them realize a fundamental shift has occurred: Power has transferred from those who create innovative products and services to mega-distributors, who are increasingly in control of the global marketplace.

Mistakenly, many marketing departments see deals with mega-distributors as the way to boost sales and market share. In reality, the Megas live by high volume and low prices. They use their powerful leverage to demand price cuts and other concessions from suppliers. Companies end up with razor thin or non-existent profit margins, even as their innovative products and services are treated like commodities by both the Megas and the buying public. Surprisingly, this transformation of the business landscape has occurred with little fanfare or real analysis.

The Blame Game

Before you think that this is merely another attempt to blame Wal-Mart Stores, Inc., GE Capital, AutoNation, The Home Depot and others for the ills of the world, let us be clear: We do not blame the Megas for the distribution trap and what it has caused. As far as we know, no one has ever been forced to sell their products or services to someone else. Megas rarely, if ever, travel to visit potential suppliers. They wait for would-be vendors to show up. And boy, do they—in great numbers, each hoping to strike it rich!

Beginning in the early 1980s, innovative firms permitted, either consciously or subconsciously, outsiders into their companies. They allowed these outsiders to gain increasing control over sales and distribution activities. Innovative firms and the people who led them were responding to what management theorists were saying at that time. The "business gurus" talked about organizational transformation— emphasizing things like resources, capabilities, innovation, technology and operational effectiveness. "Total quality management," "lean manufacturing" and "zero defects" were just a few of the solutions preached by business elites to companies of all sizes.

Drinking this elixir, thousands of companies that once had been in control of all aspects of their innovative development began to lose interest in sales and distribution, preferring instead that other companies take over this "business function." The concept of "core competencies" was provided as the justification for letting loose of control after the producing firm had exercised its unique set of value-adding activities. Why manage a string of dealers if your core competency— your basis of differentiation—is in research and development or manufacturing? Taking this advice, companies divested themselves of activities that were not perceived as value added. Sales and distribution were pushed aside.

One of the people who understood the ramifications of the new transformational thinking was Sam Walton. He and a raft of imitators stepped in to fill the power vacuum that the strategy gurus had helped create. The result was the evolution of massive distributors, which ultimately drove the sales and distribution of innovative products and services in the United States.

The Distribution Trap

Numerous manufacturers have seen their profit margins squeezed and their brands eroded because they decided to sell through the Megas. Rubbermaid, Levi Strauss, Goodyear and many lesser-known companies have been literally trashed by the relentless pressure from the Megas to cut prices. Remember Jones Soda Co.? In 2006, this company showed profits of $39 million on $406 million in revenue. A distribution strategy initially based on selling through tattoo parlors and snowboarding shops morphed into one focused on Panera Bread, Barnes & Noble and Starbucks. But in 2007, Jones Soda began to sell to the Megas (including selling a limited selection to Wal-Mart), and ended up posting an $11.6 million loss for the year.

One website summed it up: "And just exactly what is Jones Soda doing for sale at Wal-Mart? Is Jones Soda now going to market itself as a value-priced soda, except with weird flavors?" (Source: www.blogging stocks.com/2007/06/14/jones-soda-loses-its-fizz.) In September 2010, after suffering from years of quarterly losses, the company went all-out in marketing to the Bentonville, Ark., giant, agreeing to sell 6-packs of its most popular sodas to the Mega's 3,800 stores. This served to only further debase what had at one time been a popular, upstart brand.

The scope and magnitude of a Mega can quickly consume the brand equity of individual products and services. Private labels, discounting, lack of service and mass-market presentation have diluted the value of American brands. The distribution trap has squeezed margins by making products that were once viewed with respect easily substituted with either store brands or inexpensive knock-offs. In fact, the Megas can be viewed as instruments of brand dilution. The very act of discounting, which is the business model of the Megas, undermines the entire idea behind a manufacturer's brand.

In 1993, Rubbermaid, the long-time producer of high-quality storage products was named America's Most Admired Company by *Fortune* magazine. Rubbermaid offered 5,000 different items, producing nearly 400 new, innovative products each year. Most the company's history was defined by strong relationships with end-users through a network of independent distributors and dealers. However, beginning in the early 1990s, a new leadership team entered and committed to expanding sales through the Megas.

The CEO at the time, Wolfgang Schmitt, explained: "It's typically the bigger suppliers that can form the sort of close partnerships that retailing's behemoths are increasingly demanding. The goal is to boost sales and reduce costs for both sides by slashing inventories, shortening lead times and eliminating error: There is a healthy interdependence between us and people like Wal-Mart. We need them; they need us." Wal-Mart accounted for about 14 percent of Rubbermaid's business when, in 1994, disaster struck.

The key components of Rubbermaid products are polymer-based resins, which make up about one-third of the cost of any given product. The price of resins had been stable for years, but costs shot up in spring 1994 because of new global demand and a supply shortage resulting from problems at key refineries. Within 18 months, the price of resins nearly doubled—adding $200 million to Rubbermaid's costs. Focused as always on earnings growth, the company increased its prices. The price increases were met with derision by the Megas. The giant retailers objected to monthly price increases, and complained that Rubbermaid was unresponsive to the realities of the market. Wal-Mart, frustrated with the price increases, emptied shelves of Rubbermaid's "Little Tikes" line of toys, and turned the space over to Fisher-Price.

Left with no other real option, Rubbermaid felt compelled to change gears. In 1994, it began to compete aggressively on the basis of price, offering steep discounts to the Megas. Its margins quickly eroded, and cost-cutting measures were enacted, including the elimination of its dealer network, thousands of American jobs and the closure of nine plants. The company purged 6,000 color and size variations and cut the total number of products by 45 percent. These efforts produced only temporary relief. Rubbermaid was acquired by the Newell Corporation in 1998 for a mere $6 billion in stock.

The Outsourcing Compulsion

Another consequence of the distribution trap is outsourcing and off-shoring. While the academic literature is replete with theories about foreign direct investment (FDI), the real motivator for much of the 23 percent FDI that is "contracted-out" has been entirely ignored. Producers are being literally forced to invest in overseas manufacturing by their mega-distribution partners. Outsourcing is a coping mechanism in response to relentless price pressures from the Megas. Companies locked into the distribution trap can substantially lower costs by shuttering domestic manufacturing operations.

Lakewood Engineering & Manufacturing Co. is a case in point. For years, this electric fan manufacturer sold its 20-inch box fan for $20. Responding to Wal-Mart's downward price pressure, the company opened a factory in Shenzhen, China in 2000, where labor costs averaged $0.25 per hour compared with $13 per hour in Chicago. By 2003, the fan was sold at the Mega for $10. In 2008, Lakewood employees, alongside local labor organizations, protested the company's decision to close its electric heater operations and move production to China. Wal-Mart buys 80 to 90 percent of the company's heaters.

Lakewood claimed that its hands were tied because it was heavily mortgaged to Wells Fargo Bank, which refused to lend it more money. The company's relationship with the Mega resulted in the layoff of 220 workers and the outsourcing of production. All too often, the compulsive embrace of offshoring by U.S. firms is not a function of internally generated goals and objectives, but is instead driven by the sheer demands of corporate survival.

One of the consequences of the outsourcing compulsion is environmental degradation in the developing countries where distributor-forced outsourcing takes place. In many emerging markets, environmental laws are lax or simply go un-enforced. These countries may be viewed favorably by multinationals, because they constitute "pollution havens"—with the cost of pollution absorbed by the people living in those countries, not by the multinational corporations or their customers. For example, China's industrial cities are so full of air pollution that their occupants rarely see the sun. The heavy reliance on coal has polluted the air with suspended particles of liquid or solids that float in the air. These particulates—and China has lots of them floating around—are associated with respiratory problems and heart disease. In the U.S., the growth of municipal waste has grown in tandem with the contribution of retail trade to the gross domestic product. According to the Environmental Protection Agency, 55 to 65 percent of municipal waste is classified as "residential waste": It is the product of the buying habits of individuals and families. This has taken place because during the last 25 years, as consumer prices have dropped and as consumption has increased, people have purchased increasing amounts of cheap stuff from the Megas—which quickly wears out and is then discarded.

The rush to the cheapest possible price has not yet factored in these costs of environmental degradation. When that inevitably happens, prices will have to rise. In short, the offshoring of production, driven by the mega-distributors, is not sustainable. China and other emerging

Briefly

- Partnering with mega-distributors holds an irresistible lure for many companies.
- The Megas' business model depends on mass marketing, low price and volume.
- Avoiding the Megas may mean less volume, but can have other advantages.

economies have traded extremely high economic growth for polluted air, water and land. No country can pursue such a strategy indefinitely. In the coming decades, as emerging markets grow up, environmental concerns will outweigh the appetite for runaway growth, and the unreasonably low prices that Americans have come to expect as they make purchases from the Megas will end.

The Independent Solution

Falling into the distribution trap is not an inevitable outcome of American business practice. But companies like Red Ants Pants have prospered by avoiding the big-box stores and other mass-market retailers. Thirty-year-old company founder Sarah Calhoun became so frustrated with ill-fitting work pants, designed without the female figure in mind, that she started her own company. There are now 70 different sizes of the double-knee, double-seat work pants with their lower-rise front and higher-rise backs. By importing 12-ounce cotton canvas from India, and having it cut and sewn by a factory in Seattle, Calhoun is free to sell the premium priced pants ($119 a pair) to her target market: women who work for a living in the construction trades. A 1964 Airstream trailer decorated with red ants is the marketing vehicle of this small firm. Calhoun's Tour de Pants road trips allow her to make direct sales to groups of women at homes across the country. Personal contacts made through trade shows and conferences further extend her direct marketing approach.

Another example is STIHL Inc., a manufacturer of outdoor power equipment that has never sold its products through mass merchants. Instead, the company sells its innovative products through thousands of independently owned servicing dealers across America and throughout the world. An industry global leader in both market share and profitability, STIHL continues to embrace its founding principle of only selling the company's products through servicing dealers.

The Current Landscape

The rise of the Megas has created a groundswell of community-based efforts to help local independent businesses compete effectively and prevent chains and online giants from displacing local entrepreneurs. More than 100 such groups have organized in North America since 2000, including 70 affiliated with the American Independent Business Alliance (AMIBA), a non-profit dedicated to supporting these community efforts.

AMIBA facilitates group purchasing, cooperative promotions and advertising and other activities to help local businesses gain economies of scale. It also wages sophisticated "buy local" campaigns to promote the greater overall value local businesses often can provide to customers, as well as the vital economic, social and cultural role they play in communities. Lastly, these alliances are advocates for the interests of local entrepreneurs in their local government and media. As their ranks grow, AMIBA aims to shift state and national policies that favor larger corporations at the expense of smaller community enterprise. Another effort to support local business is Independent We Stand, sponsored in part by STIHL. Independent We Stand focuses on the money spent at locally owned companies and how it re-circulates throughout the community. Whether it is the taxes that are paid, the payroll of the workers or the businesses' own spending, the impact of local-driven commerce makes a community a far better place to live.

The battle lines are being drawn for a new showdown between locally focused groups like AMIBA and Independent We Stand and Wal-Mart. The mega-retailer recently announced that it is targeting urban areas with the idea of introducing smaller stores like the ones it already operates across Latin America. In a recent *Wall Street Journal*

article, Bill Simon, head of Wal-Mart's U.S. stores business, said that Wal-Mart hopes to open many of its "Neighborhood Markets" across the country. These stores will be like the smaller "bodegas" the company has set up across Latin America. According to Simon, Wal-Mart believes that the opportunity exists for "hundreds" of the smaller-sized outlets, which will offer customer staples and produce.

The Reality Check

For many companies, the lure of partnering with a megadistributor is irresistible. These giants can put products in front of hundreds of millions of customers—and potentially bring in huge gains in sales and market share. But behind these high hopes may be a faulty premise that can lead to disaster. Whether out of naiveté, arrogance or greed, innovative companies expect that the Megas will care about the success of their products and services as much as they do.

What companies forget, or ignore, is that the Megas' business model depends on mass marketing, low price and volume. Naturally, the Megas use their tremendous leverage to dictate tough terms to innovators. They insist on ever-greater price reductions and force companies to redesign products and services to better suit their needs. In the end, many producers discover that all the blood, sweat, tears and money they have poured into their products and services has been wasted: Their hard-won creations have been turned into commodities with razor-thin profit margins. From this perspective, the outcomes for the innovator are not surprising: the abandonment of brand integrity, the acceleration of the innovation into a commodity and the inevitable cost cuts that result from offshoring and outsourcing.

Having created the process and product, and invested time and money, why would companies turn the final stage of the operation over to a third party? Business leaders do it all the time. It is their choice, and they must bear responsibility for what happens.

To avoid the negative outcomes described, companies must control their own distribution. This may mean selling directly to customers online or through company-owned retail stores. Or, it may mean striking strong deals with distributors and avoiding partners who will not agree to stringent terms. Of course, avoiding the Megas may mean less volume, but the advantages of doing so are likely to make up for it. Companies that keep a tight rein on distribution have a greater ability to control pricing, customer service and after-sales service. They can also build stronger, longer-lasting relationships with their customers. And isn't that what every company ultimately needs?

Critical Thinking

1. Explain the lure for manufacturers to partner with and sell their products through mega-distributors.

2. In your opinion, do small businesses that control their own distribution and avoid partnerships with mass-market retailers stand a chance at success?

ANDREW R. THOMAS is assistant professor of international business at the University of Akron in Ohio, **TIMOTHY J. WILKINSON** is professor of marketing and Interim Dean of the College of Business at Montana State University Billings. They co-authored "The Distribution Trap: Keeping Your Innovations from Becoming Commodities" (Praeger, 2009), winner of the Berry-AMA Book Award for the best marketing book of 2010. They may be reached at art@uakron.edu and timothy.wilkinson@msubillings.edu, respectively.

Reprinted with permission from *Marketing Management*, Spring 2011, pp. 20–25, published by the American Marketing Association. Copyright © 2011 by American Marketing Association.

In Lean Times, Retailers Shop for Survival Strategies

They're cutting costs, listening to customers.

Jayne O'Donnell

An economic slowdown tends to spook the retail industry. When the economy sputters, people close their wallets and delay purchases, and stores suffer. Store chains, after all, can't survive very long without robust consumer spending.

But retailers don't just stand there and take a beating. They slim down, shut stores, trim inventory, slice payroll and take other strategic steps they hope will help them endure the pain. Some stores even thrive in recession even as others struggle.

With fears that the coming months could be the toughest for them since the 1991 recession, retailers are fighting to gain any edge they can over their rivals and to cushion themselves from the slide in customer spending. Many of them are redeploying staff and revising promotions; some are putting a new stress on low prices. In the end, they know, some of them will be winners, others losers.

"I see clients being more aggressive about promotion and reviewing the strategy by which they promote and how often they do it," says Madison Riley, a retail strategist with consulting firm Kurt Salmon Associates, whose clients include most major retailers.

The stores' strategies vary. So do their prospects for success. Much depends on how vulnerable they are in the first place.

Retailers that specialize in furnishing or refurbishing homes have been among the hardest hit. Specialty stores with highly discretionary products, such as the high- and low-end tchotchkes sold by Sharper Image and Lillian Vernon, respectively, may be worst off of all. Both retailers filed for Chapter 11 bankruptcy protection last week.

Retail chains know survival isn't in the bag, so they work even harder.

Specialty apparel stores are struggling, too. Even though some clothing, especially for growing kids or for career women, is regarded as essential, sales figures suggest that many of those purchases are being postponed.

Home Depot has slashed 500 jobs at its headquarters. Jewelry store chain Zales has announced plans to close 60 stores, and Ann Taylor plans to slash 180 jobs and close 117 stores within two years.

"The retailers accept that we're in a recession—smack in the middle of it," Riley says.

Among the most visible ways that stores are trying to ease their pain from the spending slowdown:

- **Merchandise.** Retailers must take care not to stock too little of the latest hot fashion or product—or showcase it too late. Many stores, Riley says, are working more closely with overseas suppliers to settle quickly on designs and shorten the development process.

- **Pricing.** Even retailers that try to avoid across-the-board price slashing are embracing the deep discounting trend, which Wal-Mart capitalized on so successfully last fall and holiday season.

- **More consumer input.** Retailers can't afford to wait until the end of a season to determine which trends will prove most popular. Riley says stores are stepping up consumer research and using their websites to gather real-time opinions from shoppers.

Thanks to luck, foresight or a bit of both, some retailers are better positioned to manage a downturn. Those with low, low prices—think Wal-Mart and off-price retailers including T.J. Maxx—and those that cater to the wealthy are tending to outperform those in the middle.

But opportunities exist for midlevel retailers, too. If shoppers are trading down to Wal-Mart, as its sales suggest, then more affluent people may be ready to cut back on their Bloomingdale's trips in favor of Kohl's. Tough economic times tend to diminish loyalty to stores across the spectrum.

"In this type of economy, the super shoppers get coupons out and check things online; they're going to be loyal to themselves first," says Phil Rist of the consumer insights firm BIGresearch. "Everyone's trying to find ways to make their money

	Target	Neiman Marcus and Saks	Macy's	J.C. Penney
Optimistic about the economy in next 6 months	33%	35%	36%	33%
Shopping closer to home	38%	26%	36%	44%
Shopping for sales more often	42%	22%	39%	45%
Spending less on clothing	39%	28%	35%	42%
Taking fewer shopping trips	39%	11%	34%	44%

How the Views of These Stores' Regular Shoppers Compare

Source: BIGresearch survey using national sample; responses are percentages of 2,434 people who said they regularly shopped at Target, 1,632 at Macy's, 2,723 at J.C. Penney and 32 at Neiman Marcus or Saks.

Here is how these retailers' shoppers compare with the U.S. population as a whole. Depending on who the store is targeting, they want to have close to or a higher composition of shoppers than the U.S. average. An index of 100 is considered average.

	Target	Neiman Marcus	Macy's	J.C. Penney
Age 18–34	104	99	92	89
Age 35–64	110	112	110	105
Age 65 and older	69	70	82	97
Education—high school	82	71	78	92
Education—college	112	115	113	105
Household size two or fewer	88	91	91	95
Income less than $40,000	63	55	56	75
Income $40,000–$99,000	121	96	116	120
Income $100,000 and more	155	240	186	122

Stores and Their Shoppers

Source: Claritas, a Nielsen company.

go as far as they can so there's something left for things they really want."

Christopher Maddox of Washington, D.C., says he's not giving up on Macy's, one of his favorite retailers, but is being far more cautious about his purchases this year.

"I'm only buying essentials due to the economy," Maddox says. "Luxury and big-ticket items are not in my budget due to increased costs of gas, food and utilities."

What follows is a look at the strategies of four retailers—Target, J.C. Penney, Macy's and Neiman Marcus—that draw from often-overlapping segments of shoppers.

As they brace for a possible recession, these stores are re-examining, in particular, four areas that will be most evident to shoppers: inventory, staffing, store openings and promotions.

Macy's
Frequent Big Sales and Discount Offers Won't Be Ending Anytime Soon

The nation's largest department store chain concedes that the economic slowdown has forced it to put off plans to scale back its sales and promotions.

"We still believe the strategy is a good one, but the timing is not necessarily good," says CEO Terry Lundgren.

In 2006, Macy's said it was trying to wean customers off frequent sales in favor of its "Every Day Value" pricing. Though

Lundgren says there were slightly fewer promotions in 2007 than in 2006, he says Macy's won't reduce the timing or the number of sales until consumer spending starts to bounce back.

All the great deals now in stores are one benefit of the depressing economic news, says Marietta Landon of Cambridge, Mass. She finds sales everywhere she goes. "Especially Macy's—they make every weekend a sale with saving passes and advertising galore," Landon says.

Macy's says its plan, announced earlier this month, to eliminate 2,300 management jobs in the company's central office and create 250 new ones in its local markets wasn't necessarily driven by the economy. But saving about $100 million a year sure doesn't hurt. The plan to localize decision-making "was conceived long before there was talk of a credit crunch or mortgage crisis, but executing it now in the face of a possible recession does have its benefits," says Macy's spokesman Jim Sluzewski.

The addition of Tommy-Hilfiger-branded men's and women's apparel this fall, which will make Macy's the only place to buy the brand in the USA outside of Hilfiger stores, should further boost sales, he says.

Macy's has also announced plans to close nine poor-performing stores this year. Though struggling with some of the same issues that its rival J.C. Penney faces in catering to the middle class, Macy's holds an advantageous position, says Phil Rist of BIGresearch. That's because Macy's enjoys the image of being something of a novelty in many areas since it renamed the former May department stores in the fall of 2006.

Its clientele is generally more affluent than Penney's, notes analyst Bill Dreher. Still, in times like this, even a Macy's will likely be hurt by the tendency of customers to cut back on non-essentials.

"All the department stores are vulnerable because they are about 80% apparel and 20% home goods," Dreher says. "After years of strong apparel sales, customers have full closets, and with a weak fashion cycle, there's nothing fashionistas have to run out and buy."

Neiman Marcus
Despite the Times, Life Is Still Sweet at the High End of the Retail Spectrum

Neiman Marcus is preparing for a possible sales slowdown, recognizing that while affluent customers might not trade down to lower-quality stores, they might buy less even if they remain loyal.

The luxury retailer may adjust the amount of merchandise in stores, but otherwise is "just continuing business as usual," says spokeswoman Ginger Reeder.

Neiman "knows how to react," to economic troubles, Reeder says. That means preserving its customer service and high-quality merchandise but adjusting its inventories to concede the reality that its customers may be tightening their snakeskin belts.

"We've found our customers are very resilient," says Reeder, referring to Neiman's history during past economic slowdowns. "They're not trading down but might potentially buy less."

As at other luxury retailers with strong presences in California and Florida, Neiman's sales have suffered along with their customers' finances during the housing recession, says Craig Johnson of retail consulting and research company Customer Growth Partners. But for the "premier luxury retailer in the U.S.," in Johnson's words, suffering means merely moderate sales growth—down from double-digit increases in recent years. "As the economy stabilizes and spring returns, we look for improving results," Johnson says.

Neimans focuses its promotions on two major sales a year, which Reeder says won't change.

In this economy, sales figures show, the safest demographic spot for retailers to occupy is either the low end or the very high end. "Middle-market department stores continue to bleed market share to discounters such as Wal-Mart and TJX, to high-end players like Saks and Neiman Marcus and to hot specialty stores such as Anthropologie," Johnson says.

As Reeder suggests, those who remain loyal to Neimans through economic turmoil are typically those who prize quality over price.

"I still shop at Neiman's and will continue to," says Amy Cavers, of Skillman, N.J. "If things worsen or my budget gets tighter, I may cut back on my volume if anything, but not where I shop. I still want the same quality in my purchases. . . . I would rather have fewer shoes and dresses but with the same uniqueness and flair or style that I expect."

Jennifer Stillman of Atlanta says that rather than cutting designer labels out of her apparel budget, she's buying groceries at Wal-Mart and Costco over pricier markets such as Whole Foods.

J.C. Penney
Growth Plan with Swanky Fashion Lines Calls for Full Steam Ahead

Damn the economic naysayers, J.C. Penney is designing its most ambitious five-year plan for store openings in its history and last week oversaw its largest-ever merchandise launch. Still, facing a persistent drop in consumer spending, CEO Mike Ullman says the chain is scaling back those store openings from 50 to 36 this year and will adjust its inventories to reduce the need for hefty markdowns.

Ullman hopes that Ralph Lauren's new American Living fashion, home and footwear line for men, women and kids will further invigorate the Penney brand, which has drawn more and younger customers with the addition of the Sephora makeup line and two private-label lingerie lines designed, in part, to compete with Victoria's Secret. The American Living line will be found in 600 of the chain's 1,000 stores, often with its own in-store shops.

Deutsche Bank senior retail analyst Bill Dreher questions whether now is a good time for Penney to launch a line that's about 25% higher-priced than similar merchandise already in its stores.

Under the deal, Ralph Lauren's name won't appear anywhere on the new merchandise or displays, Dreher notes. Kohl's, by contrast, was able to connect the Lauren name with its Chaps line for many years, which helped keep customers aware of the connection. The new line is "no panacea," he says.

Still, Dreher notes, Penney has successfully reinvented itself over the past decade from a chain known for "dowdy, older-lady-type fashions to one that's very much hip, on-trend and cool." More recently, Penney has recognized that its catalog business is less important now than its website, he says.

About six months ago, Penney decided to merge its store, catalog and online marketing operations; the change will result in 100 to 200 job losses. Ullman insists it's "not a cost-driven exercise," but rather one that'll give shoppers "one view of our merchandise."

"People expected us to have cost-cutting, but that's not how you grow a business," Ullman says.

Ullman says Penney benefits by serving the "middle third" of the country, where people aren't "living paycheck to paycheck." Still, all bets are off if a weak economy grows really sick.

Nick Birchfield of Garden City, Mich., is still shopping at Penney, but that could change. If the economy gets much worse and gas prices rise higher, he says, "I will not be shopping at J.C. Penney unless they are giving their merchandise away."

Target
Upscale Discounter Starts to Spotlight Low-Priced Goods in Addition to Style

"Hello goodbuy."

Couldn't that be a Wal-Mart slogan?

As the economy struggles, Target, long known as the purveyor of the well-designed product, is increasingly spotlighting its low-priced goods. "Hello goodbuy" is the tag line for ads that now focus as much on the price of its products as they do on their style. After all, in a down economy, hand-painted toilet-bowl-brush covers that cost several bucks more than the next one are seldom a major consumer priority.

That leaves Target more vulnerable in this economy than, say, Wal-Mart, says Deutsche Bank senior retail analyst Bill Dreher. It may be a discounter, but it's hard for it to compete with Wal-Mart on price, Dreher says.

"Target has historically focused more on being fashion-forward and having value-added design," Dreher says. "The problem is, consumers don't want that now. They're not redecorating or refurbishing their homes. They're looking for everyday life staples."

At the same time, Dreher says, Target is better positioned than department stores these days.

Target has been trying for years to get its low-price message across, says spokeswoman Lena Michaud. And she says its business plan will carry it through hard times: "We are very confident in our strategy going forward."

That includes trying to rein in costs in a way that customers won't notice. That may be difficult given that a key target is hourly payroll expenses. Michaud says Target is investing in technology to make sure workers are scheduled at the right times. Unlike some of its competitors, Target is sticking to its plan to open stores, about 100 of them, which Michaud says is consistent with the number it has opened in recent years.

The chain is also preparing for the departure this year of designer Isaac Mizrahi, who has a line of popular private-label apparel at Target but is leaving to join Liz Claiborne. Spokeswoman Susan Giesen says Target will still offer apparel from trendy designers, which, along with the new Converse All-Star apparel and footwear line, should fill any gaps in its clothing lines.

That might not be enough to keep clothing customers loyal. Based on BIGresearch's survey data on people who shop at Target primarily for at least one category of merchandise, these consumers are shopping around. "The folks who shop at Target for health and beauty aids—a lot of them go to Kohl's, Macy's and Penney's first for clothing," says Phil Rist of BIGresearch. "There's a lot of cross-shopping."

Critical Thinking

1. With a small group of peers from your class, conduct a comparative analysis of the four retailers discussed in the case on the dimensions of inventory, staffing, store openings, and promotion.

2. In your opinion, is it more challenging for retailers to maintain customer loyalty during tough economic times? Justify your answer.

Contributing: Erin Kutz.

The Rebirth of Retail

**Innovator: Shopkick's Cyriac Roeding reinvents retail:
Meet Cyriac Roeding, the man reinventing shopping for the mobile era.**

JASON ANKENY

The idea first came to Cyriac Roeding in 1994. The German-born business and engineering graduate student was studying Japanese management theory at Tokyo's Sophia University. "Everywhere I went, I saw people walking around with these clunky machines they called 'mobile phones,'" Roeding says. "I said, 'Wow, that's the next big thing.'"

The seed was planted, but the true form and scope of the idea remained elusive for more than a decade. In the meantime, Roeding pursued other successes. He founded a mobile marketing firm called 12snap. He served as executive vice president of CBS Mobile, where his interactive entertainment concepts were strong enough to win an Emmy Award nomination.

Still, the big kahuna—the eureka moment, the one that captured lightning in a bottle—refused to reveal itself.

"I have been looking for an idea that has the potential to become a really large company in mobile for 11 years," Roeding says. "When I started 12snap in 1999, it was during the dark ages of mobile, when text messaging was still a geeky thing even in Europe. For years I've been trying out different mobile-use cases, looking for the one with a chance to become huge."

Roeding left CBS Mobile in 2008 and traveled the world for nearly two months. Everywhere he went, from New Zealand to Nepal, he saw people on mobile phones. With each successive stop, the idea took shape.

"I wanted to develop a service where mobile meets the real world," Roeding says. "Your cell phone is the only interactive medium you carry with you in a noninteractive physical environment, and that changes everything. It makes the offline world an interactive experience."

The idea finally achieved critical mass in September 2008, when Roeding arrived at his new gig as entrepreneur-in-residence with Silicon Valley venture capital firm Kleiner Perkins Caufield & Byers. After poring over thousands of business plans submitted to KPCB's iFund (a $200 million investment initiative created to ignite software developer interest in Apple's then-fledgling iPhone) and finding nothing that crystallized his vision, he shifted his perspective from identifying a solution to pinpointing a problem.

"The number-one challenge facing every retailer in America is getting people through the door," Roeding says. "Conversion rates in the physical world are so much better than online—between 0.5 percent to 3 percent in the virtual world, and between 20 percent to 95 percent in the real world. So if foot traffic is so important, then why hasn't anyone rewarded people for visiting stores? The answer is simple: It's because nobody knows you came through the door."

So Roeding set to work on a smartphone-optimized rewards program offering customers discounts and promotions simply for entering retail stores—a model he describes as "the physical-world equivalent of an online click." Meetings with big-box retailer executives followed. "They all loved the idea," he recalls. "It was crazy. I still didn't have a company, the technology, a team or even any funding. I only had a PowerPoint presentation."

With kickbucks, retailers design their own rewards. The idea—or shopkick, as it's now formally known-launched last August, buoyed by $20 million in funding from KPCB, as well as venture firm Greylock Partners and Linked-In founder Reid Hoffman (also an investor in Facebook and Zynga). The startup's eponymous mobile application delivers "kickbucks" rewards to all registered iPhone and Android users who enter a participating retail location. Kickbucks can be collected and redeemed across any partner store and turned into gift cards, discounts, song downloads, movie tickets, Facebook Credits or even charitable donations. As of late last year, shopkick spanned 1,100 individual United States retail outlets and 100 shopping centers with partners such as Best Buy, Macy's, Target, Sports Authority, Crate & Barrel and mall operator Simon Property Group.

"Shopkick transfers the online business model to the real world," says Roeding, CEO of the Palo Alto, Calif.-based company. "We're tackling a huge market with a big problem, and we're offering them a solution that works."

Roeding speaks about ideas in a deeply reverential, almost spiritual, tone. "I love building companies," he says. "I've always said that if the right people and the right idea pop up, I will drop everything to start a company. That's why I came to the United States I wanted to build something."

Roeding's entrepreneurial aspirations took a left turn when he landed in the entertainment industry, taking the helm of CBS Corp.'s fledgling mobile entertainment unit in 2005.

"At that time Disney had 270 people in its mobile department and CBS had zero," he recalls. "I met with [CBS executives] Nancy Tellem and Leslie Moonves and asked, 'Why are you talking to me? I'm an entrepreneur. I'm not a big-company person,'" he says. "And Les said, 'Because I want to turn this company into a company of entrepreneurs.'"

Roeding left CBS Mobile after three years at the top. Along the way, he pioneered a mobile video news-alert program, produced mobile games based on the network's prime-time hits and masterminded original made-for-mobile content across the three largest United States wireless carrier networks. Roeding also inked an early location-based mobile advertising partnership with Loopt, a still-growing mobile social networking startup that predates up-and-comers like Foursquare and Gowalla by several years.

At first glance, it may appear shopkick is yet another variation on the location-specific check-in paradigm championed by those firms, but Roeding cautions that the app is not a social networking tool.

"Our vision is to transform shopping into a personal, rewarding and fun experience for everyone," he says. "Shopkick is an app that is built around the act of going out and shopping. It's not about going out and letting your friends know where you are."

And unlike other location-enabled applications, shopkick doesn't rely on GPS triangulation. "If you want to reward someone for walking in your store, you cannot use GPS," Roeding says. "It's way too inaccurate. There's an error radius of about 500 yards, meaning I still don't know if you're inside the store, out in the parking lot or across the street at a competitor."

Shopkick instead incorporates a patent-pending device located in each participating store. The box, which costs retailers less than $100 and is roughly the dimensions of a paperback novel, plugs into any power outlet, emitting an audio signal that's undetectable to the human ear but automatically picked up by a smartphone's internal microphone. Because the signal's range is limited to the perimeter of the store, users must physically enter the location to earn kickbucks. And as Roeding points out, because detection occurs via the mobile device, consumers retain control over the privacy of their presence information.

Retailers determine how many kickbucks a shopper receives for entering their business. Roeding says each walk-in can earn as many as 100 kickbucks, with 875 kickbucks earning a $25 restaurant gift certificate, for example. Retailers can leverage the shopkick app to deliver special offers, like a discount on specific merchandise.

The concept also extends beyond retail: In partnership with brands including Kraft Foods and Procter & Gamble, shopkick offers smaller rewards for scanning product barcodes, which extends the network to about 230,000 additional stores nationwide.

Shopkick receives a small commission fee for each kickbuck a customer earns. "It's essentially a cost-per-click equivalent, only we charge cost-per-visit," Roeding says. If a shopper makes a purchase after using the app, shopkick claims a percentage of that transaction as well.

Not only is the shopkick model different from services like Foursquare, its users are different.

"Eighty percent of Foursquare users are male and 70 percent are between the ages of 19 and 35," Roeding says. By contrast, he notes, "55 percent of our users are female. Forty-nine percent of all users are aged 25 to 39, and 13 percent are 40 or older. Only 6.5 percent are 13 to 17. It's the perfect shopper demographic."

Retailers credit shopkick with kicking their customer traffic into a different gear. Sporting goods chain Sports Authority has rolled it out to more than 100 of its United States locations. In late 2010 the chain doubled—and in some cases even tripled—kickbucks rewards to determine the potential effect on walk-ins. The promotion ultimately increased shopkick user walk-in growth 50 percent to 70 percent.

"You have to innovate in retail to be relevant," says Jeff Schumacher, Sports Authority's chief marketing officer. "We looked at other applications, but we felt shopkick's strategy was the best fit. Their focus is on driving frequency, and in retail, frequency is a powerful metric. Anything that incents the customer to come into the store more often is a win-win for us."

Schumacher declines to reveal how many Sports Authority customers actively use the shopkick application, but says the company is "quite pleased" with it. "We're trialing shopkick in our major markets, which is where we see the greatest density of smartphones," he says. "Our customers love it. Some of them are even asking for it in markets where we don't have it. Feedback has been very positive."

Shopkick's rapid growth corresponds with surging consumer interest in leveraging mobile technology to shop smarter. Shoppers relying on mobile solutions to search for price and product information, check merchandise availability, compare prices at nearby stores, browse product reviews and even purchase goods accounted for $127 billion in consumer spending during the 2010 holiday season—which represents 28 percent of the $447 billion the National Retail Federation forecasts United States consumers spent over the period—according to a survey conducted by research firm IDC.

"We're seeing a fundamental shift in how consumers are accessing information at the point of purchase," says Cathy Halligan, senior vice president of marketing and sales at PowerReviews, a company in San Francisco that provides social commerce solutions (including customer reviews) to retailers and brands. "Consumers now have access to product information while they're standing in the store. They've never had that before. It's a game-changer."

As of October, nearly 61 million United States consumers owned smartphones, up 14 percent from the preceding three-month period and translating to one out of every four American wireless subscribers in all, researcher comScore reports. And as smartphone penetration grows, the opportunity for startups like shopkick flourishes.

"We made the decision to focus only on smartphones—it makes the most sense," Roeding says. "There will be 150 million smartphone users across the United States by the end of [2011], and consumers who can afford to shop are overrepresented in that group."

His idea is growing, too. Shopkick is extending its platform into the small-business sector: At press time, the firm was planning to launch its SMB retail trials in the first quarter of 2011.

"We're very excited about moving into the small-business world," Roeding says. "You could never join a national program as a local player before. It just didn't work. But with kickbucks, the playing field is level."

He also plans to expand the core capabilities of the shopkick model. In conjunction with the annual Black Friday shopping frenzy, the company recently unveiled The 12 Days of Kickmas, a sweepstakes giving walk-in users a shot at winning one of a dozen daily prize packages, including a grand prize of 4.25 million kickbucks. Other initiatives are in the pipeline, and as shopkick grows and improves, retailer offers should become more sophisticated as well, with kickbucks awards and promotions eventually targeting consumers according to age, gender, geography, shopping frequency or purchase history.

"Shopkick is about shopping, and not anything else," Roeding says. "There are all kinds of things that shopping entails, and we want to improve all of them. It's about making the in-store experience amazing. It's not a tool. This is your world."

Critical Thinking

1. In your opinion, what are the traits of a true visionary?

2. Elaborate on the concept of Roeding's 'shopkick.'

3. As a consumer, how do you assess the 'shopkick' app? Suggest some ways to improve it.

Marketing Communication in a Digital Era

Marketers Should Focus Efforts on Emerging Social, Mobile and Local Trends

DONNA L. HOFFMAN AND THOMAS P. NOVAK

Today's web is all about social media. It is increasingly becoming less about technology and more about what technology lets people do. Through social media, Internet users can perform various actions online, from connecting with friends to sharing videos to buying products. But as social media applications proliferate and the dynamics of online social interaction continue to evolve, marketing managers are seeking a deeper understanding of how and why people use social media, so that consistent practices based on online consumer behavior can be developed. The need for such understanding is acute, especially as more people spend more time interacting with others through social media applications.

Trends and Implications

Before outlining a framework for how to understand consumer behavior in today's dynamically changing online environment, let's first examine five social media outlets that are poised to have a large impact on both marketing research and practice.

1. Portable Social Graphs

First coined by Facebook founder and CEO Mark Zuckerberg in 2007, a person's "social graph" is the set of data-based connections that indicate how people within a given social network are related to each other. Social graphs can be diagrammed with the people as "nodes" and "edges," or lines connecting the nodes indicating how people are connected to each other. Such diagrams are typically called sociograms and describe the connections among one's "friends" in a particular social network.

Since April 2010, Facebook has significantly broadened the reach of users' social graphs via "social plug-ins," or embedded features on external websites that keep people connected with friends from their Facebook social graph. Through these plug-ins, a person can, for example, broadcast that she "likes" a certain story on another site, without first having to log in to Facebook. Instead of being limited to just the Facebook interface, actions between Facebook friends can now happen around the Web. Social plug-ins have made social graphs essentially portable.

With "like" buttons and other social plug-ins, marketers can now more easily integrate their Web presence with consumers' social networking behavior. Social plug-ins can provide social proof or legitimacy to content and increase reach when used in the right situations (for example, if a customer were to like a particular movie on IMDb, Amazon could access those likes via Facebook and serve product recommendations to that user based on her IMDb likes). In addition, the use of social plug-ins can drive traffic, promote word of mouth, increase interaction and generate marketing insight into consumer behavior (through website traffic data and demographics accessible through the Facebook Insights Dashboard). Besides the "like" button, other examples of popular social plug-ins include the activity feed that shows users what their friends are doing on the marketer's site (through "likes" and comments) and the recommendations plug-in that provides a marketer's page recommendations personalized to users.

Currently, 250 million people use Facebook through other sites, instead of through direct visits to Facebook.com. But as the social graph becomes increasingly portable and users are able to take their friends with them as they travel around the

---

Briefly

- Track consumers' online behavior via their social graphs, "likes," "check-ins" and "information shadows."
- Analyze social media's evolution using the "4Cs" as a framework: connect, create, consume and control.
- Focus your social media efforts using the LEAD model: listen, experiment, apply and develop.

Web, we are left with the question of where this trend will lead. We have two predictions that we think will have important consumer behavior and marketing practice implications.

First, we believe that people will increasingly want to limit their social graph to their "real friends," ultimately ending the era of "promiscuous friending" and leading to more meaningful application of the social graph to marketing practice.

Second, because Facebook, not the marketer or the user, controls the information embedded in the social graph, we believe there will be a battle for control of the social graph, potentially leading to a backlash over ownership of social data and creating new regulatory challenges for businesses.

2. The Power of the "Like"

Social search, or human-driven search, incorporates one's social graph into any given search, giving more weight to content endorsed by users in one's social graph. A user can thus find content based on friends' shared bookmarks, tags, questions and answers, reviews and ratings. This kind of search combines artificial intelligence with human intelligence, is evolving rapidly and takes on a variety of forms. Examples of social search include Aardvark and Quora (which match a user's question to someone in his network who may be able to provide an answer), Stumpedia (in which users index, organize and review search results based on their relevance to their social graphs) and Scour (in which users vote and comment on the relevancy of search results).

At one extreme, social search results can be driven by the in-depth response of a single expert member of one's social graph, such as with Aardvark or Quora. At the other extreme, Facebook's social search, which is based upon likes, is driven by the collective behavior of a large group of people. It provides a much broader, but at the same time much shallower, dip into the social graph. When a user clicks the "like" button, it is tantamount to an endorsement of the content, which others in that user's social graph can then use as the basis for their own content searches. This "power of the 'like' vs. power of the link" phenomenon is changing the dynamics of organic search, essentially changing the way we search, from Googling to liking. More importantly, we are shifting from a reasonably objective search process controlled by a purportedly neutral third party like Google or Bing, to a mass frenzy of websites motivated to install "like" buttons out of fear that not doing so would make them invisible to Facebook's social search.

One critical problem this trend introduces is that it does not distinguish between different types of likes. There is, for example, a difference between people who like a product out of genuine preference for it and those who might be externally motivated to like a product as a result of simply seeing others perform the action. Another problem is that we don't know whether a like relates to purchase intent. Clicking "like" does not necessarily represent a commitment on the part of the consumer. A person might click "like" purely from a *wish* to buy a particular product, not because of any *plan* to buy it.

The concept of liking something is getting baked into social search. Two million sites and counting use social sign-in and all are using this social plug-in. This is a huge investment that will not be going away anytime soon, so marketers are stuck with "like" whether they like it or not. Looking ahead, marketers need to figure out how best to leverage all these connections.

3. The "Footstream"

The geolocation field is getting crowded. There are currently around 20,000 real-time location-based mobile apps through which users can "check in" and share their locations and activities. Of the 20,000, only a handful have an established following, with Foursquare currently leading the pack. Other examples include the Meebo MiniBar (a website that allows users to check in to any website and share content with friends) and Whrrl 3.0 (a social location-based game, in which users inspire each other to try new activities and experiences). Virtual check-in to a location, content or brand is analogous to a "like," and is another way the social graph is being redefined.

Not surprisingly, the check-in model is rapidly evolving and is serving as a focal point for the integration of online and offline retailing. Shopkick's mobile check-in application, for example, identifies the customer entering a participating store and gives Kickbucks points just for walking in. Check-in was, at first, largely about creating awareness and driving traffic, but it is moving in the direction of location-based points, rewards, coupons and incentive systems that draw from principles of game mechanics to encourage specific customer behaviors. For example, Foursquare has formalized seven types of marketing specials, such as the "Mayor Special" that identifies and rewards the most frequent visitor to a venue over a two-month period for loyalty. Shopkick can reward very specific consumer behaviors with Kickbucks, such as inspecting products being promoted in the store or even entering a dressing room. A merchant could also use check-in data to identify and push product specials to customers already at the store. Starbucks, for example, could use this data to push deals and coupons for a venti cappuccino.

This location data measures foot traffic, which advertisers can use to quantify return on investment. Some are calling this the "footstream," but as we've seen, the footstream goes well beyond merely counting the number of customers to measuring specific targeted customer behaviors. Many view the footstream as the solution to the "last 50 feet" problem, in that it allows marketers to engage and incent consumers when they are literally at the front door of the business. The footstream brings the social Web into the store.

4. Social Data Mining

Through basic PC sensors (such as a mouse and keyboard) and more advanced smart-phone sensors (such as a touch screen, microphone, camera, motion sensor, proximity sensor and location sensor), people are leaving what some have called "information shadows." These information shadows are a behavioral trail of one's visited websites, emails, instant messages, tweets, blog posts, photographs, videos, locations and so on.

The advent of location-based sensors that use radio frequency identification (RFID)—which use radio waves and intelligent bar codes, like smart labels—near field communication (NFC) or short-range wireless and geotags—GPS data that indicate longitude and latitude of a tagged object (it's embedded in photos and videos with GPS-equipped smartphones and digital cameras)—will lead to an exponential increase in these information shadows.

Consider this: A single tweet has 40 fields of data associated with it. How many fields of data arc associated with a person? Taking into account every upload from every location at every point in time, a single person has more fields of data than the total number of websites in the 1990s. This can be expanded if we incorporate internal sensors that monitor, for example, heart rate or other bodily functions. What we have, then, is a data mining problem that goes considerably beyond the footstream, to a veritable fire hose of data. A primary challenge for marketers in the coming decade is how to make sense of these information shadows and connect the dots for a deeper understanding of customer behavior.

Emerging technology trends suggest a convergence of augmented reality, real time, location and sensors that will make Facebook seem quaint.

---

5. Smart Signs

There are two types of smart signs. The first is the digital sign, the simplest and most common form of which is a flat-screen television playing a loop of advertisements in a public place.

Digital signage can be seen in retail stores, doctor's offices, gas stations, restaurants, gyms, airports, train stations and taxis. The advertising medium has expanded into a multibillion-dollar business and has continued to grow relatively rapidly through the economic downturn of the past several years. Digital signage is now integrating identification technologies, such as tiny facial recognition cameras, in order to tailor advertisements to match audiences, as well as to record a consumer's response to ads.

As a consumer draws near to the screen, the camera-enabled smart sign can detect the consumer's age and gender, prompting the screen to run an ad that matches the consumer's profile. Facial recognition is the most common targeting method, but other digital signage systems employ RFID, Bluetooth and social networking. Most systems do not record individual identities at present, but there is little barrier to individual identification and profiling in the future. Although somewhat cliche in the digital signage industry, the famous advertising scenes from the movie "Minority Report," in which billboards can scan a face to determine one's gender and age and present ads accordingly, are the clearest dramatization of what this medium may ultimately be capable of doing. In fact, a Japanese company has already undertaken research in this direction of "gladvertising," using emotion recognition (EMR) software to serve ads according to one's mood.

The other type of smart sign is webcam-based augmented reality (AR), in which a camera either identifies a target or pattern on a physical-world object or uses motion capture to overlay digital information on top of a physical object captured via a webcam. Examples of augmented reality include the Ray Ban Virtual Mirror, which allows users to virtually try on different styles of Ray Ban sunglasses, and the United States Postal Service Priority Virtual Box Simulator, which allows users to determine the correct box size for the item they want to ship.

Bloomingdale's Magic Mirror and Macy's Magic Fitting Room in-store AR installations allow customers to virtually try on clothing via a large-scale interactive mirror and receive remote feedback from their social network friends in the process.

Online marketers have been largely concerned about the relationship between online and offline retailing, but now they also have to worry about the convergence of online and offline with "social retailing." Digital signs (displays that recognize and target offers to individuals) and augmented reality (signs that overlay digital information on physical objects) will continue to converge in such a way that in the future, the sign will know it's you, suggest a dress just for you and digitally dress you—right there on the street. And clothing is just the beginning.

Managing What's Next

Based on a close examination of these five trends, we can expect considerable technology changes in the coming decade, driven by the fundamental laws of technology that suggest exponential increases in processing power, data storage, bandwidth and number of Internet-enabled devices. As a result, we need to step back and use a framework to address these constant changes in social media and to help manage what is coming up next, and that framework must start with consumers in mind.

In our research, we argue that the fundamental interactivity of social media allows for four higher-order goals. These "4Cs" of connect, create, consume and control not only are the fundamental defining characteristics of social media, but also define the goals that consumers pursue in connection with social media use. Thus, social media enable and facilitate interactions that "connect" people. These social media conversations occur through Web- or mobile-based applications that people use to "create" (i.e., post, upload, blog) and "consume" (i.e., read, watch, listen to) content. Finally, social media applications give individuals a greater ability to manage their reputations and control content (e.g., page layout, tagging, rating) and online settings such as profile and privacy options.

All five of the trends we have discussed can be viewed through the lens of the 4Cs to understand why these trends have captured the attention of today's consumers. This understanding provides the starting point for developing digital strategy as social media continues to evolve. The chart on the next page summarizes the marketing implications of the five trends we examined in this article, in the context of our 4Cs.

Take the LEAD

Digital communications are increasingly becoming social, mobile and local. The Web is moving far beyond its current state of connecting people and content, as billions of devices

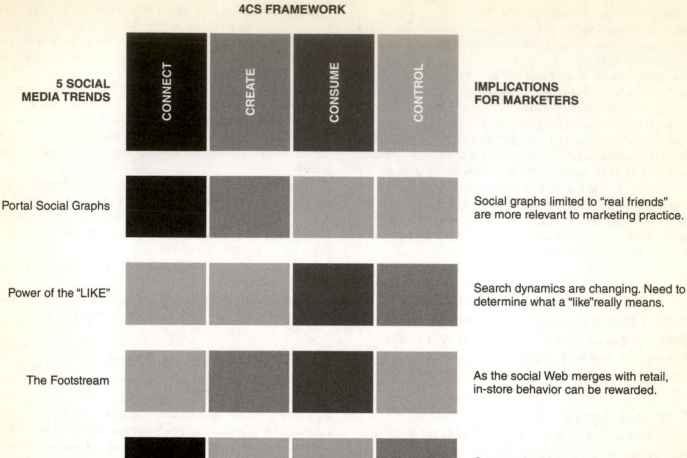

Marketing implications of five social media trends

with embedded mobile functionality create an "Internet of things." Emerging technology trends suggest a convergence of augmented reality, real time, location and sensors that will make Facebook seem quaint. The Web is evolving rapidly, driven by exponential changes in technology and a thrilling abundance of innovation. Marketers have no choice but to keep up or fall far behind.

One way marketers can not only keep up, but also get ahead is to use our LEAD model. With the LEAD model, marketers listen, experiment, apply and develop to help focus their companies' social media efforts against what sometimes feels like dizzying and dynamic change.

Listen

Marketers need to formally monitor and analyze what their customers are saying about them online, as well as what they are doing online. Ideally, marketers should put a formal process in place to monitor and analyze the conversations that customers are having about their brands, using the information as an early warning system, but ad hoc is better than nothing.

Experiment

Marketers can't just monitor. Start with simple pilot social media experiments, such as a Facebook brand page, YouTube videos or a Twitter stream. While ROI metrics for social media are still in the early stages, it's clear that these experiments pay off big-time in terms of increased customer awareness and brand engagement. Marketers can take first steps toward co-creation, and reach out to their customers through collaborative efforts to conceive new offerings and ad campaigns. Be aware that there really aren't any best practices or established business "models' yet, so marketers just need to get as much experience as they can as quickly as they can.

Apply

As experimentation proceeds, marketers are ready to gather the successes and start applying them systematically and on a larger scale. At this point, measuring impact is paramount, so it is important to track the results.

Develop

This involves developing integrated marketing programs that effectively integrate social media in marketing campaigns and go beyond simply viewing social media as just another channel for advertising.

By using a framework like the LEAD model, and remembering the 4Cs' fundamental aspects of how consumers behave online, marketers will be prepared as social media trends continue to evolve.

Critical Thinking

1. Describe the five social media trends discussed in the article.

2. According to the authors, what are the four goals that consumers pursue in connection with social media use?

3. With a small group of peers in your class, evaluate the LEAD model. Do you agree or disagree with the implications?

DONNA L. HOFFMAN is Chancellor's Chair, professor of marketing and co-director of the Sloan Center for Internet Retailing at the University of California in Riverside, Calif. **TOM NOVAK** Is Albert O. Steffey professor of marketing and co-director of the Sloan Center, as well. They may be reached at Donna.Hoffman@ucr.edu and Tom.Novak@ucr.edu, respectively.

From *Marketing Management*, Fall 2011, pp. 37–43, published by the American Marketing Association. Copyright © 2011 by American Marketing Association.

Selling Green

Marketing a business as green requires a blend of transparency, practicality and savvy. Here is *Entrepreneur's* five-step guide to how to do it right.

MATT VILLANO

In the world of marketing, green is the new black.

Have a recycling program? That's green. Use LED light bulbs? That's green, too. Heck, if you go so far as to encourage employees to carpool to work, you might as well be able to say your business is green.

And yet, green marketing—that is, *successful* green marketing—isn't nearly as easy as it seems.

It turns out there's more to eco-consciousness than simply being conscious of the environment. We asked a number of entrepreneurs and experts for insights on the components of green marketing that works. The gist: Green only yields green when messaging blends transparency, practicality and savvy.

1. See What Your Customers Want

Marketing your business as green is a great idea—provided your customers are into that sort of thing. Executives at Bardessono, a luxury hotel and spa in Yountville, Calif., learned this the hard way.

When the 62-room property opened in 2009, executives trumpeted the hotel's Platinum status from the Leadership in Energy and Environmental Design (LEED) program—the resort was one of only two such honored hotels in the United States. While the facility was a hit among environmentalists and green-obsessed journalists, it struggled with perhaps its most important group of constituents: customers.

The problem? Travelers accustomed to the luxury hotel experience perceived "green" to mean "sparse" and "uncomfortable" and booked elsewhere.

"Our messaging was great for occupancy but not so good for the average daily rate," says Jim Treadway, the hotel's general manager. "We had lost sight of the fact that our core customers value a luxury experience above all else."

Naturally, in 2010 Bardessono changed its tune, tweaking marketing messages to emphasize luxury first and green second. Almost overnight, bookings—at full price, mind you—soared.

The lesson: Never assume everybody will love you just because you're green.

"It took us a while to realize the best message for our customers was, 'We're a world-class hotel and, oh yeah, we're green,'" Treadway says. "That might not be intuitive, but when you consider that your customers are the top priority, targeting your messages to their lifestyle certainly makes sense."

Beware of 'Greenwashing'

While marketing your company as green has undisputed benefits, misrepresenting one's greenness—a process known as "greenwashing"—can be disastrous to a company's credibility.

ConAgra, the food product company, is facing a class-action lawsuit for labeling its cooking oils as "natural," even though they're made with genetically modified ingredients.

Then there's Sigg. The Switzerland-based reusable-bottle manufacturer told its customers that its products were BPA-free, even though the bottles contained the chemical in their liners. When news of this hit the mainstream media, sales dropped precipitously.

Apparently, greenwashing is getting worse. According to the 2010 Greenwashing Report from the TerraChoice Group, an environmental marketing agency based in Ottawa, Ontario, more than 95 percent of all consumer products claiming to be green were found to commit at least one of the "Seven Sins of Greenwashing," which include not providing evidence, being vague or flat-out lying.

The best way to avoid these claims, according to Shel Horowitz, CEO of Greenandprofitable.com, is to keep messages consistent and support every claim with incontrovertible evidence.

"Transparency and honesty is the best approach," he says. "If you're accused of greenwashing and there's some stick to it at all, you're dead."

2. Define What Green Means to You

Describing something as "green" can be dicey, since the word often means different things to different people.

In one instance, it could summarize an off-the-grid production facility powered by solar energy. In other cases, it could signify the existence of a telecommuting program that helps reduce a carbon footprint.

Jenny Grayson, a Los Angeles-based consultant who helps companies go green, says it behooves companies to be totally honest and to define exactly what "green" means to them.

"Everyone right now, from Clorox to Huggies, is marketing themselves as 'natural,' but what does that really mean?" she asks. "Environmentally savvy consumers can become quickly disillusioned with a company when it doesn't live up to its eco-friendly claims," or when it doesn't explain how it's eco-friendly in the first place.

Personal explanations usually work best. Ava Anderson Non-Toxic, a personal-care-product manufacturer (and one of *Entrepreneur's* "Entrepreneur of 2011" award winners), explains on the company website how its founder, as a 14-year-old girl, became disillusioned with chemicals in beauty products due to their hazardous health effects.

Bill and Jane Monetti offer similarly personal insights on the website for their company, Eco-Command, which produces GoFlushless, a spray that neutralizes the odor of urine and reduces the need to flush a toilet. The Monettis detail how the product was born out of necessity when they purchased a home in the environmentally sensitive area of Maryland's Eastern Shore.

"Along with our new home, we acquired a well, septic tank, drainage field and an extreme awareness of every drop of water we use," they write. With this, it's easy to understand the company mission of "saving water, saving energy."

3. Connect the Dots

No matter how well a company defines green, being green alone is not enough—there has to be some substance behind the messaging to make it work.

Park Howell, president of Park&Co, a sustainable marketing firm in Phoenix, says that in the current economy, emphasizing how people can save *their* green by going green is the most effective approach.

"In these overwhelming efforts to come across as eco-friendly, most small businesses taking their products to market miss the most important differentiators: quality and price," he says. "Something that's good for the planet is nice, but in this day and age, the masses simply don't care about it as much."

Howell contends that the best green marketing campaigns address the "three Ps" of *profit, people* and *planet,* effectively answering consumers' questions in the following order:

- Is it good for my budget?
- Is it good for my family?
- Is it good for the planet?

Do Customers Care?

With businesses in just about every industry vying to market themselves as green, it's natural to ask: To what extent do customers care? The answer depends on where you look.

Some data indicates that increasing numbers of Americans are seeking out green products; according to the Organic Trade Association, organic food sales have grown about 20 percent per year over the last decade. What's more, Wal-Mart, that mass-market juggernaut, is now the world's largest buyer of organic cotton.

Still, when most companies gauge customers about what matters most to them, answers such as "greenness" or sustainability frequently come in behind key issues such as usefulness and price.

Saul Kliorys, environmental programs manager for Great Lakes Brewing Company in Cleveland, has taken surveys of this nature, and says green is always near the top but never finishes first. "On the whole," he says, "greenness doesn't sell products; products sell products."

Still, to be fair, certain demographics appear to be more concerned than others with whether products are, in fact, green.

Women, for instance, account for a majority of household spending, and many may be worrying about the chemicals in their kids' shampoo, or might be trying to avoid purchasing genetically modified food at the grocery store.

The bottom line: Green likely isn't the sole factor determining customer behaviors in today's economy, but it undoubtedly is one of the few.

"Customers want good-performing products at prices they can afford that are healthy for their families and easy to get," says Park Howell, president of Park&Co, a sustainable marketing firm in Phoenix. "If a product has met all of those considerations and it's green, that's even better."

Howell adds that in most cases, green campaigns should avoid the word *green* and avoid incorporating green leaves into a logo. "Really, these tactics are just camouflaging a brand differentiator," he says. "Finding another way to tell your story will always end up delivering a targeted message to the people you want to reach."

4. Practice What You Preach

In an age when just about anyone can find out just about anything about the inner workings of a company online, transparency is key. For this reason, it's important for companies that market themselves as green to operate sustainably in many of their day-to-day operations.

At Green Apple Cleaners, a non-toxic dry cleaning business in New York City, this has meant no print advertisements

Green Allure

Jennifer Kaplan is a partner in green marketing firm Green-hance and the author of *Greening Your Small Business*. She is also an entrepreneur in her own right, having recently founded VineCrowd.com, a website designed to connect artisanal, independent wineries with consumers to buy, sell, discuss, compare and share. Kaplan compiled this ranking of green marketing innovators from the past decade for the Green Marketing and Communications class she teaches at Golden Gate University in San Francisco.

1. Tide Coldwater Challenge

This landmark 2005 marketing campaign addressed the money saved by washing in cold water and the product's deep cleaning and whitening abilities, making green the ancillary benefit. The far-reaching campaign included national advertising, in-store programs, product sampling, a strong Internet presence, consumer promotions and strategic alliances.

2. Jamie Oliver

The outspoken English chef and advocate of healthy food is a brand in and unto himself. He uses "disruptive media and public visibility" to communicate and motivate, creating a new kind of "infotainment."

3. Diesel Clothing: Global Warming Ready

In print ads promoting its 2007 spring/summer collection, the Italian clothing company depicted landscapes transformed by environmental disaster. The campaign proved that green marketing and tongue-in-cheek humor-when done well—resonate with young audiences.

4. GE Ecomagination

A massive 2008 multimedia campaign for Ecomagination established GE's green position in a competitive marketplace where credibility and believability are paramount to success. The resulting creative was simple, beautiful and compelling and delivered the message in engaging ways.

5. HSBC: There's No Small Change

A highly successful 2008 print campaign elevated HSBC's environmental credentials and consolidated the bank's environmental leadership position—all without TV or radio.

6. TOMS Shoes: Project Holiday

For the month of December 2008, TOMS promoted its Project Holiday campaign to sell 30,000 pairs of shoes so it could give the same number of protective rubber shoes to kids in Ethiopia. The company exceeded its goal by 23 percent and raised unprecedented awareness for its cause—all without paid media.

7. Toyota Prius: Harmony

This 2009 multimedia campaign showed how the Prius delivers extra power, space, safety, advanced technology and superior gas mileage.

8. Timberland: Earthkeepers

This 2009 global campaign showcased the Earthkeepers collection of eco-friendly apparel and included TV, print and retail ads, as well as social media and a microsite that used 3D technology.

9. Method: Just Say No to Jugs

This cheeky 2010 campaign is typical of Method's marketing, mocking mainstream cleaning products as feeding a household's "jug" habit. The campaign relied only on print and online ads.

10. BMW Diesel: Ch-ch-changes

This 2011 campaign launched at Super Bowl XLV, communicated valuable information and a relevant message to the American audience about the environmental benefits of and changes in diesel technology.

---

whatsoever, steering away from the traditional approach within the industry. Instead, founder and CEO David Kistner has opted for virtual (and therefore paperless) services such as Groupon and Google Offers to bring in new customers.

"Could you imagine if one of our coupons came in the mail?" he says, assuming eco-conscious customers wouldn't remain patrons for long.

Other businesses have opted for different strategies. At Eco-Command, owners Bill and Jane Monetti have installed in their home water-efficient shower heads, aerators for sink fixtures and an Energy Star clothes washer. GreenChoice Bank, a green-themed bank in Chicago, issues debit cards with a 100 percent recycled plastic core and boasts electric car chargers in all of its bank parking lots.

Consultant Shel Horowitz, author of *Guerilla Marketing Goes Green,* says it doesn't matter how a company embraces eco-consciousness, so long as it does so on some quantifiable level.

"You need to walk the walk to some extent," he says. "The minute a customer calls credibility into question, that customer will start shopping somewhere else."

5. Reinvest in the Community

One of the most important attributes of sustainability is reinvesting dollars and energy into the surrounding community. It's a simple step—but it's also an initiative many green companies overlook.

Reinvesting in the community can take many forms. Green Choice Bank offers flexible loan terms to commercial clients who build sustainably. Ben & Jerry's, one of the first green companies, continues to donate significant money to nonprofits more than a decade after it was purchased by Unilever.

Great Lakes Brewing Company, a brewery in downtown Cleveland, has taken a different approach: It sources locally. All told, the brewery's restaurant uses local vegetables and herbs in dishes whenever seasonally available, as well as local eggs, milk, cream, butter and locally raised meats. Saul Kliorys, the company's environmental programs manager, says the brewery has gone so far as to manage and till part of the 16-acre Ohio City Farm in Cleveland, growing many of the herbs and vegetables itself.

"Why source from elsewhere when we can get what we need right here?" Kliorys says. "Being green isn't always about making the best choices for the planet at large; sometimes it's about making the best choices for the people in your own backyard, too."

Critical Thinking

1. What are the five steps to effective green marketing proposed in this article?

2. Define "green washing" and discuss the possible negative impact(s) it may have on a company's image and credibility.

3. With a small group of peers in your class, explain the following statement: "Green only yields green when messaging blends transparency, practicality and savvy". Do you agree with this statement?

MATT VILLANO is a Freelance Writer and Editor Based in Healdsburg, Calif.

What's Your Social Media Strategy?

A new study shows four ways companies are using technology to form connections.

H. James Wilson et al

A global bank executive recently described to us a challenge for our times. It turns out that a customer who normally would qualify for the lowest level of service has an impressive 100,000 followers on Twitter. The bank isn't doing much yet with social media and has no formula for adapting it to particular customers, but the executive still wondered whether the customer's "influence" might merit special treatment.

It's the kind of perplexing question many companies face as they formulate their thinking about social media. To understand how businesses are approaching the challenge, we analyzed strategies and practices at more than 1,100 companies across several industries and continents, and conducted in-depth interviews with 70 executives who were leading social media initiatives. Our research revealed four distinct social media strategies, which depend on a company's tolerance for uncertain outcomes and the level of results sought.

The "predictive practitioner." This approach confines usage to a specific area, such as customer service. It works well for businesses seeking to avoid uncertainty and to deliver results that can be measured with established tools.

To increase Clorox's virtual R&D capabilities, the social media team created Clorox Connects—a website that enables brainstorming with customers and suppliers. A typical query posted there: "We're working on X product idea. What features would you like to see included?" To encourage participation, Clorox uses incentives borrowed from gaming. For example, people who post answers or add rating comments are awarded points. The site features different levels of difficulty, and contributors who demonstrate expertise can advance to problems requiring greater creativity, knowledge, and involvement. The sharpest contributors gain visibility, making participation rewarding and sticky. One early success came after Clorox posted a question about a specific compound for its salad dressings. Five responses quickly came in. The company decided on a solution within a day and brought the problem solver into the product development process.

The "creative experimenter." Companies taking this approach embrace uncertainty, using small-scale tests to find ways to improve discrete functions and practices. They aim to learn by listening to customers and employees on platforms such as Twitter and Facebook. Sometimes they use proprietary technologies to conduct internal tests.

The IT services giant EMC is a creative experimenter. It pays particular attention to how its 40,000 global employees use internal social media to locate needed expertise within the company. In an effort to reduce the use of outside contractors, it created a test platform, called EMC/ONE, that helped employees (many of whom were new because of recent acquisitions) network and connect on projects. "We were very clear that in two months we might unplug this and try a completely different approach," says Len Devanna, the director of social strategy. "This was the reason we were inside the firewall: To be free to make mistakes and learn our lessons before exposing ourselves to the outside." Within a year EMC/ONE was delivering substantial benefits. For instance, a division that needed to produce a sales video connected with an in-house production group, saving $10,000 as a result. The company estimates that EMC/ONE has generated more than $40 million in savings overall.

The "social media champion." This involves large initiatives designed for predictable results. It may depend on close collaboration across multiple functions and levels and include external parties.

Consider Ford's 2009 Fiesta Movement campaign, used to prepare for the car's reintroduction in the U.S. It required joint efforts among marketing, communications, and the C-suite. Ford decided to lend 100 Fiestas for six months to recipients who would use social media to discuss their experiences with the cars in an authentic, direct way. It held an online contest to select candidates, carefully choosing drivers with large social media followings. To further reduce uncertainty, it required them to regularly produce content on themed "missions" (for example, volunteerism) and designed a schedule for postings. Within six months the drivers had posted more than 60,000 items, which garnered millions of clicks, including more than 4.3 million YouTube views. The $5 million campaign created a prelaunch brand awareness rate of 37% among Millennials, generated 50,000 sales leads to new customers, and prompted 35,000 test-drives—a level of results that might be expected from a traditional campaign costing tens of millions of dollars.

Understanding Your Current Social Media Strategy: A Quiz

A company's social media strategy is generally oriented toward one of four types. This quiz can help you identify your dominant approach (the category with the highest total). Then consider whether you're using the strategy that best suits your resources and goals, or perhaps diffusing your efforts over multiple approaches when you would be better served by focusing on one.

	Don't Agree			Strongly Agree
Predictive Practitioner				
Each of our social media projects is owned by a specific functional group or department.	0	1	2	3
There is little or no cross-functional coordination among projects.	0	1	2	3
Each project has a clear business objective.	0	1	2	3
We can measure each project's impact with existing metrics.	0	1	2	3
			TOTAL	
Creative Experimenter				
Our overall objective is to learn from our social media projects.	0	1	2	3
In particular, we aim to enable engagement and to listen and learn from resulting conversations.	0	1	2	3
We position our projects as experiments within discrete functions or departments.	0	1	2	3
We are not overly concerned with predefining outcomes.	0	1	2	3
			TOTAL	
Social Media Champion				
We have a centralized group and specific leaders dedicated to coordinating and managing social media projects across departments and functions.	0	1	2	3
This centralized group develops policies and guidelines for social media use.	0	1	2	3
We enlist executive champions and other evangelists, including external influencers, to promote and participate in our projects.	0	1	2	3
We share best practices and lessons learned from various projects throughout the organization.	0	1	2	3
			TOTAL	
Social Media Transformer				
Our portfolio of social media projects involves both internal employees and external stakeholders, such as customers and business partners.	0	1	2	3
Our social media technologies are tightly integrated with how we learn and work.	0	1	2	3
Our projects typically encompass multiple functions and departments.	0	1	2	3
We have centralized groups tasked with thinking about how social media can inform our business strategy and culture in light of surprises and emerging trends.	0	1	2	3
			TOTAL	

What Happens When Companies Lack a Social Media Strategy?

Here's what often occurs when companies encounter a new technology: One group begins a small experiment. So does another . . . and another. The various groups' efforts are typically ad hoc; there's little coordination and no effective way to share lessons learned. One manager summed up the social media experiments in progress at his company this way: "It's a free-for-all."

Sometimes companies start out with a clear strategy but lose focus as the effort expands. One professional services firm gave its marketing department a limited mandate to use Twitter and other social networks to try to increase its lead generation. The group began well enough, devising specific policies, practices, and metrics for increasing conversations with potential clients—behavior that placed it firmly on the predictive practitioner track. Made heady by early successes, however, it pushed to increase the scale of the initiative and ended up haphazardly pursuing elements of both the social champion and creative experimenter strategies. It struggled to recruit executive champions for an internal community and also urged all employees to blog and tweet about the company's services. Lacking a strategic mandate or clear learning objectives, and without much buy-in outside the department, it tried to drum up support by offering prizes for participation and asking HR to make blogging a job requirement. Today it's hard to say what this company's social media strategy is; it's as if the firm has been using a shotgun to try to hit its target.

Companies that are still taking a small-scale, experimental approach to social media need to be strategic about ramping up. Long-term success is rarely found in a free-for-all.

The "social media transformer." This approach enables large-scale interactions that extend to external stakeholders, allowing companies to use the unexpected to improve the way they do business.

In 2010 Cisco launched Integrated Workforce Experience (IWE), a social business platform designed to facilitate internal and external collaboration and decentralize decision making. It functions much like a Facebook "wall": A real-time news feed provides updates on employees' status and activities as well as information about relevant communities, business projects, and customer and partner interactions. One manager likens it to Amazon. "It makes recommendations based on what you are doing, the role you are in, and the choices of other people like you. We are taking that to the enterprise level and basically allowing appropriate information to find you," he says.

Cisco also makes extensive use of video. It conducts most of its training and meetings virtually, through video streamed to desktops and available via video-on-demand. Like Facebook, the system lets users tag and comment on videos. These technologies have accelerated "time to trust" among Cisco's stakeholders, quickly establishing collegiality and knowledge sharing among new geographically dispersed teams.

Putting Strategy into Practice

The strategies are temporal, and many organizations will progress from one to another. Companies with clear objectives for using and measuring social technologies in a specific part of the organization should begin as predictive practitioners. They should look for a group (marketing, for instance) that wants to become more social in its business.

Creative experimenters are driven in part by small budgets; labeling a project "experimental" can exempt it from ROI constraints. Both the predictive practitioner and creative experimenter strategies can quickly create significant results and learning and serve as a training ground for larger efforts.

Other companies should use—or migrate toward—a larger-scale strategy if they want significant results. A social champion strategy can help companies identify and enlist enthusiasts to expand initiatives inside and outside the organization. As Ford's Fiesta Movement showed, carefully engaging those who have a sizable influence in social networks can reduce risk.

With all else being equal, the social transformer strategy can have the largest impact on an enterprise, affecting everything from R&D and operations to channel partners and customers. However, moving from a champion to a transformer strategy requires major, companywide changes to such things as incentive systems, business processes, resource management, and leadership styles. The social transformers we've seen often have broader social business objectives and view social technologies as a key enabler of—but not the final answer to—those objectives.

It's worth remembering that despite their ubiquity, Twitter and Facebook are only five and seven years old, respectively. Who knows what new technologies lie ahead? Understanding how company strategies are evolving to use existing social media not only will be of use today but also should guide managers as they adapt to platforms developed in the years to come.

Critical Thinking

1. List and summarize the four social media strategies proposed in this article.

2. With a small group of peers from your class, brainstorm some alternative social media strategies that companies could pursue to better target the college students segment.

H. James Wilson is a senior researcher at Babson Executive Education. PJ Guinan and Salvatore Parise are associate professors of information systems at Babson College. Bruce D. Weinberg is the chair of the marketing department at Bentley University.

Advertising's New Campaign

JENNIFER WANG

"Mothers," as *Calvin and Hobbes* cartoonist Bill Watterson proclaimed, "are the necessity of invention."

Look around online, and there's no doubt it's true: When it comes to innovation in digital commerce and media, moms rule. The current generation of moms is tech-savvy, highly educated and controls a dominant 85 percent of household income. Moms are also the most social demographic—which means that when they see something they like (or dislike), everybody and, well, their mother, hears about it.

Many companies are attempting to tap into this base, but one has found a way to do so that goes beyond traditional advertising. BlogFrog, co-founded in April 2009 by Rustin Banks and Holly Hamann in the startup-friendly city of Boulder, Colo., provides free tools for mom bloggers to power their own online communities, live discussions and video broadcasts, then connects these platforms with brands like Coca-Cola that are willing to pay to be a visible part of those conversations.

"Brands have glommed on because we can get them out of the sidebar and into the main bar," says CEO Banks, referring to online advertisers' age-old struggle to get users to click on banner ads. Such ads are seen as a distraction, since successful ones force customers to click away from their original purpose; social media product placement, meanwhile, can seem pushy, while mass-pitching bloggers for reviews is seen as distasteful. BlogFrog's "conversational marketing" products have disrupted business as usual, allowing advertisers to relate to customers via "brand communities" and "sponsored conversations."

BlogFrog's platform promotes a new type of social network, one that bases connections on what you're interested in, rather than on who you know. BlogFrog has 125,000 active members and 65,000 bloggers with a reach of 10 million parents per month, making it the largest mom-blogger network in the country. Tight communities have formed on the platform around topics such as food and fashion, as well as more serious issues related to military spouses, infertility and special-needs kids. Some of these communities are even transcending the virtual world—in internet speak, BlogFrog members are meeting F2F (face-to-face) and ending up friends IRL (in real life).

"Moms are the most powerful consumer segment, and also the most underserved and misunderstood," says Hamann, who serves as vice president of marketing. "Before us, nobody was going there."

Many other services, such as Ning and Go Social, allow users to create niche social networks monetized by ad sales; the idea is that the aggregated blogs have increased power when it comes to traffic and search engine optimization, resulting in higher ad revenue. BlogFrog, however, goes the extra step and offers a way to monetize the content of the blogs themselves, through brand integration.

In a mere 18 months, BlogFrog has signed on major clients such as ABC News, the UN Foundation, Lego, Procter & Gamble and Intuit, as well as Coca-Cola. Annual revenue is on track to reach the multimillions (revenue doubled from the first to the second half of 2011); the staff has quadrupled from just five employees at the end of 2010; and the company is in its third office, a sprawling 9,500-square-foot space that's a far cry from the 600-square-foot room in which it launched. In March, BlogFrog closed on $3.2 million in funding, led by Washington D.C.-based Grotech Ventures.

Here's how it works. The network's brand communities are led by a team of bloggers, or "community leaders," carefully matched by topic interest and level of influence. (BlogFrog collects data based on metrics like quality of posts, blog traffic and Facebook rankings.) Marketers pay a flat monthly fee depending on the number of bloggers, their reach and type of campaign. Sponsored conversations generally involve a larger blogger group that's asked to pose a question and call for reader contributions in the form of personal stories and comments, votes or photos. Responses are aggregated and distributed to the brand's hub pages and to what BlogFrog calls "conversational ad units"—widgets that show campaign results in real time and serve to amplify the conversation and spread it across the web. Sponsored conversations, too, are cost-dependent on influencer reach and type of campaign; say, $20,000 for a four-week campaign with 40 bloggers with a combined readership of 2 million.

For example, organic dairy company Horizon signed on for a campaign around the question, "How do you sneak Omega-3s into your family's diet?" (No surprise: Milk has a bunch.) Thirty bloggers were asked to talk about picky eating and get the community to share kid-friendly recipes. Not one word was company-supplied "advertorial." The campaign resulted in 2.1 million social media impressions on Twitter and Facebook and 3.7 million ad-unit impressions. Horizon has since sponsored three BlogFrog conversations and has signed an annual contract for 2012.

"Consumers want to be connected to relevant brands, yet so much of advertising today is irrelevant. BlogFrog is an attempt to bridge that gap and be genuinely helpful . . . and 2012 is about scaling and applying our products to categories beyond moms, and working with other kinds of influencers, like You-Tube stars," Hamann says.

"Right," Banks agrees. "Elevated, authentic editorial brought to you by a brand is the future."

Banks started working as an engineer at Ball Aerospace in 2005. He'd moved to Boulder with his wife, Tara, and their 18-month-old, and they didn't know a soul. Stuck at home and stir-crazy, Tara began blogging and soon amassed a decent-size audience. Banks noticed that even though readers left plenty of encouraging comments, they couldn't communicate with one another directly. A simple fix occurred to him: a widget that would allow his wife to form her own online community.

Banks had coded his first Bulletin Board System (think an old-school online chat room and forum) and hosted it from his parents' closet at the age of 12, so after a few nights and week-ends studying HTML, he managed to code a prototype and put it on his wife's blog. Fellow bloggers snatched up the technology like a new Baby Einstein product, and Banks realized he had a business opportunity on his hands.

Boulder's close-knit startup community steered him to Hamann, who 18 years earlier had packed up everything she owned in Maryland and driven west. She found herself in a startup utopia, where you could "have a good idea one day and be doing something about it the next."

When Banks approached her, Hamann (who has a 16-year-old) had already built teams and executed marketing for six startups, several with successful exits. Banks' idea to use technology to connect moms sounded like "nirvana" to her, and after several months of discussion, Hamann quit her job as vice president of marketing at a now-defunct music-event invitation service to work on the business plan full-time. A month later, in May 2009, Banks did the same.

"It was fun," Banks recalls, describing lengthy coffee-shop meetings and huddling on the front steps of the downtown branch of the library, leeching Wi-Fi. They hustled, attending mom-blogger conferences and talking to every brand agency they knew. By February 2010, they'd raised about $300,000—enough to hire a couple of staffers and secure proof of concept and a small office for their company, whose name riffed off the concept of "blog hopping."

As traction grew, BlogFrog got the attention of David Cohen, founder of the TechStars incubator, who led a second funding round of $600,000 in early 2011. At that point the team, which had been focused on the blogger community tools and brand communities, launched its first sponsored conversations.

Caitie Ramsburg, director of client services, says BlogFrog's strength is in its level of customization. "We dig deep for what brands want to get out of the campaign. We tie that into what women are already talking about and come up with an elevated topic or question," she says, noting that on average, the brain-storming sessions last a couple of days.

Then, with the help of a sophisticated algorithm that scores influence levels in a way that allows bloggers at all levels a shot at being picked, the team recruits the group that is most aligned with campaign goals. "A brand might want a health blogger in a particular income group with kids under the age of 10," Hamann says. "We have that information because we look at who they are and who they're connected to on several levels."

The advertising world is still feeling out social media's place in its future. "In advertising, you clinch the customer by being emotive," says veteran account manager Elaine Marino, and traditionally that has been done through TV and video. Now, she says, "we're going after the blog space."

Many agencies, eager to tap into the power of these social media influencers, have gotten behind the BlogFrog concept. "It's a better way for brands to approach marketing, because they make sure bloggers actually want to work with you," says James Clark, founder of Boulder-based boutique marketing agency Room 214, which brought Horizon to BlogFrog and has recommended similar campaigns for several other clients. Clark believes the conversational marketing method inspires more activity and loyalty than merely sending samples to random bloggers and hoping for a plug.

The process is also said to yield more honest feedback. Community members are more willing to respond and participate in discussions that are led by their peers, and the conversations give brands a chance to listen in, participate and attempt to boost their own likeability and perception as helpful. Horizon, for example, brought in expert nutritionists and food scientists to answer readers' questions. "We let community leaders run with it," Clark says. "We tell them the topics we like and if we're interested in getting opinions about something, but the communities are self-sustaining."

Other blog networks are partnering with BlogFrog, too. Chuck Moran—chief marketing officer of Burst Media, which represents indie websites across many verticals—is using the community-platform technology to syndicate content across his MomIQ parenting channel. "From a branding perspective, nothing is more powerful than having your target audience participating in a conversation, whether or not it's about a specific product," he says. Reader response to the sponsored conversations has been so great that Burst recently rolled out the platform for its Ella channel (targeting females 18 to 35 with relatively high disposable incomes) and plans to do the same for other communities.

BlogFrog's bloggers are also seeing benefits. The most successful blogs, which can have larger audiences than reality TV shows, can earn their domain owners six-figure incomes. In addition to obvious revenue streams like traffic-driven ad revenue, sponsored posts and product endorsements, popular bloggers can earn money from social media consulting gigs, e-book sales and sponsored conversations and communities like those on BlogFrog.

Last year, BlogFrog paid out more than half a million dollars to its bloggers, who are sent monthly checks based on the communities and campaigns they lead, with the most influential and active making upward of $10,000 a year. Some bloggers who join the network see revenue increase an average of 50 percent, according to the company. BlogFrog's user metrics have also determined that bloggers on its platform see average time on their sites increase fivefold and page views per visit go up by 10.

Laurie Turk is behind TipJunkie.com, a blog that aggregates DIY and craft tutorials and gets about 7 million page views per month. She notes that bloggers' income depends on skill set, influence, traffic and contacts, but there's really no limit to how much they can make. "I don't need to use BlogFrog," she says, noting that when Banks first tried to recruit her, she refused until the platform had developed into a product that was relevant to her community. She also admits to being skeptical that the brand relationships would feel authentic. However, she says, "now I use BlogFrog for engagement, because they stay relevant."

What's most important to her is that the company provides mom bloggers the opportunity to wield their power and influence. "They're at the forefront of helping 'mom blogger' become a profession," Turk notes.

Shannon Shaffer, a former accountant and the voice behind the blog For the Mommas, agrees. As a BlogFrog community leader, she spearheads several brand campaigns per month—representing a small sliver of the income she generates from her site, which has approximately 500,000 unique visitors per month. "I only say yes to campaigns I think readers will enjoy," Shaffer says—like a recent one for Kraft Foods in which she shared easy recipes, some involving the brand's ingredients.

"BlogFrog does a really good job of matching, so it's a good relationship," she says. "It's not like in an ad network where you don't have the opportunity to say no. I'm a foodie, and I love saving money. BlogFrog has done a really good job of introducing brands to our readers without it being invasive. It's genuine information. If the brand is Kraft, it isn't that we're asking readers to buy Kraft products—it's recipes, easy weeknight recipes that we're coming up with and providing resources for. It's real, true content."

The bloggers themselves—and the amount of trust they are able to engender among their readers—are perhaps the biggest determining factor in BlogFrog's model. Although the company's method of increasing the distance between advertising message and consumer should result in greater trust, authenticity isn't guaranteed, notes Prashant Malaviya, associate professor of marketing at Georgetown University's McDonough School of Business. That depends on how transparent the blogger is in divulging her association with a brand, how loyal her readers are, how relevant the discussions are to readers' lives and even the ways in which readers find out about the community—via the brand itself or elsewhere on the internet. Blogs, Malaviya says, can lose influence if they're discovered to have "sold out," and those that discuss "deeper subjects are perceived to be more authentic."

On a crisp winter Friday afternoon, Banks and Hamann are showing off BlogFrog's new Boulder headquarters. A running trail abuts the back of the office building, just east of a hip downtown shopping area where healthy-looking denizens with shiny MacBook Airs are a common sight, even at the nicer restaurants.

Banks and Hamann seem an unlikely pair. Wearing a Blog-Frog T-shirt, Banks looks the part of the classic startup guy, with laid-back energy and a genial, two-handed handshake. Hamann is trim, well-spoken and professional in a sharp suit jacket.

The new office has a rooftop perfect for big summer gatherings, and plenty of room for growth. But at the moment, it's mostly empty. The team of 21 sits together (by choice) in a bullpen, and the conference rooms, named after famous frogs like Kermit and Jeremiah, are identified by taped-up sheets of paper. At least one animal-cracker box is being used to hold file folders. The walls are decorated with frog-theme paintings, the efforts of staff and friends from the last holiday party—most notably, a frogified version of Van Gogh's The Starry Night (by Hamann) and a surreal image of a frog peeking out of a blooming flower (courtesy of Banks' wife).

The office's makeshift, ephemeral decor is a fitting metaphor for the company's promising, if still nebulous, trajectory. "The landscape of the competition changes daily, and the demands are great," says vice president of engineering Doug Cotton.

On the consumer side, the platform needs to be scalable and intuitive to use on every device and browser; for enterprises to sign on, there must be proof, metrics-wise, that the system works. One never-ending task is to find ways to make BlogFrog more viral—coming up with more campaigns, more brand products and more tools. The latest, released in January, is Conversation Networks, which lets bloggers pool small niche communities into one larger one. Titus Stone, the company's lead front-end developer, likens it to a moving target.

"We take requests," he says, only half joking. "When the Live Discussion feature was launched, we started writing code and pushing it out while we were on the phone with bloggers asking us if it could do this or that."

While remaining based in Boulder, the BlogFrog team plans to open a New York office this summer to go after East Coast clients. Meanwhile, it is preparing to extend its network beyond moms to include blogs about food, fitness, fashion, entertainment and tech. Up for grabs? A share of the rapidly growing social media advertising space—which Forrester Research expects to rise from $1.59 billion in 2011 to nearly $5 billion in 2016.

Critical Thinking

1. In what way is the current generation of moms different than previous generations?

2. With a small group of peers in your class, discuss the appeal of blogs in today's digital communication arena.

3. Elaborate on the following statement from the article: "From a branding perspective, nothing is more powerful than having your target audience participating in a conversation, whether or not it's about a specific product."

UNIT 4

Global Marketing

Unit Selections

41. **Emerging Lessons,** Madhubalan Viswanathan, José Antonio Rosa, and Julie A. Ruth
42. **KFC's Radical Approach to China: To Succeed, the Fast-Food Giant Had to Throw Out Its United States Business Model,** David E. Bell and Mary L. Shelman
43. **Retail Doesn't Cross Borders,** Marcel Corstjens and Rajiv Lal

Learning Outcomes

After reading this Unit, you will be able to:

- What economic, cultural, and political obstacles must an organization that seeks to become global in its markets consider?

- Do you believe that an adherence to the "marketing concept" is the right way to approach international markets? Why, or why not?

- What trends are taking place today that would suggest whether particular global markets would grow or decline?

- Which countries do you believe will see the most growth in the next decade? Why?

- In what ways can the Internet be used to extend a market outside the United States?

Student Website
www.mhhe.com/cls

Internet References

International Trade Administration
   www.ita.doc.gov
World Chambers Network
   www.worldchambers.net
World Trade Center Association OnLine
   www.iserve.wtca.org

"All too often, cultures are insufficiently studied or wrongly interpreted. It might seem that responsiveness to cultural differences should be second nature to marketers and therefore virtually reflexive. However, cultural differences continue to challenge marketers and can negatively affect the marketplace. Many times, disregarding local idiosyncrasies is like the introduction of a destructive virus on a culture."

—Michael Czinkota and Charles Skuba

It is certain that marketing with a global perspective will continue to be a strategic element of United States business well into the next decade. The United States is both the world's largest exporter and largest importer. In 1987, United States exports totaled just over $250 billion—about 10 percent of total world exports. During the same period, United States imports were nearly $450 billion—just under 10 percent of total world imports. By 2010, exports had risen to $5131.3 trillion and imports to $6641.6 trillion—roughly the same percentage of total world trade.

Regardless of whether they wish to be, all marketers are now part of the international marketing system. For some, the end of the era of domestic markets may have come too soon, but that era is over. Today, it is necessary to recognize the strengths and weaknesses of our own marketing practices as compared to those abroad. The multinational corporations have long recognized this need, but now all marketers must acknowledge it.

International marketing differs from domestic marketing in that the parties to its transactions live in different political and cultural units. It is the "international" element of international marketing that distinguishes it from domestic marketing—not differences in managerial techniques. The growth of global business among multinational corporations has raised new questions about the role of their headquarters. It has even caused some to speculate whether marketing operations should be performed abroad rather than in the United States.

The key to applying the marketing concept is understanding the consumer. Increasing levels of consumer sophistication are evident in all of the world's most profitable markets. Managers are required to adopt new points of view in order to accommodate increasingly complex consumer wants and needs. The

Kevin Phillips/Getty Images

markets in the new millennium will show further integration on a worldwide scale. In these emerging markets, conventional textbook approaches can cause numerous problems. The new marketing perspective called for by the circumstances of the years ahead will require a long-range view that looks from the basics of exchange and their applications in new settings.

The articles in this unit were chosen to provide an overview of world economic factors, competitive positioning, and increasing globalization of markets—issues to which each and every marketer must become sensitive. "Emerging Lessons" describes how understanding the needs of poorer consumers can be both profitable and socially responsible for multinational companies.

The next article in this unit is intended to spark a discussion about one of today's growth markets: China. HBR's "KFC's Radical approach to China" addresses how the fast-food giant's success in China required that they throw out their United States model. In the final article of the section, "Retail Doesn't Cross Borders," the authors investigate possible reasons why the grocery industry is still dominated by local players in most countries, and most grocery retailers that have ventured overseas have failed as often as they have succeeded.

Emerging Lessons

For multinational companies, understanding the needs of poorer consumers can be profitable and socially responsible.

MADHUBALAN VISWANATHAN, JOSÉ ANTONIO ROSA, AND JULIE A. RUTH

Businesses, take note: An underserved and poorly understood consumer group is poised to become a driving force in economic and business development, by virtue of sheer numbers and rising globalization.

They are subsistence consumers—people in developing nations like India who earn just a few dollars a day and lack access to basics such as education, health care and sanitation.

As these consumers gain access to income and information over the next decade, their combined purchasing power, already in the trillions of dollars, likely will grow at higher rates than that of consumers in industrialized nations. The lesson for multinational companies: Understanding and addressing the needs of the world's poorest consumers is likely to become a profitable, as well as a socially responsible, strategy.

A characteristic associated with low-income consumers, and one that has major implications for doing business with them, is that many struggle with reading and math. Like the 14% of Americans estimated to be functionally illiterate in a U.S. government survey, subsistence consumers have difficulty reading package labels, store signs or product-use instructions, or subtracting the purchase price of an item from cash on hand—all of which hampers their ability to put their limited incomes to best use.

Our research shows that low-literacy consumers process market information and approach purchasing decisions differently than other groups of shoppers. As a result, companies may have to alter marketing practices such as packaging, advertising, pricing, store signage and the training of retail-store employees in order to communicate with them more effectively and win their business.

Here is what we learned from our studies on low-literacy, low-income consumers in the U.S. and subsistence consumers in developing markets, and our recommendations on how marketers can improve the value these groups get from product purchase and use.

Concrete Thinking

One of the key observations we made is that low-literacy consumers have difficulty with abstract thinking. These individuals tend to group objects by visualizing concrete and practical situations they have experienced.

They exhibited what science would call a low grasp of abstract categories—tools, cooking utensils or protein-rich foods, for example—which suggests low-literacy consumers may have difficulty understanding advertising and store signs that position products that way. Their natural inclination is to organize merchandise according to the ingredients needed to make a particular dish or the products needed to complete a specific task, such as doing laundry or cleaning the bathroom, and that is often what they are envisioning as they navigate store aisles, deciding what to buy.

This is reminiscent of research on low-literacy peasants in Central Asia in the early 20th century, who, when presented with a set of objects such as hammer-saw-log-hatchet and asked to select the three that could be placed in one group or be described by one word, didn't derive abstract categories such as "tools" even when prompted. Instead, they grouped the objects primarily around envisioned tasks such as chopping firewood.

Being anchored in the perceptual "here and now" also interferes with the ability of low-literacy consumers to perform mathematical computations, especially those framed in abstract terms. For example, when we asked low-literacy shoppers in the U.S. to estimate whether they had enough cash to pay for the groceries in their cart, many needed to physically handle cash and envision additional piles of currency or coins to accurately estimate the cost of goods in their cart; when the sensorial experience of counting cash was taken away, they often were at a loss.

Because handling cash while walking store aisles isn't advisable, many low-literacy consumers arrive at checkout counters not knowing whether they have enough money to cover their purchases. All too often, they hand all of their cash to the register attendant and hope for an honest transaction.

One of the most potentially detrimental results of concrete thinking, however, is the difficulty that low-literacy consumers have with performing price/volume calculations. They tend to choose products based solely on the lowest posted price or smallest package size, even when they have sufficient resources for a larger purchase, because they have difficulty estimating

For Further Reading

See these related articles from MIT Sloan Management Review.

Strategic Innovation at the Base of the Pyramid

Jamie Anderson and Costas Markides (Fall 2007)
   Strategic innovation in developing markets is fundamentally different from what occurs in developed economies.
   http://sloanreview.mit.edu/smr/issue/2007/fall/16/

The Great Leap: Driving Innovation From the Base of the Pyramid

Stuart L. Hart and Clayton M. Christensen (Fall 2002)
   Companies can generate growth and satisfy social and environmental stakeholders through a "great leap" to the base of the economic pyramid.
   http://sloanreview.mit.edu/smr/issue/2002/fall/5/

Has Strategy Changed?

Kathleen M. Eisenhardt (Winter 2002)
   Globalization has quietly transformed the economic playing field.
   http://sloanreview.mit.edu/smr/issue/2002/winter/10/

The Need for a Corporate Global Mind-Set

Thomas M. Begley and David P. Boyd (Winter 2003)
   Many international business leaders consider a global mind-set desirable, but few know how to embed it companywide.
   http://sloanreview.mit.edu/smr/issue/2003/winter/3/

The Dynamic Synchronization of Strategy and Information Technology

C.K. Prahalad and M.S. Krishnan (Summer 2002)
   The authors' work with 500 executives revealed that few managers believed their information infrastructure was able to handle the pressures from deregulation, globalization, ubiquitous connectivity and the convergence of industries and technologies.
   http://sloanreview.mit.edu/smr/issue/2002/summer/2/

the longevity and savings that come from buying in larger volumes. Some base purchase decisions on physical package size, instead of reported volume content, or on the quantity of a particular ingredient—such as fat, sodium or sugar—but without allowing for the fact that acceptable levels of an ingredient can vary across product categories or package size.

Misspent Energy

We found that low-literacy consumers spend so much time and mental energy on what many of us can do quickly and with little thought that they have little time to base purchase decisions on anything other than surface attributes such as size, color or weight.

They tend to think in pictures, so any change in visual cues such as sign fonts, brand logos or store layouts can leave them struggling to locate a desired product category or brand. Price displays can cause confusion because of the many numbers presented, such as original prices, discounted percentages and discounted prices. Even estimating the price of two gallons of milk if the price of one is known may require a pencil-and-paper calculation unless the price is set in whole or half-unit increments, such as $3 or $3.50.

Because so much shopping time is devoted to deciphering product labels and locating products, we found that low-literacy consumers are less able than other groups to assess the value of products based on subsurface attributes—this computer has more memory and will do what I need more effectively, for example.

When shopping in unfamiliar stores, some low-literacy consumers will choose products at random, buying the first brand they see once they locate a desired product category or aisle. Others simply walk through the store, choosing items that look attractive based on factors such as packaging colors or label illustrations, without regard to whether they even need the product.

When shopping in familiar stores, many low-literacy consumers buy only the brands they recognize by appearance or have purchased previously. While this approach reduces the incidence of product purchases for which the consumer has no use, it precludes the adoption of new and improved products as a category evolves and improves over time.

The pitfalls and uncertainty that come from choosing products at random, based on surface attributes or out of habit provoke anxiety in many low-literacy consumers, leading us to another finding: Shopping takes a heavy emotional toll on this group.

Buying the wrong items, running short of cash at the register or having to ask for help in the aisle to locate products are recurring worries, even cause for despair. The anticipation of such stressful experiences prompts some low-literacy consumers to avoid new, large or what they perceive to be threatening shopping venues or to delay shopping until family or friends can assist, even if waiting means doing without essentials. Although low-literacy consumers tend to be passive in public settings, they will remember episodes of poor treatment by service personnel and won't patronize stores or brands they associate with disrespectful treatment.

Despite the significant constraints that low-literacy consumers face, their ingenuity in coping and positive outlook are a testament to human adaptiveness. For instance, subsistence consumers overcome many of the challenges that come from not being able to read or do math problems by relying on their interpersonal networks—family and friends who may have complementary skills and knowledge. In many situations, the network includes the owners of neighborhood stores who offer very limited product assortments and high prices, but who can answer questions and offer advice to consumers unable to read the labels and determine the value of products on their own.

Subsistence consumers are resource-poor but likely to be relationship-rich, and this must be taken into account by businesses seeking to serve them.

Drawing Them In

To win and enhance customer loyalty in developing markets, manufacturers and retailers need to understand the difficulties faced by low-literacy consumers and create shopping environments that make them feel less vulnerable. Here are a few ways that companies can help customers make better purchases and avoid embarrassment:

- Display prices and price reductions graphically—a half-circle to indicate a 50% markdown, for example, or a picture of three one-dollar bills to indicate a purchase price of $3. Price products in whole and half numbers to make it easier for low-literacy consumers to calculate the price of, say, two bags of rice. These pricing practices are critically important in marketplaces where general stores and kiosks are being replaced by self-service stores, where there is less interaction between customer and store owner.

- Clearly post unit prices in common formats across stores, brands and product categories to make it easier for low-literacy consumers to perform price/volume calculations.

- Include illustrations of product categories on store signs to make it easier for low-literacy consumers to navigate new or refurbished stores. Similarly, use graphical representations of sizes, ingredients, instructions and other information to communicate product information more effectively in shelf and other in-store displays.

- Put the ingredients required for the preparation of popular local dishes in the same section of the store. This would be helpful to low-literacy consumers who often envision the sequence of activities involved in fixing specific dishes to identify the ingredients and quantities they need to purchase. The same can be done for other domestic tasks.

- Incorporate familiar visual elements—such as color schemes or font types—into new store concepts or redesigned brand logos to minimize confusion and anxiety among low-literacy shoppers and increase the likelihood that they will try new products and stores.

- Create a friendly store environment by training store personnel to be sensitive to the needs of low-literacy shoppers and by verbally disclosing and consistently applying store policies. In addition, allow employees to form relationships with consumers by learning their names and offering small amounts of individualized assistance. This is particularly important for global brands and companies entering markets where foreigners are mistrusted or have accrued a history of mistreating people.

As subsistence markets become more attractive, additional opportunities to serve low-literacy consumers will probably become available. Because literacy deficiencies are likely to be addressed at a slower pace than the pace at which poor consumers gain discretionary income and the ability to spend it on products and services, the companies that respond to this group's needs early on will have an advantage. Low-literacy consumers can be a profitable and loyal customer group if treated properly.

Critical Thinking

1. According to the articles what are some of the challenges associated with marketing to subsistence consumers?

2. You have been assigned as a consultant for a business that is looking to target subsistence consumers. Prepare a list of DOs and DON'Ts to help it attract and retain this target market.

DR. VISWANATHAN is an associate professor of marketing at the University of Illinois at Urbana-Champaign in Champaign, Ill. **DR. ROSA** is a professor of marketing and sustainable business practices at the University of Wyoming in Laramie, Wyo. **DR. RUTH** is an associate professor of marketing at Rutgers University in Camden, N.J. They can be reached at reports@wsj.com.

KFC's Radical Approach to China

To Succeed, the Fast-Food Giant Had to Throw Out Its United States Business Model

DAVID E. BELL AND MARY L. SHELMAN

Global companies face a critical question when they enter emerging markets: How far should they go to localize their offerings? Should they adapt existing products just enough to appeal to consumers in those markets? Or should they rethink the business model from the ground up?

The typical Western approach to foreign expansion is to try to sell core products or services pretty much as they've always been sold in Europe or the United States, with headquarters watching closely to make sure the model is exported correctly. This often starts with selling imported goods to the expat community or opening one or two stores for a trial run. Once such an approach is entrenched, companies are reluctant to rethink the model. United States retailers and food corporations that have spent years saturating the huge home market tend to cling to what has worked in the past. Domino's Pizza nearly failed in Australia because it underestimated the need to adapt its offerings to local tastes; only after it turned the country over to a local master franchisee did Domino's become the largest pizza chain there.

A master of adaptation is the Swiss food giant Nestlé, which has created an array of products that incorporate differing regional flavors—and cater to local tastes—in coffee, chocolate, ice cream, and even water. For a hundred years Nestlé's country managers have been empowered to say no to the head office if a product or a campaign doesn't suit their locales. Perhaps the greatest tribute to the strategy is that many consumers around the world believe Nestle is a local company.

One of the most impressive stories of a United States. multinational in an emerging market is unfolding right now in China: KFC is opening one new restaurant a day, on average (on a base of some 3,300), with the intention of reaching 15,000 outlets. The company has achieved this success by abandoning the dominant logic behind its growth in the United States: a limited menu, low prices, and an emphasis on takeout.

We recently studied KFC China's transformation of the business model that had made Kentucky Fried Chicken a global brand, and we learned how, in the process, the company accumulated strengths and competencies that now pose formidable barriers to competitors. KFC China offers important lessons for global executives who seek to determine how much of an existing business model is worth keeping in emerging markets and how much should be thrown away.

Five Competitive Advantages

In 1987, when the first Chinese KFC opened in Tiananmen Square, Western-style fast-food restaurants were unknown in China. Many Chinese still wore the tunic suits of the Mao era, and bicycles were the main means of transportation. KFC was a novelty, a taste of America. It was a place where residents with spending money could go for a special occasion. Although customers didn't like the food much, KFC made steady progress, according to Sam Su, now the chairman and CEO of Yum! Brands China Division, which owns KFC and a number of other brands in the country.

> **KFC China's menus typically include 50 items, compared with about 29 in the United States.**

In 1992, after the Chinese government granted foreign companies greater access to markets, KFC China's managers gradually developed the blueprint that would transform the chain. Like every other multinational in China, KFC made its way up the learning curve by trial and error. But the strategy that emerged was remarkably clear and embodied five truly radical elements: turning KFC into a brand that would be perceived as part Chinese; expanding rapidly into small and midsize cities; developing a vast logistics and supply chain organization; extensively training employees in customer service; and owning rather than franchising the restaurants.

KFC China's executives believed that the company's United States. model, although good enough to do moderately well in the largest Chinese cities, wouldn't lead to the level of success the company sought. They understood that in China, as in many

KFC China's Blueprint for Success

KFC China's success in winning over Chinese consumers grew out of a deep understanding of the differences between established and developing markets and a willingness to radically alter the United States business model. KFC's approach may not apply across the board, but it suggests a mind-set that can position multinationals to win in emerging markets.

other developing countries, food is at the very heart of society, inextricable from national and regional cultures, and that an abundance of flavors and an inviting ambience would be necessary to win over consumers in great numbers.

Execution of the strategy turned on a fluke of corporate ownership. With a closely involved parent, KFC China might not have been free to pursue its homegrown strategy. But the chain was then a unit of PepsiCo, which took a hands-off approach—it was more concerned with beating Coca-Cola than with selling fried chicken. As long as KFC China's financial results were good, PepsiCo was happy. Su (who joined KFC China in 1989) created a knowledgeable, motivated top management team, hiring ethnic Chinese and painting a scenario they could believe in: The company they would build would make China a better place.

KFC China's five competitive advantages all depart from the United States. model.

Infusing a Western Brand with Chinese characteristics.

The company's managers sought to stretch the brand so that consumers would see KFC as part of the local community—not as a fast-food chain selling inexpensive Western-style items but as restaurants offering the variety of foods and the traditional dishes that appeal to Chinese customers. They enlarged the outlets, which are about twice the size of those in the United States., to allow for bigger kitchens and more floor space where customers can linger. They made a special effort to welcome extended families and groups. In the United States, by contrast, KFC outlets are designed primarily for takeout—most of the dining is done at home.

KFC China's menus typically include 50 items, compared with about 29 in the United States. The menu variety adds traffic and encourages repeat visits. The company introduces about 50 new products a year (some of them are offered only temporarily), compared with one or two in the United States. Its executives have what they consider to be a very aggressive program for new product development, which is handled by a committee of managers from marketing, operations, product safety, and the supply chain. Menus offer spicy chicken, rice dishes, soy milk drinks, egg tarts, fried dough sticks, wraps with local sauces, and fish and shrimp burgers on fresh buns. Spiciness levels are very important to customers. In the chain's early days, when the same recipes were served at all outlets, Shanghai customers complained that dishes were too hot, while diners in Sichuan and Hunan complained that they were too bland. So the company changed its recipes to suit the regions. It also offers congee, a popular rice porridge that is hard to make at home, which is KFCs number one seller at breakfast.

The extended menu means that food preparation is more complex in Chinese KFCs than in American ones and requires more hands (thus the bigger kitchens). These outlets typically employ 60 people—nearly twice as many as in the United States. Often one of those employees is a hostess who greets customers and organizes pastimes, such as learning English songs, for young children in play areas.

With all this activity to support, KFC can't position itself as the cheapest dining option—nor does it want to. Customers spend the equivalent of $2.50 to $3.50 per visit, a price point that puts KFC way above street vendors and local restaurants and even somewhat above other fast-food chains. Although young "white collars" in Shanghai might eat a KFC lunch with friends once or twice a month, a family in a smaller city might go once or twice a year, to celebrate a special event.

Localize Offerings By Country and Region.

In an effort to please local consumers, the company reinvented its menu and varied spiciness levels from region to region.

Move Quickly to Establish a Broad Presence.

KFC established 16 beachheads as a way of quickly expanding throughout the country.

Take Charge of the Supply Chain.

In the absence of logistics providers, KFC China created a distribution system to ensure adequate and high-quality supplies.

Become a Learning Organization.

Across the company, from logistics to food preparation to customer service, employees require extensive training, and experienced managers must be constantly developed as the company grows and changes.

Maintain Flexibility.

Focusing on owned restaurants rather than franchises enabled the company to make changes where necessary to meet local needs.

Guard Against Backlash.

Concern in the West over high-fat, high-carbohydrate foods prompted the company to begin changing its menu and educating consumers about health.

Expanding Rapidly.

Rejecting the measured growth of its China competitors and of KFCs in other countries, KFC China set its sights on rapid expansion. One factor in this decision was the presence of McDonald's in China's four largest cities. Rather than go head-to-head with the Big Mac, KFC decided to embrace smaller cities and to build a national business with outlets all over the country. Scale allows the company to reduce costs, and being the first to enter a city means getting the pick of locations with good foot traffic and visibility. Being first also means garnering free publicity when officials celebrate an outlet's opening as marking the city's coming of age. Moreover, a national presence means that KFCs (and other Yum! outlets) are popular with mall developers.

KFC rushed to establish a presence in 16 locations from which it could grow and develop. By 1999 it was opening dozens of restaurants a year, and in 2002 it picked up the pace even further. (In 2008 Yum! Brands' annual opening rate in China surpassed 500 restaurants, most of them KFCs—compared with 103 new KFCs in the United States.) From site selection to grand opening, it takes KFC China four to six months to bring a new restaurant into the world— about half the time required in the United States. Some 700 Chinese cities now have outlets.

With KFC as its flagship chain, Yum! has become China's largest restaurant company by far, with more than 250,000 employees and about 40 percent of the market for fast-food chains. KFCs rapid expansion in China has allowed the company to widen the gap between itself and competitors: McDonald's has about one-third as many outlets and owns a 16 percent market share.

Developing a Logistics Network.

In the United States and Europe, fast-food chains rely on networks of distributors to ensure that food is handled properly and kept refrigerated from the farm to the restaurant. No such networks exist in many of the world's emerging markets. To meet this challenge, KFC China established a distribution arm in 1997, building warehouses and running its own fleet of trucks. This was an expensive undertaking, but necessary if the company was to expand rapidly, carry a lengthy and complex menu, and introduce new products quickly. That same year the company implemented a supplier rating system that allows managers throughout China to concentrate purchasing with the suppliers that perform best.

Food safety is a matter of paramount importance, especially given Chinese consumers' concern in recent years over incidents involving tainted milk powder and contaminated livestock feed. KFC China had a brush with this issue a few years ago, when a colorant that had been linked to cancer was found in one of the company's sauces. Although the problem was resolved quickly, Yum! China reported a resulting 30 percent drop in operating profit in the second quarter of 2005.

KFC China closely monitors the entire supply chain, all the way back to animal feed companies and other input providers, and it trains employees in personal hygiene, including how to dress for the workplace and how often to wash their hands. It now has the most advanced and integrated cold-chain system in China, with 11 full-service logistics centers and six satellite centers serving every province except Tibet. To circumvent the traffic jams that sometimes extend for miles in the winter, it relies on contingency plans that involve renting temporary warehouses and reserving space on cargo airlines.

Most products are sourced in China. Buying locally is essential to keeping costs low, and it strengthens the parent company's relationship with the Chinese government. The policy has a few unavoidable exceptions, including certain herbs and spices—for KFCs "secret" fried chicken recipe—that can't be obtained in China. But the company works with its suppliers to build their capabilities and capacity; it is even working with growers to introduce United States varieties of sweet corn.

Training Employees in Service.

When KFC opened in Beijing, it was one of the first companies to promote excellent customer service—a concept then unfamiliar in China after decades of communism. But despite an abundance of willing workers, staffing is a perennial obstacle. In fact, it is the limiting factor in the chain's expansion, according to Sam Su. To maintain its current restaurant-opening rate, KFC needs at least 1,000 new managers and 30,000 new crew members a year, and they must be ready the minute an outlet opens, because it is likely to be packed. The company prides itself on being a "learning organization." Teams of new employees work side by side with experienced ones in established outlets; once trained, they move to a new location.

New recruits at KFC often have to be taught basic people skills in order to interact with customers.

Teaching employees how to interact with customers is no small matter. One-child families and the proliferation of home computers mean that Chinese children interact less with other people than they did in previous generations. New recruits at KFC often have to learn basic people skills and teamwork.

Many other companies have followed KFCs example in customer service (last year McDonald's announced that it was opening a Hamburger University in China), but KFCs training program functions exceptionally well, churning out a continual stream of new managers. This, like the company's extensive logistics network, is an advantage that is difficult for any competitor to emulate.

Focusing on Ownership Rather than Franchising.

In KFCs early days, China required foreign companies to have local partners; but when the country became more receptive to wholly owned foreign enterprises, KFC China switched to a strategy of company-owned outlets—another way in which it challenged the dominant logic. (More than 90 percent of Yum!'s outlets in China are company owned, compared with 12 percent in the United States. and 11 percent in other international markets.)

The Chain Restaurant Landscape in China

Ever since KFC China opened its first outlet, in Beijing in 1987, the number of foreign-owned chain restaurants has grown steadily in China. Here's a look at some of them.

Burger King has about three dozen restaurants in China, where its first outlet opened in 2005. In 2010 an executive said that Asia would be the brand's largest growth engine within three to five years but that BK planned to proceed cautiously in China.

Dairy Queen has some 300 Chinese outlets.

Mcdonald's opened its first restaurant in China in 1990 and plans to double the number of outlets there to 2,000 by 2013. The company says its strong sales in the Asia/ Pacific, Middle East, and Africa regions are led by results in China, and it cites the appeal of such conveniences as delivery, drive-through, and extended hours. Some 70 percent of McDonald's Chinese outlets are open 24 hours a day.

Papa John's plans to increase the number of its outlets in China from 155 to 300 within three years.

Pizza Hut is a part of the Yum! portfolio; it has some 500 dine-in restaurants and 120 delivery-only outlets. Like KFC, it has undergone a transformation in China, it now offers a lengthy menu that includes seafood pizza, beefsteak, and fried squid, and it attracts an older and more affluent crowd than KFC does.

Starbucks opened in China in 1999 and has about 450 shops there; the company plans to have 1,500 by 2015. Executives say they believe there is huge potential to drive coffee consumption in China.

Taco Bell was similarly positioned by Yum! as an upscale restaurant, but it was shut down in China after a five-year experiment. Mexican food, with its emphasis on dairy and beans, didn't appeal to Chinese consumers.

Wendy's/Arby's has only about 300 restaurants outside North America. It announced earlier this year that it was considering expansion in China.

Franchising has long been a mainstay of the fast-food industry, because it reduces investment costs and risk and enables rapid geographic expansion. It works well when a pool of experienced, entrepreneurial candidates are available to run franchises and when restaurant operations are relatively simple—built around, for example, a limited menu of easy-to-make products. But KFC China's model was more complex and evolving rapidly. Owning the restaurants allows the company to closely control every aspect of their operation, from menu to decor, and to monitor results and the success of new products. It permits centralized purchasing, which reduces costs, and gives the company a larger share of outlet profits.

The Risk of a Backlash

KFC China's rapid growth poses challenges: A highly visible company could easily become the target of a consumer or government backlash against the perceived negatives of fast food. Some Western health problems are already showing up in China. The 2002 China National Nutrition and Health Survey revealed that 22.8 percent of Chinese adults were overweight, up from 6 percent in 1982. The number of overweight and obese children aged seven to 17 has tripled to 8.1 percent over the past 10 years, according to the same agency.

In the mid-1990s a fellow participant at a seminar in the United States. asked Su why he would want to bring "junk food" to China— a question that started him thinking deeply. Aware of a growing sense in the West that high-fat, high-carbohydrate foods play a role in the obesity epidemic, Su asked himself how Yum! Brands could take action to forestall such problems in China.

In 2005 the company developed the concept of a "new fast food" that would be "nutritious and balanced" and promote "healthy living." It eliminated "supersize" items and added roast chicken, sandwiches, fish, shrimp, and more fruit and vegetable dishes to its menus. KFC's children's meals are served with vegetables and juice, although fries and soda can be substituted on request. Tray mats carry educational messages. Nutrition information is printed on every package. Hostesses teach lessons on nutrition to kids.

A Confident, Dynamic Company

The results of the strategy of heavy localization have been impressive: In the first half of 2011 sales at Yum! China locations that had been open a year or more rose 16 percent, compared with

Taking on a New Challenge: Chinese Food

Yum! China's strengths in service, logistics, and training have positioned the company to support additional restaurant formats, including a local one with which it had no experience: Chinese fast food.

In recent years Yum! has experimented with developing **East Dawning,** a chain that takes its name from a line in an ancient Chinese poem. The clean, efficiently run restaurants have Chinese decor and serve Chinese food exclusively—no United States-style fried chicken, no pizza, no burgers. The chain, which opened in Shanghai in 2005, offers such favorites as beef rice and bean curd at prices similar to KFC's.

Yum!'s initial hope was to create a large national chain, but Chinese food poses significant challenges in a fast-food context: Noodles and vegetables must be prepared just before serving; customers are highly discerning about freshness and traditional flavors; and tastes vary widely across regions. The chain has relatively few outlets, and nationwide expansion is still a distant goal.

Recently, Yum! has focused on acquiring a competitor, **Little Sheep,** a Hong Kong-listed chain of hundreds of Mongolian-style hot-pot restaurants. By 2010 Yum! held a 27 percent stake in Little Sheep, and earlier this year it proposed to increase its ownership level to 93 percent.

a decline of 2 percent at United States. locations. The restaurant margin for those six months was 22 percent—well above the United States margin of 11 percent. Yum! China revenues and operating profits in 2010 were $4.1 billion and $755 million, respectively; comparable figures for the overall company were $11.3 billion and $1.77 billion. The third quarter of 2010 marked the first time that China revenue (more than $1.1 billion) had surpassed United States. revenue, and many analysts expect that Yum!'s China business will be twice as large as its United States business within five years.

Over time, KFC China has come to reflect China itself in some respects: It is large, growing, confident, and eager for variety and new experiences. Most of all, it is, like China's economy, dynamic and capable of expanding still further—at a remarkable pace. Much of what the company has accomplished is the result of its homegrown strategy—and of the independence that PepsiCo gave Su and his leadership team in the early days. If there is an overriding lesson to be drawn from KFCs experience in China, it is that when entering an emerging market, a multinational must decide whether it wants to garner quick extra sales or to establish a long-term presence. If it's there for the long haul, it should install local managers whose vision is to build an organization that will last.

Critical Thinking

1. In your opinion, how far should global companies go to localize their offerings?

2. List and summarize KFC China's five competitive advantages.

3. "One of the most impressive stories of a United States multinational in an emerging market is unfolding right now in China." With a small group of peers in your class, discuss KFC's recipe for globalization success.

DAVID E. BELL is the George M. Moffett Professor of Agricutture and Business and a senior associate dean at Harvard Business School. **MARY L. SHELMAN** is the director of the Agribusiness Program at Harvard Business School.

From *Harvard Business Review*, November 2011, pp. 137–142. Copyright © 2011 by Harvard Business School Publishing. Reprinted by permission.

Retail Doesn't Cross Borders

Marcel Corstjens and Rajiv Lal

Here's Why and What to Do About It

Globalization's lure is almost irresistible. With the United States economy struggling to expand and Europe on the brink of recession, fast-growing markets in the developing world offer the best opportunities for boosting revenues and profits today. Many companies in the developed world are keen to follow in the wake of corporations in a variety of industries—such as Boeing, Coca-Cola, DuPont, General Electric, Hewlett-Packard, IBM, Oracle, Unilever, and Disney—that appear to have succeeded in going global.

Globalization is no panacea, however. Success abroad varies widely, and it's often tough to boost profits by investing overseas. Because most studies look at **cross**-industry patterns to draw lessons about how to succeed at globalization, they can be misleading. When we focused on one industry—grocery retailing—we found that, with a few exceptions, globalization's benefits had not accrued to retailers.

In contrast to other industries, grocery **retail** is still dominated by local players in most countries. International players are almost entirely absent from even the largest **retail** markets. And every grocery retailer that has ventured overseas has failed as often as it has succeeded. Moreover, our research shows that on average, the extent of internationalization does not have a significant effect on retailers' revenue growth rates or their profit margins. Some industries clearly can't travel across **borders** as well as others.

A few grocery retailers have succeeded in globalizing by developing strategies that take into account the idiosyncrasies of their industry—and have found new paths to growth at home as well. Extrapolating from their experience, we propose some **retail**-specific rules for globalization that may also be useful for any company venturing abroad.

The Pressure to Globalize

Retailers wish to enter global markets for a number of reasons. Common ones include a quest for greater economies of scale and scope, a need to diversify risks, a desire to attract fresh talent and create new opportunities for existing leaders, and a need to make up for constraints imposed by regulatory agencies when a retailer becomes too big for its home market.

Growth is the main impetus for globalization, though. Retailing is a low-margin business, so companies have to expand rapidly if they wish to remain attractive to investors. One example: In 2009 Walmart's expected sales growth, as per its stock price valuation, was 8.5 percent. That implied an increase in sales of $34 billion that year, and a rise in revenues from $400 billion to $600 billion over five years, according to the stock investment database ValueLine. In contrast, investors expected the consumer goods giant P&G to grow by just 5.5 percent. That meant sales growth of $4.5 billion in 2009 and an increase in sales from $83 billion to $108 billion over the next five years—less than a fifth of Walmart's expected sales.

Because of the unrelenting pressure to grow, many globalization gambits are opportunistic and jeopardize carefully crafted long-run strategies. For example, Walmart's move into the UK in 1999 through the purchase of Asda was unplanned. The American retailer had intended to invest in its undersized German operation at the time, but quickly stepped in when Asda announced its plans to merge with a British white goods retailer, Kingfisher. It jumped at the opportunity because Asda was a good fit with its positioning and operations, but the move was internally controversial—Walmart's international head, Bob Martin, eventually resigned over the matter.

Retail's pattern of geographic expansion is puzzling. The sales of the world's 10 biggest retailers tripled from 2000 to 2011, but their global sales more than quintupled—admittedly from a very low base. It would be logical to expect that grocery retailers would enter the world's biggest markets—the United States, Germany, Japan, the UK, and France—to boost revenues and profits. Yet no retailer is present in all of them today. Walmart **doesn't** operate in either continental Europe or Japan, and neither of the other two biggest American chains has made an overseas investment yet. France's Carrefour, the world's second-largest retailer, **doesn't** have a presence in the United States, Japan, or Germany, although it has tried to break into all three countries. Britain's Tesco, the world's third-largest chain, has had no European business since it pulled out of France and has only recently developed a small presence in Japan and the United States.

Every retailer has tasted failure abroad. Walmart has succeeded in Canada and Mexico, but it had to pull out of Germany and South Korea. Tesco has carved out market share in

South Korea and Malaysia, but it failed to establish a presence in France or Taiwan. Germany's Metro took off in Poland and Romania, but its forays into the UK and Denmark ended in failure. Carrefour has exited several markets in Europe—including Austria, the Czech Republic, Germany, Norway, Portugal, Slovenia, and the UK—but it has broken through in others, such as Spain, Belgium, Greece, Italy, Romania, Poland, and Turkey, during the same period.

It could be argued that the grocers' failures are due to differences in consumer tastes, particularly for food products. However, companies like Mars, Nestle, Kraft, P&G, Danone, and Unilever have succeeded in creating global food brands. These suppliers have had presences in the biggest retailing markets for more than 15 years, so international retailers' lack of success must be attributable to other factors.

To be sure, some companies are making inroads. Big retailers, especially those from the United States and France, have invested in Latin America, and the European giants have targeted Central and Eastern Europe. Still, international players are remarkably absent in most countries. In numerous markets, local retailers occupy the number one and number two spots suggesting that standard globalization strategies haven't worked in **retail.**

Globalization's Financial Impact

Given this spotty track record, it seemed worthwhile to investigate whether globalization helps retailers meet financial goals. We conducted an econometric study comparing international and predominantly national grocery retailers. Growth rate in sales and increases in net profit margin were the two performance indicators we used, and internationalization was one of the independent variables.

Our findings surprised us:

- The degree of internationalization, measured by any yardstick, doesn't significantly affect a retailer's sales growth rate or profit margin.
- The GDP growth rate of the home market is a major driver of the retailer's sales growth rate.
- The sales growth rates at home have a significant impact on the retailer's profit margin.
- Neither the size of the home-market population nor the retailer's size, measured by sales, influences its sales growth rate or profit margin.

Clearly, retailers need to rethink their attitudes toward globalization as well as their strategies. If they are investing overseas to boost sales and margins in the short run, they will be sorely disappointed. Globalization is likely to contribute to revenues and profits only in the long run. Paying closer attention to the domestic market will be important in the meantime, not just to achieve faster growth but also to boost margins. Whatever the retailer decides to do globally, the home market is critical to its performance. This may be as true for big retailers as it is for small ones.

Factors That Influence Retailers' Globalization Strategies

Since few have achieved universal success, retailers should think hard before entering foreign markets. Their decision-making processes should take into account the unique characteristics of their industry. Three factors stand out:

Retailers Face Many Barriers to Entry in Foreign Markets

It's tough for retailers to enter overseas or foreign markets by acquiring local players. In developed markets, few retailers want to sell. Even well-established chains have trouble making acquisitions work—as Walmart's trials in South Korea and Carrefour's tribulations in Japan and Belgium show. It's equally difficult for grocery retailers to grow organically because of real estate costs, entrenched competition, and the lack of suitable sites. In emerging markets, few chains have developed large networks of stores. Retailing is usually local in those nations, and the industry is highly fragmented.

Moreover, foreign entrants struggle to bring offerings to developed countries that shoppers perceive as new, different, and valuable. The mixed response to Tesco's new United States venture, Fresh & Easy, illustrates this problem. Consumers didn't feel the format was novel enough, and the choice of locations left much to be desired. Even more worrisome, the team Tesco had sent to get the venture off the ground was made up of its brightest and best executives. In developing countries, on the other hand, consumers perceive foreign retailers to be premium players, even though they may not offer the services that local grocers do, such as free delivery, credit, and custom packaging. In addition, in many parts of the world, including the otherwise open market of India, laws protect local retailers from foreign competition.

Grocery Retailing is a High-Fixed-Cost, Low-Margin Business with Returns that Accrue Only Over Time

Companies have to operate a large network of stores in each country to benefit from the economies of purchase, supply chain investments, and technologies that drive worker productivity. However, most retailers don't enter a country all at once; they enter one city, then another, then a region, and so on. The process of building a network of stores to a profitable scale takes a long time and entails large investments that may not pay off for decades. Walmart broke even in China in 2010, after 15 long years of investment.

Moreover, unlike grocery suppliers, which can profitably cater to one consumer segment across a country, mass-market retailers must compete for every consumer in the economically diverse trading area of each store. They don't enjoy the luxury of selecting slices of consumers; they have to make every store profitable despite the mix of clientele in the surrounding area.

Foreign Entrants Often Have to Take on Incumbents that Operate Exclusively in One Country

These "country killers" understand local preferences and tailor offerings to local consumers' needs. Outsiders, on the other hand, have to respond to large variations in shopping habits across an extensive network of stores, which makes them prone to errors. Moreover, the advantages of global supply chains vary greatly by product category, with food products offering fewer global buying opportunities because of the heterogeneity in local tastes and habits. Gains grow when nonfood offerings become more important.

How Retailers Can Get Globalization Right

None of this means that retailers should avoid moving into foreign markets. However, the nature of the business is such that globalization isn't for every retailer: Each player must think through the unique challenges the industry poses, understanding that even successful chains won't reap financial rewards for a long time. Retailers will do better overseas if they apply four rules:

Rule 1: The Home Market is the Linchpin of Globalization

Retailers often make two mistakes when they venture overseas. One, they perceive opportunities outside the home market to be larger, less constraining, and easier to tap into than those in the home base. Two, they divert their attention from what's happening at home. Both errors can prove costly.

The stronger the retailer's market position at home, the better its chances of sustaining overseas investments. Walmart's leadership position in the United States is undoubtedly the key to achieving its global ambitions. Conversely, Carrefour's problems spring from its precarious position in its home base, where it has lost market share and its profits fell by 40 percent in the first half of 2011.

Retailers must also remember that there are no mature markets; only mature managers. Even in the most developed markets, retailers can generate the resources they need to go global by patiently applying innovative growth strategies to their home bases.

Rule 2: Always Bring Something New to Market

Without an element of novelty, it will be difficult, if not impossible, for retailers to overtake entrenched rivals. For example, the slow but persistent expansion of the discount supermarket retailer Aldi shows that if grocers can offer new value propositions, shoppers may be willing to switch. The German chain's "hard discounter" proposition extends across borders better than other formats do because nearly every country has a sizable segment of consumers interested in low-price, no-frills offerings. By pioneering the concept of small stores Aldi has grown successfully in Europe, Australia, and the United States.

The keys to Aldi's success have been the format's simplicity and a focus on lowering operating costs, which results in lower prices. Aldi limits the number of SKUs in a category to ensure that its mostly private-label suppliers produce sizable volumes of each item and can extract the greatest possible economies of scale. The simplicity of store layouts, and the consequences for logistics and operations, help Aldi offer products at prices 40 percent lower than supermarkets can. Both factors also translate into shopper convenience: It may take a couple of hours to shop at a supermarket; Aldi cuts that time in half.

Being innovative often allows retailers to break into new markets successfully. In the mid-1990s, Jerónimo Martins, a leading Portuguese grocery retailer, decided to enter Poland, the biggest Eastern European market, by acquiring first a cash-and-carry business and then a small chain of Polish hypermarkets.

As Poland attracted the attention of other European retailers, Jerónimo Martins adopted a new approach. Lacking the resources to compete with the new entrants, it sold off the cash-and-carry business and the hypermarkets and focused on developing Biedronka, a chain of 48 small stores, as a hard discounter. A local team applied retailing principles that were new to Poland: very small stores, low prices, limited assortments (800 SKUs), quality private-label products that accounted for 60 percent of sales, and obsessive cost efficiency in all activities.

Jerónimo Martins then went a step further. It ran Biedronka as a stand-alone business with no operational links to its other businesses. Polish shoppers saw the brand as one of their own in a market full of foreign interlopers, and the company reinforced this image by procuring 95 percent of its products from Polish suppliers. Fifteen years after its acquisition, Biedronka operates 1,800 stores in Poland and plans to open another 1,200 by 2015. With Biedronka generating 60 percent of its sales and 90 percent of its profits, Jerónimo Martins has effectively become a Polish company with a subsidiary in Portugal.

Rule 3: Differentiation is More Important than Synergies

The benefits from international expansion are often supposed to accrue from increased scale and scope economies. However, small local players often outperform international players because the synergies from globalization are not always as big as anticipated.

Back-office efficiencies, IT, finance, real estate management, logistics, and central purchasing are part of the potential cost efficiencies that can result from international expansion. However, the share of central purchases in retailers' sales is never as large as expected; more than 70 percent of sales usually originate from local producers. Notwithstanding their claims, most multinational retailers aren't organized enough to capture gains from global procurement. Even if they are, they run the risk of overloading local assortments with products from global suppliers. These retailers end up selling what they have bought instead of buying what they can sell.

Economies of scope are beneficial only if the retailer's core competencies are relevant for a new market. Walmart struggled in Germany partly because its low price proposition didn't stand out in a market where hard discounters control 47 percent of grocery sales. It couldn't gain benefits from using its IT and logistics systems because of the operation's lack of scale. Finally, Walmart's people policies were out of tune with the unionized, high-wage German labor force.

Leveraging synergies globally while providing each country operation the independence to adjust to local needs is a critical balancing act. For instance, the more consumers value local food products, the fewer synergies the retailer will be able to derive and the more it will struggle to compete with country killers. The key is to find synergies that add to the consumer offering rather than conflict with it.

Rule 4: Timing is Critical

Retailers need to think carefully about when to enter a market. They often enter markets too early. For instance, Carrefour, the most international retailer, failed in several developed markets because shoppers weren't ready for the hypermarkets concept. Also, it usually takes retailers longer than they expect to grow in overseas markets, which frustrates them because the business is capital-intensive. This is particularly a problem if the retailer is expanding in scattered markets rather than trying to build critical mass in a few.

At the same time, internationalization can't be postponed forever. Strategic windows close, especially for retailers operating in large home markets. If Kroger and Target, the number two and number three United States grocery retailers, wait much longer, they may miss the most attractive opportunities overseas and their future growth will be limited. One key dimension in determining the optimal time to enter a market is format. Cash-and-carry retailers can enter a country early because they can serve mom-and-pop stores. Hard discounters can also enter fairly early because there will always be some shoppers interested in their value-for-money proposition. However, if hard discounters go in too soon, they will face issues such as the lack of reliable private-label suppliers or few other formats present in the market, making it difficult to set up a differentiated value-provider positioning.

The number of countries in which a retailer operates should never be a proxy for its international success. Even grocery retailers that have gone global would do well to stop planting flags and focus instead on a limited set of opportunities where they are most likely to be successful in generating operations of scale. They can do that by using strategies similar to those they use at home—such as moving into more locations, deploying more formats, and offering more products and services. Only then will global retailers' expansion become aligned with a superior understanding of shoppers' needs and wants.

Room for Global Growth

In most countries, the number one retailer is a local player or a multinational whose home base is that country. Clearly, retailers must rethink their attitudes toward globalization and develop new strategies in order to tap the enormous opportunity for growth in global markets.

Why Retailers Go Global

Grocery retailers' sales are much larger than those of grocery suppliers, but investors still expect retailers' earnings to grow faster. Since retailing is a low-margin business, big chains have been forced to move into overseas markets.

Expected Earnings Per Share Growth Rate

Grocery Retailers	Carrefour 20 percent
	(2011 Sales: $10 Billion)
	Walmart 10 percent
	($422 Billion)
	Tesco 9 percent
	(94 Billion)
Grocery Suppliers	Coca-Cola 9 percent
	($35 Billion)
	Danone 6 percent
	(23 Billion)
	P&G 2 percent
	(80 Billion)

*Average EPS growth rates implicit in company valuations
Source Thomson-One banker database.

How Retailers Fare

Grocery retailers offer shelf space, pretty much a commodity, whereas consumer goods manufacturers must tailor their products to local tastes in every market. Yet suppliers have successfully entered many more countries than retailers have.

Number of Countries in Which the Company Operates

Grocery Retailers	Carrefour 38
	Walmart 15
	Tesco 13
Grocery Suppliers	Coca-Cola 200
	(Approx.)
	Danone 120
	(23 Billion)
	P&G 180

Source: Planet **Retail** and company reports.

The Retailer's Golden Rules of Globalization

- First explore all options for profitable growth in your home market.
- Continued success in the home market is necessary, but not sufficient, for success internationally.
- Unless you enter by acquiring a strong local player, make sure you bring something new to the market.
- Focus on local success and differentiation in each new country before exploring and leveraging synergies across your portfolio of countries.
- Don't enter too early; you will fail.
- Don't wait too long. Opportunities dry up, and competitors may become unassailable incumbents.

Idea in Brief

Many companies, especially those in the developed world, have tried to grow faster by investing abroad, and retailers are no exception. But it's tough to make money overseas, particularly for retailers.

Local retailers still dominate most markets, and almost every chain that has ventured overseas has tasted failure. In fact, the data suggest that traditional globalization strategies don't work well in **retail.**

Research also shows that the extent of internationalization **doesn't** contribute significantly to either retailers' revenue growth or their profit margins; the home market's growth is the major driver.

Retailers face serious obstacles in going global: It takes time to break into foreign markets, returns accrue only over time, and foreign entrants have to take on well-established local incumbents.

Some retailers' experiences suggest that to succeed abroad, firms must bring new things to market; focus on differentiation, not synergies; and enter at the right time.

Strategies for Growing the Home Market

The hype about globalization shouldn't blind retailers to opportunities in their home markets. Here are three ways retailers can grow faster at home.

Grow Existing Formats

Some retailers, such as Spain's Mercadona, the Netherlands' Jumbo, and Dollar General in the United States, have found room to grow even in mature markets. And their success isn't because of the size of the opportunity; they represent small (Jumbo), midsize (Mercadona), and large (Dollar General) home bases.

Mercadona, for example, is obsessed with satisfying the shopper, whom the company calls The Boss. Mercadona is able to offer high-quality products at low prices because it manages operations extraordinarily well. Founded as a family-owned supermarket in 1977, the company generated sales of more than €16 billion from 1,200 locations in 2010. Sales per employee have risen consistently over the past 13 years, more than doubling over the period to €232,000 per employee.

Expand into New Formats

Another option is to expand the number of **retail** formats at home. Sainsbury's in the UK, Denmark's Dansk Supermarked, and Walmart Mexico, which operates independently from Bentonville, Arkansas, have all grown by serving different customer segments and offering different kinds of experiences such as bulk, top-up, and convenience shopping.

Wal-Mex, as it is commonly known, has built a $25 billion business this way. Its Bodega Aurrera and Mini Bodegas cater to less affluent segments, while Walmart Supercenter, Sam's Club, and the convenience-store format, Superama, focus on more-affluent consumers. Wal-Mex operates VIPS restaurants on the same premises as its hypermarkets; it also has a casual clothing chain, Suburbia.

Using different formats to focus on different consumption occasions and segments allows Wal-Mex to compete for a higher share of wallet. For example, within a two-mile radius of Mexico City, Wal-Mex has as many as 17 stores. What's more, with a portfolio of formats, Wal-Mex can take advantage of a variety of real estate opportunities as they become available. By contrast, a company with a single format must find locations that fit its format. Flexibility is another benefit; when a community becomes richer, for instance, Wal-Mex can convert a low-end store into a hypermarket and thereby keep pace with consumer needs.

Leverage the Brand

Retailers must leverage the equity—values, beliefs, and perceptions—they enjoy with customers by identifying new product categories and services that are consistent with those qualities. We call that a "weightless" brand strategy because it allows retailers to float into new markets, escaping the forces that keep them in their traditional areas of expertise.

Consider, for instance, Tesco, the British retailer, which is expanding into banking and insurance as a way around the UK Competition Commission's concerns about its 30 percent grocery market share. By capitalizing on the trust consumers have in the company along with its value-for-money reputation, Tesco hopes to keep growing.

Critical Thinking

1. Define globalization. In your opinion, what is the lure of globalization for retailers?

2. Discuss some factors that may influence retailers' globalization strategies.

3. With a group of peers in your class, summarize and discuss the four rules to successful globalization proposed in the article. Can your group suggest some other rules that may ensure success in global markets?

MARCEL CORSTJENS is the Unilever Chaired Professor of Marketing at Insead. **RAJIV LAL** is the Stanley Roth Sr. Professor of Retailing at Harvard Business School.

Acknowledgements—Harvard Business Review Notice of Use Restrictions, May 2009 Harvard Business Review and Harvard Business Publishing Newsletter content on EBSCOhost is licensed for the private individual use of authorized EBSCOhost users. It is not intended for use as assigned course material in academic institutions nor as corporate learning or training materials in businesses. Academic licensees may not use this content in electronic reserves, electronic course packs, persistent linking from syllabi or by any other means of incorporating the content into course resources. Business licensees may not host this content on learning management systems or use persistent linking or other means to incorporate the content into learning management systems. Harvard Business Publishing will be pleased to grant permission to make this content available through such means. For rates and permission, contact permissions@harvardbusiness.org.

Glossary

This glossary of marketing terms is included to provide you with a convenient and ready reference as you encounter general terms in your study of marketing that are unfamiliar or require a review. It is not intended to be comprehensive, but taken together with the many definitions included in the articles themselves, it should prove to be quite useful.

A

acceptable price range The range of prices that buyers are willing to pay for a product; prices that are above the range may be judged unfair, while prices below the range may generate concerns about quality.

adaptive selling A salesperson's adjustment of his or her behavior between and during sales calls, to respond appropriately to issues that are important to the customer.

advertising Marketing communication elements designed to stimulate sales through the use of mass media displays, direct individual appeals, public displays, give-aways, and the like.

advertorial A special advertising section in magazines that includes some editorial (nonadvertising) content.

Americans with Disabilities Act (ADA) Passed in 1990, this U.S. law prohibits discrimination against consumers with disabilities.

automatic number identification A telephone system that identifies incoming phone numbers at the beginning of the call, without the caller's knowledge.

B

bait and switch Advertising a product at an attractively low price to get customers into the store, but making the product unavailable so that the customers must trade up to a more expensive version.

bar coding A computer-coded bar pattern that identifies a product. *See also* universal product code.

barter The practice of exchanging goods and services without the use of money.

benefit segmentation Organizing the market according to the attributes or benefits consumers need or desire, such as quality, service, or unique features.

brand A name, term, sign, design, symbol, or combination used to differentiate the products of one company from those of its competition.

brand image The quality and reliability of a product as perceived by consumers on the basis of its brand reputation or familiarity.

brand name The element of a brand that can be vocalized.

break-even analysis The calculation of the number of units that must be sold at a certain price to cover costs (break even); revenues earned past the break-even point contribute to profits.

bundling Marketing two or more products in a single package at one price.

business analysis The stage of new product development where initial marketing plans are prepared (including tentative marketing strategy and estimates of sales, costs, and profitability).

business strategic plan A plan for how each business unit in a corporation intends to compete in the marketplace, based upon the vision, objectives, and growth strategies of the corporate strategic plan.

C

capital products Expensive items that are used in business operations but do not become part of any finished product (such as office buildings, copy machines).

cash-and-carry wholesaler A limited-function wholesaler that does not extend credit for or deliver the products it sells.

caveat emptor A Latin term that means "let the buyer beware." A principle of law meaning that the purchase of a product is at the buyer's risk with regard to its quality, usefulness, and the like. The laws do, however, provide certain minimum protection against fraud and other schemes.

channel of distribution *See* marketing channel.

Child Protection Act U.S. law passed in 1990 to regulate advertising on children's TV programs.

Child Safety Act Passed in 1966, this U.S. law prohibits the marketing of dangerous products to children.

Clayton Act Anticompetitive activities are prohibited by this 1914 U.S. law.

co-branding When two brand names appear on the same product (such as a credit card with a school's name).

comparative advertising Advertising that compares one brand against a competitive brand on at least one product attribute.

competitive pricing strategies Pricing strategies that are based on an organization's position in relation to its competition.

consignment An arrangement in which a seller of goods does not take title to the goods until they are sold. The seller thus has the option of returning them to the supplier or principal if unable to execute the sale.

consolidated metropolitan statistical area (CMSA) Based on census data, the largest designation of geographic areas. *See also* primary metropolitan statistical area.

consumer behavior The way in which buyers, individually or collectively, react to marketplace stimuli.

Consumer Credit Protection Act A 1968 U.S. law that requires full disclosure of the financial charges of loans.

consumer decision process This four-step process includes recognizing a need or problem, searching for information, evaluating alternative products or brands, and purchasing a product.

Consumer Product Safety Commission (CPSC) A U.S. government agency that protects consumers from unsafe products.

consumerism A social movement in which consumers demand better information about the service, prices, dependability, and quality of the products they buy.

convenience products Consumer goods that are purchased at frequent intervals with little regard for price. Such goods are relatively standard in nature and consumers tend to select the most convenient source when shopping for them.

cooperative advertising Advertising of a product by a retailer, dealer, distributor, or the like, with part of the advertising cost paid by the product's manufacturer.

corporate strategic plan A plan that addresses what a company is and wants to become, and then guides strategic planning at all organizational levels.

countersegmentation A concept that combines market segments to appeal to a broad range of consumers, assuming that there will be an increasing consumer willingness to accept fewer product and service choices for lower prices.

customer loyalty concept To focus beyond customer satisfaction toward customer retention as a way to generate sales and profit growth.

D

demand curve A relationship that shows how many units a market will purchase at a given price in a given period of time.

demographic environment The study of human population densities, distributions, and movements that relate to buying behavior.

derived demand The demand for business-to-business products that is dependent upon a demand for other products in the market.

differentiated strategy Using innovation and points of difference in product offerings, advanced technology, superior service, or higher quality in wide areas of market segments.

direct mail promotion Marketing goods to consumers by mailing unsolicited promotional material to them.

direct marketing The sale of products to carefully targeted consumers who interact with various advertising media without salesperson contact.

discount A reduction from list price that is given to a buyer as a reward for a favorable activity to the seller.

discretionary income The money that remains after taxes and necessities have been paid for.

disposable income That portion of income that remains after payment of taxes to use for food, clothing, and shelter.

dual distribution The selling of products to two or more competing distribution networks, or the selling of two brands of nearly identical products through competing distribution networks.

dumping The act of selling a product in a foreign country at a price lower than its domestic price.

durable goods Products that continue in service for an appreciable length of time.

E

economy The income, expenditures, and resources that affect business and household costs.

electronic data interchange (EDI) A computerized system that links two different firms to allow transmittal of documents; a quick-response inventory control system.

entry strategy An approach used to begin marketing products internationally.

environmental scanning Obtaining information on relevant factors and trends outside a company and interpreting their potential impact on the company's markets and marketing activities.

European Union (EU) The world's largest consumer market, consisting of 16 European nations: Austria, Belgium, Britain, Denmark, Finland, France, Germany, Greece, Italy, Ireland, Luxembourg, the Netherlands, Norway, Portugal, Spain, and Sweden.

exclusive distribution Marketing a product or service in only one retail outlet in a specific geographic marketplace.

exporting Selling goods to international markets.

F

Fair Packaging and Labeling Act of 1966 This law requires manufacturers to state ingredients, volume, and manufacturer's name on a package.

family life cycle The progress of a family through a number of distinct phases, each of which is associated with identifiable purchasing behaviors.

Federal Trade Commission (FTC) The U.S. government agency that regulates business practices; established in 1914.

five C's of pricing Five influences on pricing decisions: customers, costs, channels of distribution, competition, and compatibility.

FOB (free on board) The point at which the seller stops paying transportation costs.

four I's of service Four elements to services: intangibility, inconsistency, inseparability, and inventory.

four P's *See* marketing mix.

franchise The right to distribute a company's products or render services under its name, and to retain the resulting profit in exchange for a fee or percentage of sales.

freight absorption Payment of transportation costs by the manufacturer or seller, often resulting in a uniform pricing structure.

functional groupings Groupings in an organization in which a unit is subdivided according to different business activities, such as manufacturing, finance, and marketing.

G

General Agreement on Tariffs and Trade (GATT) An international agreement that is intended to limit trade barriers and to promote world trade through reduced tariffs; represents over 80 percent of global trade.

geodemographics A combination of geographic data and demographic characteristics; used to segment and target specific markets.

green marketing The implementation of an ecological perspective in marketing; the promotion of a product as environmentally safe.

gross domestic product (GDP) The total monetary value of all goods and services produced within a country during one year.

growth stage The second stage of a product life cycle that is characterized by a rapid increase in sales and profits.

H

hierarchy of effects The stages a prospective buyer goes through when purchasing a product, including awareness, interest, evaluation, trial, and adoption.

I

idea generation An initial stage of the new product development process; requires creativity and innovation to generate ideas for potential new products.

implied warranties Warranties that assign responsibility for a product's deficiencies to a manufacturer, even though the product was sold by a retailer.

imports Purchased goods or services that are manufactured or produced in some other country.

integrated marketing communications A strategic integration of marketing communications programs that coordinate all promotional activities—advertising, personal selling, sales promotion, and public relations.

internal reference prices The comparison price standards that consumers remember and use to judge the fairness of prices.

introduction stage The first product life cycle stage; when a new product is launched into the marketplace.

ISO 9000 International Standards Organization's standards for registration and certification of manufacturer's quality management and quality assurance systems.

Glossary

J

joint venture An arrangement in which two or more organizations market products internationally.

just-in-time (JIT) inventory control system An inventory supply system that operates with very low inventories and fast, ontime delivery.

L

Lanham Trademark Act A 1946 U.S. law that was passed to protect trademarks and brand names.

late majority The fourth group to adopt a new product; representing about 34 percent of a market.

lifestyle research Research on a person's pattern of living, as displayed in activities, interests, and opinions.

limit pricing This competitive pricing strategy involves setting prices low to discourage new competition.

limited-coverage warranty The manufacturer's statement regarding the limits of coverage and noncoverage for any product deficiencies.

logistics management The planning, implementing, and moving of raw materials and products from the point of origin to the point of consumption.

loss-leader pricing The pricing of a product below its customary price in order to attract attention to it.

M

Magnuson-Moss Act Passed in 1975, this U.S. law regulates warranties.

management by exception Used by a marketing manager to identify results that deviate from plans, diagnose their cause, make appropriate new plans, and implement new actions.

manufacturers' agent A merchant wholesaler that sells related but noncompeting product lines for a number of manufacturers; also called manufacturers' representatives.

market The potential buyers for a company's product or service; or to sell a product or service to actual buyers. The place where goods and services are exchanged.

market penetration strategy The goal of achieving corporate growth objectives with existing products within existing markets by persuading current customers to purchase more of the product or by capturing new customers.

marketing channel Organizations and people that are involved in the process of making a product or service available for use by consumers or industrial users.

marketing communications planning A six-step process that includes marketing plan review; situation analysis; communications process analysis; budget development; program development integration and implementation of a plan; and monitoring, evaluating, and controlling the marketing communications program.

marketing concept The idea that a company should seek to satisfy the needs of consumers while also trying to achieve the organization's goals.

marketing mix The elements of marketing: product, brand, package, price, channels of distribution, advertising and promotion, personal selling, and the like.

marketing research The process of identifying a marketing problem and opportunity, collecting and analyzing information systematically, and recommending actions to improve an organization's marketing activities.

marketing research process A six-step sequence that includes problem definition, determination of research design, determination of data collection methods, development of data collection forms, sample design, and analysis and interpretation.

mission statement A part of the strategic planning process that expresses the company's basic values and specifies the operation boundaries within marketing, business units, and other areas.

motivation research A group of techniques developed by behavioral scientists that are used by marketing researchers to discover factors influencing marketing behavior.

N

nonprice competition Competition between brands based on factors other than price, such as quality, service, or product features.

nondurable goods Products that do not last or continue in service for any appreciable length of time.

North American Free Trade Agreement (NAFTA) A trade agreement among the United States, Canada, and Mexico that essentially removes the vast majority of trade barriers between the countries.

North American Industry Classification System (NAICS) A system used to classify organizations on the basis of major activity or the major good or service provided by the three NAFTA countries— Canada, Mexico, and the United States; replaced the Standard Industrial Classification (SIC) system in 1997.

O

observational data Market research data obtained by watching, either mechanically or in person, how people actually behave.

odd-even pricing Setting prices at just below an even number, such as $1.99 instead of $2.00.

opinion leaders Individuals who influence consumer behavior based on their interest in or expertise with particular products.

organizational goals The specific objectives used by a business or nonprofit unit to achieve and measure its performance.

outbound telemarketing Using the telephone rather than personal visits to contact customers.

outsourcing A company's decision to purchase products and services from other firms rather than using in-house employees.

P

parallel development In new product development, an approach that involves the development of the product and production process simultaneously.

penetration pricing Pricing a product low to discourage competition.

personal selling process The six stages of sales activities that occur before and after the sale itself: prospecting, preapproach, approach, presentation, close, and follow-up.

point-of-purchase display A sales promotion display located in high-traffic areas in retail stores.

posttesting Tests that are conducted to determine if an advertisement has accomplished its intended purpose.

predatory pricing The practice of selling products at low prices to drive competition from the market and then raising prices once a monopoly has been established.

prestige pricing Maintaining high prices to create an image of product quality and appeal to buyers who associate premium prices with high quality.

pretesting Evaluating consumer reactions to proposed advertisements through the use of focus groups and direct questions.

price elasticity of demand An economic concept that attempts to measure the sensitivity of demand for any product to changes in its price.

price fixing The illegal attempt by one or several companies to maintain the prices of their products above those that would result from open competition.

price promotion mix The basic product price plus additional components such as sales prices, temporary discounts, coupons, favorable payment, and credit terms.

price skimming Setting prices high initially to appeal to consumers who are not price-sensitive and then lowering prices to appeal to the next market segments.

primary metropolitan statistical area (PMSA) Major urban area, often located within a CMSA, that has at least one million inhabitants.

PRIZM A potential rating index by ZIP code markets that divides every U.S. neighborhood into 1 of 40 distinct cluster types that reveal consumer data.

product An idea, good, service, or any combination that is an element of exchange to satisfy a consumer.

product differentiation The ability or tendency of manufacturers, marketers, or consumers to distinguish between seemingly similar products.

product expansion strategy A plan to market new products to the same customer base.

product life cycle (PLC) A product's advancement through the introduction, growth, maturity, and decline stages.

product line pricing Setting the prices for all product line items.

product marketing plans Business units' plans to focus on specific target markets and marketing mixes for each product, which include both strategic and execution decisions.

product mix The composite of products offered for sale by a firm or a business unit.

promotional mix Combining one or more of the promotional elements that a firm uses to communicate with consumers.

proprietary secondary data The data that is provided by commercial marketing research firms to other firms.

psychographic research Measurable characteristics of given market segments in respect to lifestyles, interests, opinions, needs, values, attitudes, personality traits, and the like.

publicity Nonpersonal presentation of a product, service, or business unit.

pull strategy A marketing strategy whose main thrust is to strongly influence the final consumer, so that the demand for a product "pulls" it through the various channels of distribution.

push strategy A marketing strategy whose main thrust is to provide sufficient economic incentives to members of the channels of distribution, so as to "push" the product through to the consumer.

Q

qualitative data The responses obtained from in-depth interviews, focus groups, and observation studies.

quality function deployment (QFD) The data collected from structured response formats that can be easily analyzed and projected to larger populations.

quotas In international marketing, they are restrictions placed on the amount of a product that is allowed to leave or enter a country; the total outcomes used to assess sales representatives' performance and effectiveness.

R

regional marketing A form of geographic division that develops marketing plans that reflect differences in taste preferences, perceived needs, or interests in other areas.

relationship marketing The development, maintenance, and enhancement of long-term, profitable customer relationships.

repositioning The development of new marketing programs that will shift consumer beliefs and opinions about an existing brand.

resale price maintenance Control by a supplier of the selling prices of his branded goods at subsequent stages of distribution, by means of contractual agreement under fair trade laws or other devices.

reservation price The highest price a consumer will pay for a product; a form of internal reference price.

restraint of trade In general, activities that interfere with competitive marketing. Restraint of trade usually refers to illegal activities.

retail strategy mix Controllable variables that include location, products and services, pricing, and marketing communications.

return on investment (ROI) A ratio of income before taxes to total operating assets associated with a product, such as inventory, plant, and equipment.

S

sales effectiveness evaluations A test of advertising efficiency to determine if it resulted in increased sales.

sales forecast An estimate of sales under controllable and uncontrollable conditions.

sales management The planning, direction, and control of the personal selling activities of a business unit.

sales promotion An element of the marketing communications mix that provides incentives or extra value to stimulate product interest.

samples A small size of a product given to prospective purchasers to demonstrate a product's value or use and to encourage future purchase; some elements that are taken from the population or universe.

scanner data Proprietary data that is derived from UPC bar codes.

scrambled merchandising Offering several unrelated product lines within a single retail store.

selected controlled markets Sites where market tests for a new product are conducted by an outside agency and retailers are paid to display that product; also referred to as forced distribution markets.

selective distribution This involves selling a product in only some of the available outlets; commonly used when after-the-sale service is necessary, such as in the case of home appliances.

seller's market A condition within any market in which the demand for an item is greater than its supply.

selling philosophy An emphasis on an organization's selling function to the exclusion of other marketing activities.

selling strategy A salesperson's overall plan of action, which is developed at three levels: sales territory, customer, and individual sales calls.

services Nonphysical products that a company provides to consumers in exchange for money or something else of value.

share points Percentage points of market share; often used as the common comparison basis to allocate marketing resources effectively.

Sherman Anti-Trust Act Passed in 1890, this U.S. law prohibits contracts, combinations, or conspiracies in restraint of trade and actual monopolies or attempts to monopolize any part of trade or commerce.

shopping products Consumer goods that are purchased only after comparisons are made concerning price, quality, style, suitability, and the like.

single-channel strategy Marketing strategy using only one means to reach customers; providing one sales source for a product.

Glossary

single-zone pricing A pricing policy in which all buyers pay the same delivered product price, regardless of location; also known as uniform delivered pricing or postage stamp pricing.

slotting fees High fees manufacturers pay to place a new product on a retailer's or wholesaler's shelf.

social responsibility Reducing social costs, such as environmental damage, and increasing the positive impact of a marketing decision on society.

societal marketing concept The use of marketing strategies to increase the acceptability of an idea (smoking causes cancer); cause (environmental protection); or practice (birth control) within a target market.

specialty products Consumer goods, usually appealing only to a limited market, for which consumers will make a special purchasing effort. Such items include, for example, stereo components, fancy foods, and prestige brand clothes.

Standard Industrial Classification (SIC) system Replaced by NAICS, this federal government numerical scheme categorized businesses.

standardized marketing Enforcing similar product, price, distribution, and communications programs in all international markets.

stimulus-response presentation A selling format that assumes that a customer will buy if given the appropriate stimulus by a salesperson.

strategic business unit (SBU) A decentralized profit center of a company that operates as a separate, independent business.

strategic marketing process Marketing activities in which a firm allocates its marketing mix resources to reach a target market.

strategy mix A way for retailers to differentiate themselves from others through location, product, services, pricing, and marketing mixes.

subliminal perception When a person hears or sees messages without being aware of them.

SWOT analysis An acronym that describes a firm's appraisal of its internal strengths and weaknesses and its external opportunities and threats.

synergy An increased customer value that is achieved through more efficient organizational function performances.

systems-designer strategy A selling strategy that allows knowledgeable sales reps to determine solutions to a customer's problems or to anticipate opportunities to enhance a customer's business through new or modified business systems.

T

target market A defined group of consumers or organizations toward which a firm directs its marketing program.

team selling A sales strategy that assigns accounts to specialized sales teams according to a customer's purchase-information needs.

telemarketing An interactive direct marketing approach that uses the telephone to develop relationships with customers.

test marketing The process of testing a prototype of a new product to gain consumer reaction and to examine its commercial viability and marketing strategy.

TIGER (Topologically Integrated Geographic Encoding and Reference) A minutely detailed U.S. Census Bureau computerized map of the United States that can be combined with a company's own database to analyze customer sales.

total quality management (TQM) Programs that emphasize long-term relationships with selected suppliers instead of short-term transactions with many suppliers.

total revenue The total of sales, or unit price, multiplied by the quantity of the product sold.

trade allowance An amount a manufacturer contributes to a local dealer's or retailer's advertising expenses.

trade (functional) discounts Price reductions that are granted to wholesalers or retailers that are based on future marketing functions that they will perform for a manufacturer.

trademark The legal identification of a company's exclusive rights to use a brand name or trade name.

truck jobber A small merchant wholesaler who delivers limited assortments of fast-moving or perishable items within a small geographic area.

two-way stretch strategy Adding products at both the low and high end of a product line.

U

undifferentiated strategy Using a single promotional mix to market a single product for the entire market; frequently used early in the life of a product.

uniform delivered price The same average freight amount that is charged to all customers, no matter where they are located.

universal product code (UPC) An assigned number to identify a product, which is represented by a series of bars of varying widths for optical scanning.

usage rate The quantity consumed or patronage during a specific period, which can vary significantly among different customer groups.

utilitarian influence To comply with the expectations of others to achieve rewards or avoid punishments.

V

value added In retail strategy decisions, a dimension of the retail positioning matrix that refers to the service level and method of operation of the retailer.

vertical marketing systems Centrally coordinated and professionally managed marketing channels that are designed to achieve channel economies and maximum marketing impact.

vertical price fixing Requiring that sellers not sell products below a minimum retail price; sometimes called resale price maintenance.

W

weighted-point system The method of establishing screening criteria, assigning them weights, and using them to evaluate new product lines.

wholesaler One who makes quantity purchases from manufacturers (or other wholesalers) and sells in smaller quantities to retailers (or other wholesalers).

Z

zone pricing A form of geographic pricing whereby a seller divides its market into broad geographic zones and then sets a uniform delivered price for each zone.

Test-Your-Knowledge Form

We encourage you to photocopy and use this page as a tool to assess how the articles in *Annual Editions* expand on the information in your textbook. By reflecting on the articles you will gain enhanced text information. You can also access this useful form on a product's book support website at www.mhhe.com/cls

NAME: DATE:

_____

TITLE AND NUMBER OF ARTICLE:

_____

BRIEFLY STATE THE MAIN IDEA OF THIS ARTICLE:

_____

LIST THREE IMPORTANT FACTS THAT THE AUTHOR USES TO SUPPORT THE MAIN IDEA:

_____

WHAT INFORMATION OR IDEAS DISCUSSED IN THIS ARTICLE ARE ALSO DISCUSSED IN YOUR TEXTBOOK OR OTHER READINGS THAT YOU HAVE DONE? LIST THE TEXTBOOK CHAPTERS AND PAGE NUMBERS:

_____

LIST ANY EXAMPLES OF BIAS OR FAULTY REASONING THAT YOU FOUND IN THE ARTICLE:

_____

LIST ANY NEW TERMS/CONCEPTS THAT WERE DISCUSSED IN THE ARTICLE, AND WRITE A SHORT DEFINITION:

NOTES